# Urban History Yearbook 1988

Editor
**Richard Rodger**

Leicester University Press

First published by Leicester University Press 1988

Typeset by J & L Composition Ltd, Filey, North Yorkshire
Printed in Great Britain by Antony Rowe Ltd, Chippenham

**British Library Cataloguing in Publication Data**
Rodger, Richard
Urban History Yearbook
1988 – 1. Cities and towns – History – Serials
909'.09732

ISBN 0–7185–6088–4
ISSN 0306–0845

# Contents

Page

v  Editorial note

1  **Did urbanization secularize Britain?** by Callum G. Brown

15  **Immigration and population growth in early fourteenth-century Norwich: evidence from the tithing roll,** by Elizabeth Rutledge

31  **Assessed taxes as sources for the study of urban wealth: Bristol in the later eighteenth century,** by Elizabeth Baigent

49  **Property transfers and the Register of Sasines: urban development in Scotland since 1617,** by Richard Rodger and Jennifer Newman

58  **Town histories and Victorian plaudits: some examples from Preston,** by A.J. Vickery

65  **Nordic urban history and urban historians in the last decade,** by Jan Eivind Myhre

78  **Conference reports,** compiled by Richard Rodger

89  **Review of periodical articles,** by R. Malcolm Hogg, Peter Borsay and Richard Trainor

109  **Research in urban history: a review of recent theses,** by David Reeder

118  **Current bibliography of urban history,** compiled by Diana Dixon and Nicholas Wilson
Outline of the classification
Journal abbreviations
Index of towns

171  **Reviews of books** (book review editors: Joyce Ellis and John Walton)
1 General and thematic
2 Individual towns and regions
3 Methodology and sources
List of books reviewed

# Editorial note

Few historians would disagree that in an expansionary phase more initiatives are possible than in contraction. Yet in the face of the attack upon higher education, the drastic reduction of research funds and postgraduate studentships in urban, social and economic history by the reconstituted Economic and Social Research Committee, and an ethos which rewards relevance rather than scholarship, urban history has continued to transmit positive signs of life. A contributory factor has been the stewardship of David Reeder as editor of the *Urban History Yearbook* from 1978 to 1987. Others, rightly, will evaluate the worth of the *Yearbook* and its contribution to urban history, but in difficult times, David Reeder has stabilized the number of subscriptions, reformulated the editorial team, and during a period when urban history has itself spawned discrete sub-groups, sustained a varied temporal and disciplinary coverage in the articles published in the *Yearbook*. Judged by the articles alone, no one could accuse the editor of a chronological preference or the lack of an interdisciplinary perspective. Ever aware of the financial constraints on researchers without recourse to institutional funds and on postgraduates and temporary staff, and of the erosion of salaries in higher education, and with the collaboration of Leicester University Press, David Reeder has endeavoured to contain the cost of the *Yearbook*; between 1981 and 1986 the cost of the *Urban History Yearbook* has increased by 32 per cent compared to an average price increase of 48 per cent in books generally, according to the most recent data from the Publishers Association. In real terms the cost of the *Yearbook* is less now than in 1981, and on the basis of words per page and per £ subscription, the *UHY* represents good value for money in relation to many journals. Notwithstanding this immense editorial labour spanning nine *Yearbooks* between 1979 and 1987, David Reeder has also undertaken to survey recent theses in urban history, to act as review editor, to coordinate the bibliography when production problems have emerged, and generally to act as sweeper for an editorial board scattered throughout Britain – all while maintaining his own research, teaching and publication, and an active role in the Urban History Group in various capacities. It is particularly reassuring to a new editor not only to inherit a durable product central to the international dissemination of urban history, but also to be able to enlist the experience of David Reeder as a member of an editorial board whose other members are themselves deeply committed to urban history and supportive of the editor.

It is as a research tool that the *Urban History Yearbook* remains most widely used. Articles providing historiographical surveys, methodological insights, appraisals of source materials, and an annual average of 1000 indexed bibliographical items culled from approximately 560 periodicals and innumerable monographs and edited collections, provide indispensable assistance to those intent upon new lines of research, as well as to 'old hands' and reference librarians. Cross-referenced by town and classified thematically, these entries offer a convenient method by which, annually, to update reading lists or embark upon research projects at a time when few higher education libraries can afford even 1 per cent of the titles screened. Most issues have included a 'state of the art' piece in a specific field from current practitioners – municipal socialism (Kellett, 1978), politics in the Victorian city (Fraser, 1979), community and social geography (Dennis and Daniels, 1981), social mobility in the city (Kaelble, 1981), political and economic systems in medieval and early modern towns (Reynolds and Goose, 1982), city systems (King, 1983), new urban history (Mohl, 1983), central and local government relations (Hennock, 1984), urban elites (Trainor, 1985), and religion and secular society (McLeod, 1978; Brown, 1988) are some examples. Judged by the admittedly imperfect criteria of citations in periodicals, subscribers' comments, and bar chat at urban history meetings, consumer reports hold such wide-ranging survey articles in high regard.

Editorial policy, therefore, remains committed to the pursuit of excellence in the form of urban historiographical surveys and new methodological perspectives. Shorter articles on source materials are always welcome. In addition, a steady flow of detailed research articles, often stemming from recent Ph.D. theses, have found the *Urban History Yearbook* a suitable outlet for publication, and in this respect the *Yearbook* has been in the vanguard of disseminating new research findings. It is hoped that that flow of substantive research-based typescripts will continue to land on this editorial desk (the address for contributors is given at the end of this note).

A regular feature of the *Yearbook* has been its interest in non-British urban history. Most conspicuously this has taken the form of surveys of recent developments in the urban history field of a particular country or regional grouping. For example, the spotlight was successively turned on Australia (1979, 1984), Japan (1980), India (1981), the United States (1983), New Zealand (1984), South Africa (1985), Ireland (1986), China (1987) and in this 1988 issue, the Nordic countries of Sweden, Denmark, Norway, Finland and Iceland. Research findings and trends, important monographs, new techniques, bibliographical guidance, and where appropriate, the relevance to British and North American urban history, have been highlighted by scholars prominent within their respective countries. The insider's perspective on new academic developments is particularly valued, based as it often is on access to publications in languages other than English, and on access to information systems and personal networks which, for the foreigner, are difficult to comprehend, far less utilize. Further surveys of this type are in preparation.

A new departure for the *Yearbook* in the field of international urban history is the overtly comparative study. Though the 1988 edition retains a firmly British flavour, from 1989 the *Urban History Yearbook* will confront the need to pursue cross-cultural comparisons in the search to understand the nature of urban processes. The initial setting, perhaps predictably given the nature and volume of publications, is North Atlantic – Britain, Canada and the United States. In this respect future *Yearbook* initiatives may further subscribe to a view of urban history advanced by its first editor H. J. Dyos, namely that while specific urban locations convey local colour, of more fundamental interest are the general processes shaping urban development. This is not to say that process is invariably more important than locus. Clearly urban history needs an amalgam of case studies and general theories. But by embracing an international dimension it is hoped that the features and more general mechanics of urban change may be exposed.

This editorial commenced by remarking on the continuing flow of research in urban history, a trend which owes much to the deep reservoir of interest among local historians concerned to set the specific urban experience of their town or region within the context of broader themes in urban history. How typical, how unusual was the urban experience of a particular town in relation to its neighbours, rivals, or boroughs with allied economic or other functions is an approach which is commonly adopted. The *Urban History Yearbook* has faithfully attempted to incorporate such interests – specifically scanning local history journals and citing relevant material in the annual bibliography. But it is also hoped that the thematic articles contained in the *Yearbook* participate in a two-way process by contributing approaches and ideas which provide the context and overview for many of these local urban history studies. In the current academic climate it is clear that much high-quality urban scholarship continues outside the precincts of universities and polytechnics, and in this respect, editorial policy, as initially fostered by both Jim Dyos and David Reeder, remains committed to encouraging typescripts from new authors and from those who may not have previously considered the *Yearbook* an appropriate outlet for their work. Perhaps this more expansive explanation of the perceived functions of the *Urban History Yearbook* and of editorial policy will continue the *Yearbook*'s longstanding support for and encouragement of researchers about to embark upon publication.

The sheer volume of work required from the editorial board is yet another indication of the range and breadth of urban historical interest and the *Yearbook*'s attempt to survey it. Mention of the number of annual bibliographical entries has already been made. The scale of this task imposes considerable burdens and requires special organizational skills. The *UHY* took the unusual step of adding a second bibliographer to the editorial team, and to complement the sterling work from Nick Wilson were fortunate to entice Diana Dixon out of her 'retirement'; 1986 remains the only year since the foundation of the *Yearbook* in 1974 that she has not acted as bibliographer. The survey of periodical literature, that feat of annual magic Rick Trainor has managed to perform by seeing connections between the most unlikely articles often published in the most unusual places, has also been 'double teamed', with early modern and medieval urban history articles admirably surveyed by Peter Borsay (assisted by Malcolm Hogg). If other members of the editorial team are not mentioned by name it is certainly not because there was less for them to do; more it is a reflection of their continuing stalwart efforts. No less cooperative have been Peter Boulton and Susan Martin of Leicester University Press who have dealt sensitively and patiently with a particular form of urban ritual, the baptism of a new editor. Their efforts are appreciated.

The current crop of articles in the fifteenth issue of the *Yearbook* spans the medieval to the present day. Callum Brown provides a masterly examination of declining church attendance and the social significance of late-Victorian religion and doubts whether this was simply a product of urbanization. Jan Eivind Myhre evaluates the contemporary urban history scene during a hectic decade of official town histories to commemorate the founding of numerous towns in five Nordic countries. Elizabeth Baigent shows how tax data and record linkage provide useful insights into the structure of eighteenth-century wealth. Elizabeth Rutledge, by using tithing rolls to argue that the population of Norwich, like that of York, continued to expand in the early fourteenth century, contributes to the ongoing debate as to whether medieval towns continued to increase up to the Black Death or faced decline after 1300. Richard Rodger and Jennifer Newman examine the background to property registration in Scotland in the early seventeenth century and claim that the Register of Sasines, a neglected source, has considerable research potential for urban history from the seventeenth to the twentieth century. A. J. Vickery scrutinizes town histories, directories and guides to show what Victorians thought of their urban environment and how this can be interpreted.

Substantive case studies, methodological issues, comparative surveys, essays in bibliography and historiography, and accounts of sources and methods of interest to urban historians in all periods are welcome. Intending contributors should send typescripts to:

Richard Rodger, Department of Economic and Social History, University of Leicester, Leicester LE1 7RH (tel. 0533–522586).

*Back issues*

Back issues for 1974 to 1984 inclusive (except 1979, which is out of print) are available at the special price £2 each plus postage & packing, for a limited period. Issues for 1985 onwards are available at £19.50. Order direct from:

Leicester University Press, University of Leicester, Leicester LE1 7RH (tel. 0533–523334).

# Did urbanization secularize Britain?

There are few issues in British history about which so much unsubstantiated assertion has been written as the adverse impact of industrial urbanization upon popular religiosity. Urban history undergraduates are plied each year with the well-worn secularizing interpretation of urban growth which emanated with the Victorians (mostly churchmen) and which has since been reassembled by modern investigators in forms suitable for digestion in ecclesiastical history, social history (Marxist and non-Marxist), historical sociology, and historical geography. This 'pessimist' school of thought has reigned virtually unchallenged since the nineteenth century, giving rise in its endless repetition to simplistic historiographical myths. Arguably, systematic inquiry has suffered because modern urban society has been regarded as inimical to religion.

An important start to disentangling the web of confusion has already been made by Jeff Cox in his admirable but underrated *The English Churches in a Secular Society*, a study of Lambeth between 1870 and 1930.[1] In the first and final chapters of that book, Cox commenced the assault on the 'pessimist' school, pointing out in necessarily blunt language the illogicality and empirical weakness in the arguments of many historians and sociologists of religion. That book should have a reserved space on every reading list dealing with this issue. The present article attempts to expand on what might be called the 'optimist' school of thought concerning the impact of urbanization upon religion: that the churches survived urbanization in the eighteenth and nineteenth centuries. While Cox adduced from his research on the 1870–1930 period that the great decline of the churches had not occurred before then, the following pages shift the focus to a reassessment of the evidence on the preceding 100 years. The approach is first to review the 'pessimist' thesis, isolating the key qustions which require systematic investigation. The second and third sections focus on two of them: the statistical relationship between urban growth and churchgoing, and the social composition of churchgoers. The fourth section assesses the fortunes of urban religion over the long term from the beginning of industrial urbanization through to the twentieth century in Glasgow – with the exception of London, the largest and fastest growing industrial city to emerge in nineteenth-century Britain, and notorious for social problems that posed the greatest possible challenge to the churches.

## I

Many early nineteenth-century churchmen wrote about the adverse impact of urban growth upon the churches. One was Dr Thomas Chalmers of the Church of Scotland, and later leader of the Disruption which created the Free Church in 1843. Based on his experience in Glasgow, his *The Christian and Civic Economy of Large Towns*[2] was extremely influential in broadcasting the view that manufacturing cities destroyed the system of parochial supervision which had operated in the countryside for centuries, bonding together the common people, social elites and the church. It should be noted, however, that though his view was widely held, it was far from unanimous. The Congregationalist Robert Vaughan drew attention to the vibrancy of cities, their creativity and energy, illustrating the evangelical dissenter's sense of the urban conjunction of economic and religious individualism.[3] But the pessimist view is the one that dominated: and while ecclesiastical historians are wont to pinpoint particular eras when clergy were very concerned with the rise of irreligion, the truth is that churchmen have been voicing this concern almost continuously from the 1780s down to the present day.

Interpreting this clerical worry is important. Their primary measure of irreligion has always been the extent of non-churchgoing, and despite the contrary impression that might be gained from writers such as Chalmers, this was not a phenomenon born with the industrial city. Evidence from the early-modern period shows that the problem existed then in rural areas – often as in the north of England and large tracts of Scotland merely because of the phenomenal size of parishes which made churchgoing impracticable, and because of the shortage of church accommodation.[4] But the reason that sharp concern with non-churchgoing emerged in industrial society was not so much that the problem grew, but rather it was because the new commercial and industrial society encouraged a pluralistic view of religion. Churchgoing became optional, a choice for the civil population to make. This was a complete change from pre-industrial society, both urban and rural, where the church had represented the parochial or local state. People's links with the church had previously come through a series of statutory and enforced ties – the most important of which were church taxes, and the *de facto* judicial functions of the parson or, as in Scotland, the kirk session. The early-modern concern was with popular submission to the paternalistic, fiscal and judicial authority of the church, rather than with churchgoing.[5]

It was the fracturing of the social structure and the weakening of traditional relations between social 'ranks' that fuelled concern with the religious condition of industrializing Britain. The city was the pinnacle, but by no means the only representation of this; it was also to be found in agricultural and industrial villages. But it is worth remembering that much of the concern in the late eighteenth and early nineteenth centuries occurred amongst Established Churchmen who felt their position threatened by the rise of non-Established religion: Methodism and Nonconformity in England and Wales, Presbyterian dissent in Scotland, and Irish-immigrant Catholicism in many urban, industrial and mining districts.

It was this denominational rivalry (primarily between Establishment and Protestant dissent) as much as irreligion that led to the taking of Britain's one and only state census of churchgoing on Sunday 30 March 1851. This produced the most famous and influential statement of the 'pessimist' school – that by the census compiler Horace Mann in his report accompanying the tables of statistics that were presented to Parliament. What has to be said, and has to be said bluntly, is that every statement he made implying that non-churchgoing had grown, and about the identity of the non-churchgoers, was entirely unsupported by the census itself. Referring to 'the emergency' of 'the alarming number of non-attendants', he wrote:

> Even in the least unfavorable aspect of the figures just presented, ... it must be apparent that a sadly formidable portion of the English people are habitual neglecters of the public ordinances of religion. Nor is it difficult to indicate to what particular class of the community this portion in the main belongs. ... More especially in cities and large towns it is observable how absolutely insignificant a portion of the congregations is composed of artizans.

Of these 'unconscious Secularists' he said: 'These are never or but seldom seen in our religious congregations.'[6] Mann's report fuelled the idea that there had been a decline in churchgoing levels; but the census did not and could not show this, as it was a 'snapshot' of churchgoing levels at one moment in time. Since it also involved absolutely no occupational or social-class analysis, all of Horace Mann's statements on these matters were entirely speculative.

In the century and a half since the religious census, Mann has become the most frequently cited authority to support the contentions that churchgoing declined with urbanization, and that those who lost their church connection were the industrial working classes. Historians have been at odds over when this loss occurred. In the 1910s, for instance, the Hammonds wrote of the power of the 'Evangelical Revival' amongst the working classes until the 1830s:

At the beginning of the Industrial Revolution the Established Church hardly counted in the spiritual life of the districts where mines and factories began to collect these vast populations. ... The Church offered no function to the poor man.... The Chapel invited him to take a hand in the management of the affairs of his religious society: perhaps to help in choosing a minister, to feel that he had a share in its life, responsibility for its risks and undertakings, pride in its successes and reputation. As a mere exercise in self-government and social life, the Chapel occupied a central place in the affections and the thoughts of people who had very little to do with the government of anything else.[7]

But in the 1950s and early 1960s, researchers stressed the *early* origins of working-class alienation from the churches. E. R. Wickham, in his pioneering study of Sheffield, came to the firm conclusion that:

From the emergence of the industrial towns in the eighteenth century, the working class, the labouring poor, the common people, as a class, substantially, as adults, have been outside the churches. The industrial working class culture pattern has evolved lacking a tradition of practice of religion.[8]

This theme was taken up by K. S. Inglis whose 1963 book *Churches and the Working Classes in Victorian England* retains a prominent position in undergraduate reading lists. He pointedly stated that the issue was not one of when the churches lost the working classes:

If it is a mistake to imagine that the typical late-Victorian working man went to public worship for part of his life and then stopped, it may be almost as unwise to substitute a picture of his early-Victorian father or his Georgian grandfather worshipping for a time and then staying away. Before wondering why people stop doing something it is worth asking whether they ever started; and the social historian of religion in modern England could find a worse guide than the clergyman who remarked in 1896: 'It is not that the Church of God has lost the great towns; it has never had them.'[9]

This view has had enormous influence in the teaching of urban history (and especially in the framing of examination questions). However, it has sat beside – though often estranged from – a whole mass of research which suggests contrary conclusions. There have been two main reasons. One is that the conflicting evidence comes from research which has not been directly focused on the social history of religion but on other themes; the other reason is that intellectual disparities make it pedagogically difficult to set these themes beside the often less demanding statements from church historians. Much of the research can be encompassed by one broad interpretational framework called the 'midwife of class' thesis. This term emanates from Harold Perkin's *The Origins of Modern English Society 1780–1880* which described how religion acted as a *temporary* focus of social identity for the new social classes which emerged from early industrial urbanization. Dissenting churches were staging posts for some, though never all, of the middle and working classes on their centuries-long route from the Established Church to the secular life:

Old Dissent [Presbyterians, Congregationalists, Baptists, Quakers and Unitarians] was no more than the core of the middle class, as it had been of the middle ranks [of pre-industrial society], and if one door led into it from the Church [of England], another led out of it to sophisticated forms of unbelief; and Methodism was but one religion of the working class, and as often as not the gate through which large numbers of working men passed to secularism or religious indifference, the ultimate spiritual state of the majority in the great towns of the industrial age.[10]

Considerable support for this treatment has developed, E. P. Thompson's seminal *The Making of the English Working Class* drew attention to Methodism's 'gains among the new industrial working class', especially between 1790 and 1815. In his account, Methodism promulgated the industrial work ethic, turning the labourer 'into his own slave driver', indoctrinating the proletariat through the evangelical Sunday schools and Wesleyan preaching. A 'component of the psychic processes of counter-revolution', Methodism's revivalist emotionalism and its emphasis on the after-life made it 'the chiliasm of the defeated and the hopeless'.[11] Thompson's book raised other, more sophisticated issues concerning the nature of working-class culture and consciousness, but it attracted considerable hostile commentary from social historians of religion who objected to various epithets describing Methodism ('psychic masturbation' being the favourite) and to the emphasis on Methodism as crude bourgeois social control over the working classes.[12]

But the general treatment became academically popular. Another Marxist historian, Eric Hobsbawm, acknowledged that in the birth of industrial society and of the Labour Movement 'religion remained inseparable from the ideology of the common people and provided the main language for its expression', yet saw it as a temporary feature:

> The question of workingclass religion becomes confused, partly because the characteristic workers of proto-industrialization (handloom weavers, journeymen artisans, miners, etc.) were much given to religious excitement or heterodoxy, partly because much of industrialization took place in villages and small towns. Yet 'beyond any possible doubt' [Hugh McLeod[13]] workers in cities took less part in formal religious practice than others, and relative workingclass indifference or irreligion is recorded by practically all enquiries at all dates. ... Migration, normally from country to city, and contact with the city, led to a decline in religious practice, in certain cases even among the peasantry.[14]

Amongst the mostly non-Marxist social historians of religion, this broad interpretation became something of an axiom in the 1970s. In their encyclopaedic compendium of British religious statistics, Currie, Gilbert and Horsley wrote that 'industrialization created an urban population quite remote even from such desultory religious ministrations as obtained in many country places. ... [Shortage of church accommodation] prevented any church from counteracting the secularizing tendencies of industrial technique and an industrial, urban life-style.'[15] In other books, Alan Gilbert expressed satisfaction that statistical reanalysis of the 1851 religious census, together with qualitative investigations such as Wickham's on Sheffield, supported Mann's link between urbanization and institutional secularization.[16] Yet it was Gilbert who produced the firm statistical evidence of *increasing* church membership per capita during most of the nineteenth century. Accounting for this is the thorniest problem for the 'pessimist' school. Gilbert employs an approach derived from Perkin's 'midwife of class' theory. Despite the advance of 'secular' education, welfare and local government between 1830 and 1914, Gilbert argued that:

> religion enjoyed continuing social prominence because, fortuitously, the conflicts, tensions, political alignments precipitated during Britain's transition to urban society and liberal democracy coincided precisely with inherited religious confrontations between 'Church' and 'chapel'.

Thus, 'religion's inherited social prominence and continuing involvement in mainstream politics masked the impact of secularization because it guaranteed, at least temporarily, the Churches' institutional significance.' Defying the statistical evidence, Gilbert urges us to relocate secularization from the twentieth century – to which period the decline of church membership per capita is almost totally confined – to 'the Victorian era when growth ceased to be progressive and became marginal'.[17] Given his work in collecting and computing the data, this may seem a rather cavalier dismissal of what they show.

Gilbert's interpretation hinges on the sociological concept of 'modernisation' which, he maintains, undermined the parochial community that sustained the social role of religion. While religion remained temporarily important in the transitional proletarian villages of the early Industrial Revolution, he views cities as essentially preventing the formation of a 'viable community' in which religion could play a role: religion was incapable of 'fashioning communities out of an amorphous urban population, or of mobilising the particular kinds of communities which do emerge in urban contexts'.[18] The problem with this argument is that so little research has been conducted on the role of religion in large cities during the early Industrial Revolution. Apart from Wickham's work on Sheffield, which concentrated almost completely on church *accommodation* as a gauge of popular religion before 1850, research on large cities has tended to concentrate on the late-Victorian and Edwardian period (1880–1914) when evidence of secularization is clearly to be found in many forms: declining churchgoing, stagnating church membership per capita, collapsing religious voluntary organizations (especially Sunday schools), the secularizing effects of middle-class suburbanization, and the Labour Movement's erosion of evangelical social policy, amongst other things.[19] Moreover, much of the research has concentrated on London which, because of its unique early-modern experience as a metropolis, seems to have established a wholly different community framework for religion from that which developed in other places.

Large cities, then, and the working classes in them, have been fairly generally condemned for their religious indifference and apathy. Much of the academic literature suffers from over-generalization, untested hypotheses, and in some cases gross distortion. The accounts by ecclesiastical historians can be particularly alarming. In justifying concentrating solely on the Church of England in his two-centuries study of *Church and Society in England*, E. R. Norman offers a cascade of at best arguable and at worst demonstrably refutable statements. The Church of England, he wrote, had:

> a relationship to public life which has placed it far above the other Churches in its engagement with temporal questions. On most issues ... the social teachings of the Church of England can be taken as reasonably typical ... [and it] has exercised a leadership of the other Protestant Churches in social questions.

On social composition, Norman refutes the notion of working-class church membership:

> If the weight of the establishment is in the upper-middle and upper classes, then the weight of Protestant Dissent is certainly not working class, as is often supposed. It is middle and lower-middle class, touched with additions from the 'aristocracy of labour', the skilled artisans, pushing upwards through status aspiration to lower-middle-class gentility. *This has always been the case* with a few local exceptions where there have been real working-class Churches, like the Durham mining villages or the South Wales Chapels, where, anyway, urban living is still mixed with strong surviving rural qualities. The Roman Catholic Church has had a strong working-class element. But the Irish immigrants who formed it tended either to defect from the faith in the second generation or to move up the social scale.[20] (My italics)

Even the essays on religion in the celebrated Dyos and Wolff collection on *The Victorian City* perpetuate the myths with scant qualification. John Kent wrote: 'Back in the years 1815–48, when the new cities were at their most chaotic, it had looked as though working-class Christianity would vanish'; and the 'Victorian period saw the drying up of organized, institutionalized popular religion.' David Mole wrote of Birmingham: 'the majority of the working classes, though avowing membership of some religious body, were by accident or design, lost to organized religion, and were scarcely or never seen in the churches or chapels, for whom they formed a vast and increasing mission field.'[21]

To proceed in this field of inquiry, it is important to state clearly the questions to be investigated. It is proposed that the initial ones are these. First, what relationship, if any, was there between urbanization and rates of church affiliation? Second, who were the churchgoers? This essentially comes down to two *discrete* questions: what proportion of churchgoers were working-class, and what proportion of the working classes went to church? And third, how did organized religion fare in the large industrial city, as distinct from a small one, throughout the whole period of the Industrial Revolution from 1770 to 1914? The remainder of this article seeks to tackle these in turn.

## II

There are a number of possible ways of approaching the statistical exercise of calculating the effect of urbanization upon church adherence and practice. One is the simple task of comparing church accommodation (either number of churches or, a more precise variable, the number of church seats) to population at various dates during the process of urban growth. This requires considerable knowledge of local history sources to obtain a reasonable sample of towns. Where it has been done, the answer seems clear.[22] During the stages of sharpest urban expansion, which for most towns fell between 1780 and 1850, the ratio of church accommodation to population declined. Churches, and especially the Established Churches of England and Scotland, could not keep pace with urban growth because of legal difficulties and because of a disinclination to pass resources from rural to urban districts. But after about 1850, churchbuilding improved, and either kept pace with or exceeded population growth.

Another technique would be to examine levels of church membership per capita for a selection of cities over the course of the period. However, this would be an exceptionally time-consuming task, since membership statistics for localities would have to be painstakingly disaggregated from national figures collected by the individual denominations.

An easier method is to use the 1851 religious census. This is a notoriously difficult set of statistics to handle, and there is no space here to enter into the problems associated with it.[23] It is a much-quarried source of information, but it has tended to be used to provide illustrative examples from selections of localities rather than for systematic statistical scrutiny. However, two historians sought to relate size of town to rate of churchgoing on that census Sunday. Harold Perkin grouped towns into five sizes and totalled the attendances per capita for each group (given in brackets): London (25 per cent), towns over 100,000 population (27 per cent), towns between 50,000 and 100,000 people (35 per cent), 20,000 to 50,000 people (40 per cent) and all places under 20,000, both urban and rural (45 per cent).[24] Pickering carried out a very similar exercise. He grouped towns according to whether they had attendance figures in percentage terms of over 60, 50–9, 40–9 and under 40. He found that the distribution of towns with over 100,000 population was weighted to the lower percentages, and towns under 50,000 to the higher percentages, with towns of intermediate size being more evenly distributed but with a concentration in the 40–59 per cent groups.[25] These were fairly simple and apparently revealing statistical techniques. However, Pickering's results are somewhat skewed because he seems to have used the figures for the separate London boroughs, rather than a single figure for the metropolis.

In any event, a more sophisticated technique is regression analysis. This was undertaken on the figures for church attendances per capita for each of the 63 English and Welsh towns and 53 Scottish towns tabulated in the census, using the

*Table 1: Church attendance and population in British towns, 1851: regression equations and coefficients of determination* (t *statistics in brackets*)

| | | | | | |
|---|---|---|---|---|---|
| 1 $Attn_{Eng}$ = | 60.973 − | 0.0000096$Pop_1$ − | 0.2423△$Pop_2$ − | 0.3574△$Pop_3$ | $R^2 = 0.04$ |
| | (13.33) | (−1.61) | (−1.35) | (−0.65) | |
| 2 $Attn_{Sco}$ = | 88.185 + | 0.0000185$Pop_1$ + | 6.158△$Pop_2$ − | 10.739△$Pop_3$ | $R^2 = 0.25$ |
| | (13.66) | (0.23) | (1.50) | (−4.13) | |
| 3 $Attn_{Sco}$ = | 92.881 − | 9.265△$Pop_3$ | | | $R^2 = 0.26$ |
| | (16.89) | (−4.21) | | | |

$Attn_{Eng}$ = church attendance rates in towns, England and Wales 1851; $Attn_{Sco}$ = church attendance rates in towns, Scotland 1851; $Pop_1$ = population of towns 1851; $Pop_2$ = rate of growth of towns' population 1841–51; $Pop_3$ = rate of growth of towns' population 1801–51.

*Sources*: Data on church attendances were taken from Census of Great Britain, 1851: Religious Worship, England and Wales, PP 1852–3, LXXXIX; Census of Great Britain, 1851: Report of Religious Worship and Education, Scotland, PP 1854, LIX; data on population are from the censuses of population for 1831 and 1841, and from the 1851 Religious Census and the population census for that year. See note 26.

I am extremely grateful to Jayne Stephenson for assistance in collecting the religious data; to Dr Clive Lee, Dept. of Economic History, University of Aberdeen, for interpretation and presentation; and to Dr Stephen Tagg, Director of the Social Statistics Laboratory, University of Strathclyde, and Mr Fred Shakespeare, Computing Division, Lancashire Polytechnic, for computing.

crude attendance figures (the aggregate of morning, afternoon and evening attenders). In respect of Scotland, the high level of non-reporting (over 20 per cent) was compensated by attributing to each non-reporting congregation attendances equal to the congregational average for the locality. (The uncorrected Scottish attendance figures produced similar results, and are not given here.) These sets of figures were then correlated to three variables for *each town*: population size in 1851, per annum growth rate of population for 1841–51, and the per annum growth rate of population for 1801–51.[26] The results are shown in Table 1. What becomes apparent is how unsatisfactory the variables were in accounting for churchgoing rate. This failure was particularly acute with towns in England and Wales (equation 1). The coefficient of determination ($R^2$), when multiplied by 100, shows that less than 5 per cent of the variation in churchgoing rate amongst those towns can be accounted for by the variables, and each of the variables' *t*-statistics (calculated by dividing the parameter above it by the standard deviation) was considerably short of the value 2 which is required to show statistical meaning. In short, the English and Welsh religious census of 1851 showed no statistically significant relationship between churchgoing rate and population size or growth for towns and cities.

The results from Scottish towns show a somewhat better, though still not very significant result. But even this slight improvement is important, and may well have a bearing on the English and Welsh situation. Equation 2 shows that the first two variables were again not significant, but the third, growth rate over 50 years, was significant. $R^2$ indicated that 25 per cent of the churchgoing rate was accounted for by the variables, and the *t*-statistics indicate that all of that figure comes from the third variable – population growth over 50 years – in an inverse relationship. The $R^2$ for that variable alone, given in the third equation, shows that it actually accounted for 26 per cent of the variation in churchgoing rate. Thus, towns with higher population growth rates over the period 1801–51 tended to have lower rates of church attendance, but only one-quarter of the variation can be accounted for by this factor.

The Scottish result is significant because the Scottish religious census, unlike the one south of the border, included towns of every size from 2,364 inhabitants (Dingwall) to 344,986 (Glasgow); 41 of the 53 places classified as towns in Scotland had lower populations than the smallest town (Kidderminster with 18,462 inhabitants) included by Horace Mann in his calculations on urban areas in

England and Wales. For this reason, the Scottish census was far more sensitive to the impact of urban growth and size across the full range of community size up to large industrial city. Small towns of between 2,000 to 20,000 inhabitants were an important characteristic of the early Industrial Revolution, with economic growth centred on industries like handloom-weaving, spinning, calico-printing and mining. As we have seen, such proto-industrial communities are central to the analyses of Gilbert and Hobsbawm. They ascribe unusually strong religiosity to such places – a religiosity that was allegedly not evident in larger towns and cities. But the results of this investigation tend to discount this hypothesis; they indicate that town *size* did not determine churchgoing levels, but that town *growth* over the long term (i.e. 50 years) did account for a quarter of the variations discovered by Horace Mann in Scotland.

Clearly, further analysis of the 1851 religious census can and should be undertaken; churchgoing rates can be calculated for more urban districts from the enumeration returns for England and Wales, and other variables can be introduced. In the interim, the Scottish result would seem to show that the problem for organized religion in the cities during the first half of the nineteenth century was *partly* the logistical failure in the construction of enough churches for the expanding population. As already noted, churchbuilding caught up with or exceeded growth in urban population between 1850 and 1890 and, arguably, increased the social significance of religion in British cities. The reasons for this were probably closely linked to the changing social composition of urban congregations.

## III

Given the direction of historiographical debate, social-composition analysis would seem to be a fundamental necessity in the study of cities and secularization. Yet, despite widespread reference to, and indeed assertion concerning the extent (or more precisely, in most cases, the absence) of working-class church attendance, there has been surprisingly little research on the issue.[27] Analysing the social make-up of congregations and religious voluntary organizations is an extremely time-consuming task, matching names from communicants lists, baptismal registers and so forth to occupations found in street directories or elsewhere. Ideally, the selection has to include a fairly large number of people from a given congregation, a reasonable cross-section of denominations, and a meaningful proportion of all the congregations within a given locality. The rewards seem small in relation to the hundreds of tedious research hours needed, and in point of fact the ideal has never been attained.

But the little research that has been conducted provides us with fairly clear-cut conclusions. Table 2 summarizes the results of two of the largest studies – by Gilbert on English Dissent and Hillis on Glasgow Presbyterians – and also provides an example drawn from one congregation. Despite the enormous problems of classifying occupations (between skilled and unskilled manual for instance), and despite variations in the classification systems used by researchers, it is clear that a significantly high proportion of churchgoers were composed of skilled working-class groups. However, as the results from John Street Church in Glasgow show, there could be significant changes in the composition of a given congregation over a relatively short period. This is an important phenomenon, and one little remarked upon in the literature. Nineteenth-century city dwellers were highly mobile both spatially and socially. Congregations of all denominations (but especially Dissent) were continuously moving to newer and more expensive churches as the wealth and status of their membership rose. Thus, in the 1830s, the Royal Commissioners on Religious Instruction in Scotland found that in Edinburgh and Glasgow usually a *minimum* of two-thirds, and in many cases the *total* membership of Dissenting congregations, together with normally one-half of Established Church congregations, were composed of 'the working classes and the poor'.[28] This was noted especially of two prominent denominations – the Relief Church and the Secession

*Table 2: Social composition of church members*

| (Numbers) | Gilbert England c.1800–37 Dissent (10,997) % | English society (n/a) % | Hillis Glasgow Presbyt. dissent 1845–65 (2,397) % | Ch. of Scot. 1855–65 (1,269) % | John Street Relief/United Presbyterian Church, Glasgow 1822–32 (161) % | 1853–57 (148) % |
|---|---|---|---|---|---|---|
| 1 Upper class/high status; aristocracy, merchants, manufacturers, professional | 2.2 | 3.6 | 19.1 | 12.8 | 6 | 10 |
| 2 Farmers | 5.3 | 14.0 | | | | |
| Low status middle class | | | 20.7 | 8.6 | 11 | 27 |
| Tradesmen | 7.1 | 6.2 | | | | |
| 3 Skilled manual/artisans | 59.4 | 23.5 | 48.0 | 54.2 | 75 | 50 |
| 4 Unskilled manual | 17.4 | 19.5 | 12.3 | 24.4 | 9 | 13 |
| 5 Unclassified | 8.6 | 33.2 | | | | |
| | 100.0 | 100.0 | 100.0 | 100.0 | 101 | 100 |

*Sources*: A. D. Gilbert, *Religion and Society in Industrial England* (1976), 67; P. Hillis, 'Presbyterianism and social class in mid-nineteenth century Glasgow: a study of nine churches', *Journal of Ecclesiastical History, 32* (1981), 47–64; John Street Relief/UP Church, Glasgow, baptismal register, Scottish Record Office, CH3/806/12.

Church. However, 20 years after these denominations merged in 1847 to form the United Presbyterian Church, the congregations were renowned for their middle-class wealth. In 1871, for instance, the lowest rate of illiteracy amongst Scottish brides and grooms signing marriage registers was to be found in UP Churches.[29]

As churches moved up the social scale, and especially after 1850, so congregations commenced the massive evangelization schemes noted by all historians of the second half of the nineteenth century. These schemes invariably entailed a mission station at which working-class adherents were encouraged to become self-financing congregations. Arguably, the vast bulk of new urban churches in the 1850s, 1860s and 1870s were formed in this manner. Thus, there was constant recruitment from the 'unchurched', predominantly upwardly-mobile members of the working classes.

To understand this operation, it seems crucial for historians of urban religion to consider the mechanism of in-migration to cities and how the churches coped with it. For most of the nineteenth century, more than half of all inhabitants in large industrial cities were born elsewhere. This created a staggering logistical problem for the churches: to meet and recruit newcomers. The best known recruitment is probably that of Irish Catholic immigrants whose church could not keep pace with the number of in-migrants to British cities such as Liverpool and Glasgow until after 1850.[30] One of the few studies of Protestant migrants is that by Withers of Highland Presbyterians moving to Glasgow, Edinburgh and Aberdeen in the late eighteenth and early nineteenth centuries.[31] What studies of both Catholic and Protestant recruitment show is that the receiving congregations induced a social hierarchy with clergy and middle- or upper-working-class lay members socializing arriving migrants to the social mores and aspirations of city society. If the facilities for worship (church and mission halls, and prayer meetings in schools, houses and places of Sunday work) provided by religious voluntary organizations are added to the rising urban church accommodation of the second half of the century, then it seems inescapable that popular, working-class involvement in organized religion increased.

There are, of course, many writers who refer to contrary evidence.[32] The issue, though, is largely one of investigators' perception and methods. Those looking for non-churchgoing by the working classes will find it wherever they look, and can quite plausibly conclude that the majority of the working classes did not attend church either regularly or at all. But if research attempts to assess the proportion of churchgoers who came from the working classes, then it is becoming clearer that the answer is at least half – i.e. the majority.

This raises a whole series of questions about the extent of middle-class churchgoing which have really not been investigated.[33] In any event, the inevitable conclusion seems to be that we should not underestimate the extent of working-class religious observance in the nineteenth-century city. Chapel, church, religious and quasi-religious events (such as teetotal walks) sustained the role of religion in working-class communities. Though research has shown the importance of employers in supplying and controlling churches for their workers (especially in smaller industrial towns of the kind found in Lancashire and Lanarkshire),[34] considerable evidence has also been presented of proletarian self-management in religious organizations and activities for all periods in the nineteenth century.[35] Social control and class consciousness could co-exist within chapel, Sunday school and Rechabite tent. The divide in religious practice was thus not so much that between middle and working classes, but that *within* both classes.

## IV

Explaining how religion adapted to urban society in Glasgow is long and complex.[36] Much of the explanation is wrapped up in the story of churchbuilding, which in turn relates to the timing and nature of social fragmentation in the industrializing city. Rising demand for church accommodation from middle-class and upper-working-class groups led initially in 1780–1830 to the progressive exclusion from existing Established Churches of the lower working classes and also of many artisan families. The mechanism for exclusion was the pew rent, which, while not a new phenomenon, nonetheless overtook pews set aside for paupers and 'the lower class of inhabitants'. Pew rents, rising rapidly on the supply-demand mechanism, prevented lower-income groups from being able to afford to attend church.[37] This led to waves of churchbuilding, first between 1790 and 1830 by Dissenters, followed in the 1830s by disenchanted lower-middle and upper-working-class groups *within* the Church of Scotland. The latter created 20 new evangelical congregations which laid the basis for the great Disruption of 18 May 1843 when, in Glasgow, over half the worshippers in the state Church (and 40–50 per cent in Scotland as a whole) walked out to form the Free Church of Scotland, commencing another wave of churchbuilding.

Throughout all these church extensions, the proportion of the population able to be accommodated in church was diminishing as the number of Glasgow's citizens doubled about every 20 years. The Catholic Church, for instance, had only three chapels in the city in 1840 to cater for up to 40,000 adherents. But after 1850, churchbuilding by all denominations rose in a frenzy of evangelizing recruitment, improving church accommodation for the population. Pew rents continued to be exacted in Scotland to a greater extent than in England, but in the mission stations and halls there was more often free access, permitting attendance by lower-income groups. However, the pew rent became the symbol of worldly and spiritual 'success', the gauge of economic and religious salvation. Working-class congregations were reported to be particularly keen on paying rents, and on setting the scale of rents by congregational vote.

Another part of the explanation is the evangelical 'home mission' – the evolution of new 'agencies' to recruit the non-churchgoing. This was where the adaptation to urban society was most apparent as the traditional urban paternalism of the early-modern period disintegrated. The first and always the largest agency was the Sunday chool,[38] which by 1851 held more children than day schools. Sunday-school teachers – including significant numbers of future wealthy entrepreneurs – were the mainstay of the evangelical movement, undertaking home visitation to recruit children first for Sunday school and then, after 1840, for church day schools, Bands of Hope and other youth organizations. They were also important in the mission to adults, starting first with tract-distribution societies in the 1810s, but from the 1820s, they assisted 'home missionaries' (divinity students and, after 1850, young ministers). In the 1850s, 60s and 70s, it became *de rigeur* for fully sanctioned Protestant congregations to set up mission stations where fledgling working-class churches were nurtured to full status and financial self-reliance, and for congregational members to assist in large numbers as 'district visitors'. It was home visitation, which the non-churchgoing experienced at least three times a year in the 1850s and once a month by the 1880s, that contributed so much to the evangelical hegemony of 'respectable' popular culture and ideology in the second half of the century. Teetotalism and revivalism (in the mould established by visiting Americans such as Charles Finney, Edward Payson Hammond, Dwight Moody and Ira Sankey) were the two dominant themes after the 1860s. Many might and did reject the patronizing attitude of the evangelizers, but few could escape the ideas and influence of religion, so intense was the evangelizing of the city and so important was religion to organized leisure pursuits.

A third part of the explanation was the role of local government. In Glasgow as in many Victorian cities, outwardly secularized bodies like the Corporation, the poor-relief authority and (after 1872) the school board were dominated by churchmen (laity and clergy) who pushed the evangelical agenda of social-reform issues (such as intemperance, immorality, irreligion and inadequate education) to the forefront of municipal politics. On the same agenda, of course, there also appeared 'secular' issues: municipalizing the gasworks and the trams, laying main sewers, bringing fresh water to the city, and doing something about insanitary and overcrowded housing. But these issues emanated from within the evangelical community. Evangelical councillors voted across party lines for such measures from as early as the 1830s, trying to use municipal collectivism to create the 'Godly Commonwealth'. Religious visions of 'democratic cities of God' were important to the advance of social welfare at local level in the nineteenth century, and churchmen organized religious campaigns for social reform. In Glasgow, the Rev. Robert Buchanan, a Free Church minister, marshalled his presbytery (the church court for the city) to stave off one of the periodic ratepayers' reactions to the cost of the mammoth Loch Katrine water project of the 1850s. The same minister's experience in evangelizing a city-centre slum inspired a co-partnery of 22 businessmen and councillors secretly to buy up large tracts of slum property. The intention of improving or replacing the housing proved too expensive, so councillors on the group (including six successive Lord Provosts) used their position to get the property bought by the Corporation under the Glasgow City Improvement Act of 1866. Again, during the fever epidemics of the 1860s, the Council's sanitary officers used congregational district-visiting societies to distribute leaflets giving advice on hygiene and counter-measures.

These kinds of linkages between municipal improvement schemes and the churches abounded – with Glasgow being not unexceptional.[39] It helped to cement the ubiquity of the religious world view in civic life. Weekly church connection may have involved a minority of adults (though this may still admit of dispute), but it was a large minority that commanded the rules by which social mobility, economic success and 'respectability' were determined. Moreover, few could have been untouched at some point in their lives. In 1891, the number of enrolled Sunday-school scholars represented 65 per cent of Glasgow children aged 5–15 years. A census in Glasgow's adjoining industrial burgh of Clydebank in the same year showed that, despite rapid suburbanizing in-migration from Glasgow itself, 56 per cent of adults attended church one summer Sunday from amongst the 72 per cent who were church members.[40]

Late-Victorian society was thus very far from the irreligious state that many commentators both then and now would have us believe. It was arguably the point in British history when religion attained its greatest social significance. It did this not merely through churchgoing, but through a religious dominance of organized leisure (and leisure venues), social-policy formation and implementation, publishing, and many other facets of the nation's (urban) life. The fact that the majority of the population did not attend church on a given Sunday does not negate this. There were a whole host of levels of contact between individuals and religious activities and ideas. Glasgow was certainly an epicentre of evangelical innovation and enterprise; it was dubbed 'Gospel City' by one young churchman in the 1830s.[41] But it was not untypical of the progress of religion in other British cities, and was by no means the nation's 'most religious' urban community. Throughout the country, religion adapted to the new urban circumstances – at first rather slowly, but by the second half of the century with extraordinary skill and success.

## V

The early and mid 1890s were the peak for organized religion in Britain from which decline set in. Historians have given considerable attention to the crisis that befell the churches and religious voluntary organizations at the turn of the century.[42] Church attendances started to decline dramatically, church membership growth slowed down and in some cases declined per capita of population, and most religious and temperance voluntary organizations went into rapid and unremitting decay. Every major statistical indicator of religion's social significance shows a downturn in either absolute or relative terms between 1890 and 1914.

The reasons are complex. They involve the suburbanizing of the middle and expanding lower-middle class groups, the advance of the Labour Movement, the rise of state welfarism, the decline of church influence in secular affairs as local elected agencies such as school boards were abolished, and the leisure and sports revolution. But the one major reason that cannot account for it is urbanization. It is in the years before the First World War that the proportion of the British population living in cities started to stabilize at around 80 per cent. Many big cities like Glasgow, Manchester and Liverpool, together with a very large number of small and medium-sized industrial towns, attained very nearly their maximum proportions. It was at this point of stagnation in the urbanization process that all the measurable indicators of religion showed, for the first time, that religion was in decline.

Other evidence seems to support this view. In his examination of the Thompson–Vigne oral history material, Hugh McLeod found considerable regional variation in the extent to which the 500 socially-representative respondents born between 1872 and 1906 claimed that their parents were 'regular' church attenders: very high in Wales and Scotland (over 50 per cent of both mothers and fathers), medium in Lancashire and Yorkshire (over 40 per cent mothers, 32–40 per cent fathers), lower in the Potteries, north Midlands and the north-east (40 per cent mothers, 20 per cent fathers), and very low in London (24 per cent mothers, 20 per cent fathers).[43] Yet these results did not seem to suggest that either size or economic base of a town was an operative factor determining the extent of active church connection. Moreover, analysis of the results produced by the Bible Society censuses of churchgoing, conducted between 1979 and 1984, shows clearly that, with the exception of the strongly religious Western Isles of Scotland and north Wales, the areas of highest church attendance are mostly industrial or formerly industrial regions: west central Scotland (especially the Glasgow conurbation), South Wales, and Lancashire. Indeed, the regional variations are very similar to those uncovered by McLeod from the oral testimony for the turn of the century. Figures for highly urbanized districts varied considerably above and below the national average – from 19 per cent for Glasgow and 14 per cent for Merseyside, to 9 per cent for London, Tyne and Wear and the west Midlands.[44] Once again, urban community *size* appears to have little bearing on differences between towns in churchgoing rate.

From the 1900s down to the present day, church decline has been virtually continuous; only brief and small rises in church membership were apparent in the period after the Second World War.[45] Twentieth-century forces – such as world wars, economic depressions, dramatic rises in standards of living, and sustained growth in leisure time – seem to have assisted the process. It is important for historians to focus much more attention on these and other developments during the period when the weight of evidence suggests religious decline mainly or exclusively occurred – the twentieth century. The bulk of secularization took place in cities but, it has been suggested here, the causes were not the size of cities, only partly the rapidity of growth of cities, and not because the nineteenth-century urban working-classes were non-churchgoers.

**Callum G. Brown**
University of Strathclyde

## Notes

1 J. Cox, *The English Churches in a Secular Society: Lambeth, 1870–1930* (1982). For a review of the international literature, see H. McLeod, 'Religion in the city', *Urban History Yearbook* (1978).
2 T. Chalmers, *The Christian and Civic Economy of Large Towns*, 3 vols (1821–6).
3 B. I. Coleman (ed.), *The Idea of the City in Nineteenth-Century Britain* (1973), 87–94.
4 A. Gilbert, *Religion and Society in Industrial England: Church, Chapel and Social Change 1740–1914* (1976), 98–103; C. G. Brown, *The Social History of Religion in Scotland since 1730* (1987), 101, 106–7.
5 M. Spufford, 'Can we can count the "Godly" and the "Conformable" in the seventeenth century?', *Journal of Ecclesiastical History*, 36 (1985); Brown, *Social History*, 90–100.
6 Census of Great Britain, 1851: Religious Worship, England and Wales, PP, LXXXIX (1852–3), clviii, clxvii.
7 J. L. Hammond and B. Hammond, *The Town Labourer 1760–1832: The New Civilisation* (1917), 268–71.
8 E. R. Wickham, *Church and People in an Industrial City* (1969 edn), 14.
9 K. S. Inglis, *Churches and the Working Classes in Victorian England* (1963), 14.
10 H. Perkin, *The Origins of Modern English Society 1780–1880* (1969), 196.
11 E. P. Thompson, *The Making of the English Working Class* (1968 edn), 386, 393, 419.
12 *Ibid.*, 'Postscript', 916–23.
13 H. McLeod, 'Class, community and religion: the religious geography of nineteenth-century England', *Sociological Yearbook of Religion*, 6 (1973), 47.
14 E. Hobsbawm, 'Religion and the rise of socialism', *Marxist Perspectives*, 1 (1978), 14, 18.
15 R. Currie, A. Gilbert and L. Horsley, *Churches and Churchgoers: Patterns of Church Growth in the British Isles since 1700* (1977), 85.
16 Gilbert, *Religion and Society*, 113.
17 A.D. Gilbert, *The Making of Post-Christian Britain* (1980), 74, 78–9.
18 Gilbert, *Religion and Society*, 113–14.
19 S. Yeo, *Religion and Voluntary Organisations in Crisis* (1976); H. McLeod, *Class and Religion in the Late Victorian City* (1974); P. Thompson, *Socialists, Liberals and Labour: The Struggle for London 1885–1914* (1967); R. Gray, 'Religion, culture and social class in late nineteenth and early twentieth century Edinburgh', in G. Crossick (ed.), *The Lower Middle Class in Britain 1870–1914* (1977); Cox, *Lambeth 1870–1930*; Brown, *Social History*.
20 E. R. Norman, *Church and Society in England 1770–1970: A Historical Study* (1976), 7.
21 J. Kent, 'Feelings and festivals: an interpretation of some working-class religious attitudes', and D. E. H. Mole, 'Challenge to the Church: Birmingham 1815–65', both in H. Dyos and M. Wolff (eds), *The Victorian City*, vol. 2 (1973), 866, 868, 821.
22 Wickham, *Church and People*, 70–89, 108–9, 127, 148–56; R. B. Walker, 'Religious changes in Liverpool in the nineteenth century', *Journal of Ecclesiastical History*, 19 (1968); R. Peacock, 'The Church of England and the working classes in Birmingham, 1861–1905' (unpublished M.Phil. thesis, University of Aston, 1973, appendix 1); Brown, *Social History*, 100; C. G. Brown, 'Religion and Social Change', in T. Devine and R. Mitchison (eds), *People and Society in Scotland 1750–1830* (1988).
23 See K. S. Inglis, 'Patterns of Religious Worship in 1851', *Journal of Ecclesiastical History*, 11 (1960); W. S. F. Pickering, 'The 1851 Religious Census – a useless experiment?', *British Journal of Sociology*, 18 (1967); D. M. Thompson, 'The 1851 Religious Census: problems and possibilities', *Victorian Studies*, 11 (1967); D. J. Withrington, 'The 1851 Census of Religious Worship and Education: with a note on church accommodation in mid-nineteenth-century Scotland', *Records of the Scottish Church History Society*, 18 (1974); R. Dennis, *English Industrial Cities of the Nineteenth Century: A Social Geography* (1984), 29–32; Brown, *Social History*, 59–83.

24 Perkin, *Origins*, 201.
25 Pickering, '1851 Census', 402.
26 For two towns, Ashton and Rochdale, growth rate figures for 1801–51 were calculated on population totals for districts which conformed as closely as possible to the borough boundaries used in the 1851 Religious Census. London refers to the Census Registration Division. In the Scottish Religious Census, the data for Airdrie and Musselburgh actually refer to the parishes of New Monklands and Inveresk respectively; the figure for Banff includes the burgh of Macduff; and the figures given for 1851 population in Forfar, Glasgow, Paisley and Perth were untraceable in or mistranscriptions from the population census, and were substituted.
27 For a review of the literature, see H. McLeod, *Religion and the Working Class in Nineteenth-Century Britain* (1984).
28 Royal Commission on Religious Instruction, Scotland, First Report, PP, XXI (1837), 29, Second Report, PP, XXXII (1837–8), 17. For an English example of high religiosity amongst unskilled workers, see E. Hopkins, 'Religious dissent in Black Country industrial villages in the first half of the nineteenth century', *Journal of Ecclesiastical History, 34* (1983).
29 Brown, *Social History*, 151.
30 C. Johnson, *Developments in the Roman Catholic Church in Scotland 1789–1829* (1983); J. E. Handley, *The Irish in Scotland 1798–1845* (1945) and *The Irish in Modern Scotland* (1947); L. H. Lees, *The Exiles of Erin: Irish Immigrants in Victorian London* (1979).
31 C. W. J. Withers, 'Kirk, club and culture change: Gaelic chapels, Highland societies and the urban Gaelic subculture in eighteenth-century Scotland', *Social History, 10* (1985).
32 Mole, 'Challenge to the Church'; T. C. Smout, *A Century of the Scottish People 1830–1950* (1986), 181–208.
33 But see H. Meller, *Leisure and the Changing City, 1870–1914* (1976) on Bristol, and J. Kent, *Holding the Fort: Studies in Victorian Revivalism* (1978), which though misleading as to the middle-class monopoly of this socially widespread phenomenon, provides some useful perspectives.
34 P. Joyce, *Work, Society and Politics: The Culture of the Factory in Later Victorian England* (1980), and A. B. Campbell, *The Lanarkshire Miners 1775–1874* (1979).
35 T. W. Laqueur, *Religion and Respectability: Sunday Schools and Working Class Culture, 1780–1850* (1976); A. J. Ainsworth, 'Religion in the working-class community and the evolution of socialism in late nineteenth-century Lancashire: a case of working-class consciousness', *Histoire Sociale, 10* (1977).
36 C. G. Brown, 'Religion and the development of an urban society: Glasgow 1780–1914' (unpublished Ph.D. thesis, University of Glasgow, 1982).
37 C. G. Brown, 'The costs of pew-renting: church management, church-going and social class in nineteenth-century Glasgow', *Journal of Ecclesiastical History, 38* (1987).
38 C. G. Brown, 'The Sunday-school movement in Scotland, 1780–1914', *Records of the Scottish Church History Society, 21* (1981).
39 See for example E. P. Hennock, *Fit and Proper Persons: Ideal and Reality in Nineteenth-century Urban Government* (1973), and R. V. Holt, *The Unitarian Contribution to Social Progress in England* (1938).
40 Figures calculated from *Glasgow Sabbath School Union, Annual Report* 1892; and *Clydebank and Renfrew Press*, 22 August 1891.
41 *Autobiography of a Scotch Lad* (1887), 30.
42 See note 19 above.
43 H. McLeod, 'New perspectives on Victorian working-class religion: the oral evidence', *Oral History Journal, 14* (1986), 33.
44 C. G. Brown, 'Religion', in R. Pope (ed.), *Atlas of British Social and Economic History* (1988), map 12.2.
45 Currie *et al.*, *Churches and Churchgoers*; R. Currie and A. Gilbert, 'Religion', in A. H. Halsey (ed.), *Trends in British Society since 1900* (1972).

# Immigration and population growth in early fourteenth-century Norwich: evidence from the tithing roll

Estimates of urban population before the Black Death have been hampered by a lack of suitable data. Although it is common knowledge that many towns reached a physical size in the late thirteenth and early fourteenth centuries that was not exceeded until the early-modern period, little definite is known about the gross urban population at this date.[1] Where attempts have been made to estimate urban populations these have traditionally depended on multiplying from one arbitrary sector of the community, such as property owners, taxpayers or freemen, or on back projections from the late-fourteenth-century poll tax returns.[2] The problem with such an approach is not only that there is little independent basis for the multipliers used, but also that the relationship between any such arbitrary sector and the urban population as a whole may alter from town to town as well as from time to time within the same community. An exception to this approach has been the recent work of Derek Keene, who has used other indicators of population size and pressure, namely land values, the extent of the built-up area and density of settlement, to estimate the early-fourteenth-century populations of Winchester and London.[3] It may be significant that this method has produced considerably higher population figures than had been reached by the more traditional approach. In this uncertainty, any source that purports to record the whole of a demographically defined section of the population is of considerable interest. Norwich is fortunate in the survival of such a source in an early-fourteenth-century tithing roll for the leet of Nedham and Mancroft (hereafter Mancroft), one of the four leets of the city.[4] An urban tithing roll should list all adult males within the area covered and so the Mancroft roll presents an unusual opportunity to study the total adult male population of one quarter of a medieval town. Moreover, any apparent changes should be the direct result of population change within the leet rather than just the result of extrinsic economic and governmental factors. This paper seeks to establish the credibility of the Mancroft tithing roll not only as a population source for the date when it was first drawn up, but also as an indicator of population change during the period that it was in current use. As such the roll has been used to attempt to quantify population growth and mobility in a way that has rarely been achieved in a medieval context.[5] Much of the work has involved comparing the tithing populations with more usual urban sources, namely deeds and the 1332 subsidy assessment, and throws light on some problems inherent in their use.

This interpretation of the Mancroft tithing roll has been helped greatly by the Norwich Survey plans which reconstruct the pattern of property ownership at Norwich from the deeds enrolled on the court rolls, 1285–1340 (hereafter the Reconstructions).[6] No original work has been done on the enrolled deeds for this paper and (unless otherwise specified) all details of the ownership of freehold property and of wills have been taken from the Reconstructions.

I

The physical size of Norwich in the early fourteenth century may have been out of proportion to its apparent wealth. Although only one other county, apart from Middlesex, enjoyed a higher average assessment per square mile than Norfolk in the 1334 lay subsidy, Norwich ranked only seventh among provincial towns in terms of wealth taxed that year.[7] Its hinterland was populous as well as (in subsidy terms) wealthy; the population of eastern Norfolk was such that a density approaching 500 persons per square mile has been suggested for some districts.[8]

The geographical area of Norwich reflected this populous hinterland. The two and a half mile circuit of the walls, completed by 1343, together with the river enclosed a square mile containing more than 50 parish churches. Naturally there were open spaces within the walls, but to appreciate the extent to which street frontages were developed by the early fourteenth century one need only look at Hochstetter's plan of Norwich in 1789 as redrawn by James Campbell.[9] A few side streets were built up in *c.*1789 where there were no houses in the early fourteenth century and there are a few areas of fourteenth-century development where there was open land at the end of the eighteenth century, but generally the similarity between the pattern of development in these two periods is remarkable. In the eighteenth as in the early fourteenth century most building took place within the city walls, with minor suburban development to the south and west. Only along Pockthorpe St to the north-east and beside the river to the north-west did some eighteenth-century development extend beyond the fourteenth-century bounds. The Reconstruction evidence suggests that not only was Norwich before the Black Death comparable in built-up area to the late-eighteenth-century city, but also that it was still growing into the early fourteenth century. It is difficult to get much general impression of the results of the numerous divisions and amalgamations of property in the more heavily developed parts of the city, but overall there appears to be a gradual

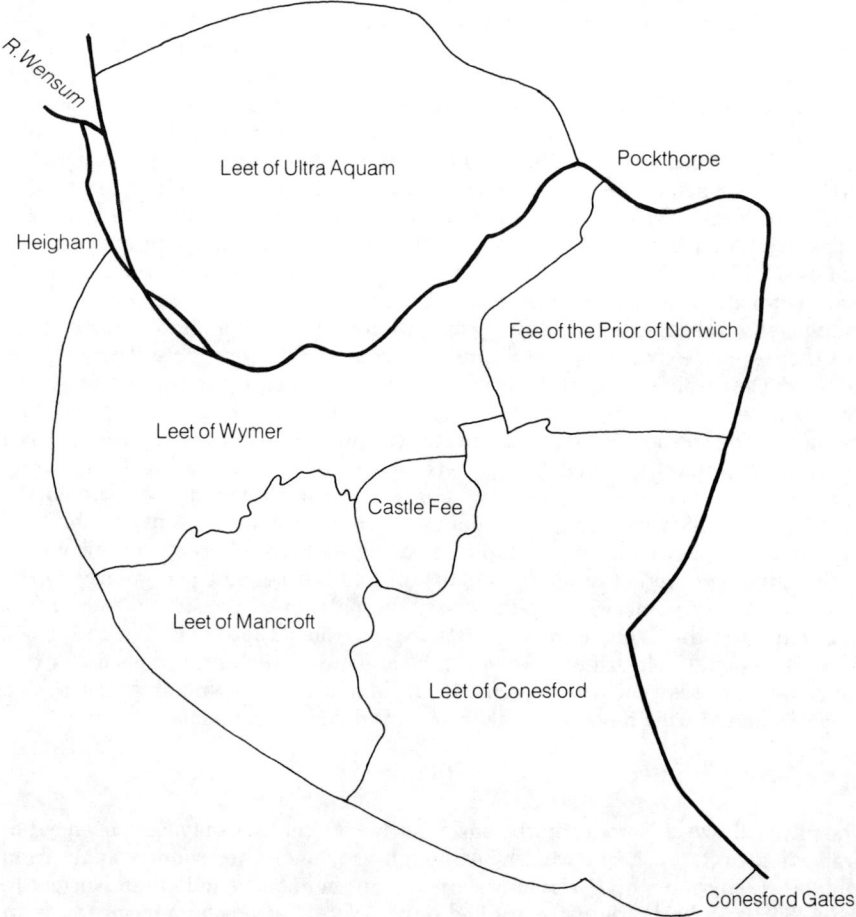

Figure 1. Norwich *c.*1300. The prior also held a small area within the leet of Ultra Aquam.

extension of housing over the period 1285–1340 into areas previously described as land; exceptions to this general expansion may occur to the south near Conesford Gates and in the north-west corner of the city near the wall where a few properties may be reverting to land towards the end of the period. An expectation that the demand for housing would continue may have been a factor behind two moves made by the city about this time. One was a dispute with the escheator over the right to profit from the revenues from waste grounds, which was settled in the city's favour in 1330; the other was the purchase of the Castle Fee in 1345, the grant of which specifically referred to the rent of places to be inhabited in the future.[10]

The quarter of Norwich covered by the Mancroft tithing roll lay to the west of the castle, where the French borough with its huge market place had been founded soon after the Conquest (figure 1).[11] As the leet of Mancroft it was one of the four leets into which medieval Norwich was divided but consisted of only two parishes, St Peter Mancroft (hereafter St Peter) and St Stephen. St Stephen in its turn comprised the areas of Nedham and Great Newgate. Nedham was the western part of the parish and the road leading from the castle to St Stephen's gates was known as Nedham St (*vicus de Nedham*); Great Newgate was the southern area to the east of Nedham St (figure 2). Although both the parishes in the leet of Mancroft stretched south and west from near the castle to the city walls, they were very

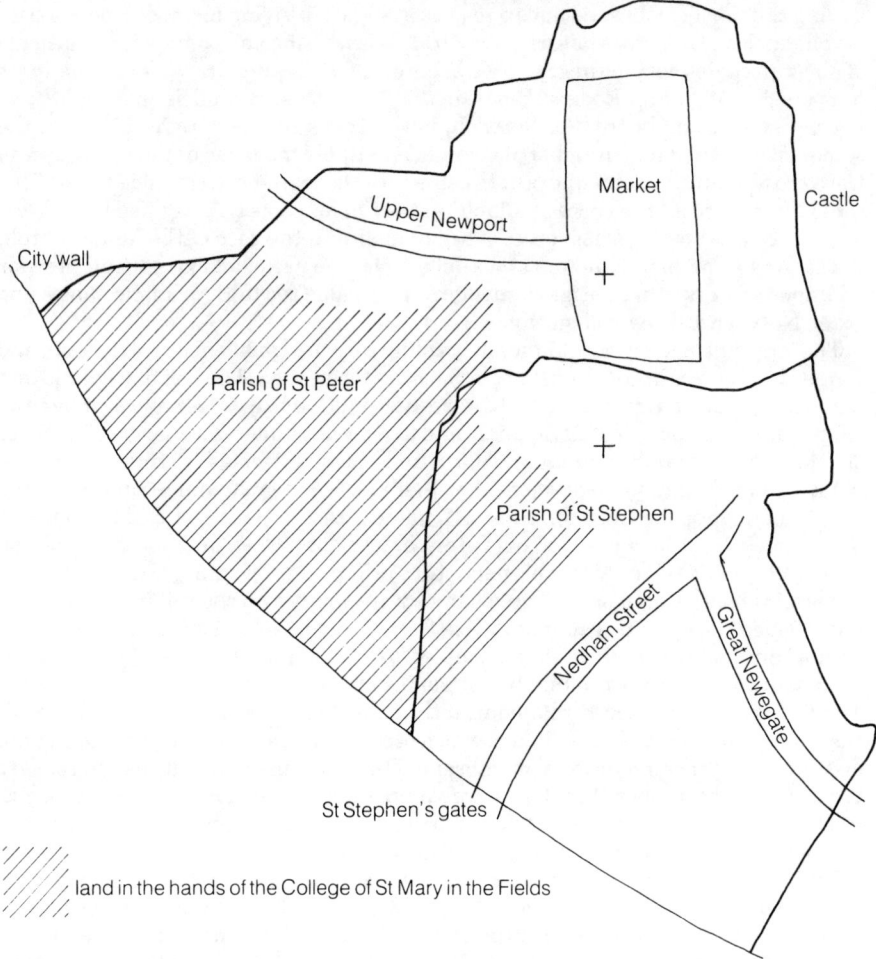

Market

Castle

Upper Newport

City wall

Parish of St Peter

Parish of St Stephen

Nedham Street

Great Newegate

St Stephen's gates

land in the hands of the College of St Mary in the Fields

Figure 2. Mancroft Leet *c.*1300.

different in character. Almost the whole of the western half of the parish of St Peter was open land (generally described as the croft) in the hands of the College of St Mary in the Fields. Apart from a short stretch along Upper Newport to the north of this section, all the development in the parish was concentrated around the market place. Part of the croft of the College also lay in the parish of St Stephen, but the area held was smaller and had little impact on the character of the parish as a whole. St Stephen's extended from near the edge of the market to the north to the city wall to the south and included the large mainly undeveloped area to the south-east that was referred to in Edward I's reign as the street and fields of Great Newgate (figure 2).[12] Thus, as well as providing a picture of the population of Mancroft leet as a whole, the tithing roll also makes it possible to compare a heavily built-up central market area (St Peter's) with a parish with room for development on the outskirts of the city (St Stephen's).

## II

The method of community policing known as the frankpledge system, which prompted the creation of tithing rolls, is well known.[13] In particular the system prevailing in Norwich, together with many aspects of the Mancroft roll, has been described by W. Hudson in *Leet jurisdiction in the city of Norwich*.[14] The Mancroft tithing roll itself can best be understood as a single surviving member from a series of rolls such as L. R. Poos has used for rural Essex.[15] At some point, a list was made of all adult males within the leet area. Where new rolls were drawn up annually, as happened at Margaret Roding, Essex, in the 1320s, this original listing would have needed little amendment. At Norwich, however, as in other areas of Essex, the same roll was used for a number of years.[16] Inevitably men died or moved away and were crossed off the list while others came into the leet and were added to it. This could go on until all the space available on the roll for some tithings had been filled, when presumably the whole process began again. In the case of the Mancroft roll, the start of a completely new list was delayed by the use of an extra membrane for additions after the three original membranes became too full. As implied above, no other Norwich tithing roll survives.

The original list on the Mancroft tithing roll was published by Hudson and Tingey in *The records of the city of Norwich*.[17] It is headed 'The leet of Nedham and Manecroft and of Great (*Magna*) Newegate' followed by 242 names under the subheading 'The parish of St Stephen' and 618 names under 'The parish of St Peter de Manecroft', making a total of 860 names for the leet as a whole. Although Hudson and Tingey say elsewhere that there were only 690 names on the tithing roll,[18] their published list contains 247 names for the parish of St Stephen and 615 names for the parish of St Peter, a total of 862. The first state of the Mancroft tithing roll used for this paper thus differs in a few minor particulars from the original list as published. These names were written on the roll in two columns and divided into groups ranging in size from 5 to 29. Not every group made up a tithing and two or more could be coupled together under one capital pledge, or representative, so that the number of names in each tithing ranged from 5 to 67. The first state is written throughout in the same hand and there is no break with the change to the parish of St Peter, which occurs near the top of the second column on the dorse of the first original membrane. The roll is undated, but the reference to Great Newgate implies that it was drawn up after jurisdiction over that area was granted to the city in 1305.[19] By comparing the names of capital pledges Hudson demonstrated that the tithing roll pre-dated one of the surviving Norwich leet rolls, itself dated only to the 'sixth year'.[20] Using his knowledge of the Norwich enrolled deeds, Hudson took this to be 6 Edward II or 1312–13, as the eighteenth-century Norwich antiquary Kirkpatrick had done before him, and all available evidence supports this dating. As the Norwich leet courts were held around Easter, this leet roll dates from early 1313.[21] The Mancroft tithing roll was probably drawn up several years before the leet roll, as one tithing had already changed capital pledge twice by then; the second pledge, John de Wroxham, had his will proved in 1312. Detailed work done on tithing men owning property in these two parishes supports Hudson's date of about 1311.

However, as has already been mentioned, the Mancroft tithing roll does not just consist of the first state as published by Hudson and Tingey but contains numerous additions. New entries were made in a number of different hands and slightly differing inks presenting the possibility of establishing a chronological sequence. To depend just on palaeographic techniques would probably lead to a high degree of error, but fortunately some sixteen groups of entries can be easily identified, irrespective of ink or handwriting, by a series of dots and dashes used before and/or after the name. Some examples of this are: a name followed by two dashes, a name followed by three dots, two dots before a name and two afterwards, and two dots before a name and one afterwards. This exercise is also helped by the move to the additional membrane. The different tithings are identified on this extra membrane by their capital pledges, whose names appear to have been written in all at the same time in the same hand that was used to squeeze in a few final entries on the other membranes. The use of the new membrane means that newcomers to the leet after the move can be clearly distinguished from those who came in before. Where groups of entries can be identified, they appear in the same order throughout the roll. This suggests that whenever the tithing roll was reviewed one clerk was responsible for adding names to all the appropriate tithings.

New names appear to have been added to the tithing roll on about 40 different occasions between c.1311 and the last entry on the additional membrane. If alterations were made annually, the roll would cover a period of about 40 years. It seems improbable that the list should have been in regular use over so long a period and other tithing rolls are known to have been drawn up more frequently. There is an interval of only two years between the extant Leicester rolls and none of the pairs of surviving rolls used by Poos are more than 29 years apart, the others being annual or separated by 8 or 15 years.[22] Another possibility is that the Mancroft tithing roll was updated twice a year, perhaps at a view of frankpledge at Michaelmas and around Easter when the Norwich leet courts were held.[23] This would bring the tithing roll up to about 1331. In fact the roll appears to end in 1333. It presumably post-dates the 1332 lay subsidy assessment as 6 of the 51 taxpayers who can be identified on the roll were crossed off before it was abandoned.[24] On the other hand, three tithingmen not removed from the roll are known from the Reconstructions to be dead by 1334. This gives the Mancroft tithing roll a lifespan of approximately 22 years. The move onto the additional membrane would seem to have taken place five to six years before the roll was abandoned, which dates it to c.1327–8.

Hudson has dealt at length with the question of who was entered on the Mancroft tithing roll.[25] All lay adult males in a town were required to enrol in tithing. Though it is nowhere stated, it may be assumed that Norwich followed the usual practice of enrolling boys at the age of 12; this is the age given in the articles of the view of frankpledge which were copied into the Norwich Book of Customs early in the fourteenth century.[26] There is no evidence that Mancroft men were removed from tithing because they were too old, as at Leicester,[27] but a couple of men are marked 'sick' (*eger*) and may have been removed because of ill health. Clerics were generally exempt, but this probably did not apply to those only in minor orders as Richard, clerk of the church of St Peter de Parmentergate, was presented for not being in tithing in 1291.[28] Maintenance of the system of frankpledge was taken seriously by the city authorities and the Norwich leet rolls, 1288–1313, contain many presentments and amercements of men out of tithing and those who harboured them.[29] These include fathers who harboured sons, masters who harboured servants and even a taverner for harbouring a lodger who was not enrolled. Although Bracton suggests that a man need not be in frankpledge if he holds '*rem immobilem*' in a city, it is clear from the Reconstructions that in Norwich ownership of real property did not give exemption.[30] Nevertheless Hudson did suggest that a small number of substantial citizens may have been above the obligations of frankpledge.[31] It is difficult to see, however, how such exemption could have worked. It could not have been on the basis of wealth alone, as those who can be identified on the tithing roll make up a cross-section, in wealth, of the taxpaying population of 1332. Even if wealth were the criteria, a man would presumably be entered in a tithing before his wealth was acquired. Another possible hypothesis is that there was a group of leading families, whose members were exempt. However, if we look at the bailiffs, who were the chief officers of the city until the early fifteenth century, this too appears unlikely. Four bailiffs were elected each year and so Mancroft, as one of the four leets, might be expected to provide one-quarter of the bailiffs. Of those serving during the 22-year period 1312–33, a possible 21 are to be found on the tithing roll; some years there is no identifiable bailiff but in other years two or even three of the bailiffs apparently came from the leet of Mancroft. Furthermore, of the 64 men who served as bailiff between 1300 and 1340, 17 appear on the Mancroft roll and of the 38 who served as Members of Parliament for Norwich during the same period no fewer than 10 are named on the tithing list.[32]

It is therefore surprising to find that only about half the men named in the Mancroft section of the Norwich 1332 lay subsidy assessment can be identified on the Mancroft tithing roll.[33] One factor was probably the instability of surnames that can make identification so difficult at this date.[34] The name under which a boy was entered at the age of 12 need not have been the same as that by which he was generally known in later life. Ralph de Burwode is a case in point. In the Mancroft section of the 1332 subsidy he was assessed to pay 12s.; he served as Member of Parliament for Norwich in 1306 and as bailiff in 1325, 1330 and 1333; by 1293 he already held a capital messuage in the parish of St Peter, which he left by will in 1334; his wife was amerced for brewing in the leet of Mancroft in 1313.[35] Here is a man, apparently resident in the parish of St Peter, whose wealth and status might appear to absolve him from enrolling in a tithing. Moreover, no Ralph de Burwode appears on the Mancroft list. Fortunately, in his case, we can tell from the Reconstructions that he was also known as the son of Roger the hatter and Ralph the son of Roger le Chapeller is duly entered on the first state of the roll.

The other possible explanation helps to define the nature of the male population as entered in tithing. Not all those assessed for tax under Mancroft in 1332 need have been primarily resident in the leet. In fact some need not have been resident in the leet at all. In the late thirteenth and early fourteenth centuries movable wealth was assessed where it lay and not where the taxpayer lived.[36] It would not be surprising if merchants not living in Mancroft leet found it convenient to store goods near the market in the parish of St Peter and were assessed on these rather than on household items. A probable example of this is Simon de Lopham. Simon was one of the six subsidy-men on the Mancroft tithing roll who was crossed off before the roll was abandoned. Although entered and owning property in the parish of St Peter, his name was marked *'alibi in leta de Wymer'*, in which leet he also owned property. (Wymer was the leet adjoining Mancroft to the north.) Nevertheless he was assessed to pay 16d. in the Mancroft section of the 1332 subsidy roll.[37] More common, however, may have been the assessment of merchants, many of whom owned real property in Norwich, who were accustomed to spend time in the city on business but whose primary residence was elsewhere. Such men would have been like Robert de Collyngebourne at Winchester, who although in the Winchester assessment played little part in civic life and may have been principally associated with Collingbourne in Wiltshire.[38]

It thus appears that the Mancroft tithing roll is a list of all adult males primarily resident in the area and settled there for over a year, with the exception of religious and clerics in higher orders, possibly a small number of the infirm and men who evaded enrolment. The last group may have been fairly small. Capital pledges were required to present anyone who was not in tithing and were amerced for concealment if they failed to do so, while the penalties for 'harbouring' must have led fathers, masters and landlords to encourage enrolment. It is impossible, however, to tell whether the small number of presentments of men out of tithing in 1313 (six for the leet of Mancroft) was the result of success in enrolling all who were liable or of failure to identify those who were not enrolled.[39]

However complete the c.1311 tithing list may be, quite different problems arise when considering the final state of 1333. It is impossible to estimate the size of the adult male population of the leet of Mancroft at any stage between c.1311 and 1333 because it is not known when names were crossed off the roll, but a list of all the names that were never taken off should, theoretically, give the tithing population at the date when the roll was abandoned. This would only be the case if all men dying or leaving the area were removed from the roll. To test the probability of this having happened, we need to look both at the roll and at external sources. Throughout the tithing roll some names are struck through. Occasionally this is explained by the note 'mortuus' or 'alibi', but usually no explanation is given. It is clear from the inks used that the deletions took place at different times and the practice continues onto the additional membrane, so that men who had only been entered in the last couple of years were crossed off before the roll was abandoned. In addition to the names struck through, some are marked with a cross. This appears not to be tantamount to removal from the roll. Some names have two crosses against them before they are crossed off; other men, though their names are so marked, probably survived until 1333. John Brid, for example, appears on the 1332 subsidy assessment and John the son of Peter Flint buys and sells property in the mid 1330s. Hudson, quoting from the early-fourteenth-century Norwich custumal, explains that a cross usually meant absence without leave and refers to this use of crosses among the names of capital pledges on the Norwich leet rolls.[40] It seems likely that their use here indicates a requirement to attend the view of frankpledge and/or the leet courts and heavy dots beside other names may have fulfilled the same purpose. Such marks were probably not made very often, but are one indication of the practical use to which the tithing roll could be put and for which it would need to be kept with reasonable accuracy.

Another sign of the care shown in maintaining the Mancroft tithing roll is an apparent response by the compilers to the problem, in a growing population, of identification. This shows itself in an increasing use of occupations and 'double' surnames when describing tithingmen coming onto the roll and occasionally an occupation was added to a name already there. For example, Reginald de Bauburgh from the c.1311 state of the roll was followed by Reginald le Fevre de Bauburg and Reginald Hering de Bauberg; John de Aylsham and John son of Thomas de Aylsham, both from c.1311, were followed by John son of Simon de Aylsham; while Roger de Brok was distinguished from both Roger de Brok carpenter and Roger de Brok fishmonger. The use of such 'double' names and occupations rises from 22 to 32 per cent of the total roll population between c.1311 and 1333.[41] The practice was so successful that the increase in the number of men described in exactly the same way as someone else failed to keep pace with the rise in population, let alone made the type of proportional increase that might be expected.[42]

Inevitably external evidence is only available for the more wealthy members of the tithing population. The Reconstructions show, either through wills or references to widows and executors, that 18 of the men on the Mancroft tithing roll were dead by 1333. All except one of these, William Bele, were crossed off the roll before it was abandoned. It is more difficult to quantify evidence that men whose names were left on the roll were still alive in 1333, but something can be done by considering the fate of a particular group, those who owned real property in c.1311. It appears from the Reconstructions that 109 of the men listed on the first state of the roll may have owned the property in which they lived. Of these, 62 died or moved and were crossed off the list. Twelve of the remainder were named as taxpayers in the 1332 subsidy assessment and eight more appear in the Reconstructions, either buying and selling or in abuttals, in or after 1333. Another six were alive shortly before 1333 as they are mentioned in the Reconstructions in 1327, 1330 and 1332. There is no information available on 20 of the remaining 21 men after the early 1320s. The twenty-first was William Bele who was not taken off the roll although he is known to have been dead by 1318. (His son and widow conveyed property in the parish of St Peter in that year.) It is hard to see why he should have been left on the roll. He was a capital pledge and the '*cap*' before his name was crossed through, but not the name itself. One possible explanation is that he had a second son of the same name who came into the tithing at about the time of his father's death; his son Simon was entered on the roll in *c*.1312.

Even if the name 'William Bele' was left on the list in error, the Mancroft tithing roll was probably accurate in its treatment of 81 per cent of this group of 109 men and it is highly unlikely that all the remaining 20 names should have been crossed out. The Mancroft roll was a working, not a formal, document, much of whose point would have been lost had it not been kept with reasonable care. Any document of this type may be expected, through ignorance or carelessness, to contain errors and there were probably men whose names should have been removed and were not, in the same way that there were men who should have been in tithing but were not enrolled. It appears, however, that the tithing roll was kept with quite as high a degree of accuracy as could reasonably be anticipated and any errors are unlikely to be on such a scale as to invalidate the drawing of conclusions from the final state of 1333.

## III

Between *c*.1311 and 1333 the number of adult males listed on the Mancroft tithing roll rose from 860 to 1513, an increase of 76 per cent. The rate of increase was not standard throughout the leet. The tithing population of the parish of St Peter rose by only 59 per cent (618 to 981), while that of St Stephen rose by a massive 120 per cent (242 to 532) or more than doubled over the period. Nor was the rate of growth the same in both parishes. Whereas men entered on the tithing roll after the additional membrane was begun (*c*.1327–8) made up 16 per cent of the final male population for the leet as a whole (237 out of 1513), this group made up only 11 per cent of the final tithing list for St Peter's (111 out of 981), but 24 per cent of the final total for the parish of St Stephen (126 out of 532). This was not because the flow of men into St Peter's had reduced by *c*.1327–8, but because of a much increased rate of turnover in the parish after that date.

There are two main methods of expressing movement in any community for which there exist two or more lists of population. One is to calculate the percentage of the earlier population that also appears on the later list/s (the persistence rate). The second method is to express the number leaving the first list (exits) as a percentage of the earlier population and those coming into the area (entries) as a percentage of the later population (turnover rates).[43] The persistence rate for the leet of Mancroft as a whole was 47 per cent, for the parish of St Peter was 42 per cent and for the parish of St Stephen was 59 per cent. This last figure may seem surprisingly high for a period of 22 years, but it must be remembered that the tithing roll only lists men aged 12 and above. The Princeton Model West life tables quoted by L. R. Poos in his study of Essex tithing lists indicate how much lower the death rate is likely to be in a population of this age where infant and child mortality are excluded. Thus, according to the table quoted by Poos, given a life expectancy for males at birth of 39.16 years the percentage of deaths per annum among males of over 12 would be 2.62 per cent.[44] This figure would produce a persistence rate of almost 59 per cent (58.76) over 20 years. The turnover rate for the whole leet, *c*.1311–33, was 53 per cent for exits, 73.3 per cent for entries, an average of 63.15 per cent. Once again, the rates show up differences between the two parishes. For the parish of St Peter the turnover rates for exits and entries were 57.9 and 73.5 per cent respectively, an average rate of 65.7 per cent; turnover rates for the parish of St Stephen were 40.5 per cent for exits and 72.9 per cent for entries, the average being only 56.7 per cent. These differences are accentuated if one looks not only at the exits from and entries to the populations of *c*.1311 and 1333, but also at the number of men who both came into the leet and left again between these two dates.[45] Altogether, 273 of the males who were entered on the Mancroft tithing roll after the first state of *c*.1311 had been crossed off before the roll was abandoned in 1333; 221 of these were entered for the parish of St Peter and 52 for the parish of St Stephen. When these figures are added to the other exits and entries, the turnover rates for the whole leet rise to 84.7 per cent for exits, 91.3 per cent for entries with an average rate of 88 per cent; the amended rates for the parish of St Peter become 93.7 per cent for exits and 96 per cent for entries, average 94.85 per cent, while for the parish of St Stephen they are 62 per cent for amended exits, 82.7 per cent for entries, average 72.35 per cent. This contrast between the two parishes is particularly noticeable in the period after the move to the additional membrane (*c*.1327–8). Of the men entered on this membrane for the parish of St Peter 52 per cent (120 out of 231) were crossed off as against only 6 per cent (8 out of 134) of the St Stephen's entries over the same period.

These differences in turnover between the two parishes that made up the leet of Mancroft would appear to lend support to the accuracy of the tithing roll. As at the biennial reviews the same clerk went through the whole roll adding names as necessary (p. 19), it is probable that deletions were made throughout the roll at the same time and that both parishes were treated in the same way. Assuming this to be true, the parish likely to experience the greater degree of error was St Peter, with its higher population and density of housing and tithings which were less clearly defined on the ground (later, p. 24). The situation might be made worse by increased mobility in a market area with more opportunities for casual labour. Thus, if the growth in population suggested were attributable to failure to remove tithing men from the roll, this is where the apparent growth would be greatest. Moreover, there would be no reason for the two parishes to show such differing rates of turnover. The picture that emerges from the Mancroft roll is far otherwise. Although the rise in the tithing population of the parish of St Peter is greater in number than the rise in St Stephen's (364 to 290), it is much smaller as a proportion of the *c*.1311 population in the two parishes (59 to 120 per cent). After *c*.1327–8 even the number of men staying on the roll is smaller in the parish of St Peter (111 to 126). Add to this the greater mobility of the central parish as shown by its lower persistence rate (42 opposed to 59 per cent) and higher turnover rates (average 94.85 as against 72.35 per cent) and the tithing roll produces a credible pattern of settlement moving to the outlying parishes as the centre of Norwich becomes saturated.

Turnover rates calculated from tithing rolls are bound to appear lower than those calculated from lists of the population as a whole. One reason for this has already been mentioned, the fact that infant and child mortality are excluded. A second is that the tithing roll essentially records only the more stable part of the population. No man was entered on the roll until he had been in the city at least a year and a day and in a community the size of Norwich this must often have meant in the area of the leet for a year and a day. As names were added twice a year a man could be living in Mancroft for almost eighteen months before even becoming liable to enrol. Those unable to find work and accommodation, or servants hired for a limited time, could move on and never come within the purview of the frankpledge system.[46] These considerations do not affect the comparison of turnover rates in Norwich with those of the four rural Essex communities studied by Poos, as the information for both comes from early-fourteenth-century tithing rolls.[47] To compare them it is necessary to restate the Norwich figures as annual turnover rates to allow for the differing lengths of time between the rolls used. This is achieved by dividing the overall rates by the number of years between two lists. Assuming the Mancroft tithing roll to have been in use for 22 years, the annual turnover rate for exits from the list was 2.41 per cent and for entries was 3.33 per cent. The mesnes of the crude annual rates for the Essex tithing areas were 4.68 per cent for exits and 5.63 per cent for entries, reducing to 4.2 and 5.2 per cent respectively when weighted in proportion to community size. It would probably be wrong to assume from these figures that mobility was much greater in rural Essex than in Norwich at this date. Two factors may depress the Mancroft, compared to the Essex, rate of turnover. One is the 22 years that separate the first from the final state of the Mancroft tithing roll. The further apart two listings are, the less realistic will their turnover rates become, because of the failure to allow for intermediate movement. It is, for instance, impossible over 20 years to achieve an annual turnover rate of more than 5 per cent, but the Essex statistics are affected by a turnover at Margaret Roding of 14.7 per cent in only one year. Another possible factor is the size of the communities involved. The smaller the community listed, the greater is the likelihood that men will move out of it to find work and accommodation. At first glance this would help to explain the lower turnover in Mancroft as the smaller of the two parishes (St Stephen's) had almost twice as many tithingmen as the largest of the Essex communities (242 to 133). The difficulty is in knowing within how large an area a Mancroft tithing man could move without changing his tithing.

The wide variation in the size of the Mancroft tithings (p. 18) suggests that they were organized to some extent on a territorial basis. This was clearly considered desirable, as may be gathered from a thirteenth-century tract which recommends that at least one guardian (*custos*) be assigned to each area or street (*vicus*) of a town (*burgi*).[48] Such an arrangement existed at Nottingham where one or more capital pledges presented at the great tourn for each street, while Hudson has demonstrated how the capital pledges of 1288 for the Conesford leet of Norwich were distributed throughout the district.[49] A similar pattern has been sought for the leet of Mancroft. The tithingmen for *c*.1311 and 1333 have been compared with property owners named in the Reconstructions, on the assumption that the correct pattern would produce the greatest number of men apparently living in their own property. The results of this exercise suggest that, as at Nottingham, the tithings in the parish of St Stephen were organized by street. This is at its clearest in the case of the two main tithings for Great Newgate, where the first tithing covers the east end of the street and the second west end. This strict demarcation of tithing area is unusual in Mancroft and probably springs from the fact that the jurisdiction over Great Newgate had been acquired so recently by the city (p. 18) that the overlaps and uncertainties apparent elsewhere had not had time to develop. In the rest of the parish of St Stephen the tithing boundaries are by no means so clearcut and several tithings may cover the whole length of one street. On the whole these tithings are not entered on the list in any topographical order. This is not surprising, as there are changes in sequence even between the main roll and the additional membrane. In the parish of St Peter different forces came into play. There the dominating factor was the market place and the tithings were arranged around this in an anti-clockwise spiral starting from the church and working from the edge of the market outwards. The later tithings covered not only the areas furthest from the market place but also possible recent encroachments south of the market and to the east of the church, as well as the site of the former jewry south-west of the castle. This system led to considerable overlap and it was by no means unusual for a member of one tithing to become the capital pledge of another covering more or less the same area.

In short, although the Mancroft tithings appear to have been arranged on a topographical basis, their boundaries were very flexible. This may well have resulted from previous amalgamations and divisions of tithings such as can be seen to take place during the lifetime of the Mancroft roll. The result was that the size of community within which a tithing man could move without changing tithing was perhaps as large as the largest Essex community used by Poos in the case of the parish of St Stephen and double this in the case of the parish of St Peter.[50] Even taking size of community and the length of time between the lists into account, however, it is clear that population turnover in Norwich in the early fourteenth century was no higher than in rural Essex and was probably lower. Such stability may have been encouraged by the tendency towards zoning of occupations in medieval towns; once a man had acquired some expertise, he would be likely to find similar work within the same area.[51] It also implies that the urban expectation of life before the Black Death was appreciably higher than that recently suggested for the fifteenth century.[52]

This emphasis on the relative stability of the Mancroft population is not intended to rule out the possibility of movement within the leet, although there is little evidence of this on the tithing roll. There are only 39 cases of men possibly moving between the two Mancroft parishes and other evidence suggests that families tended to stay within the same small area. It is noticeable that surnames common in one parish will be completely absent from, or hardly appear in, the other. Furthermore, there is virtually no evidence for movement between tithings, apart from capital pledges, within the parish of St Stephen. The situation was otherwise in the parish of St Peter where a number of men may have moved tithing. There is little point in attempting to quantify this movement, however, as there are few occasions when both parties are described in such a way as to make identification at all certain and many of the possible 'movers' may be two different individuals. All such movement, of course, will be included in the turnover rates given above. On the other hand, it must be re-emphasized that the men recorded on the tithing roll were those relatively settled in the parish. Moreover, as has already been indicated, a tithingman in either parish could probably move within quite a wide area, up the street or elsewhere on the same side of the market, without having to change his tithing. Nothing in the Mancroft roll precludes rapid mobility over very short distances similar to that found in fifteenth-century Cheapside.[53]

If stability was one circumstance contributing to the growth of population in Mancroft in the early fourteenth century, immigration into the leet was surely another. Over the 22 years following the first state of c.1311, 1,393 men were newly entered on the Mancroft tithing roll, an average of just over 63 a year. A comparison of the numbers coming in before and after the move to the additional membrane in c.1327–8 indicates that the average remained about the same throughout the period.[54] The new entrants were divided between the two parishes roughly in accordance with the number of tithingmen they contained; the proportion entering the parish of St Stephen increased after c.1327–8 as its share of the leet population grew. Some of the new tithingmen were undoubtedly the sons of existing inhabitants who had just reached the age of 12. However, even assuming a birthrate as high as 40 per 1,000, the possible result of a previous wave of immigration, fewer than half of those coming onto the roll could be accounted for in this way.[55] Some of the remainder would have come from other parts of the city or from within Mancroft leet itself. It can reasonably be assumed, however, that a high proportion of the new tithingmen came from outside Norwich, though there is no direct evidence for this apart from a few rural-sounding surnames. (For example: William son of Bartholomew late Medwo de Felmingham, Nicholas son of Robert le Shephird.[56]) The incentive for such immigration is not far to seek. Bruce Campbell has shown how, in Norwich's densely populated hinterland, land hunger was creating ever smaller holdings, leading to subsistence farming.[57] In these circumstances the opportunities for work offered by Norwich must have lured many into the city. Such immigrants were probably both young and single. Only in a few instances (nineteen) are two or more members of a family apparently entered together on the Mancroft roll, while an influx of young men shortly before c.1311 would help to account for the high persistence rate in the parish of St Stephen. There is no obvious pattern of immigrants moving from the outskirts of the city into the centre or vice versa; the numbers moving between the two Mancroft parishes are more or less in relation to their populations. Twice as many men possibly moved out from the parish of St Peter to that of St Stephen (26) as moved in the other direction (13).

It is probable that most of these immigrants were poor. It is clear from the early-fourteenth-century Norwich custumal that Norwich already contained an appreciable number of day labourers by the turn of the century and immigrants squeezed out of the rural property market must have increased the proportion of the population with neither capital nor security of income.[58] The effect of this can be seen in the changing proportion of the Mancroft tithing population identifiable on the Reconstructions as owning real property. Between c.1311 and 1333 this proportion dropped from 13 (109) to 6 per cent (96).[59] The failure of newcomers to purchase was such that although tithingmen from c.1311 made up only 27 per cent (404) of the Mancroft tithing population in 1333, 37.5 per cent (36) of the 1333 owner-occupiers were already in the leet by c.1311 and 25 per cent (24) were not only in the leet but already in possession of property 22 years before. Moreover, only two out of the 237 men who were newly entered on the tithing roll after c.1327–8 and not crossed off by 1333 had acquired real property before the roll was abandoned. This fall in the percentage of Mancroft tithingmen owning real property was not occasioned by the wealthy turning to leasehold rather than freehold. No fewer than 40 (78 per cent) of the 51 Mancroft subsidymen who can be identified on the tithing roll owned freehold property within the leet. Moreover, of all the 112 Mancroft taxpayers in 1332, 66 per cent (74) owned freehold property within the leet and a further 3.5 per cent (4) owned it elsewhere in the city.[60] Personal wealth may also have been concentrated in the hands of well-established residents of the leet, but difficulties in identification make this less certain.[61]

The settled adult male population of Mancroft, as listed on the tithing roll, provides a possible basis for estimating the total population not only of that leet, but of the city of Norwich as a whole. There has been one previous published attempt to do this, when Russell took Hudson's figure of 690 names on the roll and calculated a city population of 13,000 on the assumption that all tithingmen were heads of households.[62] James Campbell rightly rejected Russell's figure on the grounds that this assumption was incorrect and, taking into account an earlier estimate by Hudson of 4,000, based on the lists of freemen, suggested an early-fourteenth-century population of 5,000–10,000.[63] However, 10,000 would appear to be on the low side even if the leet of Mancroft held at least a quarter of the total city population. When the Mancroft tithing population of 860 in c.1311 is doubled to allow for adult women and increased by a further 45 per cent to include children under 12, it produces an established lay population for the leet of 2,494.[64] Multiplied by four, this gives an established lay population for the four leets of 9,976. For the population of the city as a whole one must add to this figure the religious and clerics (Norwich had one priory, four friaries and several hospitals and minor religious foundations), those resident within the liberties of the prior of Norwich and of the Castle Fee, a floating population that had been in the city for less than a year to eighteen months and those men who managed to evade enrolment. By 1333, moreover, the established lay population of Mancroft had grown to 4,388 (1,513 × 2.90), suggesting a much higher gross population figure.

Any attempt to estimate the gross population of the city from the Mancroft tithing roll comes up against the problem of what proportion of the population of Norwich lived in the leet of Mancroft. A possible answer to this question can be calculated from the Reconstructions. Mancroft was in area the smallest of the four leets (see figure 1) and with a large part of the leet open land in the hands of the College of St Mary in the Fields (see figure 2) only about half the district was available for housing. On the other hand, the area around the market was heavily developed, in contrast to the situation in the leet of Conesford which contained mainly ribbon development along its two main roads with considerable areas of open land between. The measurement of occupied frontages would not take into account housing density and instead an estimate has been made of the number of habitable properties in each leet. This exercise is not without its difficulties. Quite apart from the frequent divisions and amalgamations, property descriptions are inconsistent and it is often impossible to tell exactly when open land was built up. To reduce these difficulties, properties have been counted according to their latest description; shops are counted when sold separately but not when sold with a messuage and groups of cottages or shops are counted as only one. The effect of this is perhaps to overestimate the amount of housing in the leet of Mancroft as shops round the edge of the market were often sold off individually. Market stalls have not been counted.

According to these calculations, the four Norwich leets contained approximately 1,870 habitable properties by 1340. Of these 360 (19 per cent) lay in the leet of Mancroft. Because the latest description has been used to calculate the housing stock, these figures are best applied to the Mancroft tithing population of 1333. Assuming the leet of Mancroft held 19 per cent of the population, as it held 19 per cent of the habitable properties, the established lay population for the four leets in 1333 was 23,095 (4,388 × 100 ÷ 19). On this basis and taking into account the religious, the clerks, residents of the liberties, short-term residents and evaders, the total population of Norwich in 1333 cannot have fallen far short of 25,000. It also becomes possible to make a more realistic assessment for c.1311. It is unlikely that other parts of the city grew as fast as the leet of Mancroft in the early fourteenth century and the possible reduction of housing on the edges of the leets of Conesford and Ultra Aquam (p. 17) suggests that the population may indeed have reached its peak sooner in these areas. This would mean that Mancroft held a smaller percentage of the population of the four leets in c.1311 than in 1333. Certainty is impossible, but if, for example, 15 per cent of the population lived in Mancroft in c.1311, the total population of Norwich at that date could have been as high as 17,000 (2,494 × 100 ÷ 15 = 16,627). This continuing growth of Norwich in the early fourteenth century must be contrasted with Poos's picture of a declining population in rural Essex after the 1315–17 famine.[65] Rural population decline, however, would not necessarily rule out urban growth, though incompatible with the possible reasons for immigration given above. It is, however, not certain that the Norfolk rural population was also in decline. On the contrary, Bruce Campbell suggests that the rise in population in eastern Norfolk continued up to the Black Death.[66]

## IV

Despite the many qualifications inherent in this study, it does appear possible to use the Mancroft tithing roll to measure population size and change. It would be unrealistic to suppose that such a document was kept with complete accuracy. Nevertheless, the degree of care apparent makes it improbable that the conclusions reached are entirely due to errors on the roll. Precise figures based on this one source should be used with caution, but this need not invalidate the general trends which emerge. Inevitably there is little extrinsic evidence for the suggestions made in this paper, though the Reconstructions do support the contention that Norwich was growing in size into the fourteenth century. Moreover, the suggested population figure of 25,000 does not seem impossible in the light of Norwich's populous and land-starved hinterland, or in terms of a city that in built-up area was almost identical to that which housed at least 37,000 towards the end of the eighteenth century.[67]

The figure of 25,000 for the population of Norwich in 1333 exceeds previous estimates not only for Norwich, but also for other provincial towns before the Black Death. It is not, however, out of line with Derek Keene's proposed 10,000 to 12,000 for Winchester or 80,000 for London at this date.[68] If accepted, such estimates bring into question the relation between certain sectors of the population and the whole. While, as already indicated, the relationship between any arbitrary sector and the gross population of a town is unlikely to be constant, it is perhaps worth mentioning that in spite of a suggested population of 25,000 in the 1330s, only 418 persons were listed in the Norwich subsidy assessment for 1332 and on average only 34 men were recorded as taking up the freedom each year at Norwich during the five years 1343/4–1347/8.[69] These figures may seem extreme, but just how low a proportion of the population was represented by the number of 1332 Norwich taxpayers can also be demonstrated from the 1,870 'habitable properties' calculated for the purpose of comparing the leets (p. 27). While this figure almost certainly underestimates the number of dwellings in the city and still more the number of households, and so cannot be used to establish the number of persons per household, it does nevertheless provide a minimum for the number of householders in Norwich at this date. On the basis of 1,870 properties the number of 1332 taxpayers was at most 22 per cent of the number of householders. Taking into account properties in the jurisdiction of the prior of Norwich and within the Castle Fee, which are not included in the 1,870, and the artificial nature of the calculation of the 'habitable properties', and allowing for multiple occupation, the true proportion was probably very much lower.

The fortunes of towns in the half century before the Black Death are a matter of debate.[70] The Mancroft tithing roll shows the population of the leet growing rapidly up to 1333, with the edges of the city near the walls becoming more heavily populated as the pressure in the centre increased. Though the rise in population may not have been so great in other areas of Norwich, or may have reached its peak sooner elsewhere in the city, Norwich as a whole was expanding. To judge from the Mancroft evidence, this growth was fuelled by immigration from the countryside, but the population, once sufficiently settled to appear on the tithing roll, shows a high measure of stability within the parish. Whether this physical growth was accompanied by economic growth is beyond the scope of this paper, but within the leet of Mancroft real wealth became concentrated in the hands of a smaller proportion of the population, while immigration probably increased the number of urban poor. It is therefore quite possible that while Norwich grew in size and population during the early fourteenth century, it may have declined both in relative wealth and in social cohesion.

**Elizabeth Rutledge**

## Notes

Acknowledgements are due to the Norwich Survey and the British Academy for helping to fund this paper, to Dr Derek Keene and Dr Roger Virgoe for their helpful criticism, to Margot Tillyard for making the Reconstructions available and to the staff of the Norfolk Record Office.

 1 Published comments include: 'No reliable estimate can be made of her pre-Black Death population', M. D. Lobel and E. M. Carus-Wilson, 'Bristol', 11 n.5; 'No figures relating to population exist before the poll tax of 1377', M. D. Lobel, 'Cambridge', 12. Both from *The Atlas of Historic Towns*, ed. M. D. Lobel, II (1975).
 2 For example, E. Miller's estimate of over 8,000 for York in 1334 is based on entries to the freedom. 'Medieval York', in *A History of Yorkshire: the City of York*, ed. P. M. Tillott (Victoria County History, 1961), 84–5. A. Saul suggests a pre-1348 population of over 4,500 for Great Yarmouth from the 1377 poll tax figures. 'Great Yarmouth and the Hundred Years War in the fourteenth century', *Bulletin of the Institute of Historical Research*, 52, no. 126 (1979), 105.
 3 Derek Keene, *Survey of Medieval Winchester*, Winchester Studies, 2 (1985), 368 and *Cheapside before the Great Fire* (1985), 19–20 and a paper given to the Anglo-American seminar on aspects of the late medieval economy and society (Historical Geography Research Group) Norwich, July 1986. The Winchester figure of 10,000–12,000 is based on a much increased estimate for the fifteenth century. The London figure is more or less double the conventional estimate of 40,000–50,000.
 4 Norfolk Record Office (hereafter NRO), Norwich City Records (hereafter NCR), case 5, shelf c.
 5 Mobility in rural Essex in the early fourteenth century is the subject of L. R. Poos, 'Population turnover in medieval Essex: the evidence of some early-fourteenth-century tithing lists', in *The World We Have Gained*, eds L. Bonfield, R. M. Smith and K. Wrightson (1986), 1. Derek Keene discusses urban mobility in the fifteenth century in *Cheapside before the Great Fire*, 17.
 6 For details of the methods employed in the Reconstructions see M. Tillyard, 'The acquisition by the Norwich Blackfriars of the site for their church c.1310–1325' in S. Kelly, E. Rutledge and M. Tillyard, *Men of Property, an Analysis of the Norwich Enrolled Deeds, 1285–1311* (1983), 5ff. At present the plans are held by the Centre of East Anglian

Studies, University of East Anglia. When finalized they will be deposited in the Norfolk Record Office.

7  The other county was Oxfordshire. R. E. Glasscock, 'England circa 1334', in *A New Historical Geography of England*, ed. H. C. Darby (1973), 141, 184.

8  Bruce Campbell, 'Population pressure, inheritance and the land market in a fourteenth-century peasant community', in *Land, Kinship and Life-cycle*, ed. R. M. Smith (1984), 92.

9  James Campbell, 'Norwich', in *The Atlas of Historic Towns*, ed. M. D. Lobel, II (1975), 11 and map 2. In the following discussion this map is being compared to the Reconstructions.

10  W. Hudson and J. C. Tingey (eds), *The Records of the City of Norwich* (1906–10), I, 23–7; II, 226/7.

11  For more detailed plans and a concise history of the development of Norwich see James Campbell, 'Norwich'.

12  Campbell, 'Norwich', 11.

13  The standard work is W. A. Morris, *The Frankpledge System* (1910).

14  W. Hudson (ed.), *Leet Jurisdiction in the City of Norwich during the 13th and 14th Centuries with a Short Notice of its Later History and Decline* (Selden Society, 5, 1892).

15  Poos, 'Population turnover'.

16  *Ibid.*, 8, 13–14.

17  Hudson and Tingey, *Records*, I, 372–81.

18  *Ibid.*, II, cxix; Hudson, *Leet Jurisdiction*, xlviii.

19  Hudson and Tingey, *Records*, I, 18–20.

20  Hudson, *Leet Jurisdiction*, xlviii–1.

21  *Ibid.*, xxiv–xxvi.

22  M. Bateson (ed.), *Records of the Borough of Leicester*, II (1901), 153–4, 157; Poos, 'Population turnover' 8–9.

23  The clause from Magna Carta requiring view of frankpledge to be held at Michaelmas was among those copied into the Norwich Book of Customs in the early fourteenth century (NRO, NCR, case 17, shelf b, f. 30d) but there is no evidence that it was followed. The Essex tithing rolls were drawn up in May and June – Poos, 'Population turnover', 7–9.

24  Public Record Office, E179/149/9m.79.

25  Hudson, *Leet Jurisdiction*, lxv ff.

26  NRO, NCR, case 17, shelf b, fos 37–8.

27  J. C. Russell, *British Medieval Population* (Albuquerque, 1948), 293.

28  Hudson, *Leet Jurisdiction*, 41.

29  NRO, NCR, case 5, shelf b.

30  H. de Bracton, *De legibus et consuetudinibus Angliae*, f. 124b.

31  Hudson, *Leet Jurisdiction*, xlii.

32  H. le Strange (ed.), *Norfolk Official Lists* (1890), 93–5, 132–4.

33  51 out of 112. Of the 112, 5 were women, one name cannot be read and one man is only identified as the brother of John de Marsham.

34  The instability of peasant surnames at this date is discussed by Zvi Razi in 'The Toronto School's reconstitution of medieval peasant society: a critical view', *Past and Present, 85* (1979), 142–4; Poos discusses the problems this produces in comparing different tithing lists in 'Population turnover', 14–15. In *The Origin of English Surnames* (1967), 331, 338–41, P. H. Reaney gives examples of name changes in early-fourteenth-century London but found the printed records of Norwich threw little light on the question. Hudson, however, from his knowledge of the records of about 1300 believed 'the same person will figure sometimes with a name of origin, sometimes with a name of occupation, sometimes with a nickname, and to a casual reader his identity will be altogether unsuspected', *Leet Jurisdiction*, xcii.

35  Public Record Office E179/149/9 m. 79d; Le Strange, *Norfolk Official Lists*, 132, 94–5; Reconstructions; leet roll 1313, NRO, NCR, case 5, shelf b.

36  This point is implicit in much of J. F. Willard, *Parliamentary Taxes on Personal Property, 1290 to 1334. A Study in Medieval English Financial Administration* (Cambridge, Mass., 1934). It has also been made by A. R. Bridbury in 'English provincial towns in the later middle ages', *Econ. Hist. Review*, 2nd series, *34* (1981), 18.

37  There were apparently two Simon de Lophams owning property in Wymer. W. Rye (ed.), *Calendar of Norwich deeds enrolled in the court rolls . . . . . . 1307–1341* (1915), *passim*. Public Record Office E179/149/9 m. 79.

38  Keene, *Survey of Medieval Winchester*, 294–5. Special arrangements were made to tax London merchants at their place of residence but this may not have applied where they held 'foreign' tenements. Willard, *Parliamentary Taxes*, 153ff.

39  Leet roll 1313, NRO, NCR, case 5, shelf b.

40  Hudson, *Leet Jurisdiction*, xlii and li.

41  193 and 860 and 483 out of 1513 respectively. Unless otherwise apparent, all numbers in this paper have been rounded up or down to the nearest whole number.

42  The numbers rose by 70.69 per cent from 56 to 94, whereas the population rose by 76 per cent. All other factors being equal, the duplication of names in a population of 1,000 will be more than twice that in a population of 500.

43  Turnover rates are used and discussed in Peter Laslett, *Family Life and Illicit Love in Earlier Generations* (1977), Ch. 2, 50ff.

44 Poos, 'Population turnover', table 1.2.
45 Laslett showed that the turnover rate for the French parish of Langueness rose from an average of 40.5 per cent to one of 81 per cent over 12 years when intermediate movement was taken into account, *Family Life*, 82–3.
46 Similar comments are made in Poos, 'Population turnover', 17.
47 *Ibid.*, 12 and table 1.1.
48 F. W. Maitland and W. P. Baildon (eds), *The Court Baron* (Selden Society, 4, 1891), 80.
49 W. H. Stevenson (ed.), *Records of the Borough of Nottingham* (1882–1900), I, 200ff; Hudson, *Leet Jurisdiction*, lix–lxi.
50 A tithing population for Birdbrook of 133. Poos, 'Population turnover', table 1.1.
51 The loose occupational zoning in Norwich at this time is discussed by Serena Kelly in Kelly, Rutledge and Tillyard, *Men of Property*, 13ff.
52 J. Hatcher, 'Mortality in the fifteenth century: some new evidence', *Econ. Hist. Review*, Ser.2, no.39 (1986), 19–38. One-third of the Canterbury monks studied may have died of plague.
53 Keene, *Cheapside before the Great Fire*, 17.
54 There is a difficulty in not knowing exactly when this move took place. If it was after 16 years the average number of new tithingmen would have been slightly higher in the earlier period; if it took place after 16 years and 6 months the reverse was the case.
55 High levels of immigration tend to increase the proportion of the population of reproductive age and so increase the birth rate. P. Corfield, 'A provincial capital in the late seventeenth century: the case of Norwich', reprinted in *The Early Modern Town*, ed. P. Clark (1976), 235. The *c.*1311 Mancroft tithing population of 860 suggests a possible total leet population of 2,494. (For the methods used to calculate this see p. 26.) The resulting 100 births a year would be female as well as male and the number of boys coming into the leet would be reduced by mortality before the age of 12.
56 This statement is not intended to conflict with the use Reaney has made of Norwich surnames to show immigration patterns, *Origin of English Surnames*, 332ff. The issue here is whether particular individuals were first-generation immigrants.
57 Campbell, 'Population pressure', 87ff.
58 The custumal mentions the problem of day labourers, working for 1d. a day, who had no goods to be attached. Hudson and Tingey, *Records*, I, 189.
59 For reasons which cannot be gone into here, these figures probably underestimate the true extent of owner-occupation. It is hoped to go into this question in more detail at a later date.
60 Reconstructions and Rye, *Calendar of Norwich Deeds, passim*.
61 At least 33 per cent (17) of the 51 subsidymen whose names appear on the Mancroft tithing roll had been living in the same parish since *c.*1311. Another 24 per cent (12) may have been in the leet since *c.*1311, but as some names appear more than once on the roll this group overlaps to some extent with the 24 per cent (12) of the subsidymen who may only have come into the area since *c.*1327–8. 8 per cent (4) of the names of men assessed for the subsidy appear for the first time on the additional membrane. Misidentification is a particular problem with the 1332 subsidy assessment because it consists of a bald list of names for the leet of Mancroft as a whole and gives no additional information. Identification between men named on the Mancroft tithing roll and the owners of property who appear on the Reconstructions is often more satisfactory. Richard Cole de Wymondham illustrates this point. He appears described as such both on the tithing roll and in the Reconstructions. On the subsidy assessment, on the other hand, there is only a Richard Cole who has been assumed to be the same man because there is no other Richard Cole on the tithing list. It is accepted that the possibility of misidentification exists throughout this paper.
62 Russell, *British Medieval Population*, 292–3.
63 Campbell, 'Norwich', 10; Hudson and Tingy, *Records*, II, cxix, cxx.
64 Nothing is known about female immigration into Norwich at this period and so it has been assumed that the number of women was equal to that of men. The 45 per cent figure for children under 12 is also a little arbitrary. Russell approves of the addition of 50 per cent to the poll tax returns to allow for children under 14, *British Medieval Population*, 9. This multiplier of 2.90 lies towards the higher end of the range used by Poos in estimating the total population of Essex communities from tithing lists, 'Population turnover', table 1.1.
65 L. R. Poos, 'The rural population of Essex in the later middle ages', *Econ. Hist. Review*, Ser.2, no.38 (1985), 521.
66 Campbell, 'Population pressure', 97ff.
67 Campbell, 'Norwich', 21.
68 See note 3.
69 Public Record Office E179/149/9 mm. 79–80; Old Free Book NRO, NCR, case 17, shelf c,f.30ff. Lists of admissions were copied up from 1317–18 but are only continuous from 1343–4.
70 The difficulties experienced by some of the cloth towns in the early fourteenth century are discussed by E. M. Carus-Wilson in *Medieval Merchant Venturers* (1954), Chs IV and V. York was expanding both physically and economically, Miller, 'Medieval York', 84–5. J. F. Hadwin opposes the view that many towns were close to their (economic) nadir in 1334 in 'The medieval lay subsidies and economic history', *Econ. Hist. Review*, Ser.2, no.36 (1983), 212.

# Assessed taxes as sources for the study of urban wealth: Bristol in the later eighteenth century

Little is known of the value of eighteenth-century rates and taxes as sources for the urban historian. Corfield, in her study of eighteenth-century Norwich, stated in 1976 that 'the stereotyped nature of eighteenth-century tax assessments precludes use of fiscal data from national sources'[1] and this is a fair reflection of the then and to some extent the current orthodoxy, despite Rudé's pioneering studies of the 1960s in which he used land tax and poor rate returns to estimate the wealth of the electorate of Hanoverian London and Middlesex.[2] Schwarz, in a study of late-eighteenth-century London, could still comment in 1979 that for eighteenth-century rates and taxes 'little is known beyond general impressions'.[3] Recently, however, Wright has thrown interesting light on the use of the Easter books and poor rates of early-modern towns and cities,[4] and the 1986 volume on the land tax edited by Turner and Mills, although still largely concerned with the use of rural land tax assessments, includes three chapters on the value of the assessments in urban and industrial history.[5] The writers hope that city rate and national tax returns might play a fuller role as historical sources, but their optimism is tempered with caution because of the returns' intractability and inconsistency. It is hoped here to reinforce both their enthusiasm and their caution, to reveal additional pitfalls and suggest ways to avoid them and in particular to extend the debate to the neglected pre-1780 assessments and to the city of Bristol.

In the 1770s Bristol, the 'Metropolis of the West',[6] was at its zenith as a port in the American trades and was the second largest city in the country. Despite its prominence relatively little is known about its social and economic structure. The sources available to the historian are fragmentary and research has reflected this: there are detailed accounts of small groups of Bristolians, such as Quakers or the Merchant Venturers, but no more general account against which to set these particular histories.[7] To provide such a broad account of Bristol society and the groupings and divisions within it a 'census' has been constructed with information about name, sex, occupation(s), place of residence, wealth and political allegiance for as many Bristolians as possible for the later eighteenth century by linking information from several sources. 1774–5 was chosen as the date for the 'census' since there are Poll Books from the general election of 1774[8] plus a city directory from 1775[9] and a good number of city rate and national tax returns[10] for these years. A prerequisite to the construction of the 'census' was the careful examination and linking of these fiscal returns.

Using the fiscal returns it was hoped to compare the wealth of Bristolians in 1774–5. Assumptions were made: first that the wealth of heads of households could be used as a proxy for the wealth of the whole population; second that a suitable measure of a household head's wealth was the worth of his place of residence; third that such a measure might best be ascertained through the use of valuations of his house made under the city rates and national taxes. The first assumption does not imply that the contribution of the head alone determined the wealth of the household, as other members could bring to it both capital and earnings; but it simply assumes that the wealth of the head reflected that of the household. The second assumption avoids the controversy over the value of an individual's real property compared with, for example, movable assets or earnings, in making up his overall wealth, since it is immaterial whether he owns his dwelling house or not: it simply assumes that a householder's wealth will be broadly reflected in the worth of the house in which he lives. The third assumption, that assessed tax valuations might reveal the worth of these dwelling places, is more contentious. We have to be sure that the returns tell us the names of occupiers, rather than owners, of dwelling houses, although these categories are not of course mutually exclusive; and that the rateable values of those dwelling houses bear some consistent relation both to other such rateable value within the city and to the actual worth of the houses. It is not necessary that rateable values be current market value, since we are interested in relative rather than absolute levels of wealth; or that they be precise, since we attempt to infer only broad categories of wealth from them; or that they be consistent with assessments for other areas or for other dates, since the study is confined to Bristol in 1774–5.

### Bristol city rates and national assessed taxes

In Bristol there was a longstanding tendency on the part of the Corporation to obtain Acts of Parliament which increased its own functions, and hence import- ance, by the provision of new amenities and services. These were financed by local rates comprising by the later eighteenth century a poor rate, a lamping and scavenging rate, a pitching and paving rate and a bridge tax. A sewer rate was levied on the 269 properties in the city served by a particular sewer.[11]

The land tax was established under 4 William and Mary c.1, 1693, and was designed as a general income tax. All incomes from land were to be taxed at 4s. in the pound at the rack rent, without respect to repairs, taxes, parish duties or other taxes. The land tax proved very difficult to administer and quotas were fixed for each county, so that the assessment in the returns reflected not the current market rent of the property, but a proportion of a pre-determined sum. Where the quota for a place was high houses were charged at the rack rent and empty buildings were charged; where the quota was low collectors were altogether more lenient.[12] Under the window tax, revised in 1747, there was a basic charge of 2s. per house, on top of which houses with 15 to 19 windows were charged at 9d. per window and those with more than 20 windows were charged at 1s. a window.[13]

### (a) The city rate and land and window tax returns

Information given in the returns includes the name of the rate- or taxpayer; the 'real' or 'rent' value of the property, the amount of money collected, and occasionally other information such as other rateable assets ('stocks' or 'personal estate'); the nature of the property ('loft', 'tenement', 'stable'); the condition of the property ('ruined', 'under construction', 'void'); and information about the rate- payer ('poor', 'widow'). The terms 'rent' or 'real', which head the column under which assessments were noted, refer to the value of the 'real' estate property expressed as the amount *per annum* which it could bring in at rack rent. The two are used interchangeably and may be considered as the rateable or taxable value of the property.

### (b) The basis for valuation and assessment

The intention is to compare rate assessments for different parishes in Bristol so it is important to know whether the basis for rate assessment and/or collection varied from parish to parish. The city of Bristol was treated as a unit for the poor rate since the setting up in 1696 of the Incorporation of the Poor which provided for the poor of the entire city. The poor rate was collected with the bridge tax, parish by parish. The lamping and scavenging and pitching and paving rates were collected and disbursed parish by parish prior to 1806. The sewer rate was levied parish by parish on those households which benefited. The total amount needed for a particular purpose (watching, lighting, and so on) for a year or half-year was fixed and then expressed as a rate in the pound which, based on the previous year's assessment, would yield this sum. The rates were administered by parish officials and the collectors' books show that similar or even the same people collected all the rates except the watching rate, working parish by parish. The watching rate was administered by a ward official, the chief constable; it was collected by ward rather than by parish and this caused some problems because of the overlap of wards and parishes.[14]

The assessments were intended to be comparable from one area of the city to the next. 7 & 8 William III c.32 stated that the poor rate was to be a 'Taxation of every inhabitant and of all Lands, Houses, Tythes inappropriate, appropriation of tythes and all stock and estates in equal proportion according to their respective worth and values'. 28 George II c.32 stated that, to provide a watch, 'an equal rate' was to be levied on occupiers of lands and properties and this again suggests that assessments were to be comparable throughout the city.

It is often suggested that property valuations made for assessed rates and taxes were not revised and so rapidly ceased to reflect the market value of a property. The land tax assessments for Clifton in Bristol were a notorious example of this as they had been fixed when the parish contained only agricultural land and were not adjusted when it became an elegant residential area.[15] Recently it has been suggested that revaluation under the land tax did take place regularly and systematically within townships, although valuations never precisely equalled market value.[16] The Acts instituting or amending the collection of rates used in this study were all passed in the eighteenth century, often only shortly before 1774–5, but it is not clear whether new valuations were made for the new rates. The window tax assessments were easier to keep up to date and to compare with one another since they were based on a simple count of windows.

There is some doubt about what was liable to be rated. The quotation from 7 & 8 William III c.32 above is a formula common to many rates. In practice, although many city merchants must have had valuable stocks, these were very rarely assessed separately and the assessments were excluded from the study. A further complication is that rateable value was not based solely on the quality of the property. 28 George II c.32 stipulates that the watching rate will be levied with 'regard being had . . . as well to the abilities of the occupiers of such houses etc. as to the yearly value of them'. One would expect the wealth of the occupants to be reflected in the rateable value of their houses, but not for that wealth to contribute directly to the calculation of the rate. Similarly pitching, paving and cleansing of the streets are to be paid for by a rate upon the inhabitants 'according to their general abilities'. Conversely the sewer rate was assessed on the basis of property valuation only and was to be levied 'in proportion to the yearly rent or value of such houses etc.' served by the sewer. Theoretically then there was some variation in what was liable to be rated, but the returns make it clear that the rates were in practice based on the worth of a property and consideration of stocks or the 'general abilities' of the ratepayer were ignored or subsumed under the general category of 'rent' or 'real'.

### (c) Exemptions and evasion

Exemptions make the returns less comprehensive especially with regard to the poor. In Bristol exemptions from rates were made on grounds of poverty: houses under the value of £7 p.a. and tenements under £10 p.a. rack rent escaped rating under many Acts. Often poor rate practice was the basis for exemption: houses exempt from poor rates were also exempt from the window tax.[17] Despite this, many poor people are listed in the returns, sometimes simply with their address and the label 'poor', but sometimes with an assessment and a note that the rate was not levied. Institutions such as almshouses were exempt and this further reduces information about the poor.

Evasion could be more serious than exemption. Tales of corruption in the administration of the window and land taxes were legion. The parish assessors were independent of Treasury appointment and had absolute discretion in deciding appeals and settling the rates. Corruption abounded, with the assessors reported to be excusing whom they chose or entirely failing to make surveys of the areas under their jurisdiction.[18] Beckett considers that, as Bristol had so many small parishes, boundary anomalies resulted in 'massive evasion' of payment of the land tax.[19] Certainly the collectors were not always sure where parish boundaries ran, but since rate and tax data were gathered for more than 6,700 heads of households in a population of about 55,000[20] evasion cannot be said to have been 'massive'.

### (d) Owners or occupiers

The purpose of this study was to evaluate the wealth of as many Bristolians as possible so it was important to know the value of dwelling houses and the names of their occupiers, rather than to have a list of the relatively small number of urban property owners and their real estate holdings. Recourse to the Acts authorizing levy of rates should have clarified the point; but, as before, the wording in them is vague and often varies from Act to Act. 28 George III c.32 states that the watching rate was to be levied on 'persons who inhabit, hold, occupy, or enjoy land, house, shop, warehouse, or other tenement'. This could mean either occupier or non-resident owner. 6 George III c.34 makes it clear that the occupier of the property shall pay the rates and, when the occupiers have paid the rate, landlords shall deduct the amount paid from rent owing. Tenants then were to hand over the money to the collectors (i.e. 'pay' in the sense of being recorded as payer in the returns) while the landlords finally footed the bill, though their contribution was unrecorded. If houses were empty the owner was to pay the rate but the Act was not at all clear in its treatment of houses with many tenants, as it simply stated that the rate 'shall be paid by one or more of the Tenants or Occupiers of such houses' (6 George III c.34). 33 George II c.52 stated that the tenant or occupier was to pay the bridge tax, only half of which was recoverable against rent due; but on the issue of multiple occupancy it unhelpfully stipulated that 'the whole house shall be charged with the whole rate' and that the tenants shall refund the payer accordingly. This gave no clue as to who was to be recorded as the payer. The land tax was to be paid by the tenant and deducted from the rent due to the owner,[21] but experience from other areas has shown that it was usually the owner who was recorded in land tax assessments.[22]

It is clear after examination of all the Acts and collectors' books that it is in most cases the occupier rather than an absentee owner who was recorded as the payer of the levy. This inference is confirmed by the land tax book of 1775 for St James's Outparish and by isolated land tax returns for St Michael's Parish. These give the name of both the owner and the occupier(s) of each property; in other fiscal returns which cover the same streets and which list only one name it is that of the occupier.

There are, however, some exceptions to this. Where one name appears several times within one street or in adjoining streets it is not clear whether the ratepayer was using all the properties or simply owned them all. For some buildings two names were given with no explanation. One cannot then state categorically that every name recorded was that of the occupier of the property, but this seems to be true in almost all cases. Neither those who drew up the Acts nor the collectors had a very precise idea of the procedures to be followed. Some confusion and vagueness is then inevitable as no amount of careful study can eliminate inherent inaccuracies; one can hope only to avoid creating further confusion.

### (e) Rates and taxes compared

In theory the window and land taxes seem to be far less promising a source than the city rates. The window tax valuations are expressed in windows and not pounds and this makes comparison difficult. The land tax, however, has proved on many grounds to be the most useful fiscal source, despite the infamy it enjoyed in the eighteenth century as a fund-raising device and the suspicion with which it is regarded by most historians today.

Apart from the fact that it is far more comprehensive than any other rate or tax the land tax in Bristol appears to have been collected more carefully and conscientiously than any other levy. Land tax collectors visited unsavoury ends of streets such as Lewin's Mead and Horse Fair in St James's Parish, while the rate collectors confined their attentions to the wealthier ends. Where rate collectors simply noted that buildings were 'void', for example in Philadelphia Street in St James's Parish, land tax assessors gave the valuations of those buildings. Where rate collectors generalized, land tax collectors gave details: where the watching rate collectors simply wrote 'Sixty Tenements' in their return for Pill or Pile Street, St Mary Redcliff Parish, the land tax collectors recorded names and valuations for many of them. Similarly in St James's Outparish they gave details of both occupiers and owners of buildings. The conscientiousness of the land tax officials, though obviously due in part to different exemption rules amongst the various rates and taxes, was evident throughout.

As to misgivings over the meaning of 'rent' under a system where quotas were fixed years previously, comparison did show the land tax returns generally to have lower 'rent' values than rate returns for identical buildings; but this does not necessarily invalidate their use. There was enough variation in the 'rent' values to make it clear that 'rent' had not ceased to reflect the worth of the property, even though it was not current rack rent. Of course if a quota is fixed for each place and thus 'rent' represents only a proportion of that fixed sum, comparison from place to place should not be attempted. The city of Bristol, however, was treated as a unit for land tax purposes and so 'rent' values within it should be broadly comparable; we can test this by testing returns against other sources (table 5).

## Nominal record linkage of rate and tax returns

### (a) The returns

Rate and tax books for all parishes[23] for 1774–5, together with isolated books for 1773–77 were examined (table 1). The nearest extant return to 1774–5 for each rate was used, but some flexibility was necessary to ensure that a reasonable number of returns was used. Fifty-one returns covering the city parishes, the Liberty of Castle Precincts and Trinity and Temple wards were used. Unfortunately no rate returns exist for Clifton Parish, which was outside the city boundary before 1789 and this is only a church rate in which properties are not listed by street. As the land tax returns for this parish are unusable by this time, Clifton was unfortunately excluded from the study.

*Table 1: Rate and tax returns used*

| Rates and taxes | Parishes | | | | | | | | | | | | | | | | | | |
|---|---|---|---|---|---|---|---|---|---|---|---|---|---|---|---|---|---|---|---|
| | 1 | 2 | 3 | 4 | 5 | 6 | 7 | 8 | 9 | 10 | 11 | 12 | 13 | 14 | 15 | 16 | 17 | 18 | 19 |
| Poor | 1 | | 1 | 1 | 1 | 1 | 1 | 1 | | | | | | | 1 | 1 | | | |
| Lamp | 1 | 1 | 1 | 1 | 1 | 1 | 1 | | | 1 | 1 | 1 | | | 1 | | | | |
| Pitch | | | | 1 | | | | | | | | | | | | | | | |
| Watch | 1 | 1 | | 1 | | | | | 1 | 1 | | | | | 1 | 1 | | 1 | 1 |
| Sewer | | | | | | | | | | | | | 1 | | 1 | | 1 | | |
| Window | | | | | | | | | | 1 | | | 1 | | 1 | | | | |
| Land | 1 | 1 | | 1 | 1 | 1 | 1 | 1 | 1 | 1 | 1 | 1 | 1 | 1 | 1 | | | | |

List of parishes: see note 21.
1 = Rate or tax return extant and used in study.

The returns were linked to form one source. A schedule was drawn up for each street with rows for ratepayers and columns for the amounts for 'rent' under various taxes. The valuations of the properties rather than the rates or taxes payable were recorded as the latter vary from rate to rate, whereas the valuations should have been fairly similar. With a few exceptions, collectors grouped properties by street with the names of the inhabitants in topographical order. In other areas, by contrast, collectors lumped together all the properties owned by one person.[24] This makes it virtually impossible to link the returns, but from the Bristol records it was easy to identify individual properties and to devise procedures to cope with changing occupiers. There was some turnover in population, but because each property was easy to identify, assessments made in returns for years other than 1774–5 could easily be credited to the occupier of the building in 1774–5.

After all the rate and tax entries had been combined to give some 450 schedules, each referring to one street and recording valuations made under all the various rates and taxes, it was discovered that some blocks of houses were assessed in one street for one rate and in another for a second. In St Peter's Street the same group of houses was assigned in one return to St Peter's Parish and in another to St Mary le Port. Sketchley's directory and contemporary maps were used to assign such groups to one of the streets and parishes named. There was now a set of schedules for streets covering mutually exclusive blocks of houses for which all relevant rent values had been noted. This information was then transferred to a computer file and its distribution analysed.

Table 2 shows the striking quantity of information: there are 6,735 properties with ascribed ratepayers. This corresponds to 6,375 household heads, about 12 per cent of the population of around 55,000[25] or between 1:1.5 and 1:2 heads of household.[26] The table also shows the large number of missing entries or assessments. Only the land tax has assessments for more than half the properties, and the pitching and paving and sewer rates have assessments for fewer than 5 per cent of the properties.

*Table 2: Statistical description of the fiscal data*

| 1 | 2 | 3 | 4 | 5 | 6 | 7 | 8 | 9 |
|---|---|---|---|---|---|---|---|---|
| Label | No. good cases | % good cases | No. missing cases | % missing cases | Lowest score | Highest score | Mean | Standard dev. |
| Poor | 1,642 | 24.4 | 5,093 | 75.6 | 1.00 | 500.00 | 10.63 | 15.02 |
| Lamp | 2,844 | 42.2 | 3,891 | 57.8 | 0.14 | 500.00 | 16.04 | 17.60 |
| Pitch | 285 | 4.2 | 6,450 | 95.8 | 5.00 | 70.00 | 16.50 | 10.59 |
| Watch | 1,590 | 23.6 | 5,145 | 76.4 | 0.14 | 100.00 | 18.74 | 14.06 |
| Sewer | 269 | 4.0 | 6,466 | 96.0 | 0.06 | 70.00 | 13.20 | 11.50 |
| Window | 643 | 9.6 | 6,092 | 90.4 | 1 | 60 | 12.18 | 7.19 |
| Land | 3,780 | 56.1 | 2,955 | 43.9 | 0.00 | 100.00 | 6.84 | 8.52 |

Column 2: Number of good cases, i.e. cases in the file for which datum ('Rent' value or number of windows, as appropriate) is present.
Column 3: Number of good cases as a percentage of the total number of cases (6,735).
Column 4: Number of missing cases, i.e. cases in the file for which datum ('Rent' value or number of windows, as appropriate) is absent.
Column 5: Number of missing cases as a percentage of the total number of cases (6,735).
Columns 6–9: Values are in pounds or number of windows, as appropriate.

Table 3 shows how unevenly the data are distributed in the file and how little overlap there is between some of the returns. The pitching rate is the worst in this respect: almost all of its small total number of entries are for properties which also have assessments under the poor rate and land tax; the overlap with the other taxes and rates is small or non-existent. Watching rate returns were made for wards rather than parishes and it was difficult to match these returns with others; so despite a relatively high total number of entries (1,590) overlap with other rates is often problematically small. Land tax assessments do not coincide with others partly because of different principles of collection, for example a return exists for St James's Outparish whose inhabitants were not liable for the city rates; partly because returns have survived for otherwise ill-served parishes such as St Leonard, St Werburg and St Nicholas and partly because more poor people are mentioned in the land tax books than in any others. This last is shown in the range of values recorded in the returns. For the land tax, while the highest assessment of £100 is high, the lowest assessment is £0 and the mean value at £6.84 is extremely low, nearly half as low as the next lowest mean, that of £13.20 for the sewer rate. The statistical description confirms the impression that many of those recorded in the land tax books were 'poor' or lived in 'tenements' or properties whose assessments were in shillings and pence rather than the normal pounds.

Table 3: Distribution of the fiscal data

|          | Poor  | Lamp  | Pitch | Watch | Sewer | Window | Land  |
|----------|-------|-------|-------|-------|-------|--------|-------|
| Poor     | 1,642 | 679   | 231   | 215   | 16    | 185    | 659   |
| Lamp     | 679   | 2,844 | 265   | 537   | 161   | 427    | 1,839 |
| Pitch    | 231   | 265   | 285   | 0     | 11    | 1      | 1     |
| Watch    | 215   | 537   | 0     | 1,590 | 2     | 415    | 521   |
| Sewer    | 16    | 161   | 11    | 2     | 269   | 5      | 156   |
| Window   | 185   | 427   | 1     | 415   | 5     | 643    | 518   |
| Land     | 659   | 1,839 | 1     | 521   | 156   | 518    | 3,780 |

The figure in each cell is the number of rateable properties which have valuations under the rate or tax shown at the head of its row and its column: e.g. 679 properties have assessments under both the Poor and Lamping rates.

To use any one rate or tax as a wealth indicator would be unwise. The obvious choice would be the land tax which survives for 16 out of 20 parishes and lists 3,780 taxpayers. Yet this is the source of which one would *a priori* be most wary and to use it would be to disregard the 2,955 for whom there are rate but not land tax returns. It would also be to ignore the opportunity which nominal record linkage gives for creating new sources from records which are individually useless but collectively valuable. It was decided to use all rates and taxes except for the window tax, which had only a small number of cases and posed the fundamental problem that assessments are recorded in number of windows, not 'rent'. It had been useful to compare the window tax returns with other sources, but they were now excluded from the study.

### (b) The inconsistency of valuations

The most disconcerting, although not unexpected, finding to emerge from the linking was the inconsistency amongst the valuations of a property made under different rates and taxes. In theory 'rent' values should have remained constant or varied in constant proportion from one rate to the next, but this was manifestly not the case.

Table 4 shows a particularly bad example, but other entries are also discrepant and this means that there is no immediate way of comparing the 'rent' and hence wealth of a ratepayer for whom we have only a land tax assessment with that of a second ratepayer for whom we have only a lamping rate assessment. This discovery was discouraging but, like the preceding statistical analysis, vindicated the decision to use all available data rather than to decide *a priori* that one source was more useful than another.

The fiscal data were checked against other sources, to see if they bore any resemblance to the true value of properties. It was known that certain streets had large elegant houses and that other courts and alleys had squalid tenements. Table 5 compares the valuations for Queen Square, an elegant early eighteenth-century

*Table 4: The incompatibility of rateable values*

Castle Street, Castle Precincts

| Name | Lamp and scavenging rate 1774–5 | Watching rate 1774–5 | Land tax 1775 |
|---|---|---|---|
| Dagg, Abel | 16 | 14 | 6 |
| Chambers, Charles | 12 | 12 | 5 |
| Bray, Robert | 16 | 12 | 9 |
| Lawson, Robert | 21 | 20 | 9 |
| Taylor, Thomas | 14 | 14 | 6 |

All figures represent rateable values in pounds.

square where many wealthy overseas merchants lived, and John Ball's Lane, a street too mean to appear on many contemporary maps and which housed many officially declared 'poor'. Table 5 shows that the recorded 'rent' values in these streets conform broadly to our knowledge of real property values and this conformity was evident throughout the city. Since 'rent' values did bear some relation to market rent values it was decided to adapt the data so that they could be used to compare the wealth of ratepayers in the city.

*Table 5: Comparison of 'rent' values for streets of inhabitants with known levels of wealth*

Queen Square, St Stephen's Parish

| Name | Poor 1775 | Lamp 1774–5 | Watch 1774–5 | Window 1774–5 | Land 1775 |
|---|---|---|---|---|---|
| Freeman, William | 23 | 50 | 50 | 35 | 16 |
| Harris, Thos. Esq. | 16 | 30 | 32 | 32 | 12 |
| Farrell & Jones | 35 | 70 | 70 | 42 | 24 |
| Masters, John | 13 | 24 | | 28 | 10 |
| Davis, Gilbert | 15 | 30 | 30 | 21 | 12 |

John Ball's Lane, St Michael's Parish

| Name | | Lamp 1775 | Land 1775 |
|---|---|---|---|
| Hartland, Widow | Poor | 4 | 2 |
| Totten, John | | 6 | 3 |
| Cahler, John | Poor | 4 | |
| Welsh, John | Poor | 3 | |
| Alford, Richard | Poor | 4 | 1:10 |

*(c) Estimation of data*

There were 6,735 rateable properties with named ratepayers. These formed rows in the matrix, which had six columns, one for each possible rate valuation. Many of the cells in the matrix were empty. The object was to provide for each ratepayer's property one adjusted valuation to allow comparison amongst cases. The adjusted figure was to be derived by the most statistically satisfactory means, but because the data were incomplete and non-randomly distributed some desirable statistical procedures would be impossible.

Missing values were estimated using multiple regression techniques[27] or, where this was not possible because of lack of overlap in the data, simple regression. We shall consider the ratepayer who had assessments under the poor, lamp and watching rates but not under the pitching and sewer rates or land tax. Using the 161 cases in the file which had entries for both sewer and lamp rates, a regression equation was produced which showed the relation of all sewer rate assessments to all lamp rate assessment. Using this equation a value was estimated for his sewer assessment based on his valuation under the lamp rate. To estimate his pitching rate assessment a three-way regression equation was produced using the 228 cases in the file which had entries under the pitching, poor and lamp rates. Gradually as many as possible of this and all other ratepayers' assessments were estimated, using multiple or simple regression.

At the end of this process some gaps remained. There were, for example, no properties at all with valuations for both pitching and watching rates so it was clearly impossible to regress the one on the other. New regression runs were made to calculate values for cells in the matrix which remained empty using all the data in the new file, i.e. original plus estimated data. This was not ideal, but it was unavoidable given the patchy distribution of the data. At the end of the process each property with its ratepayer had assessments for each of the six rates/taxes.

The original file has 6,735 cases:
viz 40,410 (6 × 6,735) entries, of which:
30,000 (74.24%) are missing
10,410 (25.76%) are present.
The final file has 6,735 cases:
viz 40,410 (6 × 6,735) entries, of which:
10,410 (25.76%) are real values
21,989 (54.41%) are estimated using real data
8,011 (19.82%) are estimated using real and estimated data.

Finally a mean of all valuations, original and estimated, was produced for each rateable property to be used as an indicator of wealth for the property's ascribed ratepayer.

Given that the 'rent' values appear broadly to reflect real property values and given the statistically sound methods by which the estimated data were calculated, it seems reasonable to use the combined real and estimated data to analyse broad differences in individuals' wealth, unless there is a more suitable alternative indicator.

*(d) Other indicators of wealth*

It is possible to infer the wealth of a citizen indirectly. If a person's occupation is known, for example from reference to a contemporary directory or Poll Book, the expected financial rewards from his occupation may be inferred from guides such as Campbell's *London Tradesman* or the anonymous *General Description of Trades*,[28] which give details of apprentice fines, journeymen's wages and masters' capital for numerous urban trades. The disadvantages of this method are, first, that it equates wages with wealth, which is dangerous for the eighteenth century when the wage economy was by no means mature and when seasonal fluctuations in earnings were very pronounced in many trades; second, that data on women's and children's wages and employment are very sparse, despite their often important contribution to the household budget; and third, that it masks most of the 'within trade' variation in wealth. It assumes, for example, that all butchers have a common level of wealth; it does not systematically test the wealth of individual butchers.

Other direct indicators of wealth prove to be far from comprehensive. Phillips and Walton drew on taxes assessed on such things as hair powder, men-servants, carriages and armorial bearings, as well as windows in their discussion of urban wealth in the mid nineteenth century: but these are all taxes on luxury and ostentation and as such applied to only a tiny fraction of the urban population.[29] Schwarz used income tax returns to estimate the wealth of Londoners in the late eighteenth and early nineteenth centuries, but stated that 'this is a very rough estimate indeed, since only those earning £60 a year and above were liable to pay income tax at all, so the working classes escaped the net.'[30] Schwarz and Jones turned to insurance policy details, but these too proved unsatisfactory, even for the tiny proportion of the populace who insured their possessions.[31]

For individual towns or areas within towns there are useful rentals. In his study of Gloucester in 1455 Langton used a rental which gives names and occupations of all lessees and sublessees, together with the amount of rent they paid.[32] Jones used a 1638 London tithe rental to comment on the distribution of wealth in various parishes.[33] Such rentals presumably exist for towns or parishes in the eighteenth century, but they will be found only sporadically and cannot be regarded as a satisfactory alternative to the assessed tax returns. Other sources used to good effect by early-modern historians are the hearth tax returns and probate inventories:[34] but the hearth tax returns peter out in the eighteenth century, as do the probate inventories, which were in any case never comprehensive.

There is then no obvious alternative to the assessed taxes if we want a direct indicator of wealth for more than a tiny proportion of the population in an eighteenth-century city. The amended returns for Bristol were therefore analysed.

## The distribution of wealth in Bristol in 1775

The data give an indication of wealth for 6,735 Bristolians who were heads of household and who were not the very poor who were homeless, who lived in institutions for the poor, since these were exempt from rating, or who lodged in another's household. The wealth of the head of household is by extension the wealth of the household.

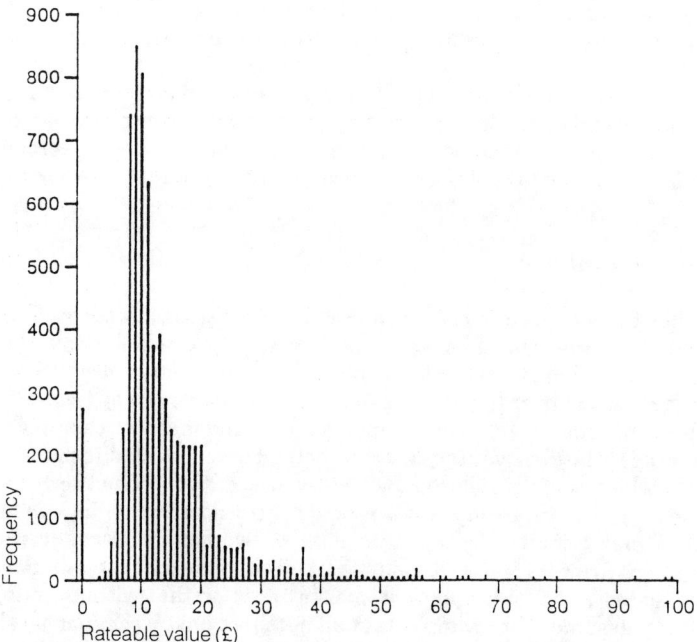

Figure 1. Frequency diagram of rateable values for the City of Bristol.

Figure 1[35] shows that the mean rateable value in the city was £13.1 which falls low within the range of values of £0 to £99. This gives the distribution a marked positive skew and a long 'tail' since there were relatively few properties of higher rateable value. The variation in the rateable values is remarkably large, given the manipulation which they had undergone. After any estimation procedure which uses averaging techniques the data will tend increasingly towards the mean. Here we consider a mean of six valuations produced at least in part by estimation based on regression. Since at each stage variation tends to decrease, the variation which remains is remarkable and this increases confidence in the inferences drawn from the figures.

### (a) Variation by parish

A wealth classification was drawn up (table 6). The class divisions correspond to breaks in the frequency distribution of rateable values for the city and were used to construct figure 2. This reveals the pattern of a wealthy central area surrounded by a poorer ring of suburbs, although the two rivers which wound through the city and which were heavily used by shipping distort any clear pattern. The poorest areas are St James, St Michael and St Mary Redcliff parishes and Temple ward, all of which are on the edge of the city; the richest areas are All Saints, Christ Church, St Ewen, St Mary le Port, St Nicholas and St Werburgh parishes, which are all in the centre of the city, together with St James Outparish beyond the city boundary. Separating the rich core and poor periphery are transitional parishes and parishes which do not fall readily into any group. One would expect to find the rich core and poor suburbs on both empirical[36] and theoretical[37] grounds and at first glance it seems that the pattern of wealthy centre/poor periphery identified in the mid sixteenth century (figure 3) had persisted through the late seventeenth century (figure 4) into the later eighteenth century.

*Table 6: Wealth classification*

| | |
|---|---|
| Class  I | 'Rent' less than or equal to £7 |
| Class  II | 'Rent' greater than £7: and less than or equal to £11; |
| Class  III | 'Rent' greater than £11: and less than or equal to £22 |
| Class  IV | 'Rent' greater than £22 and less than or equal to £99 |

Yet this impression of continuity belies the important changes which had occurred in the city. Topographical changes had occurred, most dramatically with new building in suburban parishes; but these changes are far from adequately documented in the fiscal sources. The returns for Clifton, a new elegant suburb to the west and north of the city where properties of very high value were being built,[38] are unusable. Those for St Michael's Parish, another suburb with fine houses and gentle residents, seem to be untrustworthy. The mean, median and modal rateable values are all improbably low and the classification into wealth bands unexpectedly puts the parish into the poorest group. It is clear from the Poll Book and city directory that this was a parish of gentlefolk and it seems that the fiscal data are in this instance unreliable. The linkage of sources again proves a useful way of testing their accuracy. The fiscal data for St Augustine's Parish do not seem fully to reflect the economic and social transition which the parish had seen. Those for St James's Outparish provide the only indications of the genteel suburban developments and this parish falls firmly into the richest band.

A special factor influencing suburban development was the Hotwell spa in St Augustine's Parish with associated development in Clifton. The peripheral location of the spa was due initially to geology, but also reflects a desire on the part of the visitors and permanent residents for isolation from the poor and the noisome trades of the city. While the wealth patterns of the old city remained pre-industrial, around it to the north and west were new developments which gave a distinctly different and modern pattern of wealth distribution.

It is unfortunately not clear whether the residents of the elegant suburban parishes were newcomers to Bristol, people who had given up business in the city having made their money, or active businessmen who carried on their trade at a separate location from their dwelling place. The only indication of the separation of

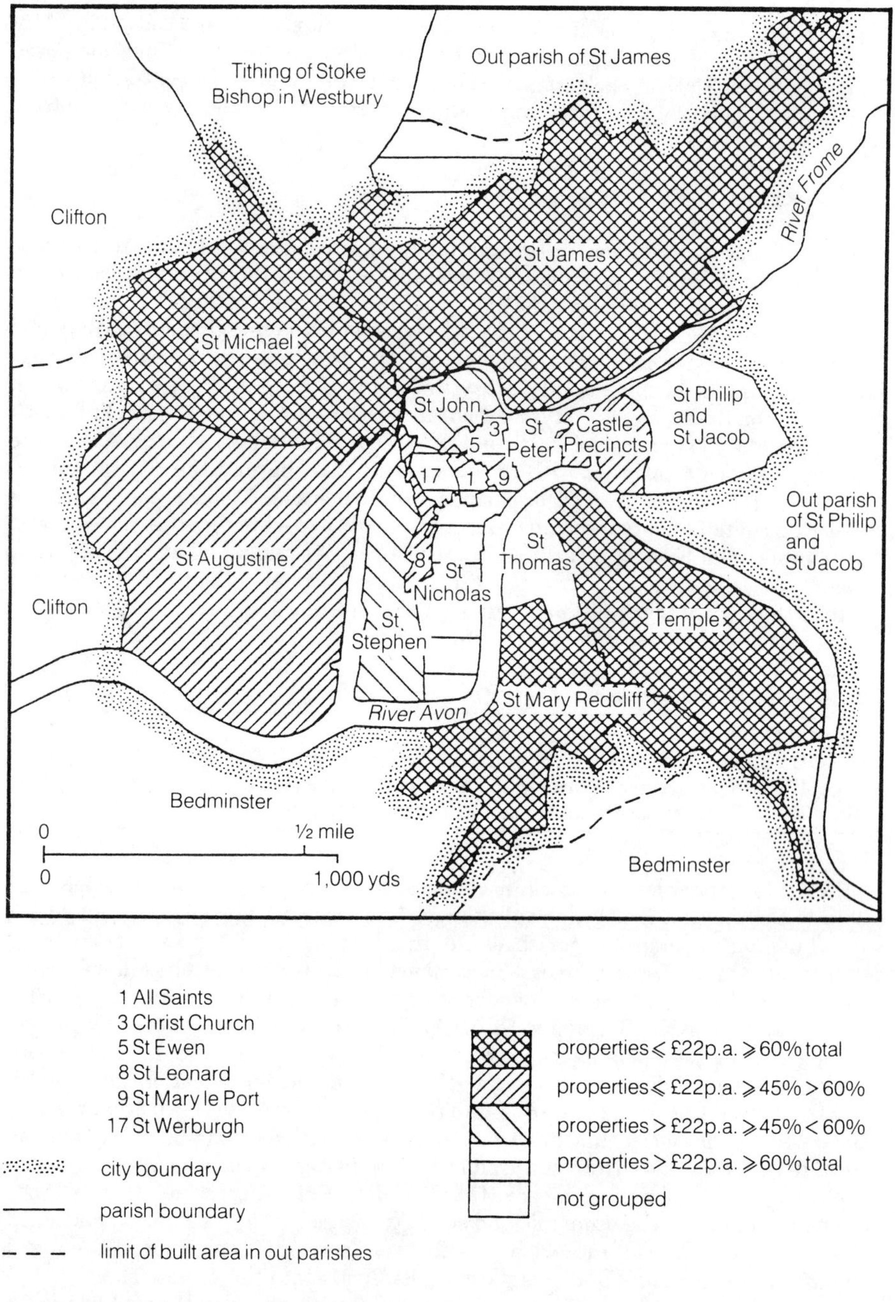

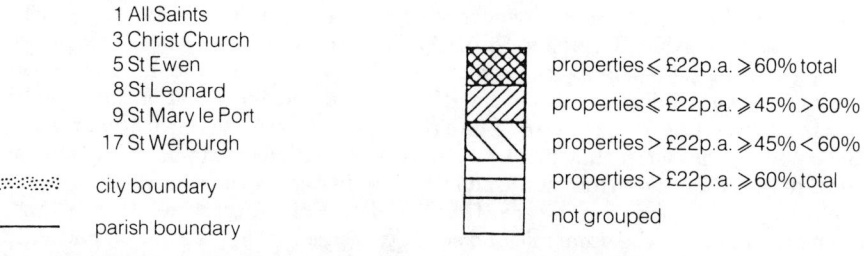

Tithing of Stoke Bishop in Westbury

Out parish of St James

Clifton

River Frome

St James

St Michael

St John

St Peter

Castle Precincts

St Philip and St Jacob

Out parish of St Philip and St Jacob

St Augustine

St Nicholas

St Thomas

Temple

Clifton

St. Stephen

River Avon

St Mary Redcliff

Bedminster

0 ½ mile

0 1,000 yds

Bedminster

1 All Saints
3 Christ Church
5 St Ewen
8 St Leonard
9 St Mary le Port
17 St Werburgh

city boundary

parish boundary

limit of built area in out parishes

properties ⩽ £22p.a. ⩾ 60% total

properties ⩽ £22p.a. ⩾ 45% > 60%

properties > £22p.a. ⩾ 45% < 60%

properties > £22p.a. ⩾ 60% total

not grouped

Figure 2. The wealth of Bristol parishes.

workplace and home comes from the directory, from which it is clear that many merchants had a counter in the Exchange in Corn Street or at another central place, and their houses and storage areas elsewhere. Thus Isaac Baugh, Esq. had an office in the Exchange but lived in St James's Square: Richard Farr, Esq. had his office on the Key but lived in Park Street. Other than cases like these it is not clear whether wealth was moving out of the centre of the city to its suburbs or coming from outside the area direct to the suburbs, so relatively little can be said about the transfer of wealth amongst Bristol parishes.

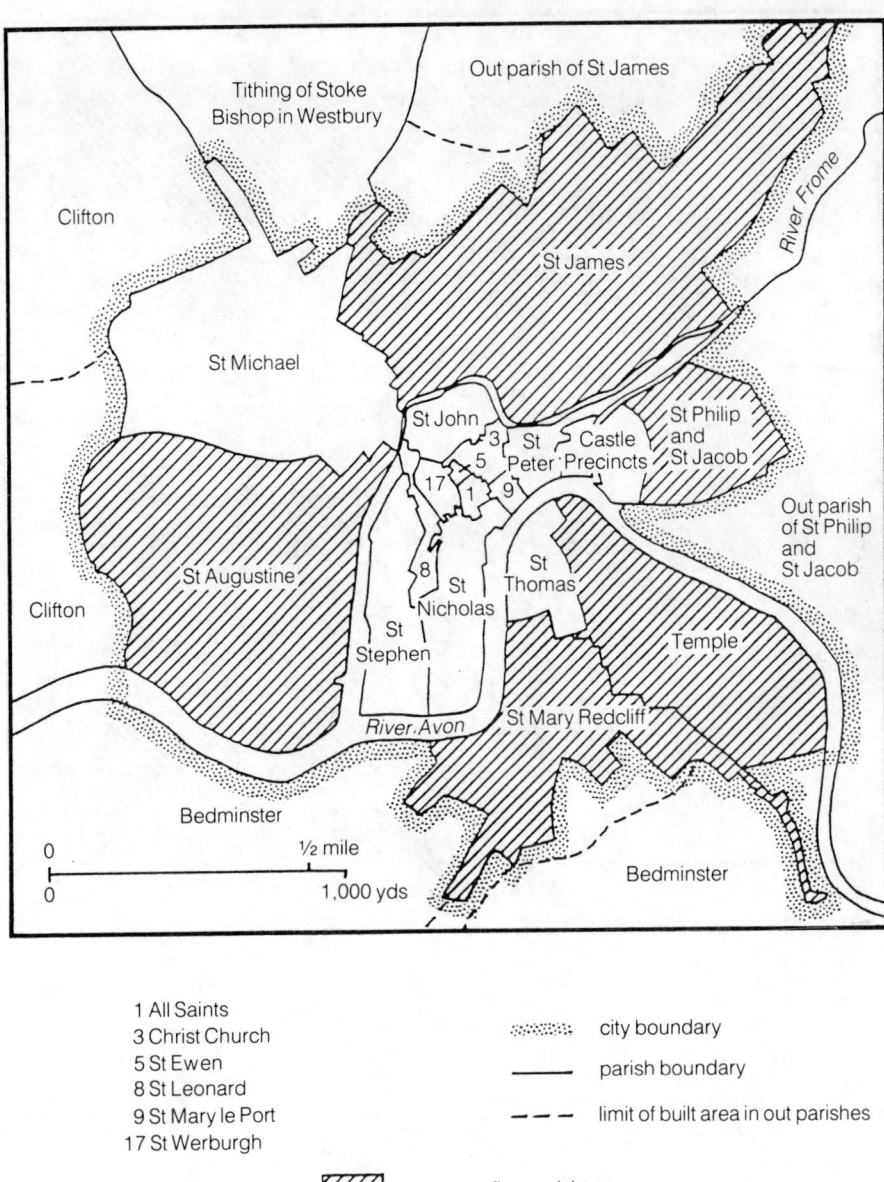

1 All Saints
3 Christ Church
5 St Ewen
8 St Leonard
9 St Mary le Port
17 St Werburgh

⬚⬚⬚⬚ city boundary

——— parish boundary

– – – limit of built area in out parishes

▨ poorest five parishes

☐ richer parishes

Figure 3. The wealth of Bristol parishes (after P.E. Slack, 'The local incidence of epidemic disease: the case of Bristol 1540–1650' in Slack *et al.*, *The Plague Reconsidered: A New Look at its Origins and Effects in Sixteenth and Seventeenth Century England*, Local Population Studies Supplement, 1977).

Forming the outer ring of the old city are the parishes of St James and St Mary Redcliff together with Temple ward which had persistently been the poorest areas in the city, associated with artisan manufactures, port activities and noisome trades. There was beginning to be an east–west divide in the city as its northern and western flanks saw new elegant development while Temple ward and St Mary

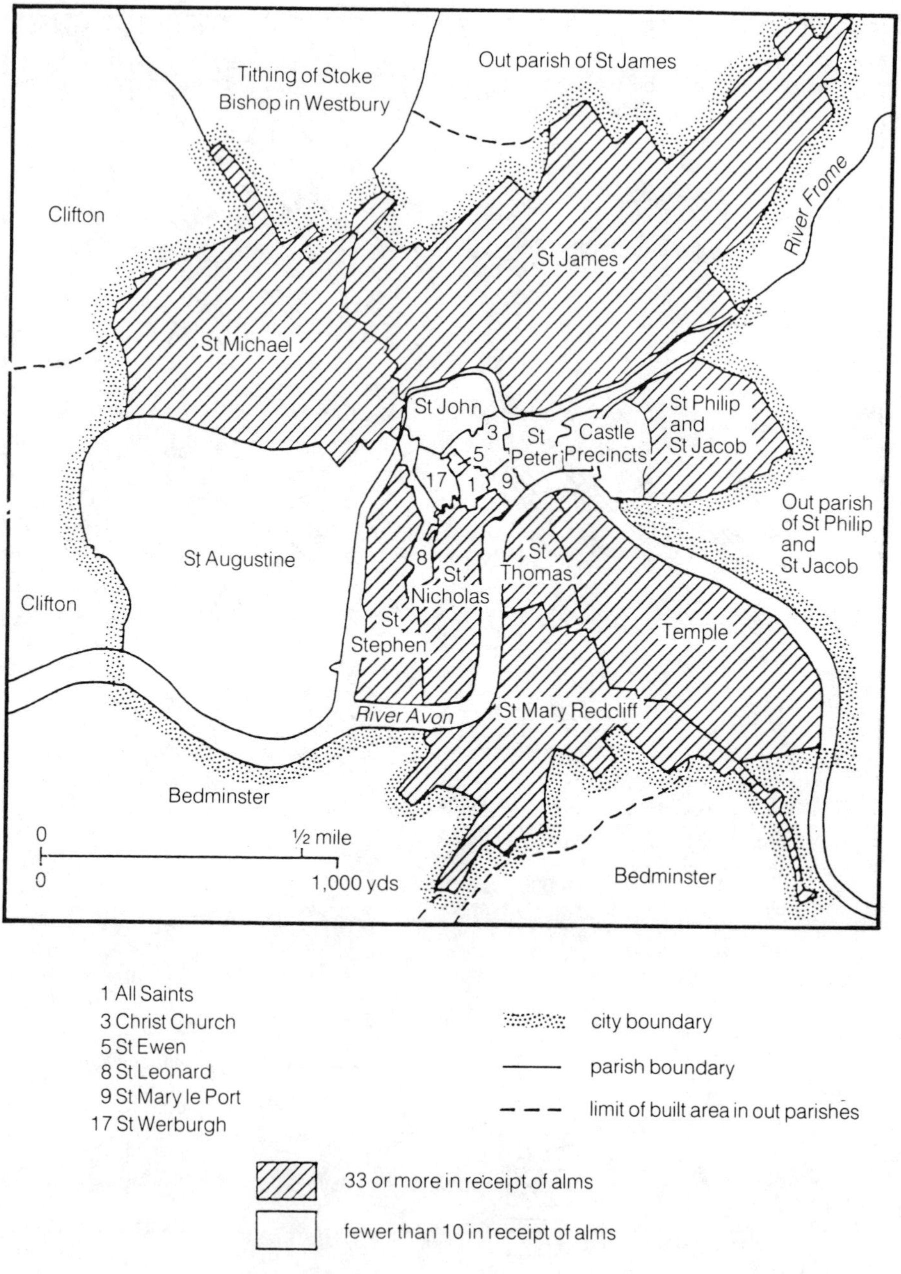

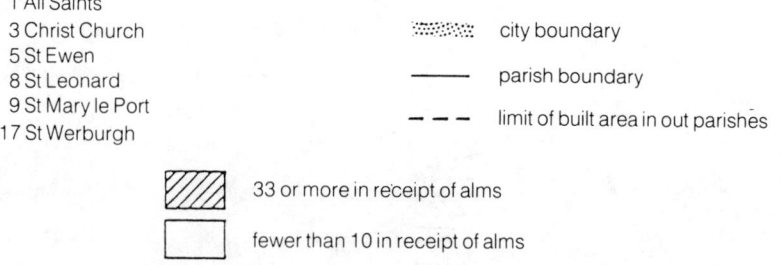

Figure 4. The wealth of Bristol parishes (after E. Ralph and M.E. Williams (eds), 'The inhabitants of Bristol in 1696', *Publications of the Bristol Record Society*, 25, 1968).

This map is based on a simple count of those in receipt of alms in 1696. Counting is influenced to some extent by the size of the parish but the relationship is not simple. St Augustine's Parish which had an area of 1541 acres and a built-up area of 739 acres had no poor at all listed. There is also a relationship with the position of almshouses: St Nicholas Parish had 13 poor, all of whom lived in the merchants' almshouse. Because of these difficulties two broad categories are drawn up: in the 'richer' class no parish had more than 10 people in receipt of alms and most had none: in the 'poorer' class all parishes had 33 or more people in receipt of alms and some, especially SS Philip and Jacob, had particularly high numbers.

Redcliff and Bedminster parishes, for the last of which there are no fiscal data, on the southern and eastern sides remained poor.

Moving in from the suburbs we find that the transitional parishes of St Augustine, St John, and St Stephen and Castle Precincts are more difficult to categorize, and St Peter, St Thomas and SS Philip and Jacob parishes were not classified at all. These were transitional areas, moving up or down the social scale. St Augustine's Parish has a high modal rateable value but a low mean and is amongst the relatively poor in figure 2. Quilici considers the parish to have undergone distinct changes in its social composition during the eighteenth century, towards the end of which numbers of wealthy gentlefolk and members of the middle class came to live in the parish, which nonetheless retained many poorer tradesmen and ships' provisioners.[39] Castle Precincts had also seen much social change.[40] It had originally been outside the city's jurisdiction and was a place of refuge for criminals and vagrants; but in the eighteenth century there was an influx of wealthier and respectable citizens.

In the centre were the wealthiest parishes, associated with domestic and overseas traders, who were traditionally the richest and most powerful men in the city. There were substantial differences in the distribution of wealth within the central parishes: St Nicholas had extremes of rich and poor; All Saints and St Ewen had large numbers of rich and fairly rich and Christ Church, St Mary Port and especially St Werburgh had extremely large numbers of very rich men. These differences emphasize that, though it is both convenient and accurate to refer to a group of central wealthy parishes, they were by no means a uniform bloc.

Both rich and poor were present in each parish. The poor, those who occupied houses worth £7 a year or less, were present in all parishes and formed 10.9 per cent of the population of the whole city and between 1.9 per cent of the population in Trinity ward and 28.0 per cent in St Mary Redcliff, if the probably erroneous figure of 35.0 per cent in St Michael's Parish is ignored. Similarly rich people were to be found in every parish. They formed 12.4 per cent of the population of the city as a whole and in the individual parishes formed between 3.1 per cent of the population in St James's City and 38.1 per cent in St Werburgh's Parish. This fits the early-modern pattern of mixing at the parish level and segregation at the street level.[41] In big cities, by the end of the eighteenth entury and generally in the nineteenth, there was far more sorting by area.[42] The significance of the development of rather homogeneous residential suburbs on the new edge of the city was obvious for those areas themselves, but also influenced other areas which inevitably became more uniformly poor as the rich moved out. Thus without any tendency to move on the part of the poor themselves, they were coming to occupy more uniformly undesirable areas of the city.[43]

## (b) Poverty

The urban poor proved elusive. The investigation of the number of properties 'under the rate' is a well-tried measure of poverty,[44] but in this study it produced improbably low figures, below 10 per cent of the total in all but two parishes. The figures say more about the practices of the collectors in the various parishes than about the real distribution of poverty in the city. The collectors neither systematically recorded nor failed to record those exempt from payment and the results reflect this inconsistency, which is exacerbated by the fact that different rate returns survive for different parishes and different exemption procedures operated for each rate. The incidence of those described as 'poor' proved just as inconsistent.

The rate and tax returns do not reveal much about the very poorest in urban society, since the homeless, lodgers and those in institutions for the poor were all excluded from assessment. Some estimation of the proportion of poor in the city may be attempted on the basis of the coverage of the returns; but this is at best indirect and approximate and it is clear that, in Bristol at least, the rate and tax returns tell us very little about the poorest in society.

*(c) Households headed by women*

Most women in the city were wives or daughters living in their husband's or father's house, but there were 1,039 households headed by women (table 7). It might have been expected that these women would have been widows or abandoned wives, often with children and in very considerable distress,[45] but in fact their households clustered in classes II and III and were neither very rich nor very poor. While there were few women amongst the wealthiest householders, a higher proportion of women than men were to be found in Class III – the relatively well off. The eligible widow of a wealthy tradesman is, of course, a stock figure[46] and it is presumably women of this type who formed the bulk of those in Class III. The abandoned or widowed destitute woman is no less well drawn a character. It is generally agreed that women of this type always greatly outnumbered men amongst paupers,[47] but it is just these paupers who were excluded from the study and so our knowledge of women in the city remains limited. An analysis of wealth by sex and parish shows that throughout Bristol households headed by women occupied less valuable property than those headed by men in the same parish: women's poverty was related to their sex rather than to the general level of wealth in the parish where they lived and this relative poverty may well have been a continuation of an earlier trend.[48]

*Table 7: Classification of rateable values for households headed by men, women and those of unknown sex*

(i) Number in each class

| Sex | Class I | II | III | IV | Total |
|---|---|---|---|---|---|
| Men | 519 | 2,199 | 1,536 | 505 | 4,759 |
| Women | 101 | 505 | 368 | 65 | 1,039 |
| Unknown | 112 | 376 | 331 | 94 | 913 |
| All | 732 | 3,080 | 2,235 | 664 | 6,711 |

(ii) Per cent in each class

| Sex | Class I | II | III | IV | Total |
|---|---|---|---|---|---|
| Men | 10.9 = | 46.2 + | 32.3 – | 10.6 + | 100.0 |
| Women | 9.7 – | 48.6 + | 35.4 + | 6.3 – | 100.0 |
| Unknown | 12.3 + | 41.2 – | 36.2 – | 10.3 + | 100.0 |
| All | 10.9 | 45.9 | 33.3 | 9.9 | 100.0 |

In conclusion it may be suggested that the use of city rates and the land tax has extended and deepened our understanding of the wealth patterns of inhabitants of the older areas of the city, although coverage of the newer suburbs is less satisfactory. The fiscal data were subsequently linked to data from a Poll Book and directory to form a 'census' for the city. This gave further opportunity to check the coverage and quality of the sources and allowed detailed discussion of the connections amongst wealth, occupation, place of residence, sex and political allegiance in Bristol at this time.[49] This gave opportunities for more subtle insight into and understanding of a pre-census city. The fiscal data played an important role, but one which was greatly enhanced through linkage with the other sources.

The use of city rate and national tax returns is then to be cautiously encouraged. With careful use they can tell us much, especially when linked with other sources: but for the unwary and the unpersistent they remain a hazard.

**Elizabeth Baigent**
St Hugh's College, Oxford

# Notes

I am grateful to the SSRC and the Bryce Fund for Historical Research for financial support and to the staff of the Oxford University Computing Service and Bristol Record Office and especially to Jack Langton for patient help and advice.

1 P. J. Corfield, 'The social and economic history of Norwich, 1650–1850: a study in urban growth' (unpublished University of London Ph.D. thesis, 1976).
2 G. E. Rudé, 'The Middlesex electors of 1768–1769', *English Historical Review*, 75 (1960), 601–17. G. E. Rudé, *Wilkes and Liberty: a Social Study of 1763–1774* (1962).
3 L. D. Schwarz, 'Income distribution and social structure in London in the late eighteenth century', *Econ. Hist. Review*, 2nd series, 32 (1979), 205–59.
4 S. J. Wright, 'Easter books and parish rate books: a new source for the urban historian', *Urban History Yearbook* (1985), 30–45.
5 M. Turner and D. Mills (eds), *Land and Property: The English Land Tax 1692–1832* (1986).
6 W. Michinton, 'Bristol – Metropolis of the West in the eighteenth century', *Transactions of the Royal Historical Society* (1954), 70–85.
7 E. Baigent, 'Bristol society in the later eighteenth century with special reference to the handling by computer of fragmentary historical sources' (unpublished University of Oxford D.Phil. thesis, 1985, 36–69).
8 Anon., *Bristol Poll Book* (1775). W. Pine, *Bristol Poll Book* (1775).
9 J. Sketchley, *Bristol Directory* (1775; reprinted 1971).
10 Rate and Tax returns in Bristol Record Office.
11 The lamping and scavenging rate was levied under 11 & 12 William III c.23, 1700; the watching rate under 28 George III c.32, 1755; the bridge tax under 33 George II c.52, 1759; the sewer rate under 6 George III c.34, 1766; and the poor rate under 7 & 8 William III c.32, 1696.
12 W. R. Ward, *The English Land Tax in the Eighteenth Century* (1953), 4,6,7,22,95.
13 W. R. Ward, *The Administration of the Window and Assessed Taxes 1696–1798* (1963), 3.
14 E. Ralph, *Guide to the Bristol Archives Office* (1971), 44–5.
15 J. V. Beckett, *Local Taxation, National Legislation and the Problems of Enforcement* (1980), 24.
16 D. E. Ginter, 'The incidence of revaluation', in Mills and Turner *Land and Property*, 180–8.
17 Ward, *Administration ... Taxes*, 3.
18 *Ibid.*, 1–7.
19 Beckett, *Local Taxation*, 20.
20 B. D. G. Little, *The City and County of Bristol: a Study in Atlantic Civilisation* (1954), 327.
21 Ward, *English Land Tax*, 4,6,7.
22 M. Noble, 'The land tax assessments in the study of the physical development of country towns', in Mills and Turner, *Land and Property*, 93–117.
23 1 All Saints; 2 Castle Precincts; 3 Christ Church; 4 St Augustine; 5 St Ewen; 6 St James City; 7 St John; 8 St Leonard; 9 St Mary le Port; 10 St Mary Redcliff; 11 St Michael; 12 St Nicholas; 13 St Peter; 14 SS Philip and James; 15 St Stephen; 16 St Thomas; 17 St Werburgh; 18 Temple; 19 St James's Outparish.
24 Noble, 'Land tax assessments', 97.
25 Little, *City and County of Bristol*, 327.
26 P. J. Corfield, *The Impact of English Towns 1700–1800* (1982), 129.
27 P-STAT, the Princeton Statistical Package, was used. It can handle large incomplete datasets and so is more suitable than many business packages for the needs of the historian.
28 R. Campbell, *The London Tradesman* (1747). Anon., *A General Description of Trades, Digested in Alphabetical Order* (1747).
29 A. D. M. Phillips and J. R. Walton, 'The distribution of personal wealth in English towns in the mid-nineteenth century', *Transactions of the Institute of British Geographers*, 2nd series, 64 (1975), 35–48.
30 L. D. Schwarz, 'Occupation and incomes in late eighteenth-century London', *East London Papers*, 14 (1972), 87–100, note to p. 100.
31 L. D. Schwarz and L. J. Jones, 'Wealth, occupations and insurance in the late eighteenth century: the policy registers of the Sun Fire Office', *Economic History Review*, 2nd series, 1 (1983), 365–73.
32 J. Langton, 'Late medieval Gloucester: some data from a rental of 1455', *Transactions of the Institute of British Geographers*, 2nd series (1977), 259–77.
33 E. Jones, 'London in the early seventeenth century: an ecological approach', *London Journal*, 6 (1980), 123–34.
34 R. Butlin, 'The population of Dublin in the late seventeenth century', *Irish Geography*, 5, no.2 (1965), 51–86. J. Langton, 'Residential patterns in pre-industrial cities: some case studies from seventeenth-century Britain', *Transactions of the Institute of British Geographers*, 65 (1975), 1–28. M. J. Power, 'The urban development of East London 1550–1700' (unpublished University of London Ph.D. thesis, 1971). D. J. Hibberd, 'Urban

inequalities: social geography and demography in seventeenth-century York' (unpublished University of Liverpool Ph.D. thesis, 1981).
35  Drawn up using SPSS (Statistical Package for the Social Sciences) (version 4:2).
36  E. Ralph and M. E. Williams (eds), 'The inhabitants of Bristol in 1696', *Publications of the Bristol Record Society, 25* (1968). P. Slack, 'The local incidence of epidemic disease: the case of Bristol 1540–1650', in P. Slack *et al.*, *The Plague Reconsidered: a New Look at its Origins and Effects in Sixteenth and Seventeenth-Century England*, Local Population Studies Supplement (1977), 49–62. J. R. Holman, 'Orphans in pre-industrial towns: the case of Bristol in the late seventeenth century', *Local Population Studies, 15* (1975), 40–4.
37  J. E. Vance, 'Land assignment in the pre-capitalist, capitalist and post-capitalist city', *Economic Geography, 47* (1971), 101–20. G. Sjöberg, *The Pre-Industrial City* (New York, 1960).
38  W. Ison, *The Georgian Buildings of Bristol* (1952; repr. 1978), 25–9. N. Pevsner, *North Somerset and Bristol*, The Buildings of England (1958), 364.
39  R. H. Quilici, 'Turmoil in a city and an empire: Bristol factions 1700–1775' (unpublished University of New Hampshire Ph.D. thesis, 1976), 38–89.
40  Ralph and Williams, 'Inhabitants of Bristol 1696', xxiii.
41  Power, 'Urban development of East London', 164.
42  J. Walvin, *English Urban Life 1776–1851* (1984).
43  Parish boundaries, of course, may not have coincided with social ones. Most of the Bristol parishes are small enough to reflect social boundaries accurately, but there were some larger more heterogeneous parishes: St James's City parish contained older, meaner houses near the centre as well as elegant new houses towards the city boundary. Analysis by street avoids this problem and is possible using computer sorting techniques but is too complicated to report here.
44  J. H. C. Patten, *English Towns 1500–1700* (1978), 190. Corfield, 'Norwich 1650–1850', 211. Power, 'Urban development of East London', 163.
45  B. Hill, *Eighteenth-Century Women: an Anthology* (1984), 156–76.
46  Corfield, 'Norwich 1650–1850', 257. W. G. Hoskins, 'The Elizabethan Merchants of Exeter', in P. Clark (ed.), *The Early Modern Town: A Reader* (1976), 150.
47  A. L. Beier, 'The social problems of an Elizabethan county town: Warwick 1580–90', in P. Clark (ed.), *Country Towns in Pre-Industrial England* (1981), 45–85, 60–1. P. Slack, 'Poverty and politics in Salisbury, 1597–1666', in P. Clark and P. Slack (eds), *Crisis and Order in English Towns 1500–1700. Essays in Urban History* (1972), 164–203, 166–7. R. W. Malcolmson, *Life and Labour in England 1700–1780* (1981), 79.
48  Holman, 'Orphans in pre-industrial towns', 43.
49  Baigent, 'Bristol society'.

# Property transfers and the Register of Sasines: urban development in Scotland since 1617

## Historical and judicial background

Walter Scott's assertion in *Rob Roy* that 'In those days possession was considerably more than eleven points of the law' overlooked a pivotal point of Scots Law, the distinction between ownership and possession. Possession or occupancy was not 'as good as title' as the sixteenth-century Scottish proverb or old French saying 'possession vaut titre' claimed. Though the distinction between ownership and possession might have seemed a nicety to Rob Roy in the sixteenth century, by 1617 a general register of titles to land, the Register of Sasines, was established in Scotland, and has continued virtually uninterrupted until the present day.[1] It is consequently a record of immense importance to urban historians.

The two Acts of 1617[2] which authorized a general register were perhaps predictably the result of refinements to several previous attempts to establish an unchallengeable record of property titles. Several sixteenth-century statutes, for example those of 1503, 1540, 1555, 1567, 1587 and 1599, extended written proof of title first from crown lands and later to all land transfers, although only in 1599 were penalties imposed for non-compliance with this obligation to record changes of title.[3] Title to land in Scotland placed enormous significance on whether investiture had taken place, and accordingly the rules of evidence by which investiture was proved were crucial. Public meetings and the symbolic transfer of land by means of physically handing over earth and stones – a ceremony known as the livery of seisin – were an early form of such verification of changes of title and were performed in front of the superior's court or, in urban land transactions, before the burgesses in the burgh court. This ceremony was certainly operative from the early fourteenth century, but by the later Middle Ages the custom had been superseded by the notarial instrument of Sasine, the sole permissible proof of transfer. At his own expense and at the risk of being sued for damages if he did not comply, the landowner (superior) was obliged to provide the vassal with a *breve testatum* as written proof of transfer, a process which had to be completed in the presence of a notary public.

The introduction of a General Register of Sasines in 1617 was therefore a product of several earlier attempts to establish an unchallengeable title to property. The early seventeenth-century attempt to regularize changes of title on a national basis owed much to the faults, loopholes and inconsistencies of earlier attempts, as well as to dissatisfaction with instances of fraud, forgery and legal malpractices. Two other sets of factors were also influential. First, there were legal conventions which assisted the standardization of property registration. In particular, Scottish feudal law required alienation and succession, that is, title transfers to a third party or an heir, to be approved by the superior and it was thus both natural and practical to record the renewal terms once the process was complete. By contrast, in England the written transmission of title deeds was unnecessary before 1677 as possession or 'uses' was deemed sufficient. The position in Scotland was fundamentally different with Sasine and its verification indispensable for the successful completion of a vassal's title to land. By the later Middle Ages the verification by means of a Notarial Instrument meant Scottish familiarity with an acceptance of a written record of title, circumstances which assisted the introduction of a General Register in 1617. Uniformity of conveyancing procedures may also have assisted the acceptability of general sasines registers, as indeed did the persistent refusal of Scots feudal law to acknowledge mere occupation as sufficient claim to land ownership: 'If a portion of deserted land be laid hold of by a private person, no length of time will transfer the property to him.'[4]

The second set of factors, more compelling in relation to the specific timing of the introduction of the General Register of Sasines in 1617, was concerned with the disposal of church property associated with the Scottish reformation.[5] The weak position of the Scottish monarchy in the second half of the sixteenth century meant that the nobility rather than the crown gained substantial tracts of land following the dissolution of church property. Even though the Annexation Act of 1587 confirmed the nobles' right to hold newly acquired land in perpetuity, rather than on conditions imposed by the crown, uncertainty remained regarding the exact boundaries of former church land. As much as half the sixteenth-century Scottish national income may have been derived from Roman Catholic lands, and given the scale of territorial upheaval – a further 38 religious institutions and their lands were disestablished between 1587 and 1625 – it was understandable that secular anxiety regarding valid title to land should exist. Pressure to introduce a General Register of Sasines was in part a repercussion of the Scottish reformation, and it dovetailed effectively with a wish for greater secularization and modernization of business and administration. It was, in fact, an early pillar of that process.

The Act of 1617 established a public register of titles, bonds, dispositions, reversionary conditions and all other issues relevant to an area of land whose boundaries were precisely stated. Within 60 days matters relating to title to land had to be recorded either in the General Register, held in Edinburgh, or the Particular Register appropriate to each county or district and maintained locally. Failure to record such sasines within 60 days might result in another transaction taking precedence. An Act of 1681 applied these procedures to royal burghs, the records being kept by the Town Clerk.

At an early stage, and certainly from 1617, any purchaser of land in Scotland could be given categorical information relating to any burdens attached to a specific property anywhere in the country. Indeed the system was likened to the ledgers of double entry book-keeping. Such assurances were only possible following laborious searches through the Minute Book aided solely by marginal annotations. The burgeoning volume of land transactions associated with the quickening pace on economic and commercial life in the late eighteenth century prompted the introduction of indices for each person and place recorded in the Minute Books. Table 1 illustrates the escalating volume of registration of titles in Glasgow and adjacent counties most affected by economic modernization. From 1821 indexes or abridgements were introduced for the county (or Particular) registers and gradually extended backwards chronologically so as to be available from 1781 (no such abridgements covered the General Register until 1871). This streamlined the consultation of Sasines records and economized on the legal fees associated with the onerous labour of searching the Sasines registers.

*Table 1: Number of sasines registered in various districts, 1780–1830*

|           | Glasgow | Lanarkshire | Renfrewshire | Stirlingshire | Perthshire |
|-----------|---------|-------------|--------------|---------------|------------|
| 1781–90   | 1,460   | 1,770       | 2,802        | 1,920         | 2,399      |
| 1791–1800 | 2,431   | 2,153       | 3,371        | 2,116         | 2,257      |
| 1801–10   | 4,176   | 2,353       | 3,701        | 2,544         | 2,844      |
| 1811–21   | 5,325   | 3,331       | 5,741        | 3,200         | 3,427      |
| 1821–31   | 6,945   | 4,027       | 6,472        | 3,734         | 4,135      |
| 1781–1831 | 20,337  | 13,634      | 22,087       | 13,514        | 15,062     |

Source: L. Ockrent, *Land Rights: An Enquiry into the History of Registration for Publication in Scotland* (Edinburgh, 1942), 10.

Between 1617 and 1868 (1681 to 1868 for royal burghs) the registration of titles had been undertaken on a dual basis. Both local (Particular) and central (General)

Registers of Sasines had to be completed, with local abridgements available from 1781. This duplication had some justification at the outset, but lack of uniformity, multiplication of errors, and delay in compiling abstracts impaired efficient searching while improved communications and postal services undermined the necessity for dual registration. Complexity of registration added to clerical work, and thus to legal fees, a recurrent nineteenth-century topic of public displeasure. The Land Registers Act, 1868, was therefore an attempt to simplify the admini-stration of recording titles, without disturbing the basic principles. The principal change was to discontinue local (Particular) land registers and establish a comprehensive General Register of Sasines, centrally located, publicly accessible, and organized on a county-by-county basis.

In the revised General Register the sasines writs were entered in a separate series of Presentment Books, Minute Books and Register volumes for each county. The Presentment Book was a continuation of a former convenience by which the presenter of a writ of sasine signed a book to establish chronological order while full registration was processed. The Minute Books remained the basic record of title, providing a complete copy of the deed which described the transfer. Appropriate extracts of titles or matters relating to them were recorded in chronological order in the new General Register of Sasines from 1871, indexing by person or place and including a cross-reference to the entry in the Minute Book. From the mid 1870s copies of the extracts were collected and entered in reference volumes under the heading of place or person, thus providing a historical outline starting with the original plot and subdividing, in urban areas, to each separate property built on that land. Computerization of the new entries to the Register of Sasines is now in effect, but inclusion of the earlier registrations will take a very considerable time in view of the volume of work involved.

## An English parallel?

The transfer of a 'Clot of earth', 'Twig of a Tree' or 'Hasp of the Door of a House' were essential English elements in the Delivery of Seisin ceremony with close symbolic parallels to the Scottish procedures.[6] But a fundamental distinction existed. In England the parties to the transfer were the outgoing and incoming tenant; the feudal lord was not involved. This absence of reference to or approval by the feudal lord on the occasion of land transfers formed the fundamental distinction between the conveyancing systems in England and Scotland for 800 years and since the feudal superior was not involved explains the early atrophy of feudal land law in England.

By separating landlord and tenant in this way English land law embarked upon a unique course by which conveyancing by private deeds resulted.[7] The customary method of transferring land became the 'bargain and sale', by which the vendor retained the legal estate and the purchaser obtained the use of the land, a mode of land transfer which would be completed by word of mouth or without livery of seisin, that is without publicity or formal record. The separation of 'legal' and 'equitable' (use) elements of land was principally a fifteenth-century device prompted by the likelihood of dispossession during the Wars of the Roses for a felony or treason.[8] The distinction between legal title and actual use of land meant landowners could protect their use or real value of land, its productivity, even if legal ownership was revoked. Such secret conveyancing was so widespread that attempts were made in 1379, 1488 and finally in 1535 to control the fraud which often resulted.[9] The Statute of Uses, 1535, attempted to reunite the 'legal' and 'use' definitions of an estate upon completion of a bargain and sale.[10] To secure publicity for such transactions a further Act the same year required the enrolment of bargain and sale agreements, either in the courts of record at Westminster or in the sessions of the counties, though this was usually evaded by the device of a conveyance by lease and release as the statute did not include bargains for a term and was confined technically to freehold.

Consequently registration of titles was never nationally undertaken in England. Limited local deeds registries were introduced, for example in 1663 in the Bedford Level area which included Suffolk, Norfolk, Ely, Huntingdon and small portions of Lincolnshire and Northamptonshire.[11] In Middlesex (1709) and in each of the three Ridings of Yorkshire – West (1704), East (1708), and North (1736) – registers of deeds were also introduced.[12] These registries of deeds, not titles, were the closest English approximation to the Scottish Registers of Sasine. Principally concerned with freehold land, the purpose was to prevent fraud by secret deeds, to warn purchasers and lenders of existing conditions attached to titles, and explicitly in the case of Yorkshire, so that woollen merchants could obtain credit on security of their house or land.

Such local registration initiatives produced some demands for a General Registry during the eighteenth century and again in 1807, but it was only after the Royal Commissions on Real Property (1829–30) and that on Registration and Conveyancing (1850) that pressure for registration mounted.[13] However, successive Bills in 1830, 1845, 1846 and 1851 all failed. A further Royal Commission on the Registration of Title reported positively in 1857 for registration though it was only after further failures in Parliament that a Bill, the Land Registry Act, finally gained approval in 1862. The purpose of this Act was to enable landowners to register their title to land, to confirm ownership, and to facilitate transactions in land. The Register was to settle boundaries and record all existing conditions affecting title to land. Two intrinsic weaknesses limited its effectiveness: voluntary registration and indefeasible title.[14] The weakness of voluntarism was self-evident, but the attempt to authenticate an absolutely flawless title to land proved cumbersome and expensive, and quickly doomed the proposal to failure. In 20 years of operation only 488 properties were registered and 131 (27 per cent) of these were subsequently deleted because of insufficient substantiation of title.[15] A further Royal Commission and an Act of 1875 did nothing to advance compulsory registration, though certain key elements of the system were refined, namely the registrar's acceptance of absolute title and 'possessory title' status while the laborious process of scrutinization was completed. Only in 1897 on the recommendation of the Privy Council or on the adoption of County Councils was compulsory registration introduced in England, though even this was only comprehensive after 1925.[16]

In only very limited areas of England was the practice of land registration applied, and then only from the early eighteenth century. According to one writer, 'Scots conveyancers, who have been brought up in a school where publicity has been almost apotheosized, are often surprised at the preference for secrecy in land transactions shewn by their colleagues in England.'[17] It is precisely because of this comprehensive national coverage in Scotland over almost 400 years that the Register of Sasines offers a unique opportunity to study property and social relations during the critical phases of urbanization.

**The research potential of the Register of Sasines**

The largest proportion of the entries in the Sasines are covered by two types of deeds: firstly, feu charters and, secondly, dispositions. The former is the granting by the superior of the right to occupy or develop a piece of land on payment of an annual feu duty by the feuar. The feuar can, in his turn, subdivide the land into plots and let them out for building purposes also using a feu contract, under the burden of an annual feu duty. Dispositions provide the confirmation of transfer of ownership of a piece of land or a building with, possibly, adjacent garden ground from one individual to another for a purchase price and including annual burdens such as feu duty, parochial and other dues. The two deeds can also be amalgamated, allowing the transfer of a property and land with permission to develop. In addition to these deeds, however, any financial transactions which affect title have also to be registered and updated if changes occur.[18]

It must be remembered that the basic intention of all these deeds is simply to establish title to land or property and that this requires no more than a description of the plot and the names of the previous and present owners and the date of the deed. These details are contained in the extract. However, most documents in the Minute Books are a mine of additional descriptive information which, in the best examples, provide the following details:

1 Superior or vendor's name, occupation and address.
2 Feuar or purchaser's name, occupation and address.
3 If a building society or other financial intermediary is concerned the names, occupations and addresses of the trustees will be included, together with the name of the society and details of the Act under which it was incorporated.
4 Any loans or mortgages against which a property or piece of land forms security will give name, occupation and address of both the lender and borrower together with a brief description of the property, the amount of the loan and the rate of interest payable.
5 The location and boundaries of a plot of land and a synopsis of its history naming the estate or holding of which it originally formed part, the superior(s) and the date on which it was divided.
6 The restrictions which must be observed if development is to take place.
7 Where a property is concerned, the address, location and reference to the feuing plan and the Feu Contract will be given together with a description of the accommodation available. The garden and other ground will be delineated and rights to shared open spaces will also be listed.
8 The purchase price and any financial burdens such as feu duty (for the whole property and for each house, if it is subdivided). Other burdens such as shared maintenance of the roof, the common stair and the back green will also be listed in the case of tenements or the maintenance of party walls, etc., where terraced properties are concerned.
9 The names and occupations of the witnesses to the signing of the deed and the name of the lawyer presenting the document are also given.

It is clear from the outline given above, that the Register of Sasines provides a substantial body of material which can be used to study landholding patterns and urban development in Scotland. As the system of recording has been established in order to ease the process of proving title to land and property, historical researchers are able to take advantage of the needs of the legal profession and can follow the process of land development backwards or forwards as required. The accumulation of land in the hands of particular owners can be studied and market influences can be assessed by examining which areas were retained and which were released for development. Owners of land put different interpretations on their role in urban development: some bodies, such as the educational trusts, were committed to influencing the style and quality of building which was erected on their land. Individuals, like Sir George Warrender, had a similar attitude and sought to achieve their aims by the feuing of land to builders under extremely detailed contracts which ensured that the terraces of the Edinburgh New Town and tenements of Victorian Marchmont were built to a uniform pattern, in the same type of stone, and conforming to feuing plans and elevations designed by well-known architects.[19] That such contracts were strictly enforced cannot be in doubt in respect of the regularity of line and the conformity of detailing in these rows of elegant houses.

Other superiors, however, were much less committed and conscientious where their lands were concerned. In Edinburgh, Alexander Learmonth and James Walker feued or sold large areas for development with no building restrictions whatsoever. Their behaviour may have been influenced by the fact that a large proportion of these lands were used primarily for working-class tenements but the same pattern is found in the sale of a large area of ground at Comely Bank for mixed development.[20] While the exterior aspect of residential developments could be carefully controlled, there was never any attempt to dictate to builders the internal requirements for housing: that was apparently a matter left to their discretion.

Because of the paucity of records of building firms in Scotland, there is extreme difficulty in following the activities of those engaged in residential and industrial development. Here the Register of Sasines can provide an acceptable proxy, allowing insight into the strategies of builders at both the management and construction levels. The use of the Sasines for this purpose has already been tested in reconstructing the career of Sir James Steel, one of Edinburgh's most prominent builders in the later Victorian period. It has been possible to follow his activities from 1867 when he first feued an area of land at Tollcross from James Home Rigg, until his death in 1904. As an impecunious jobbing builder, newly arrived in Edinburgh in the 1860s, he was only able to raise enough capital to build one tenement on his first feu and sublet all the additional stances to other builders or housing associations. This pattern continued over the next ten years with Steel gradually increasing the number of properties which he built with his own workforce until, by 1876, he was able to tender for one of the blocks in Douglas Crescent being let out at roup by the Heriot Trust. In 1887, he bought for £40,000 the Comely Bank estate which had belonged to Alexander Learmonth and, using only his own resources, developed this large area of middle-class villas and tenement houses over the next 14 years until his death.[21] The estate was completed after his death by his trustees.

Throughout his career in Edinburgh, James Steel showed considerable energy and skill in managing the land under his control. Whatever the quality of housing involved, the feu contracts which he made with other builders contained detailed requirements for standards of building and for uniformity of appearance. Site plans and elevations were provided for residential accommodation and many restrictions of use were placed on industrial developments. In many cases the superior made no such requirements in the original feuing document so Steel was free to impose his own standards of control.[22]

Though James Steel was exceedingly successful in his field, it would be equally possible to use the Sasines to chart the activities of any building firm, large or small, throughout its period of activity. Unfortunately, the Sasines can offer no firm evidence of the cost of building or the management of a firm's workforce. It can, however, give a valuable insight into the means used to raise capital. During the nineteenth century most builders obtained outside capital through loans under bond on security of the land or buildings which they controlled. It is possible through the Sasines to chart an initial loan, the interest paid, the date of maturity (repayment) and refinancing using the same security again. Any partial repayment against a bond had to be registered, as did any change in ownership (such bonds frequently formed part of the inheritance of younger generations of a family).[23]

The availability of such data has, of course, implications beyond the study of Scottish building firms. The fact that loans against property were regarded as a secure investment, giving a good return, allows investigation of the involvement of family trusts, marriage contract and widows' funds in the provision of finance for urban development.[24] The legal profession were also frequently involved in their own right, as well as on behalf of clients and many wealthy landowners regarded such loans as an acceptable form of investment.[25] Where individual borrowing for house purchase was concerned, the Register of Sasines can provide clear evidence of the spread of the services of building and friendly societies which gradually took over the role formerly played by private lenders.[26] An interesting corollary of the above is the virtual absence of bank involvement in the housing market.[27]

Although the Register of Sasines constitutes a very rich and varied source in its own right, in conjunction with other records its value can be greatly increased. The information which it provides on land acquisition can be fleshed out by incorporating the private papers of landowning families and the records of education trusts. By this means, it is possible to judge the importance of income from feu duties as compared with, for example, agricultural rents. Where the investigation of building firms is concerned, trade and street directories can be utilized to provide names and locations; sequestration papers and wills provide detailed evidence of their success or lack of it. Perhaps the most valuable additions to the Sasines data can be provided by the valuation rolls for the Scottish burghs which list each property with the names and occupations of owner, occupier and tenant plus the sum payable in rates. When these two sources are used in tandem, it is possible to study the role of builders, developers and private individuals in the provision of rented property for domestic and commercial use. Such information has been utilized to study the development of several residential areas in Edinburgh by James Steel. In 1869 and 1874 he acquired two large feus in the Dalry area of the city, close to two railway stations – the Caledonian and Haymarket – and the large industrial and food-processing complex of Fountainbridge.[28] Working-class tenement housing was built here, a small part by Steel but mostly by subletting building stances. In 1878 he acquired two more feus, further along Dalry Road at the junction with Gorgie Road, and these he began to develop from 1888 onwards, predominantly using his own workforce to produce similar small tenement houses. The same strategy for management of this housing is evident as that employed on the earlier sites: Steel retained most of the property which he constructed and let it out on annual leases to tenants who, from their occupations, appear to have been employed locally. Where he did sell, it was only on the basis of whole tenements which were taken up by investors who desired a steady income from the rental of these properties.[29] By contrast, in Comely Bank, Steel sold only a few complete tenements and pursued a policy of mixed ownership, retaining some houses for letting and selling other houses singly to owner occupiers.[30] In a few cases small groups of tenement flats were also sold to investors for letting.[31] In Comely Bank and in the middle-class areas he developed for the Heriot Trust, he retained a few villas or large terraced houses for rental but sold them fairly rapidly on completion to individual owner ocupiers.

While this material can be used to give insight into the activities of investors who provided accommodation for rental, it can also be viewed from the other end – from the point of view of the tenant. Here occupational data can be linked to local availability of work, the quality of housing (i.e. the number of houses per tenement) and the level of rates/rent which the tenant was able to meet. Where there were no property sales and descriptions of accommodation are, therefore, not available, plans held among the Dean of Guild records could be incorporated to show the number of rooms and the provision of services. In addition the velocity of turnover of tenancies and the likelihood of purchase of property by those renting it, can also be adduced together with the sources of finance.[32] Studies of several urban areas in Scotland could be used to compare the levels of demand for property for rental or purchase.

## Conclusion

Historians of urban development in Scotland have, in the Register of Sasines, a valuable collection of data which is at present greatly underutilized. For the nineteenth and twentieth centuries this source is most productive, and if less complete before 1780, remains of central importance in the comprehension of landownership and site development patterns. Admittedly the methods of registration which have evolved over the last three centuries do not aid rapid extraction of material, even when using the search books at Meadowbank House. The evolution of Sasines registration, with the cross-referencing involved, make it a cumbersome and time-consuming source to use, and if the search books accelerate research they cannot be used on their own before 1880, though patience and familiarity render the results extremely reliable and revealing. With these provisos in mind, the wealth of detailed information which is available makes the effort of utilizing the Sasines very worthwhile and a source of great interest to urban historians and others interested in the physical and social fabric of Scottish cities.

**Richard Rodger**
University of Leicester

**Jennifer Newman**
University of Essex

## Notes

The archival research upon which this is based was funded by the ESRC, project no. D00232155, and the end of grant report deposited in the British Library in June 1987. We should like to acknowledge the assistance of Albert Russell at the Scottish Record Office, and the staff of the Register of Sasines at Meadowbank House, Edinburgh for their advice and forbearance.

1. D. M. Walker, *The Scottish Legal System* (1969), 156–7; Ross, *Lectures on the History and Practice of the Law of Scotland*, 2nd edn (1822) vol.2, 201; A. M. Bell, *Lectures on Conveyancing*, 3rd edn (1882), Ch.6; J. Craigie, *Scottish Law of Conveyancing: Heritable Rights* 3rd edn (1899), 55–62, 270; *Encyclopaedia of the Laws of Scotland* (1931), paras.804–10; L. Ockrent, *Land Rights: An Enquiry into the History of Registration for Publication in Scotland* (1942), 45–55; A. B. Williamson and W. A. Wilson (eds), *Introduction to the Law of Scotland* (1980), 593; The Stair Society, *An Introduction to Scottish Legal History* (1958), 156–62, 188–93; M. Livingstone, *A Guide to the Public Records of Scotland* (1905), 166–72.
2. James VI 1617 c.12 and c.16.
3. Early Scottish Land Registration Statutes are those of James IV 1503 c.35; James V 1540 c.11–14; Mary 1555 c.21; James VI 1587 c.44,50; James VI 1597 c.17, 33, 35, 36; James VI 1600 c.22, 36; James VI 1609 c.40; James VI 1617 c.12, 16; Charles II 1672 c.16; James VII 1686 c.33; William & Mary 1693 c.22, 23; William & Mary 1696 c.18.
4. H. Home (Lord Kames), *Elucidations Respecting the Common Law and Statute Law of Scotland* (1777), 259, quoted in L. Ockrent, *Land Rights*, 47.
5. P. H. Brown, *History of Scotland* (1902), Vol.II, 287; L. Ockrent, *Land Rights*, 49.
6. C. D'O. Farran, *The Principles of Scots and English Land Law* (1958), 193, revised by C. F. Kolbert and N. A. M. Mackay as *History of Scots and English Land Law* (1977).
7. J. W. B. Innes, 'Some differences between English and Scots law: II. The origin of the land systems', *Juridical Review*, 27 (1915), 28–44.
8. W. H. Upjohn, 'The Statute of Uses and the present system of conveyancing', *Law Magazine and Review*, 4th series, 6 (1980–1), 134–6.
9. 2 Ric II St. 2 (1379); 4 Hen VII c.4(c) (1488); 27 Hen VIII c.10,16 (1535).
10. A. A. Dibben, *Title Deeds; 13th–19th Centuries* (1968), 9–11; S. R. Simpson, *Land Law and Registration* (1976), 37.
11. W. E. Tate, 'The five English district statutory Registries of Deeds', *Bull. Inst. of Hist. Research*, 20 (1944), 97–105; 15 Car II c.17 (1663).
12. F. Sheppard, V. Belcher and P. Cottrell, 'The Middlesex and Yorkshire deeds registries and the study of building fluctuations', *London Journal* (1980), 176–217; C. A. Archer and R. K. Wilkinson, 'The Yorkshire Registries of Deeds', *Urban History Yearbook* (1977), 40–7; 2 & 3 Anne c.4 (West Riding); 6 Anne c.62 (East); 7 Anne c.20 (Middlesex); 8 Geo II c.6 (North Riding).
13. E. K. Blyth, 'Land transfer and land registry', *Law Quarterly Review*, 12 (1896), 354–67.
14. H. Greenwood, 'Registration – or simplification – of title?', *Law Quarterly Review*, 6 (1890), 144–56; H. W. Challis, 'The compulsory registration of title', *ibid.*, 157–68 provides an account of efforts to register title 1862–90.
15. Blyth, 'Land transfer', 359.
16. Because of the voluntary and belated nature of English property registration before 1925, G. Green, 'Title deeds: a key to local and housing markets', *Urban History Yearbook* (1980), 84–91 makes no reference to them as a historical source.
17. L. Ockrent, *Land Rights*, 20. G. Green, 'Title deeds', 86 also refers to the secrecy of the English registration process.
18. This process has continued to the present, and these volumes can be consulted at Meadowbank House, Edinburgh, by members of the public on payment of a fee or by professional searchers and historical researchers by arrangement with the Registrar. The General Register at Register House, Edinburgh, is open to the public, with the indexes freely available and the minute books provided on payment of a fee or, without payment, through the Historical Search Room. Before 1868 the reference number is RS.27 and after 1868 RS.108. By contrast, contemporary English property registries remain closed to the public.

19 All the examples given in the following pages refer to Edinburgh and rise from a study, funded by the ESRC, of residential development in that city between 1840 and 1914. References to the Register of Sasines are given by date and name only as they appear in the indexes. See, for example, feu charter of 18 April 1876 between Heriot's Hospital and James Steel.

20 Feu charter 15 April 1869, James Walker and James Steel. Disposition 17 May 1878, Alexander Learmonth and James Steel.

21 Feu charter 9 January 1867, James Home Rigg and James Steel. Feu charter 22 March 1876, Heriot's Hospital and James Steel. Disposition 3 April 1887, William Hardinge and James Steel.

22 See, for example, feu charters of 29 May 1867 James Steel and Clunas and Wilson, builders.

23 All these points are found in the bond given over 9 Darnaway Street by James Steel to the Methuen Family on 29 May 1884, partially repaid on 1 April 1892 and the balance was repaid on 13 November 1909. It was reassigned twice in this period.

24 Marriage contract funds were sometimes used to provide the recipients with a home as in the case of Alexander Donaldson's purchase of 19 Eglinton Crescent on 19 May 1881 when £10,000 was paid out of his marriage contract fund. On 4 March 1896 the Trustees of Alexander MacTier provided £3,600 against a mixed shop and housing development at 234–41 Dalry Road.

25 James Lindesay, James Steel's solicitor, frequently provided him with funds including a loan of £2,500 on 3 January 1873 over 3 Caledonian Place. The Earl of Moray also made funds available to Steel on several occasions, including a loan of £26,000 on 15 May 1893 over 1–15 Belgrave Place.

26 The Edinburgh Mutual Investment and Building Society, the St Bernard's Friendly Society and the St Cuthbert's Co-operative Society were frequent lenders on property in Comely Bank. See, for example, the loan of £250 on 16 May 1898 to Alexander and Agnes Auchterlonie for the purchase of the northmost house on the first flat of 22 Comely Bank Avenue.

27 James Steel received only one loan from a bank – on 2 February 1871 the Commercial Bank of Scotland loaned him £7,000 over property at Lonsdale Terrace and Antigua Street.

28 Feu charter 15 April 1869, James Walker to James Steel; feu charter 9 June 1874.

29 Disposition 17 May 1878, Alexander Learmonth to James Steel; 8 March 1878 feu contract James Home Rigg to James Steel. In the Murieston Crescent development Steel sold only one tenement on 20 May 1889 to David Turner.

30 At 22 Comely Bank Avenue, for example, Steel retained three flats for rental and sold the remaining six to individual purchasers.

31 Nos. 32–6 Comely Bank Avenue were sold to two purchasers on 17 and 23 May 1898. The main door house at 32, plus the northmost flats on the first, second and third floors, were sold to Sydney Smith. The main door house at 36, with the southmost and centre flats on each upper floor, were sold to Agnes and Margaret Logan. It was very common in Edinburgh for housing to be purchased to give an income to widows and unmarried daughters. This could take the form of that adopted for the Misses Logan, by letting houses, but for those less well-endowed, the investment could take the form of providing a home for the lady concerned and she made an income from taking in lodgers. The provision of lodgings could also, of course, be made in rented accommodation, as was the case with James Steel's nieces, Susan and Mary Percival, who rented 4 Torphichen Street from him for this purpose.

32 Quite a large number of Steel's tenants in rented accommodation bought property from him at different addresses. For example, 14 May 1912, Alexander Cruickshank purchased 2 Comely Bank Grove having been a tenant at 3 Comely Bank Terrace.

# Town histories and Victorian plaudits: some examples from Preston

Charles Dickens visited Preston in January 1854 to report on the cotton lock-out of that year. What he saw contributed to his vision of the archetypal northern, urban industrial centre, Coketown:

> It was a town of red brick or of brick that would have been red if the smoke and ashes had allowed it; but as matters stood it was a town of unnatural red and black like the painted face of a savage. It was a town of machinery and tall chimneys, out of which interminable serpents of smoke trailed themselves forever and ever and never got uncoiled.[1]

Three years later a rather different topographical account appeared in Charles Hardwick's history of the borough:

> Notwithstanding the occasional carpings of a few splenetic travellers, Preston is generally and deservedly recognized as one of the cleanest and most pleasantly situated manufacturing towns in England. The cotton factories are chiefly erected to the north and east of the old aristocratic borough ... and do not as yet materially interfere with the more 'fashionable' or picturesque sections of the district.[2]

The contrast illuminates the shortcomings of the town history both as literature and historical geography; but indicates the tenor of Prestonian self-justification. It is precisely this prosaic subjectivity which makes the histories a rich source. As Peter Clark asserts, 'even fifth-rate urban historians sometimes have an important story to tell.'[3]

Unlike many other towns with long-established traditions of urban chronicling, history writing in Preston did not blossom until the nineteenth century.[4] As a result the local printed propaganda in existence is profoundly commercial in tone. Written by leading townsmen, the histories were well received because of the attention they drew to local trade and industry.[5] In his discussion of the origins of the genre, Peter Clark argues the likelihood of corporation patronage, ranging from goodwill to perquisites to occasional cash rewards.[6] Given these factors, it is hardly surprising that a uniformly confident approach is adopted and that at its very worst a town 'history' could be little more than a tourist brochure with a few historical generalizations thrown in.

Both in the case of Preston and the genre as a whole, town histories follow a predictable formula. They include a political history; an economic history; a topographical chapter, which provides the opportunity for attractive illustration; and, without fail, an account of the present government of the town, its great men and institutions. However formulaic, their very nature demands an attempt at a comparative assessment of the town through time and expression of a definable identity. As ruminations on historical change are rare in nineteenth-century urban records, town histories are a valuable source offering insight into the ideas and language available to Victorians for conceptualizing the past.

In Preston's case, the central historical drama recorded (after the Battle of Preston in the Civil War and Jacobite disturbances in the town) was the burst of industrial activity in the 1790s. In 1771 when the first cotton factory opened in the town, the population was estimated at around 6,000; by 1869 there were 77 cotton factories in the once leafy town, supporting a population of over 84,000.[7] Some kind of judgement on this transformation within a lifetime of the 'aristocratic Lancashire centre of the past' into 'the commercial emporium of the present' was unavoidable.[8] Despite the fact that these texts run the gamut from worthy corporation histories to unashamed local hymns, in their interpretations of the recent past ideological consistency is a salient and remarkable feature.[9]

In their discussion of the rapid industrialization which transformed the eighteenth-century gentry resort into the nineteenth-century cotton town, the writers disclose no hint of pastoral regret or nostalgia. As early as 1822 when Jeffrey wrote his history, the town's fashionable appeal was on the wane:

> During the greater part of the last century, the town was much resorted to as an agreeable retirement by old and respectable families, but having during the last 20 or 30 years become the seat of very extensive manufacturing the character of the inhabitants has undergone a consequent change.[10]

Historical apologists might explain that the 'railways had brought the metropolis to within a few hours of every man's door and had destroyed the motive for county families having town houses in the provinces for a little season of country gaiety.[11] Or even celebrate the dissolution of the old client economy: 'Preston had outgrown the days when the patronage of a great family was essential to its interests.'[12] But they studiously missed the point. Two or three mills might be impressive and attract tourists through their novelty. Equally the early stages of urban growth might seem pregnant with vigour and excitement. Yet too many mills, shoulder to shoulder with intensive housing, inefficient sewerage and water supply, made for an ugly squalid environment, unappealing to 'the people of birth and polished manners'.[13]

Perhaps more galling to aristocratic sensibilities, however, was the attendant social, economic, and political rise of the cottontots: Cobbett's 'seigneurs of the twist, sovereigns of the spinning jenny, great yeomen of the yarn'. Witness Frances Lady Shelley's self-conscious reminiscences of the 1790s:

> My father died when I was only six and long before his death he had become disgusted with the erection of factories near Preston – Proud Preston as it was formerly called because it was the winter residence of the nobility and county families. One day my father, in a towering passion, left his old house never to return. He had gone as usual in the morning to select the fish for dinner. On his arrival at the fishmongers, he found himself forestalled in the purchase of the finest turbot by a Mr Horrocks, a cotton spinner. This was too much for my father's sense of dignity. He pronounced Preston no longer a fit place for a gentleman to live in and immediately rented a villa about four miles out of Liverpool.[14]

This extract from her diary, though perhaps not literally true, encapsulates a genuine grumbling resentment. The gentry ceased to patronize the town, sold off their town houses and voted with their feet.[15]

Furthermore, this anecdote exemplifies an approach to urban change, seeing the town as an arena, a battleground where old property and new capital fought it out. The Preston town historians, with the interests of commerce and capital behind them, were obvious partisans in this simplified 'conflict' and interpreted history accordingly. Even in their discussions of the physical environment, their preoccupations are in evidence:

> Several ancient landmarks and historical mansions associated with many old families connected with Preston have been swept away within the last half century to make way for modern innovations in favour of trade and commerce.[16]

From the vantage point of the mid nineteenth century, the historians saw the battle won and their writing reflects this Whiggish historical confidence.

However, the histories were founded upon a contradiction. On the one hand as histories they celebated Preston's past. The town's Roman roots, medieval Charter and Georgian resort appeal differentiated the town from Burnley, Blackburn and Wigan which had no history to speak of or gentry heritage to romanticize, exaggerate or reject. Preston histories underlined the fact that it was no mere frontier town, mushrooming out of nothing. On the other hand, in explicit terms Victorian Preston was not defined against the neighbouring mill towns, but against its own past, a cardboard and colourful eighteenth century. The histories offered a caricature of the past which highlighted the superiority of the present.

Seventeenth-and eighteenth-century Preston is treated as 'The Past', an amorphous time before the commercial present; 'The Olden Days', when an equally generalized upper class had set the tone. 'We all know that in days of yore, Preston was remarkable for the gentility of its inhabitants.'[17] But in this vein the historians belittled gentility itself as an artificial non-creative state resting on prejudice: 'many of [the gentry] had indeed longer pedigrees than purses'.[18] And the effect of 'genteel' pretension on social mores and culture was roundly denounced: 'When drunkenness was a fashionable foible in the upper classes of society, Preston, always inclined to gentility was much addicted to this vice'.[19] Eighteenth-century culture was at once bestial and intemperate; 'A striking illustration of the tastes of our forefathers is to be found in their amusements: bull-baiting, bear-baiting, badger-baiting and cock-fighting ... to say nothing of their "tussles", "bloodwipes" and "scold-ducking"'[20] and simultaneously effeminate and ineffectual 'with its well-born but ill-portioned old maids and widows with aristocratic feelings and prejudices'.[21]

With a certain amount of justice, we are informed that Preston of the bad old days was no rural idyll:

> Except the main streets, the passages in and to and from the town were very narrow; ditches were wide and often deep. And in modern times a man died in one which crossed water street; the plats or bridges over them were numerous and dangerous; timber and various matters lay in the streets endangering life and limbs and even within the town the lanes were overshadowed by trees.[22]

But this approach lacked balance, as the same author complacently continued: 'When we notice our well-lighted and well-paved streets, we can scarcely believe to what inconveniences our ancestors must have been placed for want of the advantages we now possess.' In fact, the body of urban evidence undermines this picture of civic modernity and makes it clear that only a select few in the fashionable, residential developments were in a position to enjoy these urban 'advantages'.

Nonetheless, the juxtaposition was common to all the histories. The past, the static centuries, were denigrated, since that threw into relief the new vitality of urban life:

> Full are thy towns with the sons of art;
> And trade & joy, in every busy street mingling are heard.[23]

The dynamism of the present was extolled in scientific terms. All references to progress indicated that it was inexorable and irreversible.

> A fondness for and admiration of what is stationary arises from the false judgements formed concerning the truth of facts and the nature of man. If we oppose the progress of civilisation, it is only because we are under the dominion of prejudice ... The development of industry arts and sciences will appear to be what it really is, legitimate and natural ... in this movement we shall recognize the gradual march of society.

This near apocalyptic mood of expectation was reflected in letters to the editors of the flourishing local press:

> Wherever you turn your eyes behold the spirit of improvement and its rapid progress and if the 19th century shall carry on at the speed we have already gone imagination itself cannot say where we shall be at the close. Everything seems to have received new motion and every additional discovery only seems to create fresh desires for knowledge. New roads, new factories, new churches, new coaches and new discoveries of all sorts seem to be on the go.[24]

This was customary local rhetoric, suggesting that the town was on the threshold of a new era. Progress, invention and industrialization seemed bound up with inevitability and confirmed by liberal economics. There was a sense of liberation, that modernity was unleashed, at the mercy only of market forces, Adam Smith's 'invisible hand'. This progress was seen as set is motion by the actions of the commercial man, the exemplar of his class. The cotton trade truly began, according to the local historians, in 1792 when a 'yard factory' was opened by a Mr John Horrocks, an owner destined to become Preston's cotton King, founding a dynasty of MPs and mayors. In subsequent writing, he alone was credited with the trigger role in the industrialization and urbanization of the town:

> The name of Horrocks is as greatly associated with the commerce of Preston as is that of Franklin with America. A monument it is expected will be raised and placed in a conspicuous part.
> Preston may well be proud! when she has cradled an Arkwright of Cromford and adopted as her son a Horrocks of Edgeworth! The commercial part of civilized Europe will remember Preston in the annals of history to the latest posterity![25]

John Horrocks was the uncontested hero of the histories, and the commercial present contrasted with the passive, uncreative gentleman of the past. A popular story about him was recounted by Hewitson in his history. A Mr Crane, one of Horrocks's investors, was shrewdly investigating the works before he put up the money.

> And what did he see? He saw Horrocks lying on his back on the floor, near or under a machine; but he was neither lounging nor asleep. No he was oiling machinery ... in the attitude and the action he could read the man and see sufficient security.[26]

Horrocks was seen to be self-made, his achievement of MP status in 1802 being interpreted as a symbolic victory for the whole class. He was seen not only as the supreme example, but the justification of the system.[27] By individual competition anyone with energy and ability, however humble, could thrive. Thus the system was supposedly fair since in Sam Smiles's words: 'What some men are, all without difficulty might be.'[28] Moreover, this was the reward won for the nation by the socio-economic transition which Preston history was held to exemplify. It was precisely this sense of pioneering a new culture, articulated in the histories, which G. M. Young described as 'an authentic sense of war and victory, man against nature and reason against the traditions of their elders'.[29] The cotton industry was felt to be in the vanguard: 'Preston has played no insignificant part in this mighty social revolution!'[30] Literary and philosophic attempts to argue that 'revolution' was effected at the expense of the operative class were dismissed. In fact, the working class are more or less absent from the histories, at least as an active force. If presented at all it is as numbers, factory fodder or passive recipients of the 'benefits' of the cotton boom. A cynical reading of Bentham's principle of utility is absorbed in this framework of values as justification. It was argued that more production and commodities created more wealth for all. Note how a Preston owner wrote in 1790 describing a cotton mill:

A work of such general utility ... we have already spent £40–50,000 for labour since the first establishment of our works and have employed great numbers of the poor of the county. Great general benefit has been derived.[31]

The histories imply that the sole aim of industrial capitalism was the greatest happiness of the greatest number, in an attempt to make a virtue of its practice.[32] Indeed, the histories were a single-minded vindication of the industrial system as it developed in Preston. It was significant that in an era of industrial dispute, Luddism, Chartism, and riotous elections, these local historians ignored the massive industrial workforce and chose to romanticize a middle-class victory over the upper class.

But what of an appreciation of the actual environment, of the town itself, rather than a mere industrial site and symbolic battleground? Apart from blinkered topographical accounts there are few, genuine, qualitative assessments. Quantitative assessments were deemed all-sufficient; numbers of mills, production totals, numbers of steam engines and population figures abound. It was complacently observed that by breakfast time on any given day the Lancashire mills had met the demands of the home market. All the histories stressed that this was a time of unprecedented national growth in all spheres. G. M. Young's discussion of the industrial mentality and its 'vulgar pride in mere quantity the thoughtless exultation of a crowd in motion'[33] does not seem so wide of the mark. To write otherwise, to write a wider reckoning of the town would be to undermine the extent of the industrialists' triumph.

Nonetheless, some of the more sophisticated historians tried to anticipate criticisms of their self-made Coketown, recognizing that there was something to be explained, however unsatisfactorily. 'Whatever evils may be inseparable from overstrained commercial enterprise', reasoned Hardwick, 'surely they are neither irremediable in themselves nor more degrading than the vicious habits fostered by war [34] (war being an implicitly gentry pursuit). He continued to muse on:

The present with all its faults – and truly they are more than the utilitarian spirit of the hour has yet discovered or at least willingly acknowledges; – Still the despised present patronizes free schools and libraries, cheap books and periodicals, baths and wash-houses, public parks and cheap trips and other sanitary improvements, better legacies at least, to posterity than bloody victories.

He then attempted to defuse criticism, by declaring that 'mankind has gained much and lost little by the change'. And, enigmatically, he concluded: 'When the present edifice shall be completed, the ugly scaffolding, which though necessary to its construction disfigures its beauty, will be removed.' Implicit in that was the idea that the evils of industrialism and urbanism were both mere surface scars, and a stage in the evolution of capitalism. In time, all would recognize this and the new world so confidently awaited: 'will cease to be viewed through the spectacles of prejudice and personal selfishness.'[35] Essentially Hardwick was pre-empting criticism, dismissing it as deluded and nostalgic, based on a rural and probably landed stance and therefore necessarily anti-commercial and anti-urban. Thus criticism was written off as class selfishness, while the town business interest was presented as beyond reproach, representing the common good not a vested interest.

Undoubtedly town histories such as these offered a narrow interpretation of their towns' recent development, seeing it in such profoundly entrepreneurial terms. Similarly, the commercial values which leap from their pages show the liberal individualist ethos at its most stark. However, the tone and philosophy was by no means confined to this literary form. Various memoirs, autobiographies, biographies, industrial histories and county studies displayed examples of a similar historical vision.[36] What emerged was a way of looking at the quantum leap from mercantile to industrial capitalism from the point of view of vested interest: a celebration of one kind of middle-class victory. Whether or not this optimistic vision convinced the entire urban middle class in Preston and elsewhere, is another issue.[37] Indeed, the degree to which these commercial ideas can be isolated to the middle class is a moot point.

Peter Clark suggests a wide audience for such histories, among 'small manufacturers, shopkeepers, master craftsmen and lesser professional men'.[38] Town histories were a staple of modest family libraries, being a popular, everyday literary form.[39] Given that there was an obvious market for such publications, it might be fair to argue the histories fed, or at least assumed, a wider urban or perhaps even Victorian way of seeing. The interest and value of the source in the examination of urban mentalities and class language should not therefore be overlooked. The rude health of the business voice in nineteenth-century Preston is obvious. The histories read like bibles of an enterprise culture and contest recent arguments about a crisis of middle-class confidence in Victorian England.[40] This source reveals no hint of the argued polite recoil from industrial values in favour of sympathies inimical to commercial success: belief in the superiority of the pre-industrial world and the authenticity of nature.

However, these local histories could be seen as a response to this voguish, rural romanticism, in unacknowledged debate with literary and philosophical critiques of industrial capitalism. They doubtless would have applauded Walter Bagehot's attack on Dickens's sentimental radicalism in 1858:

> Nothing can be easier than to make a case against any particular system by pointing out with emphatic caricature its inevitable miscarriages and pointing out nothing else. Those who so address us may assume a tone of philanthropy and forever exult that they are not so unfeeling as other men are: but the real tendency of their exhortations is to make men dissatisfied with their inevitable condition and what is worse, to make them fancy that its irremediable evils can be remedied.[41]

Speaking with the pitiless voice of commercial justification, Bagehot might have become mayor of Coketown himself.

**A. J. Vickery**
Royal Holloway and Bedford New College, University of London

## Notes

This paper is drawn from work in progress for a London Ph.D. thesis and was given as a paper to the History Workshop Conference 'Literature and History, II' at Lancashire Polytechnic, Preston, in October 1986. I am grateful for comments and advice from the workshop participants and in particular from Michael Collinge and my thesis supervisor P. J. Corfield.
1 C. Dickens, *Hard Times* (1854; reprint, 1969), 65.
2 C. Hardwick, *History of the Borough of Preston* (1857), 426–7.
3 P. Clark, 'Visions of the urban community: antiquarians and the English city before 1800', in D. Fraser and A. Sutcliffe (eds), *The Pursuit of Urban History* (1983), 105–24.
4 It would have been useful to compare eighteenth- and nineteenth-century interpretations of local history. It is hard to disentangle the urban and commercial ethos, and a dearth of surviving records might lead one to suppose that the two are interchangeable. Certainly, these histories were written long after Preston's heyday as a gentry resort. The authors were printers, journalists, booksellers, and self-styled literary figures: P. Whittle, *A Topographical, Statistical and Historical Account of the Borough of Preston* (1821); E. Jefferey, *The History of Preston in Lancashire* (1822); P. Whittle, *History of the Borough of Preston in the County Palatinate of Lancaster* (1837); W. Dobson, *Preston in the Olden Time; Or, Illustrations of the Manners and Customs in Preston in the Seventeenth and Eighteenth Century* (1857); A. Hewitson, *History of Preston* (1883).
5 H. N. B. Morgan in his unpublished thesis, 'Social and political leadership in Preston 1820–1860' (M. Litt. University of Lancaster, 1980) stresses the extent to which the town's prominent businessmen were active in local government.
6 P. Clark, in Fraser and Sutcliffe, *Pursuit of Urban History*, 117.
7 There are no reliable data between 1760 and 1801. Nineteenth-century population figures can be found in the records of the Local Board of Health Office, Lancashire Record Office,

Preston. There is no major, modern history of Preston. For an economic survey, see Morgan, 'Social and political leadership', and for the context of national, industrial development, see M. M. Edwards, *The Growth of the British Cotton Trade, 1780–1815* (1967).

8 Anon., *Handbook and Guide* (1840), Lancashire Record Office.

9 This is not to argue that the middle classes themselves were monolithic, though this evidence in interesting in the light of recent discussion of the ideological, social and political cohesiveness of the Victorian middle class. For an introduction to the fast-developing debate, see R. Trainor, 'Urban elites in Victorian Britain', *Urban History Yearbook* (1985), 1–18.

10 Jeffrey, *History of Preston*, 11.

11 W. Dobson and J. Harland, *A History of the Preston Guild* (1862), 67.

12 *Ibid.*, 68.

13 E. Baines, *History of Lancashire* (1870), II, 472.

14 R. Edgecombe (ed.), *The Diary of Frances, Lady Shelley 1787–1817* (1912), 3. I am grateful to Michael Collinge for this reference.

15 Notably the Derby family withdrew their patronage.

16 Anon., *Handbook and Guide*.

17 Dobson, *Preston in Olden Time*, 4.

18 *Ibid.*, 4.

19 Baines, *History of Lancashire*, 472.

20 Dobson, *Preston in Olden Time*, 31.

21 Hardwick, *Borough of Preston*, 377.

22 Dobson, *Preston in Olden Time*, 31.

23 For this and the next quotation, see respectively Whittle, *Topographical ... Account*, 38; and *History of Preston*, iv.

24 *Preston Chronicle*, 28 February 1824 (British Library Colindale). From the letters to the editors of Preston's newspapers something of a local debate can be reconstructed, expressing the dichotomy between humane ethics and commercial rationalism.

25 Whittle, *History of Preston*, Frontispiece and Address, iv, v.

26 Hewitson, *History of Preston*, 167.

27 The body of their interpretation bears out Harold Perkin's assertions on the nature of the 'entrepreneurial ideal' in H. Perkin, *The Origins of Modern English Society, 1780–1880* (1969). In particular, his sketch of the active owner-manager of the industrial revolution as popular hero in *ibid.*, 222: 'The entrepreneur was the impresario, the creative force, the initiator of the economic cycle. He it was who conceived the end, found the means and bore the burden of the risk and paid out the other factors of production.'

28 S. Smiles, *Self Help*, (1859), as cited in Perkin, *ibid.*, 225.

29 G. M. Young, *Victorian England: Portrait of an Age* (1935), 5.

30 Hardwick, *Borough of Preston*, 377.

31 Lancashire Record Office, Cavendish of Holker Letters.

32 Commercial rationalism and utilitarianism were often linked in Victorian rhetoric. For example, J. Wade, *History of the Middle and Working Classes* (1833), 183: 'The utility of a class of capitalists has been demonstrated by showing the advantages derived in society from the avocations of the middle ranks, consisting of bankers, merchants, importers, wholesale dealers and retailers.' However, at the heart of this combination lay the tension between *laissez-faire* capitalism and Benthamite intervention.

33 Young, *Victorian England*, 5.

34 Hardwick, *Borough of Preston*, 378–81.

35 *Ibid.*, 380.

36 For example, *Fortunes Made in Business; A Series of Original Sketches ... by Various Writers* (1884), 10: 'As to the place the conditions ... might be regarded as the very reverse of favourable, for Preston had borne through many centuries the reputation of being proud; and pride and trade were in those days somewhat conflicting terms.' Also *ibid.*, 20: 'The various works planned and carried on by the energy of John Horrocks gave an immense impulse to the trade of the town. Shops, houses and places of business were erected on all sides and other mills rose in different quarters and the population which had stood so long at 6,000 increased with startling rapidity and the aristocratic, historical, borough cast off its old-time aspect and awoke in full activity.'

37 Discussion of this theme forms part of my research in progress, examining the ideas and inter-relationships of commercial, professional and landed elites in Lancashire society 1760–1820.

38 P. Clark in Fraser and Sutcliffe, *Pursuit of Urban History*, 123.

39 It is probably impossible to know how cynically this historical hyperbole was devised and read, whether for instance it enjoyed the status of modern advertising.

40 As argued by M. J. Wiener in *English Culture and the Decline of the Industrial Spirit, 1850–1950* (1981).

41 Cited in C. Harvie, G. Martin, and A. Scharf, *Industrialization and Culture, 1830–1914* (1970), 52.

# Nordic urban history and urban historians in the last decade[1]

## Nordic urban history – differences and similarities

To people from the Continent, like the German essayist Hans Magnus Enzensberger, Norwegians seem to be something of an urban puzzle. While crowding in towns and cities – about three-quarters of the population now live in urban settlements – the minds and lifestyles of Norwegians, their concept of the good life, are stubbornly rural.[2] More or less the same applies to the Finns. The Danes, on the other hand, are conceived as quite the opposite, a fundamentally urban nation. The Swedes fall somewhere in between.

Differences in urban attitudes, as well as other diversities between the Nordic countries, are cherished among the inhabitants themselves, although most people are well aware that the culturally unifying elements are strong, too. The variations are real, however, and different urban experiences may partly account for them. Take the case of nineteenth-century urbanization, with examples extracted from the 1977 Trondheim Nordic history conference report on urbanization.[3]

Denmark was at the beginning of the nineteenth century one of the most urbanized countries in Europe, falling behind only Great Britain and the Netherlands. Nearly one-quarter of its population was living in towns. Copenhagen was one of the few cities in Europe with a population surpassing 100,000. Denmark's urban pattern was already established to a degree that in the period 1818–99 no new incorporations were added to the existing 68 towns. However, the urban population increased four times during the century, while the level of urbanization doubled.

At the other end of the scale, Iceland's only incorporated town, Reykjavik, had a population of about 300 in 1800. As late as 1890, there were only three towns in Iceland, in addition to eight unincorporated urban places, altogether housing 12 per cent of the country's population. In 1860, Finland's official towns contained a mere 6 per cent of the total population. The figure had risen to 12.5 per cent by 1900. Between the extremes we find Norway and Sweden increasing their urban population during the nineteenth century from c.10 to 35 and 30 per cent of the total, respectively. Norway's urban pattern certainly needed filling in. From 1816 to 1866 the number of incorporated towns almost doubled, from 23 to 40.

To these different historical urban experiences, an important disparity in Nordic settlement history must be added. Norden (the Nordic term encompassing Sweden, Norway, Finland, Iceland, Denmark, Greenland and the Faeroe Islands) is divided into two parts. While in Denmark the agrarian population traditionally has clustered in villages, like the rest of Europe, in the northern part of Norden rural settlement has consisted mainly of separate farms and seldom exhibited more than a few farms grouped together. Most of Norden therefore lacked both the collective experience of village life and the numerous population nucleii from which towns could emerge. The Danish villages were rather small, compared to most of their European counterparts. Consequently in large parts of Norden, historically, most agglomerations of people, in some places even down to a few dozen people, were (and are) truly *urban* phenomena (fishing hamlets, iron works or the like being exceptions or borderline cases).[4] In contemporary public statistics, urban settlements have a lower limit of only 200 (Norway and Sweden) or 250 (Denmark) inhabitants. Accordingly, settlement history and urban history tend to mingle.[5]

The typical piece of urban history, however, is not a problem-orientated study of settlement patterns or the like, but the biography of a city or a town. Traditionally, urban history in the Nordic countries was synonymous with learned amateurs writing the chronicle of their home town. This kind of local history had its strongest base in Norway and Finland. Town and parish histories expressed – on a local level – the strong nationalism that owed its existence to centuries of national dependence. Even today several volumes of town biographies are produced every year in each of the Nordic countries. The initiatives are often local in origin, planned as prestigious projects to match or overshadow other towns. More often than not, however, these volumes are nowadays written by professionnal historians. Following in the same vein as history in general, urban biographies have n the past decade laid an emphasis on demography, social structure and economic history, paying less attention than before to urban institutions and politics.[6] Typically, town biographers have not written comparative history: their scholarly products are mainly idiographic, concerned with establishing unique urban phenomena and leaving detailed comparisons to others. One of the few exceptions to this is the three-volume history of the Swedish town of Kalmar, which emanated from a research project called The Comparative Urban History Project (PJÄS), led by Ingrid Hammarström of Stockholm.[7] Only very recently has there been a tendency for urban biographies to be written in a comparative vein.

The socio-economic bent of contemporary Nordic urban history is also evident on the nomothetic side, that is among scholars working in a comparative perspective and concerned to establish general principles of urban development. An example of this is a project carried out at the Department of Economic History, University of Stockholm: 'Stagnating metropolis: growth problems and social inequality in Stockholm, 1760–1850.'[8] Historians asking questions about urban processes in a comparative and systematic manner are still relatively few in the Nordic countries. The Swedes and the Danes seem to be the leaders in this field, while the Norwegians and the Finns are the most experienced writers of urban biographies.

Compared to countries like Great Britain, Germany and the USA, large-scale urban historical studies in Norden – omitting the biography tradition – are relatively few in number. The main reason for this is probably the comparatively small community of historians. There is simply no room for too many historical specialties; very few scholars can call themselves urban historians and organized urban studies are pursued only at the University of Stockholm. Therefore economic, political and social historians, for example, temporarily combine with historical demographers to initiate urban history projects, organized on a city, national or Nordic level. Some individual projects even stretch beyond that, as two recent books on European planning and the diffusion of service innovations illustrate.[9]

In their theoretical outlook most projects are not limited to Norden. The above-mentioned Stockholm project illustrates this point; most West European countries are represented in Søderberg's footnotes. Historians of the nineteenth and twentieth centuries seem to have received much inspiration from Anglo-Saxon sources, and, in the 1970s, from *New Urban History* in the USA.[10] The reports from the Leicester conference in 1966 and the Dyos memorial conference in 1980 are well known. The Abrams and Wrigley volume from 1978, *Towns in Societies*, seems to be gaining in influence. At the bottom of much urban history Werner Sombart is lurking with his distinction between *Städtebildern* and *Städtefüllern* (town founders and town fillers). The Kalmar historians explicitly study town growth in the perspective of Kalmar's outward economic function, its 'basic' economic activities. In the ongoing history of Oslo project, the analytical distinction between the city's external functions and its internal structure is an important one.

**Organization**

The pursuit of urban history in the Nordic countries is organized, roughly speaking, in three ways. Firstly, there are the 'scientific' projects aimed at analyzing one or more aspects of the urbanization process. Such undertakings are

usually university-based; the 'PJÄS' and 'Stagnating metropolis' projects mentioned above are examples. Four Nordic research projects are presented in a special
issue in English of the newsletter *Industrialismens bygninger og boliger*, published
by the Danish project of the same name.[11] The two Swedish projects are explicitly
urbanistic, while the Danish and the Norwegian undertakings also focus on
industrialism and social change. The principal aim of the 'Christiania project' was
to study changes in social structure during the nineteenth century in an urban
setting. However, the setting itself played a minor role in many of the dissertations
written.

Secondly there are conferences which regularly produce reports of ongoing
research, often at the Nordic level. Every three years a major conference of Nordic
historians is held. The principal topic of the 1977 Trondheim conference was the
urbanization of Norden until the First World War. The chronology was completed
in Jyväskylä in 1981, with reports on urbanization since about 1915 in four of the
Nordic countries.[12] Local historians in these countries are well organized, both
nationally and within Norden, and regularly arrange seminars in which urban
history is receiving increasing attention, as well as in local history in general. [13]
Interestingly, these seminars usually take up general and comparative problems of
urbanization. The idiographic and the nomothetic traditions are merging.
Denmark and Norway have national Committees on Urban History, acting as co-
ordinators of the isolated research efforts. The committees are also responsible for
developing national bibliographies of urban history, which are submitted to the
International Committee of Urban History.[14] The Danish Committee of Urban
History took the initiative of producing a number of historical atlases of Nordic
towns, six volumes of which were published between 1977 and 1987, and another
half-a-dozen are in the making.[15]

Thirdly, urban history is produced through city biography projects. This is by far
the bulkiest category. Two trends have been evident in the last decade: professional
historians are now almost alone in the field, and the projects are increasingly
organized with a university as their base. The two are not quite the same thing, as
local municipal committees in the past often hired professional historians to do the
job. The grants, however, are still mainly of local origin. Local histories, whether
urban or rural, are prestigious affairs, particularly in Norway and Finland, and
therefore relatively easy to finance. Of major importance here, however, is that
town histories among historians are considered scientific ventures of full value,
with ensuing professional ambitions put into them.[16] The recent or ongoing
projects involving Odense, Kalmar, Malmø, Oslo, Bergen, Trondheim, Turku (Åbo),
and Tampere (Tammerfors) are examples of such ambitious projects (see below).

### The concept of 'urban'

Nordic urban historians, like their colleagues in other countries, frequently return
to the problem of defining the term 'urban',[17] a definitional and conceptual
difficulty since medieval times in Norden.[18] The problem has two sides, which we
may label the functional and the structural aspects. The first concerns the function
in society of the (potential) town in question. Even very small clusters of people, in
early-modern as well as twentieth-century Norden, usually involve typical central
functions associated with urban phenomena, such as public administration, nodes
of communication, specialized production and retail services. The 17 towns in
Norway which were given legal status as towns between 1814 and 1900 had an
average population of 1,000 at the time of incorporation. The 17 other small urban
places which were given limited privileges as towns during the same period
averaged 780 inhabitants.[19] In early-modern Norway (1500–1800), urban settlements seem to have established stable central functions at a population of about
400. With around 40 small houses, Vadsø, a town in north-eastern Norway, was
considered a 'late medieval town' in the sixteenth century by its biographer. Vadsø
had 230 inhabitants by the time it received town status in 1833.[20] The towns of

course tended to grow beyond their formal limits, a characteristic familiar to all urban historians. Suburban growth, particularly prior to 1900, has nevertheless received scanty treatment by both town biographers and other urban historians.[21] The main reason for this is probably that the sources are meagre for the suburbs compared to the town proper, though this applies less to the twentieth century, where a few studies of suburban communities do exist.[22] In recent years, urban historians have taken an increasingly regional view of urban development, irrespective of whether their concern was with the present or earlier centuries.[23] Authors embraced Leslie Page Moth's dictum: 'The cities belong to their regions',[24] though this regional definition of 'urban' has become so problematical in the twentieth century with long-distance commuting and a blurred distinction between city and countryside[25] that Sweden dropped the legal distinction between urban and rural townships altogether in 1970.

The second aspect of the urban definition pertains to its internal structure, i.e. the patterns of urban life. Agglomerations of a few hundred people may be urban phenomena in the sense that they serve the surrounding countryside with important central functions. But do they produce lifestyles that may be labelled 'urban'? Do they possess the social differentiation characteristic of urban environments? There are indications that 'the urban threshold', to use Stuart Blumin's expression, is quite low in the Nordic countries. Due to the interest that Nordic professional historians have shown in writing town biographies, we have quite a few analyses of very small urban communities. Many deal with the periods when sources permit a close scrutiny of urban life; particularly the nineteenth century, but also the eighteenth and seventeenth centuries.[26]

The intimate relationship between town and hinterland, and the increasing difficulty in the late twentieth century of delimiting urban areas, raises problems as to the unit of study for the urban historian.[27] The history of Bergen in the period 1945–72 employs a practical solution: topography and sociological aspects are dealt with inside the narrow city limits only, while Bergen's economic development and its population growth are studied within the whole city region.[28]

## Urban typology and periodization

The question of chronological phases is also very much one of urban types and classes. The Trondheim conference in 1977 chose to highlight three periods in Nordic urban development. The first two periods at least correspond to distinct urban categories: medieval towns and the founded towns of the seventeenth and eighteenth centuries.[29] The two types show quite a few variations, however, both between the states and countries, and within them. Not all new towns in early-modern Norden were literally founded, to mention just one aspect. But the towns resembled each other in that they were part of a system of trade privileges, formally granted by the (absolutist) states.[30]

The third period scrutinized at the conference was the first phase of industrialization, defined as the period from c.1850 to around the First World War. Industrialization followed a strikingly similar course in the four biggest Nordic countries, with a breakthrough phase in the 1870s. Metal and textile industries were important in all countries and while Denmark developed agriculture-based industry, the other three were great producers of forest products. All Nordic towns felt the impact of industrialization, but quite a few of them never had any factories of their own worth mentioning, or were 'late industrializers' in the sense of that term. Industrialization thus seems to have standardized the direction of urbanization between the various countries, while it may have diversified it within each country. The first of these statements remains so far a hypothesis, as no comparative research has been carried out. However, through a number of investigations about national urban systems considerable light has been shed on the second statement.[31] A theory of uneven urban development has been launched for the Swedish case, to be explained by the economic structures and mechanisms of industrial capitalism. [32] In Finland and Norway, one important outcome of the industrial age was to spread urbanization to the interior. In 1800, 9 out of 29 Finnish towns (31 per cent) were not situated on the coast; in 1980, 58 out of 84 (69 per cent) were.[33] Norway had no incorporated inland towns in 1800, 7 by the end of the century.

Around the First World War, one urban phase ended and another started. The urbanization process slowed down and modern urban planning commenced its strikingly parallel process in the Nordic countries. But differences were also visible. The inter-war economic crisis halted Norwegian urbanization more than it did Danish or Swedish urban growth.[34] The so-called turnaround trend c.1970, a slowing down of the urbanization process, was also an inter-Nordic phenomenon, together with an increasing urban crisis, particularly in the largest cities. Urban history dealing with the last generation is far from voluminous, but growing in the 1980s.[35]

There are, however, other bases for urban categorization and periodization. The concept of the 'agrarian town' denotes an early-nineteenth century Swedish town, trying to get as much as possible out of the town common in a society where much of the peasantry was subsistence-oriented. The concept 'the town of merchant capitalism' is coined to explain the fast urban growth from the 1830s on, more than a generation before the breakthrough of industrialization.[36] The reformation in Denmark and Norway in 1536 was important because it practically ended the role of the church as a maintainer of towns. The period of absolutism constitutes separate periods in the history of Stockholm and Copenhagen. The role of the nobility in some Danish and Swedish cities in the seventeenth and eighteenth centuries separates their history from that of the towns of Norway, a country with practically no nobility at all.

The population of the Danish town of Odense in the eighteenth century stayed fairly constant at 5,000. The inhabitants nevertheless had the feeling of living in a big city.[37] This is not so surprising considering that Odense was the second biggest of Denmark's 60 or so towns, with only Copenhagen superseding it. Norden's third biggest town in 1700, Bergen counted only 10,000 people in 1700, 13,000 in 1750.[38] Nordic urban history is in many respects characterized by the many small urban places. Pre-industrial Norden boasted of only two big towns. Copenhagen and Stockholm were in fact large European cities in 1800, with populations of 101,000 and 75,000 respectively. Norden's third town, Bergen, had only 17,000 inhabitants. [39] This gives an impression of the urban dominance of these two cities. Copenhagen had in fact more than half of the urban population of Denmark (present day borders). One must remember that in 1800 Norway and Iceland belonged to Denmark, and Finland to Sweden. When the three countries achieved independence (wholly or partially), their capitals, Christiania (Oslo), Helsinki, and Reykjavik, soon reached a status akin to that enjoyed by Copenhagen and Stockholm. Oslo was one of the fastest growing cities in Europe between 1850 and 1880. Its 250,000 inhabitants in 1900 equalled the combined population of Norway's next 8 towns. Thus Nordic urban history is also the history of the supremacy of the capitals, of its 'primate cities', and accordingly, these capitals have received much attention from urban historians. For example, the city of Stockholm has, since 1941, published a series of monographs on the city's history – about 70 altogether, 23 of them published between 1978 and 1984. Interestingly, this 'primate city' approach relates less to biographies[40] and more to research projects involving monographs and articles about specific urban problems.[41]

The industrial age has given rise to some characteristic types of urban settlements, such as railway towns and small factory towns (Nordic towns based one-sidedly on manufacturing are always fairly small in size). The small factory town was very typical of Norway in the early twentieth century because of its water-power location.[42] Relatively few urban studies of the phenomenon exist, however, mainly because few of these towns were given formal town status.

*Stasjonsbyen* (the railway town) is a stock expression in Scandinavian languages. In Denmark a research project on the history of railway towns 1840–1940 was begun in 1980.[43]

## Urban growth

Nordic demographic sources are renowned for their high quality. In spite of that, urban historical demography in the Nordic countries has relatively modest dimensions. However, with an increasing number of urban databases, and the wave of social history from around 1970 onwards, progress has been made in the past decade.[44] Migration, especially in the nineteenth century, has been a central concern for urban historians, and most findings support the research evidence from outside Norden: urban migration was not a one-way movement, and the flow of migrants went in and out of both small and large towns, as well as rural parishes.[45] Another concern has been the impact of migration on natural growth, or put another way, how much of the population growth can be attributed to migration and how much to natural growth? This is a tricky question where several approaches have been attempted.[46]

The city of Stockholm is particularly interesting in two respects. Firstly, there is the so-called 'Stockholm marriage', co-habitation without wedding in the working class during the nineteenth century – in some periods, nearly half of Stockholm's births were outside marriage.[47] Secondly, Stockholm's mortality was extremely high during most of the 1800s. An investigation of the problem, comparing Stockholm to other European cities, concludes that the mortality was a phenomenon among adult males, probably caused by a rough and unhealthy labour market and alcohol consumption.[48]

Investigations of the main forces behind urban growth are often carried out in the shape of city-hinterland studies.[49] It is a well-established fact that the take-off of modern urban growth, around 1850 in Norway, Sweden, and Denmark, was *not* triggered by industrialization in the narrow sense of the word (the rise of factories).[50] In the past decade, studies of urban growth in the Nordic countries have concentrated on the building process. (Both the Danes and the Swedes have journals of building history.[51]) There are several building studies on individual towns, besides chapters in town biographies. The conclusions are similar for the Nordic capitals in their periods of rapid growth in the second half of the nineteenth century: the building industry did not follow the general business fluctuations. In the competition for scarce capital, the potential builders were the losers, partly because they were small and amateurish speculators. The hour of the builders came when the rest of the economy had passed its boom, leaving behind it a great demand for housing the increased population which was created by the boom.[52]

## Urban structure

All city and town biographies deal extensively with administration and politics. Comparative literature on the subject, however, comprises relatively few volumes. There is a Danish contribution from the Trondheim conference on urbanization and political behaviour, and a Finnish volume on services and urbanization at the turn of the century.[53] The main national effort is Finland's three-volume history of its civic administration.[54] Local political self-determination was achieved in the Nordic countries around the middle of the nineteenth century. This was less a watershed to urban municipalities than to rural ones, however, since the towns had a long tradition of self-government.[55] The history of administration and urban services probably differs less between the Nordic countries than does the history of the struggle for political power. While technological solutions and administrative practices easily diffused between the countries, the social structure and economic base varied a great deal between them.[56]

The technological side of urban administration, the construction of roads, tramways, subways, sewage and water pipes, and the supply of streetlights, gas and electricity, is a rather neglected field in Nordic urban history.[57] However, the historical study of urban planning in general is not, perhaps because this area of study has attracted researchers from disciplines other than history, such as art historians and architects. The main problems of urban planning history include the question of the role of the founded towns in early modern Norden, the origins of modern urban planning in the second half of the nineteenth century, and the challenges of post-Second World War planning. Satellite towns, dormitory suburbs, urban renewal, and the reshaping of the downtowns rank among the most important topics of the contemporary age.[58]

## Urban societies?

The urbanization process has had a certain unifying effect on the Nordic settlement pattern, and probably on Nordic attitudes as well, though there is little completed research to substantiate this latter, speculative, conclusion. Nevertheless, the national stereotypes do have historical bases. Norway, Sweden, and Finland each have an anti-urban tradition.[59] In the western world, the process of urbanization is often interpreted as urban society conquering rural society. Though valid enough for aspects of Nordic history, one may also turn this interpretation on its head: urban society, particularly in Norway and Finland, has at times been strongly influenced by rural habits and values. In a sense, in Finland and Norway the periphery (= national culture) fought the centre (= alien culture).

The history of urban mentalities and attitudes towards urban phenomena in Norden has yet to be written. The elements of such a work lie dispersed in the urban historical literature or hidden in the sources. An exciting task is awaiting the historian who wants to explore – and compare – the sources of Danish urban customs and Norwegian rural orientations; or – who knows? – reveal as false these old notions.

**Jan Eivind Myhre**
University of Oslo

## Notes

1 This article commences approximately where Ingrid Hammarström stopped, at the XVII Nordic History Conference in Trondheim 1977, whose principal topic was the urbanization process: Ingrid Hammarström, 'Urban history in Scandinavia', *Urban History Yearbook (1978)*.
    The presentation is regrettably but necessarily biased. Being written by a Norwegian specializing in nineteenth- and twentieth-century history, it will do less than justice to pre-1800 urban history, and Finnish and Icelandic urban history will suffer due to language barriers. However, the titles tell a (hi)story, too! Although they bear no responsibility for the product, I have received valuable information from Lars Nilsson, Per Boje, Marjatta Hietala, and Helgi Skúli Kjartanson.
2 Hans Magnus Enzensberger, *Norsk utakt* (Norwegian anachronisms) (Oslo, 1984).
3 G. A. Blom (ed.), *Urbaniseringsprosessen i Norden, Del 3. Industrialiseringens første fase* (The process of urbanization in Norden, vol 3. The first phase of industrialization) (Oslo, 1977). The contributors are Jan Eivind Myhre (Norway), Eino Jutikkala and Päiviö Tommila (Finland), Niels Thomsen, Per Boje, and Ole Hyldtoft (Denmark), Helgi Skúli Kjartanson (Iceland), and Bo Öhngren (Sweden).
4 Adna Ferrin Weber misunderstood the nature of Nordic urbanization when he wrote that the small 'cities' of Sweden and Norway, some of which had fewer than 500 inhabitants, were remnants of a medieval separation of town and country. A. F. Weber, *The Growth of Cities in the Nineteenth Century* (New York, 1899), 7.
5 Henrik B. Andersson, *Tätorternas bebyggelsesstruktur och förändring. En översikt över Sverige och övriga Norden* (Settlement structure and change in built-up areas. A survey of the Nordic countries) (Lund, 1977); Hallstein Myklebost, *Bosetningsutviklingen i Norge 1950–1975* (Norway's settlement structure 1950–1975) (Oslo, 1978), Summary in English; Jouko Alestalo, 'The concenration of population in Finland between 1880 and 1980', in *Fennia, 161,2* (Helsinki, 1983); Knud Prange (ed.), *Lokalsamfundene i de seneste 100 år* (Local communities in the last 100 years) (Copenhagen, 1979). This book has a

section called 'Samfundsudvikling og bosætningsstruktur' (Societal development and settlement structure) with contributions from Viggo Hansen (Denmark), Marie Nisser (Sweden), Peter Sjøholt (Norway), and Veijo Saloheimo (Finland).

6 A recent urban biography, detailed and thorough, but rather old-fashioned, is Oscar Bjurling (ed.), *Malmö stads historia*, del 2–4 (The history of M., vols 2–4, 1500–1914) (Malmö, 1977–85). Representative of the newer brand, with an emphasis on demography and social structure, is Sven A. Nilsson (ed.), *Halmstad stads historia* (The history of H.) (Halmstad, 1987). The history of Odense has elements of both 'traditional' and 'modern' approaches: H. Thrane *et al.*, *Fra boplads til bispeby. Odense til 1539* (From settlement to episcopal centre. O. up to 1539) (Odense, 1983); Erling Ladewig Pedersen *et al.*, *De fede år. Odense 1539–1660* (The fertile years. O. 1539–1660) (Odense, 1984); Aa. F. Blomberg, *De magre år. Odense 1660–1700* (The lean years. O. 1660–1700) (Odense, 1981); Anne Riising, *Gudsfrykt og oplysning. Odense 1700–1789* (Piety and enlightenment. O. 1700–1789) (Odense, 1981); Hans Chr. Johansen, *Næring og bystyre. Odense 1700–1789* (Trade and town government. O. 1700–1789) (Odense, 1983); Poul Thestrup *et al.*, *Mod bedre tider. Odense 1789–1868* (Toward better times. O. 1789–1868) (Odense, 1986); Per Boje and Henning Nielsen, *Moderne Tider. Odense 1868–1914* (Modern times. O. 1868–1914) (Odense, 1985); J. Hæstrup, *Krig og besættelse. Odense 1940–1945* (War and occupation. O. 1940–1945) (Odense, 1979).

7 Ingrid Hammarström (ed.), *Kalmar stads historia* I–III (History of the town of K., vols I–III) (Kalmar, 1979–84); Ingrid Hammarström, Rolf Hagstedt and Lars Nilsson, 'Prosjektet jämförande stadshistoria' (PJÄS), in *Historisk Tidsskrift* (Sweden, 1975). The five-volume *History of Oslo*, now in preparation, also takes a comparative approach.

8 Johan Söderberg, 'Den stagnerande staden. Stockholms tillväxtproblem 1760–1850 i ett jämförande europeisk perspektiv' (The stagnating town; Stockholm's growth problems 1760–1850 in a comparative European perspective), in *Historisk Tidsskrift* (Sweden) 2 (1985). Summary in English.

9 Thomas Hall, *Planung europäischer Hauptstädte. Zur Entwicklung des Städtebaues im 19. Jahrhundert* (The planning of European capitals in the 19th century) (Stockholm, 1986); Marjatta Hietala, *Services and Urbanization at the Turn of the Century. The Diffusion of Innovations* (Helsinki, 1987).

10 Jan Eivind Myhre, 'Tilnærminger til byhistorien. På leting etter de urbane variabler' (Approaches to urban history. In search of the urban variables), in *Historisk Tidsskrift* (Norwegian) 2(1987), summary in English; Ole Degn, *Urbanisering og industrialisering. En forskningsoversikt* (Urbanization and industrialization. A research overview) (København, 1978). Several valuable articles are printed in Thomas Hall (ed.), *Städer i utveckling. Tolv studier kring stadsförändringar tillägnade Ingrid Hammarström* (Evolving cities. Twelve studies about urban change in honour of I. H.) (Stockholm, 1984); David R. Goldfield, 'The study of cities. On urban history research in the United States and Sweden'; Bo Öhngren, 'Urbaniseringen som forskningsobjekt. Trender och problem' (Urbanization as an object of research. Trends and problems).

11 *Industrial Buildings and Dwellings. The Industrial Environment 1840–1940*, 2 (1978) (Copenhagen). Thomas Hall, 'Swedish urban enviroment. A presentation' (Svensk stadsmiljø); Bo Öhngren, 'The city and environs. Voluntary associations and urbanization in a comparative perspective 1890–1975 (Stad och omland); Ole Hyldtoft, 'Industrial buildings and dwellings – the industrial environment in Denmark 1840–1940' (Industrialismens bygninger of boliger. Det industrielle miljø i Danmark 1840–1940); Jan Eivind Myhre, 'The Christiania Study' (Christianiaprosjektet). See also Sivert Langholm, 'The Christiania Project: historians investigate the making of urban society', in *Research in Norway 1976*; Jan Eivind Myhre and Jan Sigurd Østberg (eds), *Mennesker i Kristiania. Sosialhistorisk søkelys på 1800–tallet* (People of Kristiania. Social-historical searchlight on the 19th century) (Oslo, 1979); Ole Hyldtoft, 'From fortified town to modern metropolis', in Ingrid Hammarström and Thomas Hall (eds), *Growth and Transformation of the Modern City* (Stockholm, 1979).

12 *Historica IV. Föredrag vid det XVIII Nordiska historikermötet Jyväskylä 1981. Studia Historica Jyyväskylänsia 27* (Proceedings at the XVIII Nordic Conference of Historians at J. 1981) (Jyväskyla, 1983). The contributors on urbanization were: Jan Eivind Myhre (Norway), Eino Jutikkala (Finland), Ole Hyldtoft (Denmark), and Lars Nilsson (Sweden).

13 An important report stems from the Gausdal (Skeikampen) conference in 1979: Rolf Fladby and Harald Winge (eds), *By og bygd. Stad og omland* (City and country. Town and hinterland) (Oslo, 1981). The book contains 21 articles from Denmark, Finland, Norway, and Sweden, dealing with town-hinterland relations in the demographic, economic, social, and cultural spheres. See also the Knud Prange collection mentioned in note 5 above. A Norwegian anthology, with articles from a local history conference, is Liv Martinsen (ed.), *Om byhistorie. Problemstillinger og metode* (On urban history. Problems and methods) (Oslo, 1986). It includes contributions from Rolf Fladby on modern Norwegian urban history, from Peter Sjøholt on geographical methods, from Jan Eivind Myhre on suburban history, and from Kjell-Olav Masdalen on eighteenth- and nineteenth-century sources of urban history. A report from the Nesbyen conference 1985 on the History of Oslo project is printed in *Urban History Yearbook* (1986). See also *Historisk Tidsskrift för Finland* (1981): 'Synpunkter på lokalhistoria' (Viewpoints on local history).

14 An international bibliography of modern urban history, with Nordic contributions, is in preparation at the 'Deutches Institut für Urbanistik' in Berlin. General editor is Dr Christian Engeli.

15 Scandinavian atlases of historic towns: Eino Jutikkala, *Turku* (Åbo) (Odense, 1977); Eino Jutikkala, *Porvoo* (Borgå) (Odense, 1977); Ole Degn, *Ribe*, (Odense, 1983); Niels Ahlberg og Thomas Hall, *Uppsala* (Odense, 1983); Poul Tuxen, *Stege* (Odense, 1987). The Finnish atlases are rather small, while the other three contain a large number of maps with full-bodied commentaries in two languages, of which English is one.

16 In Norway and Finland it has been commonplace for a long time for distinguished historians to write local history besides their other work. In Sweden and Denmark, however, local history has up to recently been less tempting to professional historians. Jan Eivind Myhre, 'Historien om oslohistoriene' (The History of the Histories of Oslo), in *Byminner, 3* (1986).

17 Nils Blomkvist, 'Av makt och marknadskrafter? Reflexioner kring the svårfangade stadsbegreppet' (From power and market forces? Reflections on the evasive concept of 'urban'), in Hall (ed.), *Städer i utveckling*; Jan Eivind Myhre, '"By", "tettsted", "urbanisering" – En innledning' ('Town', 'urban place', 'urbanization' – an introduction), in Blom (ed.), *Urbaniseringsprosessen i Norden 3*; Roger Andersson, *Den svenska urbaniseringen. Kontextualisering av begrepp och processer* (The Swedish urbanization. Contextualization of concepts and processes) (Uppsala, 1987), Summary in English.

18 Grethe Authén Blom (ed.), *Urbaniseringsprosessen i Norden 1, Middelaldersteder* (The process of urbanization in the Nordic countries, vol. 1, Medieval towns) (Oslo, 1977). The contributors are: Henrik M. Jansen, Tore Nyborg, and Thomas Riis (Denmark); Hans Andersson (Sweden); Erkki Kuujo (Finland); Helgi Porlákson (Iceland), and Knut Helle and Arnved Nedkvitne (Norway). See also the Swedish project 'Medeltidsstaden – den medeltida urbaniseringsprosessens konsekvenser for nutida planering. Rapport 1–' (The medieval town: implications of early urbanization for modern planning, vol. 1–). Among the important biographies are Knut Helle, *Bergen bys historie I. Kongssete og Kjøpstad. Fra opphavet til 1536* (History of B., vol. 1. From the origins to 1536. King's residence and trade centre) (Oslo/Bergen, 1982); Per Norseng and Arnved Nedkvitne. *Oslos historie I* (History of O., vol. I), forthcoming; Nils Blomkvist, *Kalmars uppkomst och äldsta utveckling. Tiden till 1300–talets mitt* (The origins and oldest history of K. until the middle of the 14th century) (Karlshamn, 1978) summary in German; Thrane *et al.*, *Fra boplads til bispeby. Odense til 1539*.

19 Jan Eivind Myhre in Blom (ed.), *Urbaniseringsprosessen i Norden 3*. In Norway, during the nineteenth century *kjøpstad* was a fully privileged town, while *ladested* had limited privileges. The corresponding Danish and Icelandic terms were *købstad* and *handelsplads*. Sweden's legal urban hierarchy consisted of *stad*, *köping*, and *municipalsamhällen*, and Finland's of *stad* and *köping*.

20 Finn-Einar Eliassen, 'Norske byer, 1500–1800: Identifikasjon, avgrensning, funksjoner' (Norwegian towns 1500–1800: Identification, delimitation, functions), in *Heimen, 3* (1987); Einar Niemi, *Vadsøs historie til 1833* (The history of V. to 1833) (Vadsø, 1983).

21 An exception is Jens Erik Frits Hansen, *Københavns forstadsbebyggelse i 1850'erne* (Copenhagen's suburbs in the 1850s) (Copenhagen, 1977). See also Thomas Lundén, 'Stockholm – a hundred years of suburban growth. Agents, flows and restrictions', in Hammarström and Hall, *Growth and Transformation of the Modern City*.

22 S. Rambusch, *Rødovre 1901–1976* (History of R. 1901–1976 [suburb of Copenhagen]) (København, 1978); Jan Eivind Myhre, *Bærum 1840–1980* (History of B. 1840–1980) (Oslo, 1982); Lars Thue, *Asker 1840–1980)* (History of A. 1840–1980) (Oslo, 1984). Bærum and Asker are two of Oslo's suburban municipalities.

23 Fladby og Winge (eds), *By og bygd.* See also the three dissertations which make up parts of the history of Kalmar: Blomkvist, *Kalmars uppkomst och äldsta utveckling*; Sven Lilja, *Kalmar under Gustav Vasa och hans söner* (K. at the time of Gustav Vasa and his sons, sixteenth and seventeenth centuries) (Karlshamn, 1983), summary in English; Lars Nilsson, *Näringsliv och befolkning i Kalmar 1910–1975* (Economy and population in K. 1910–1975) (Karlshamn, 1980), summary in English.

24 Öhngren, 'Urbaniseringen som forskningsobjekt. Trender och problem' (Urbanization as an object of research. Trends and problems), in Hall (ed.), *Städer i utveckling*.

25 Joel S. Torstenson, Michael F. Metcalf and Tor Fr. Rasmussen, *Urbanization and community building in modern Norway* (Oslo, 1985); Jan Eivind Myhre, 'Moderne byhistorie. Noen perspektiver' (Modern urban history. Some perspectives), in *Heimen, 3* (1987); Myklebost, *Bosettingsutviklingen i Norge 1950–1975*.

26 Some of these small town histories are: **Norway:** Leif T. Andressen, *Moss bys historie frem til 1700*, bind I (History of M. to 1700) (Moss, 1984); Niemi, *Vadsøs historie til 1833*; Tord Buggeland and Jacob E. Ågotnes (eds), *Lillehammer. By og bygd – gate og grend* (History of L.) (Lillehammer, 1977). **Sweden:** Stellan Dahlgren (ed.), *Enköpings historia.* Del 2 (History of E., vol. 2) (Enköping, 1979); Jörgen Björklund and Sten Rentzhog (eds), *Östersunds historia* (History of Ö.) (Östersund, 1986). **Denmark:** Peter Dragsbo, *Mennesker og huse i Aabenraa – en etnologisk studie af kvarterudvikling i en nordslesvigsk købstad 1850–1920* (People and houses in Aa. An ethnologic study of a town in northern

Slesvig 1850–1920 (1978). **Finland**: Olli Vehviläinen, *Savonlinnan kaupungin historia 3. Savonlinnan kaupunki 1876–1976* (History of Savonlinna 1876–1976), Savonlinna 1978; Viljo Rasila, *Tampereen historia 2. 1840–luvolta vuoteen 1905* (History of Tampere from the 1840s to 1905) (Tampere, 1984); E. Birck, *Nykarlebys historia II, 1810–1875* (History of Nykarleby, vol. II, 1810–1875) (Nykarleby, 1980). **Iceland**: Jon ppór, *Saga Isafjardar og Eyrarhrepps hins forna, 2 b. (The history of Isafjordur to 1920, 2 vols) (Isafjordur, 1984, 1986); Asgeir Gudmundsson, Saga Hafnarfjardar 1908–1983* 3 b. (History of Hafnarfjördur, 3 vols) (Hafnarfjördur, 1983–84).

27 Ole Hyldtoft, 'Urbaniseringen i Danmark 1914–1970', *Historica IV. Föredrag vid det XVIII Nordiska historikermötet Jyväskylä 1981*.

28 Anders Bjarne Fossen and Tore Grønlie, *Byen sprenger grensene 1920–1972. Bergen bys historie, bind IV* (The history of B., vol. IV, The city crosses its borders 1920–1972) (Oslo/Bergen, 1985).

29 Blom (ed.) *Urbaniseringsprosessen i Norden 1. Middelaldersteder*; Grethe Authén Blom (ed.),*Urbaniseringsprosessen i Norden 2, De anlagte steder på 1600–1700 tallet* (The process of urbanization in the Nordic countries, vol 2, the founded towns of the 1600s and 1700s) (Oslo, 1977). The contributors are: Ole Degn (Denmark); Bjørn Sogner (Norway); Bjørn Teitsson (Iceland); Birgitta Ericsson (Sweden); and Sven-Erik Åström (Finland).

30 See the Fladby and Winge anthology, *By og Bygd*. *Stad og omland*, where the urban economy of the mercantilist era is treated by Ilkka Mäntylä, Raimo Ranta, and Mauno Jokipii (Finland), Stein Tveite and Finn-Einar Eliassen (Norway), and Birgitta Ericsson and Anne-Marie Fällström (Sweden).

31 See the reports from the Trondheim 1977 and Jyväskylä 1981 conferences referred to above.

32 Lars Nilsson, 'Öst och väst i Sveriges urbana historia 1800–1900. Forsök till en teori om ojämn urbanutveckling' (East and West in Swedish urban history. Attempting a theory about uneven urban development), in Hall (ed.), *Städer i utveckling*; Arvo Peltonen, *Suomen kaupunkijärjestelmän kasvu 1815–1970* (Size–growth process of the Finnish town system, 1815–1970 (Helsinki, 1982).

33 Harri Andersson, 'Urban structural dynamics in the city of Turku, Finland', in *Fennia, 161*, 2 (Helsinki, 1983).

34 See the Jyväskylä reports above. Swedish urbanization took an upswing around 1930.

35 The Jyväskylä reports follow urban development up to the 1970s. The geographers, of course, are more up to date. Among the town biographies which deal with the contemporary epoch are the histories of Bergen, Kalmar, Östersund and Linköping mentioned above. There is also Veikko Laakso, *Turun kaupungin historia 1918–1970* (History of Turku 1918–1970) (Turku, 1980); Olavi Anttila, Antero Heikkinen, Erkki Pihkala and Oiva Turpeinen, *Lahden historia* (History of Lahtis since 1905) (Hämeenlinna, 1980); J. P. Clausager, *Viborg som erhvervsby* (Economic history of V.) (Viborg, 1980); Helge Paludan *et al.*, *Århus bys historie fra vikingetid til nutid* (History of Å. from the Viking age to the present) (Århus, 1984). Oslo, Trondheim, Sundsvall and Gothenburg are forthcoming. Some limited themes, like urban planning, have been brought up to the contemporary age (see below).

36 Öhngren in Blom (ed.), *Urbaniseringsprosessen i Norden, 3*. The classification stems from Gregor Paulsson's classic work *Svensk Stad* (1950).

37 Johansen, *Næring og bystyre. Odense 1700–1789*. It should be noted that the Scandinavian languages do not distinguish between 'city' and 'town'. The everyday terms are *by* in Danish and Norwegian, *stad* in Swedish.

38 Anders Bjarne Fossen, *Bergen Bys Historie, bind II. Borgerskapets By 1536–1800* (History of B., vol. II. The town of the burghers) (Bergen/Oslo, 1979).

39 Egil Ertresvaag, *Bergen bys historie, bind III. Et bysamfunn i utvikling 1800–1920* (History of B., vol. III. An evolving urban community 1800–1920) (Oslo/Bergen, 1982).

40 The new six-volume history of Copenhagen makes good popular history, but is of limited scientific value: S. Cedergren Bech (ed.), *Københavns historie*, del I–VI (History of Copenhagen) (København, 1980–3). Staffan Högberg's *Stockholms historia* I–II (History of Stockholm, vols I–II) (Stockholm, 1981), also aims at popularizing history. Its leitmotif is the role of Stockholm in the Swedish state. Oslo's latest biography of any importance dates from the 1920s, but a five-volume history is forthcoming from 1989 on. The authors are: Per Norseng and Arnved Nedkvitne (1050–1537), Knut Sprauten (1537–1814), Jan Eivind Myhre (1814–1900), Knut Kjeldstadli (1900–48), and Edgeir Benum (1948–80s). The history of Helsinki in nine volumes appeared 1950–67. Reykjavik has not had its biography written.

41 Other literature particularly dealing with the cities' function as capitals: Knut Mykland, 'Hovedstadsfunksjonen. Christiania som eksempel' (The function as capital. The Christiania example); Thomas Hall (ed.), *Städer i utveckling;* Jan Eivind Myhre, 'Fra hovedstad til hovedby. Oslo på 1800–tallet' (From capital to primate city. O. in the 19th century), *St. Hallvard 1* (1987); Knud Prange, 'Svenskekrig – stilstand – opgang' (War with the Swedes – stagnation – progress [about the towns of Zealand seventeenth to nineteenth centuries]), Thomas Hall (ed.), *Städer i utveckling;* Sven-Erik Åström, 'Town planning in imperial Helsingfors 1810–1910', Hammarström and Hall (eds.), *Growth and Transformation*.

42 Helge Dahl, *Rjukan*, 1984–5; Lasse Brunnström, *Kiruna – ett samhällsbygge i sekelskiftets Sverige, del I–II* (K. – A Swedish mining town from the turn of the century) (Umeå, 1981). A medium-sized (30,000) Norwegian town with an important industrial element is Drammen: Odd W. Thorson and Berit Nøkleby, *Drammen. En norsk østlandsbys utviklingshistorie, bd. IV* (D. – the history of a town in eastern Norway, vol. IV, 1914–45) (Drammen, 1981).

43 *Stationsbyen. Rapport fra et seminar om stationsbyens historie* (The railway town. Report from a seminar on the history of railway towns) (1980); Vigand Dann Rasmussen, *Nørrejyske jernbanebyer* (The railway towns of northern Jutland) (1981); Flemming Just (ed.), *Arbejdsrapport om Vestjyllands udviklingshistorie ca. 1750–1914* (Report on the history of western Jutland) (1984). Finnish and Norwegian examples of mixed railway and factory towns are: Jouko Hoffren, Kalevi Penttilä, *Riihimäen historia* (History of Riihimäki) (Hämeenlinna, 1979); Harald Hals, *Lillestrøms historie I–II* (History of Lillestrøm, vols I–II) (1978). The Swedish journal *Bebyggelseshistorisk tidskrift, 12* (1986) is devoted to 'Järnväg, bygd och bebyggelse' (Railways and settlements), summaries in English.

44 There are demographic databases e.g. in Stockholm, Umeå/Haparanda, Tromsø, and Oslo.

45 Kari Pitkänen, 'Stad och influensområde. Flyttningsrörelse och social förändring före industrialiseringsperioden (*c.* 1720–1850)' (Towns and spheres of influence. Migration and social change before industrialization, *c.* 1750–1820 [Finland]); Max Engman, *S:t Petersburg och Finland. Migration och influens 1703–1917* (St. P. and F. Migration and influence 1703–1917) (Helsingfors, 1983); Viljo Rasila, *Teollistumiskauden muuttliikkeet. Mikrohistoriallinen tutkimus Tampeeren seudulta* (Migration in Finland during the period of industrialization. A microhistorical study) (Tampere, 1983), summary in English; Bo Öhngren, 'Stad och omland i ett socialt-demografiskt perspektiv. Bakgrundsteckning' (Town and hinterland in a social and demographic perspective [Sweden]), both in Fladby and Winge (eds), *By og bygd. Stad og omland*; Jan Eivind Myhre, *Sagene – en arbeiderforstad befolkes 1801–1875* (S. – the peopling of a working class suburb 1801–1875) (Oslo, 1978); Jan Eivind Myhre, '"Det livligste vexel-forhold". Flyttingene til Kristiania på annen halvdel av 1800-tallet' (Migration to K. in the 19th century); Sivert Langholm, 'Frå Holmestrand til hovudstaden. Litt om røttene til handelsborgerskapet i Christiania på 1800–talet' (From the town of H. to the capital. About the roots of the Christianian bourgeoisie in the 19th century), both in Brynjulv Gjerdåker (ed.), *På flyttefot. Innanlands vandring på 1800-talet* (On the move. Domestic migration in the 19th century [Norway]) (Oslo, 1981); Sivert Langholm, '"Noget at fare med" – Angående handverksmestrene i Christiania' (Origin of the master artisans in nineteenth-century C.); Sølvi Sogner, 'Barselkvinner på flyttefot og barnefedre på flukt. En studie av flytting i forbindelse med uekte fødsel i Vår Frelsers menighet i Christiania 1731–1800' (Migration in connection with illegitimate births in C. 1731–1800), both in Sivert Langholm and Francis Sejersted (eds), *Vandringer* (Migration) (Oslo, 1980); Hans Chr. Johansen, 'In- and out–migration of Danish cities 1750–1901', Paper, seminar on urbanization and population dynamics in history (Tokyo, 1986).

46 Knud Prange, 'Geografisk mobilitet – en overset (?) faktor i lokalsamfunnenes demografi. Et forslag til nogle målemetoder' (Geographic mobility – a neglected (?) factor in the demography of local communities. Suggestion for some methods of measurement [Denmark]), in Fladby and Winge (eds), *By og bygd. Stad og omland*; Gunnar Thorvaldsen, 'Befolkningsutviklingen i Tromsø 1866 til 1900' (Population growth in T. 1866–1900 [Norway]), in *Heimen, 3* (1984); Jan Eivind Myhre, *Oslos historie 1814–1900* (History of O. 1814–1900), forthcoming.

47 Margareta Matovic, *Stockholmsäktenskap. Familjebildning och partnerval i Stockholm 1850–1890* ('The Stockholm Marriage'. Family formation and choice of partners in S. 1850–1890) (Stockholm, 1984), summary in English. See also Susanne Lindgrén, 'Äktenskap, föräktenskapliga förbindelser och sammanboende. Sociala mönster i den tidiga industrialismens Helsignfors' (Marriage, premarital relations, and cohabitation. Social patterns in early industrial Helsinki), in *Historisk Tidsskrift för Finland* (1984); Merja Manninen, 'The opportunities of independent life for women in an eighteenth-century Finnish provincial town', in *Scandinavian Journal of History* (1984).

48 Ulf Jonsson, 'Mortality pattern in 18th and 19th century Stockholm in a European perspective', Research report no. 2, Project 'Stagnating Metropolis' (Stockholm, 1984).

49 Fladby and Winge (eds), *By og bygd. Stad og omland.*; Nils Friberg and Inga Friberg, *Stockholm i bottniska farvatten. Stockholms bottniska handelsfält under senmedeltiden och Gustav Vasa. En historisk-geografisk studie* (Commercial relations of S. in the Gulf of Bothnia during the late middle ages and the reign of Gustav Vasa) (Stockholm, 1983).

50 See the reports of the 1977 Trondheim conference, above; Degn, *Urbanisering og industrialisering.* Ole Hyldtoft, *Københavns industrialisering 1840–1914* (The industrialization of Copenhagen 1840–1914) (Herning, 1984), is a detailed study of economic development in the Danish capital.

51 Denmark: *Industrialismens bygninger og boliger* (Industrial buildings and dwellings); Sweden: *Bebyggelseshistorisk tidskrift* (Journal of building history).

52 Ingrid Hammarström, 'Urban growth and building fluctuations. Stockholm 1860–1920',

Hammarström and Hall (eds), *Growth and Transformation of the Modern City*; Hyldtoft, *Københavns industrialisering*; Myhre *History of Oslo 1814–1900* (forthcoming); John Sjöström,'Industrin som bostadsprodusent. Aspekter på den moderna bostadspolitikens genombrott' (The manufacturing industry as a producer of dwellings. Aspects of the breakthrough of modern housing politics), in Hall (ed.), *Städer i utveckling*; Hansen, *Københavns forstadsbebyggelse*; Hans Chr. Johansen, Per Boje and Anders Monrad Møller, *Fabrik og bolig. Det industrielle miljø i Odense 1840–1940* (factory and dwelling. The industrial environment in Odense 1840–1940) (Odense, 1983); Truls Aslaksby, *Grønland og Nedre Tøyens bebyggelseshistorie* (the building history of G. and N. T. [Oslo, mainly nineteenth-century]) (Oslo, 1986); Kari Hoel Malmstrøm, *Fabrikk og bolig ved Akerselva. Et industrimiljø på 1800-tallet* (factory and dwelling at the Akerselva River [Oslo]. An industrial environment in the nineteenth century) (Oslo, 1982), summary in English; Lars Guldbrandsen, *Boligmarked og boligpolitikk. Eksemplet Oslo* (Housing market and housing politics. The Oslo example [mainly twentieth century]) (Oslo, 1983); Gudrun Pentén, 'Så byggdes Östersund' (How Östersund was built 1786–1986), Björklund and Rentzhog (eds), *Östersund III*; Brunnström, *Kiruna 1–2*; Rolf Näslund, *Studier i Härnösands bebyggelseshistoria 1585–1800–talets mitt* (Studies in the architectural history of H. 1585–c.1850) (Umeå, 1980) summary in English.

53 Niels Thomsen, 'Urbaniseringen og den politiske adfærd' (Urbanization and political behaviour), in Blom (ed.), *Urbaniseringsprosessen i Norden, 3*; Hietala, *Services and Urbanization*.

54 Päiviö Tommila (ed.), *Suomen kaupunkilaitoksen historia, 1–3* (The history of civic administration in Finland, vols 1–3) (Vantaa, 1981–4). The collection contains a large number of articles on urbanization, politics and administration.

55 Hans Eyvind Næss *et al.*, *Folkestyre i by og bygd. Norske kommuner gjennom 150 år* (Democracy in town and countryside. Norwegian municipalities during 150 years) (Oslo, 1987).

56 **Literature on social structure and political power**: *Stadsadministrationen i Norden på 1700-talet* (Town administration in the Nordic countries during the 18th century), Det nordiska forskningsprojektet Centralmakt och lokalsamhälle – beslutsprocess på 1700-talet. Publikation 1 (Oslo, 1982); Sivert Langholm, *Elitenes valg. Sosial avstand og politisk oppslutning blant Christianiavelgerne i 1868* (Election of the elites. Social distance and political mobilization among the Christiania electorate, 1868 [Oslo]) (Oslo, 1984), summary in English; Folke Lindberg, *Växande stad. Stockholms stadsfullmäktige 1862–1900* (Growing city. The town council of S. 1862–1900) (Stockholm, 1980), summary in English; Inger Ström-Billing, *Stockholms hamn 1909–1939. Näringsliv och politik i samverkan* (The port of S. 1909–39; the co-operation of business and politics) (Stockholm, 1984) summary in German; Birgitta Ericsson, Överheten och den fria valrätten. Borgermästartillsätningarna i Stockholm från 1770-talet til 1840-talet' (Appointing mayors in S. from the 1770s to the 1840s), in Hall (ed.), *Städer i utveckling*; Kekke Stadin, *Småstäder, småborgare och stora samhällsförändringar. Borgarnas social struktur i Arboga, Enköping och Västervik under perioden efter 1680* (Burghers of three small towns during early capitalism in Sweden) (Uppsala, 1979); Ilkka Mäntylä, 'Städernas burskaps- och näringspolitik och deras befolkning' (The politics of citizenship and trade privileges [Seventeenth- and eighteenth- century Finland]), in Fladby and Winge (eds), *By og bygd. Stad og omland*.

**Literature on urban administration and public services**: Lajos Juhasz, A series of articles on town administration (Oslo/Christiania in the journals *St. Hallvard* and *Byminner* (1977–87); Ulla Johansson, *Fattiga och tiggare i Stockholms stad och län under 1700-talet. Studier kring den offentliga fattigvården under frihetstiden* (Poor people and beggars. Poverty relief in the city and county of S. during the 18th century) (Stockholm, 1984) with a summary in German; Anne-Marie Fällström, 'Fattigvård i stad och på landsbygd' (Poor relief in urban and rural areas [Sweden, seventeenth to nineteenth centuries]), in Fladby and Winge (eds), *By og bygd. Stad og omland*; L. N. Henningsen, *Fattigvæsenet i de sønderjydske købstæder 1736–1841* (Poor relief in the towns of southern Jutland 1736–1841) (Åbenrå, 1978).

57 Some of the Stockholm monographs are exceptions, e.g. Arne Dufwa, *Trafik, broar, tunnelbanor, gator* (Traffic, bridges, subways, streets [since 1862]) (Stockholm, 1985).

58 Hall, *Planung europäischer Hauptstädte*; Thomas Hall (ed.), *Urban planning in the Nordic countries* (forthcoming, London, 1988). The contributors are: Thomas Hall (Sweden), Erik Lorange and Jan Eivind Myhre (Norway), Ole Thomassen and Bo Larsson (Denmark), and Mikael Sundman (Finland); Thomas Hall, 'The central business district; planning in Stockholm 1928–1978', in Hammarström and Hall, *Growth and Transformation of the Modern City*; Thomas Hall, 'Stadsplanering i vardande. Kring lagstiftning, beslutsprocess och planeringsidéer 1860–1910' (The coming of urban planning 1860–1910), in Hall (ed.), *Städer i utveckling*; Marianne Råberg, 'The development of Stockholm since the seventeenth century', in Hammarström and Hall (eds), *Growth and Transformation of the Modern City*; Göran Sidenbladh, *Planering för Stockholm 1923–1958* (Planning for S. 1923–1958) (Stockholm, 1981); Rolf Jensen, *Moderne norsk byplanlegging blir til* (The origins of modern Norwegian urban planning [c. 1850–1920, with an

emphasis on planning ideas]) (Trondheim, 1980), summary in English; Torstenson, Metcalf, and Rasmussen, *Urbanization and community building in Norway*; Sven-Erik Åström, 'Town planning in imperial Helsingfors', in Hammarström and Hall, *Growth and Transformation of the Modern City*; Kouppamäki-Kalkkinen, *Kaupunkisuunnittelu ja rakentaminen Helsingin Kalliossa 1880–1980* (Town planning and construction in the city of Kallio 1880–1980) (Helsinki, 1984).

59 Marjatta Hietala, 'Urbanization: contradictory views. Finnish reactions to the continental discussion at the beginning of the 20th century', *Studia Historica, 12, Miscellanea* (Helsinki, 1983).

# Conference reports

compiled by Richard Rodger

## 'History of Bury St Edmunds': Centre of East Anglian Studies meeting, Bury St Edmunds, 25 September 1987

This one-day workshop, organized by the Centre of East Anglian Studies in what was alleged to be a rare excursion across the border into Suffolk, was held in a setting that made a positive contribution to the success of the proceedings. The fabric, decoration and pictures of the Guildhall all played a part in the discussions, giving the participants a vivid sense of the reality of urban history. The importance of a 'sense of place' was in fact one of the points made by JOYCE ELLIS (Loughborough) in her wide-ranging introductory paper. This discussed the current popularity of 'Georgian' towns, emphasizing the trends in economic and social history which had restored academic respectability to the study of small towns. MARGARET STATHAM outlined the role of charities in Bury between 1570 and 1625, a period which saw the beginnings of the town's prominence as an administrative and market centre and of its close identification with the surrounding countryside. These close links were stressed in discussions throughout the day and also figured largely in the paper by PAT MURRELL on the management of Bury's 'ticklish' political interests in the late seventeenth and eighteenth centuries. They appeared again in JANE FISKE's delineation of the town's social elite between 1780 and 1830, based largely on the diaries of a local banker. RICHARD WILSON (East Anglia) rounded off the day's proceedings by highlighting some of the trends in historical research which had helped to rescue the Burys of England from academic obscurity. The impact of modern demography, of social history, of interest in consumerism and, in general, a better understanding of the dynamics of the urban economy meant that nineteenth-century disdain of 'dull Bury' was no longer valid. Sitting in the Guildhall on a sunny autumn day, it was hard to disagree.

## 'Pre-modern Towns' Conference held at the Institute for Historical Research on 5 December 1986

Nearly 100 people attended the annual meeting of the Pre-modern Towns Group on 5 December 1986. This proved one of the most successful gatherings so far, in terms both of the quality of the papers and of the discussion. The morning kicked off – after coffee – with a double-headed session on urban culture in the late seventeenth and eighteenth centuries. PETER BORSAY (St David's, Lampeter) took as his theme the rise of the performing arts after the Restoration: in drama the spread of theatre companies not only in the greater metropolis but also in many provincial towns, with purpose-built theatres by the mid eighteenth century; and for music, the growth of subscription concerts and music festivals, and the reception of opera. While Borsay stressed the elitist and metropolitan impetus behind these developments, JONATHAN BARRY (Exeter) in the second paper urged the need to examine middle-class participation in the cultural revival, illustrating his argument from Bristol. Here there was a greater concern with the arts as reflecting civic values and integrity, and a distrust of the sensual pleasures and disorder associated with gentry entertainment. In the comments which followed, speakers pointed to the continuity of developments with the pre-Civil War period and raised questions about the funding of the new cultural activities (with the drink interest not unimportant). As an envoi to the morning session SANDY JOHNSTON (Toronto) won a good deal of interest with a short paper on the Records of

Early English Drama project which has encouraged a valuable cross-disciplinary approach to the study of drama, music and popular culture in towns (and countryside) in the late medieval and Tudor and Stuart periods.

After this the famous sandwich lunch excited the collective attention, seconded by an extensive book display by Heffers. Suitably refreshed, the meeting heard a fascinating paper by CHRISTOPHER DYER (Birmingham) on marketing in the late Middle Ages, arguing persuasively for a hierarchy of consumer purchasing: the nobility buying heavily from London and the major centres; the middling landowners from smaller towns; and lesser men from the locality. Particularly interesting was his suggestion that a great deal of trading was done outside the markets, though not apparently at inns. The deflation of the medieval market town was warmly received, though early modernists were left scratching their heads about its significance for their period.

TIM HARRIS (Brown University) sought to unravel the paradoxical attitude towards crowd unrest in London held by the Tory elite during the exclusion crisis. On the one hand the Tories condemned the rabble-rousing tactics of their Whig opponents, yet on the other they deliberately courted popular support, even to the point of stirring up crowd agitation in opposition to exclusion. In the short term this merely exacerbated the problem of keeping order, since rival Whig and Tory crowds often came into violent conflict in the streets. To see why the Tories regarded the crowd as important, we need to recognize that crowd protest was not the preserve of plebeian types, but was often engaged in by people who are more accurately termed the middling sort. These people typically had political rights and could play an important part in certain areas of local government, especially in the area of law-enforcement, which depended upon the cooperation of unpaid and part-time members of the local community, either in their capacity as constables, watchmen, members of the trained bands, perhaps, or simply as informers or prosecutors of illegal activity. In fact, there could be very little difference in social status between the members of the crowd and those responsible for policing them, and often the local peace-keeping agents would be reluctant to suppress a protest for which there was much genuine local sympathy and in which their neighbours and friends might be involved. Charles I had lost control of the streets in 1640–2, because the constables and militia men refused to suppress the crowds which demonstrated in favour of the parliamentary cause. The Tory attempt to turn people against the Whigs, and the fact that they could point to a number of demonstrations in support of the Duke of York's succession as evidence of the popularity of their own position, probably facilitated them in the maintenance of order in the long term. In contrast to the early 1640s, the local peace-keeping agencies remained loyal and Charles II never had to flee a capital whose streets he could no longer control. Finally, it was suggested that the persecution of Nonconformists which followed the defeat of exclusion was so extensive because it built upon a widespread popular antagonism towards Whigs and Dissenters which the Tories had done much to encourage.

The final session on the urban economy took the form of two progress reports: one from MIRIAM CARLIN (Museum of London) on the Medieval London project study of St Botolph, Aldgate, demonstrating the varied economic and social data available for a parish which, with nearly 11,000 inhabitants by the 1630s, overshadowed all but the largest provincial towns; the second from JOHN STEDMAN (Leicester) who deployed much more fragmentary sources to survey the primitive border economy of sixteenth- and seventeenth-century Carlisle. For all the financial slings and arrows of the last few years, the London conference showed urban historians in excellent intellectual spirits.

**Pre-modern Towns Group Annual Meeting: Institute of Historical Research, London, December 1987**

With this year's meeting the group celebrated its tenth anniversary. Though, in keeping with the democratic nature of its organization, refreshments were confined to beer and sandwiches rather than champagne and caviare, the papers on offer added a good deal of sparkle to the occasion. The morning session was devoted to social conditions in the early-modern town. MARGARET PELLING (Oxford) in 'The sick poor in the sixteenth and seventeenth centuries' focused on children and young people, whom she felt needed to be explored as a group in their own right rather than as an appendage of the family. Concentrating on the area of health care and using apprenticeship indentures as her primary source, she argued that masters had a substantial (but not unlimited) responsibility for the physical welfare of their young charges. From the later Stuart period onwards, however, employers increasingly withdrew from this obligation. Not that it should be assumed these years witnessed a decline in the individual's sense of social conscience. As JOANNA INNES (Oxford) made clear in her 'Social problems and social reformers: moral reform movements in the late seventeenth and eighteenth centuries', there were many activists only too keen to intervene in the lives of their fellow creatures. Her admirably analytical treatment of the Reformation of Manners movements detected three principal phases of activity: the very late seventeenth and early eighteenth centuries, the mid eighteenth century, and the 1780s to the early nineteenth century. A comparison of these phases revealed much continuity, though the last period saw a more effective use of the printed media, greater emphasis on attacking drunkenness and rewarding virtuous behaviour, a growing role for women reformers, and a change in the political character of the movement. During the ensuing discussion, Innes expressed reservations about associating phases of warfare with those of moral reform, while Pelling emphasized the calculated nature of the Tudor and Stuart commitment to child welfare.

Any fear that the meeting might turn a little soporific after lunch was rapidly dispelled by the controversial topic of the paper presented by DAVID PALLISER (Hull) on 'The economic fortunes of towns in the fifteenth century'. He admitted that he now held a rather more optimistic view on this subject. Though urban populations in England were undoubtedly shrinking, this had to be placed in the context of a national demographic decline, a shift in the distribution of wealth in favour of the town, and rising per capita wealth among urban dwellers. Expressing scepticism about treating Coventry as a paradigm of decline, Palliser thought that its lack of port facilities made it an exceptional case among the leading towns. He felt that future research might fruitfully concentrate on the long-term fortunes of individual centres, and the impact of regional setting: and concluded by arguing that the fifteenth century should be seen as a period not of decay but of economic restructuring before renewed urban growth during the early-modern era. Inevitably much of the subsequent questioning revolved around the advisability of comparing fourteenth- and sixteenth-century tax assessments to establish the national matrix. It was suggested that the academic returns from this line of investigation had now been exhausted, and the way forward was to focus on the fate of specific centres.

For the final session the lights were dimmed and the audience treated to two illustrated papers on the urban fabric. MARK SAMUEL (Museum of London) explored 'The medieval Leadenhall' of London. Using the results of painstaking archaeological and documentary research, he reconstructed the impressive form and decoration of this mid-fifteenth-century building, and speculated on the reasons for its erection. It was probably intended to serve not only as a market, but also as a granary which could be easily secured during a period of food shortage and rioting. The city's desire to express its independence and prestige was also a motive, a point stressed by a contributor in the subsequent discussion. One questioner wondered if it was clear that Leadenhall was originally constructed as a market, though Samuel cited architectural evidence to suggest that this was so. From the study of an individual building, MICHAEL TURNER (English Heritage) directed our attention to that of a whole townscape. His 'Impact of fire: Blandford Forum 1731' primarily examined the process of rebuilding the town, after much of it had been destroyed in a devastating conflagration. Finance was largely obtained through insurance payments, the money raised on a brief, and a royal gift: and the reconstruction was (after some delay) controlled by an Act of Parliament and the body of commissioners which it established. A number of smallish changes were effected in the town's ground plan, but except in the crucial safety requirement that tile rather than thatch was to be used as a roofing material, little appears to have been done to control the architectural form of the rebuilding. Nonetheless, a fashionable brick town rapidly emerged, not least because of the contribution of the influential local Bastard family of master builders. In response to a question, Turner emphasized that what marked Blandford off from other towns unaffected by fire was the dramatic pace at which change occurred in the landscape, rather than the specific form which it took.

Rapid change has been a feature of the study of pre-modern urban history over the last decade. The PMT Group has acted as a flexible and friendly forum for these developments: let us hope it will still be doing so another ten years on.

**'London in the eighteenth century': Institute of Historical Research, 23 September 1987, the Urban History Group and the Centre for Metropolitan History**

This was a significant meeting in several regards. Ostensibly its purpose was to pay tribute to the popular and influential *London Life in the Eighteenth Century* by Dorothy George (first published in 1925), whose approach and conclusions have withstood with remarkable integrity the twin assaults of statistical analysis and revisionism. Additionally, it marked the public debut of the Centre for Metropolitan History and the first solo venture of the Urban History Group.

Significant and also successful. Participants were offered a tempting programme on the broad topic of 'Eighteenth-Century London'. There were useful pre-circulated summaries to whet the appetite and an audience of about 100 gathered to spend the day in the Institute of Historical Research ('consoling' tea in liberal supply). The papers were of variable quality and there were few overtly unifying themes, but in general the audience was not disappointed. The first contribution came from PETER EARLE (London School of Economics) who spoke on 'The Middling Sort in early-eighteenth-century London' and gave an outline summary of the contents and approaches employed in his forthcoming book on the same subject. Covering a range of objective characteristics (mentalities were not considered) from occupations, to families, households and social life, wealth and consumption, the principal conclusion seemed to be that the 'middling sort' in the early eighteenth century looked remarkably like the 'middle class' of the nineteenth century. LEONARD SCHWARZ (Birmingham) gave the second paper, on 'Occupations and economic fluctuations in London in the "Long Eighteenth Century", 1688–1815'. Manufacturing in the capital was conceptualized as 'assembly lines in the street', increasingly devoted to the finishing trades and consumer goods following the rise of provincial industry, and set in the context of a population dominated by the professions, distribution and services. This was the classic metropolitan profile, modernized but non-industrialized. Schwarz was mainly concerned with economic fluctuations, particularly the stagnation (demonstrated through a range of indices) of the years 1725–60 and later upturn. The substantive explanations and subsequent discussion were demographic in orientation, which clearly suited the inclinations of a large part of the audience, and included the possible impact of declining levels of in-migration and higher death rates during the stagnation phase. But there was no consensus on how or even why the 'demographic effect' was working. The morning ended with a short address from DEREK KEENE (Institute of Historical Research/Museum of London) on the agenda of research, seminars and services to be undertaken by and in association with the new Centre for Metropolitan History. This ambitious and much welcomed undertaking promises a bright future, despite the inevitable clouds that have attended the decline in funds available to London history.

AMANDA COPLEY (Cambridge Group for the History of Population) maintained the demographic emphasis in the afternoon with a paper, based on her doctoral work, entitled 'The population of Clerkenwell 1660–1754: a reconstitution study'. Using the kinds of innovative computer techniques that are expected of the Cambridge Group, and databases of a breathtaking scale, Copley explored aspects of the population experience of this expanding suburb. But inevitably (and properly since the project was not complete) the paper and questions revolved around methodological issues such as the representativeness of parish records of marriage, given the rise of nonconformity and the prevalence of clandestine marriages. Certain bold ideas were suggested, notably a relationship between family limitation and church marriages, though little evidence was presented here to support the thesis and cautions were offered from the floor. Nevertheless, this sort of boldness coupled to an exciting and pathbreaking statistical project (urban reconstitution has hitherto proved problematic) promises well. Bold in ideas and concept was also a suitable epithet for PETER LINEBAUGH's (Boston, Massachusetts) contribution on 'Crime and criminality in eighteenth-century London', which proved for many to be the highlight of the day, not least because of the engagingly idiosyncratic style of presentation. Of all the papers this most directly challenged the work of Dorothy George, calling into question the George thesis that crime declined in the later eighteenth century as a result of better conditions of living. Disputing the notion that criminality was an aspect of poverty, drawing on the evidence of court proceedings and the views of the informed contemporary Patrick Colquhoun, Linebaugh posited two ideas, neither of which is entirely new though they still have the power to provoke surprise among some elements in a modern audience, presently anxious about a modern crime wave. The first idea, essentially that of Colquhoun, was that crime against property was rising and was linked to a growing material gap between the rich and the poor. The second and more sophisticated idea was that late-eighteenth-century crime reflected the changing attitudes of the rich and powerful to a form of customary exchange or petty trading among the relatively poor. Crudely put, the appropriation by workers of the waste products of manufacture or trade – previously tolerated as an informal aspect of the payment system in an economy where coin was imperfectly distributed and paternalism still held sway – was increasingly regarded as criminal. This criminalization of formerly accepted practices reflected the rise of scientific business management, new technology and organization and the desire to regulate wages against a background of gradual diffusion in the money economy. But these trends coincided in the 1790s with a period of short-term financial crisis, the suspension of gold and a shortage of small coin which reinforced the role of petty dealing in waste products among the poor. It was suggested, in the discussion that followed Linebaugh's paper, that new perceptions of crime were also an aspect of broader social changes in the later eighteenth century; the rise of class, the concern for social order and fear of revolution were significant issues.

Some of these broad themes came through in the last perhaps most scholarly of the day's papers from JOANNA INNES (Somerville, Oxford) who spoke on 'Social problems and social policy in eighteenth-century London'. This was the only contribution overtly to address a broader canvas, to go beyond the essentially parochial, even myopic 'London-centred approach' and use the comparative experience of other English towns to indicate the distinctiveness of the capital. Social problems in London were different from those of other urban centres because of the differences in scale, wealth, types of business, age structures, occupations and patterns of migration. The incidence of imprisonment for debt was very high for instance. But the importance of elite attitudes in determining the scale of officially recognized criminality, vagrancy or poverty, and the consequent policies adopted to deal with these, were also stressed. Hence crime and vagrancy were seen as problems in London – a rich city with many poor migrants – whereas poverty was not a major social issue in this period. Some of the details of policy practice in London were explored in questions from a knowledgeable audience and attempts were made to draw on European comparisons (though Innes could not be tempted to speculate here). This discussion on social policy and elite attitudes was a fitting end to a day that had begun by looking at some of the concrete characteristics of those groups who were part of the elite and helped to make social policy, the 'middling sort'. With such a broad and potentially disparate topic as 'London in the eighteenth century' there would have been some benefits in having a *rapporteur* to bring the event to a tidy finish, to draw out the themes and point to the overall connections and conclusions. But this is a minor complaint. On the whole the conference was a just tribute to Dorothy George and the organizers, PAUL LAXTON (Liverpool) and LEONARD SCHWARZ, deserve praise and thanks for having concocted such an enjoyable feast of eighteenth-century London history.

### 'Victorian Scandals': Mid-West Victorian Studies Association Meeting, Newberry Library, Chicago, April 1987

Three groups of conference papers were identified by THAIS MORGAN (Arizona State University). At least eight of the papers on scandals involved women, and more generally, the issue of sexual difference. Morgan argued that emphasis on Marxist-orientated feminism with particular reference to the socio-economic aspects of gender roles was analytically helpful. A second group of papers addressed the intervention of the law in private lives of Victorians. Foucault's theory of the relation between sexuality and power, discourse and knowledge, was particularly illuminating in this respect. The psychoanalytic view of Victorian culture as 'repressive' as adapted by both Marcus and Gay was also relevant alongside Foucault's revisionist hypothesis. A third group of papers was concerned with the role of the Victorian press in the production of scandal. Analysis of newspapers, periodicals and more serious literature reveals that language played an important part in the scandals and Morgan noted that the rhetorical strategies were themselves far from being value-free.

RICHARD DELLAMORA (Trent University) analysed four scandals in his paper 'Homosexual scandal and compulsory heterosexuality in the 1890s'. The Wilde trials, the scandals surrounding the 1885 Act under which Wilde was charged, and the literary scandals connected with the publication of *The Picture of Dorian Gray* (1890) and Thomas Hardy's *Jude the Obscure* (1895) were each framed in an argument, historical and theoretical, of a crisis of masculinity in the 1890s in urban society. Whether this indeed was a crisis or a male response to the socialism, feminism and pacifism of the period requires further research. JAMES BROPHY (Indiana-Bloomington), however, reviewed the image of 'New Woman' demanding latch-keys, university education, meaningful employment and casting a critical eye at traditional values and roles associated with motherhood and marriage. His paper, 'The multifaceted image of the "New Woman" – enemy of social order' argued that the scandal of the 'New Woman' was widely publicized between 1894 and 1900. By demonstrating how varied the meaning of 'New Woman' was, Brophy argued that no consistent identity emerged, that newspapers often trivialized or parodied the term, and accordingly many intelligent women disassociated themselves from it. The term 'New Woman' also gained currency as a rallying call for anti-feminists. In this respect Brophy stressed the complexity and diversity of the nascent women's movement of the 1890s.

Enhanced female independence might have been anticipated in the wake of reform in the divorce laws. But the 1857 Divorce Act created a court which sat only in London, administered a procedure which inevitably incurred substantial litigation costs, and rigorously enforced a statute that recognized only adultery, bigamy, incest or desertion as grounds for divorce. Since expense excluded the poor, and publicity the respectable, the conventional view, that divorce served only the margins of Victorian society, has remained largely intact. Yet a one-in-ten sample of divorce petitions over a ten-year period which formed the empirical base for GAIL SAVAGE (Pennsylvania State) in her paper, 'The demand for divorce in

Victorian society 1858–68', demonstrated a much wider social base than is normally recognized. In fact the middle, and even lower middle classes of London and the home counties provided the majority of litigants, and though newspaper reports of divorce continued to entertain Victorians, they were largely atypical of divorce court proceedings and, more seriously, disguised the extent of marital unhappiness in the Victorian age.

Scandals in the Victorian theatre perhaps predictably formed part of the conference proceedings. TRACY DAVIS (Queen's University), in a paper provocatively entitled, 'Sex and the Victorian actress', claimed that the theatre's ability to disturb the behavioural norms of the Victorian urban middle class remained undiluted since actresses were cast as flamboyant women akin to prostitutes in their nocturnal habits, economically fragile and thus sexually susceptible. They were also cast as flagrant violators of the conventionally proscribed domestic sphere inhabited by the majority of women. Costumes, gestures and other images of actresses also formed part of a male sexual subculture of soft pornography which read more into actresses' performances than was perceived either by actresses themselves or other women. The self-image of the theatre was at the core of JANE STEDMAN's (Roosevelt University) paper which explained the particulars of a scandal over a breach of marriage promise in 1884 between a prominent Tory and an actress in *Iolanthe*, the theatrical press being concerned to limit damage to the dented public image of the theatre.

In 'Wrongful confinement: the ultimate argument for proper female decorum' MARILYN KURATA (Alabama-Birmingham) claimed that lunacy remained a Victorian obsession for two reasons, namely, the technical ease with which a person could legally be incarcerated, and the arbitrary medical basis for diagnosing insanity. Kurata explained that though the use of the madhouse as punishment for unacceptable behaviour was not new, what did represent an alarming nineteenth-century departure was the abuse of the lunacy laws by a male medical profession to intern women who departed from their preconception of a 'female role'. Thus an independent will could be regarded as a form of female deviance dangerously close to mental illness. It might also be viewed as subversive and so a paternalistic society enforced proper decorum for women by the threat of the madhouse.

ANN HIGGINBOTHAM (Eastern Connecticut State University) sampled the sessions papers of the Central Criminal Court in London for twelve years between 1839 and 1906 as the basis for her paper '"Scandal of the age": infanticide and illegitimacy in Victorian Britain'. Forty-two cases in which unmarried mothers were charged with the murder of their illegitimate infants, 70 per cent of which concerned new-born infants and the remainder children ranging up to several years. For the neo-naticides, common features emerged; mothers had given birth alone, concealed the birth and death of their infants, and were discovered only when changed appearances or medical complications drew attention to themselves. A simple contemporary equation that infanticide was strongly correlated with illegitimacy was no doubt essentially accurate, but it obscured the opprobrium accorded the unmarried mother, and more seriously, failed to take account of the prevailing conditions of poverty, employment and other conditions which surrounded conception. Perhaps more than any other paper this analysis of infanticide highlighted the duplicity of Victorian morality and the abyss of scandal.

The armoury of Victorian moral reform commissioned a new weapon in the National Anti-Gambling League, founded in 1890. The league claimed gambling as a great evil, second only to intemperance, but never successfully established that claim, at least judged by membership or subscriptions. No form of betting was exempt, argued DAVID ITZKOWITZ (Macalester College) in his paper 'Gambling, scandal and the National Anti-Gambling League', since racing, the stockmarket or children's bets each coarsened the human instinct in its appeal to greed, selfishness, and personal profit at the expense of others. It was difficult to escape the conclusion that the limited appeal of the league was precisely because of the temporary pleasure gambling offered to so many in a frequently unpleasant world.

Underlying many of the papers was the fine line between acceptable morality and scandal, a tension which Victorians employed to contain behaviour potentially disruptive to their social system should it overstep a perceived norm. The sanction of a scandal and the ostracization which that implied was the control mechanism; the method varied according to the nature of the behavioural transgression. The sexual overtones associated with many of the scandals presented in the papers reflected the threatening basis of changing sexuality to the *status quo* in Victorian social relations and particularly to a male hegemony.

## American Planning History Conferance: Columbus, Ohio, 24–26 September 1987

The media can play a powerful role in promoting change in the built environment. It can also assist in the development of new planning ideas. A case in point, and the subject of a paper by DAVID CLOW, was the 1947 Better Philadelphia Exhibition. The achievements in planning and redevelopment in post-war Philadelphia have won international recognition, and Clow demonstrated that 'a key turning point in the momentum of physical and political reform actually preceded these programmes and helped pave the way for their success'. This key event was the ambitious 1947 exhibition which proved to be an invaluable tool for both political reform and promotion of planning. Following the Great Depression, Philadelphia offered its citizens little to be proud of. Its physical and political image was the object of scorn and mockery in the press, a situation compounded by a general apathy among the citizens. By 1940 an effective campaign had begun to counteract the deadening effects of the corrupt bureaucracy and poor image of the city. To this end, the Philadelphia City Planning Commission was established in 1943, as was the Citizens' Council on City Planning, a citizens' action committee that sponsored the 1947 exhibition. The Better Philadelphia Exhibition was the brainchild of its technical director and designer, Oskar Stonorov, in collaboration with his co-designer, Edmund Bacon (Executive Director of the Philadelphia City Planning Commission 1949–70). Stonorov and Bacon understood the power of images; thus words and statistics were minimized. The successes of the exhibition were indebted neither to the generalized architectural image nor to the planning philosophy represented, but to the specific designs calculated to educate and inform while convincing the public to support planning: throughout the exhibition citizen action, participation and individual responsibility were encouraged.

The circuit followed by the visitor through the vast exhibition was deliberately controlled through a sequence of rooms portraying the beneficial effects of planning in a variety of ways. From the large-scale transformations of centre city to small neighbourhood projects, the present chaotic conditions were contrasted with a brighter, safer future. The message was clear and simple: without planning Philadelphia was doomed, and individually one was destined to lead a comparatively miserable life in crowded, dangerous conditions. The 'before and after' juxtaposition was most spectacular and magical in the popular downtown model of centre city Philadelphia. The large model (30ft × 14ft) was designed with rotating panels so that before one's very eyes the blighted areas of Philadelphia were replaced with the proposed changes as a recorded commentary with synchronized lighting described the 30-year redevelopment programme. The last exhibit featured a display of planning models made by schoolchildren. As parents marvelled at the creations, they were confronted with a sign on the wall asking 'What kind of Philadelphia are you going to give your children?' On leaving the exhibition, they were given the opportunity to answer. Would they support the proposed physical improvements with a rise in taxes? The majority of the 400,000 people who attended the exhibition answered positively. This was not the only testament to the effectiveness of the Better Philadelphia Exhibition. In fact, several years after the exhibition the reform Democrats overthrew the corrupt

Republican machine, and many of the proposals envisioned in the exhibition were realized. Others continue to be implemented today.

Impressed with what they had seen in Philadelphia, planners in various parts of America attempted to build similar models and exhibits in their home towns. Other examples of promoting city planning by various means were discussed, such as the immense publicity campaign to popularize Daniel Burnham's plan for Chicago, which included distributing Wacker's *Manual* (1911) to schoolchildren. Also cited was the American Institute of Planners film from 1939, 'The City'. These historic examples were important reminders that exhibitions, models, films and pamphlets are effective media in cultivating public support and awareness for urban planning and redevelopment.

### Ireland and the United States: The Transatlantic Connection 1800–1980. Cushwa Center, University of Notre Dame: 10–11 April 1987

Although the traditional interpretation of Irish–American history gave little attention to urban history this conference was dominated by the transition from an overwhelmingly rural and peasant society to urban life and the cultural continuities and discontinuities involved. In his paper, 'The Irish as urban pioneers in the United States, 1850–70', DAVID N. DOYLE (University College, Dublin), critically analysed the conventional assumption, recently challenged by Canadian historian D. H. Akenson, that Irish migrants overwhelmingly settled in cities. Doyle showed that in the mid nineteenth century Irish migrants were substantially more urbanized than native-born American or other migrant groups: that between 1850 and 1870 the urbanization tendency became more pronounced and that those who did not settle in the major cities tended to be found in smaller urban and mining communities rather than in rural areas. Doyle concluded by drawing attention to the pioneering position of the British Isles in nineteenth-century urbanization and suggested that: 'In the United States . . . the Irish put to work the lessons of urbanism learned in their then political framework of the United Kingdom, but unrealizable in its Irish component'.

One of the most commonly noted contrasts between the Irish and other migrant groups is the extent to which they retained a strong allegiance to religious practice despite the transition to an urban environment. GEAROID O'TUATHAIGH (University College, Galway), in his paper 'Faith of their fathers: the export of Irish religious culture in nineteenth-century America', outlined the reasons for this and the specific Irish contribution to US Catholicism. O'Tuathaigh emphasized that with the decline of the Irish language in the nineteenth century, religion came to represent the major badge of cultural identity. The main contributions of Irish Catholicism to their new home were substantial numbers of English-speaking clergy and laity and an expansionist mentality, while the already developed links between Catholicism and political action in Ireland, and particularly the concern with social grievance, led to significant involvement in labour and social reform movements. KERBY A. MILLER (University of Missouri) in his paper 'Paddy's paradox: emigration and America in Irish imagination and rhetoric', examined the factors which gave rise to the common Irish vision of emigration as exile. The failure of industrialization and urbanization in the post-famine economy and the simultaneously growing domination of the conservative Catholic and nationalist farming community tended to describe emigration as exile: something forced upon Irish society by British misgovernment. At the same time Irish emigrants, facing problems of adjusting from a rural, perhaps Gaelic, environment to an urbanized industrial life, tended to see themselves as exiles. The conflict in Irish and American value systems persisted into the twentieth century. In her paper 'The economic impact of the United States on Ireland 1900–1980', MARY E. DALY (University College, Dublin) examined US efforts to assist modernization of the Irish economy and the ambivalent responses it provoked in areas such as agriculture, trade and tourism. One US official in charge of Irish Marshall Aid programmes in the late 1940s noted that most Irish people responded to Ireland's economic problems with a combination of hopelessness and 'the apparent feeling that it is not Ireland's problem but that it must be solved by action entirely outside of Ireland'. She concluded that a reluctance to disturb the conservative social values which dominated Irish society delayed transition to export-led economic growth. Finally JOHN A. MURPHY (University College, Cork), in his paper 'Independent Ireland and the United States: divergent trends', suggested that the more modern, outward-looking Ireland was increasingly orientated towards Europe with consequent diminution of political and economic dependence on the US.

### Economic and Business Historical Meeting: San Francisco 23–25 April 1987

Shanghaied in San Francisco might have been the theme of this meeting, set on the edge of Chinatown, and abducted to penthouse entertainment courtesy of Wells Fargo Bank. Yet these distractions apart, there were various papers of interest to provide some competition to the attractions of a unique urban location.

In a session of astounding thematic unity TOM WINKPENNY (Elizabethtown College) and RICHARD RODGER (Leicester/Kansas) investigated the persistence of artisanal production in urban locations as diverse as Pittsburgh and Paisley. In his paper, 'From East Liverpool to Gotham: the mixed fate of the nineteenth-century artisan', Winkpenny noted how in certain urban settings hand technology endured well into the 1890s when elsewhere it had been eliminated by 1860. Urban scale could not alone explain this divergence, since the studies covered the very large cities (New York, Philadelphia), substantial cities (Cincinatti, Pittsburgh), and also small towns such as Danbury (Con), Lancaster (Pa), East Liverpool (Oh). Intrinsic skill, as with Pittsburgh puddlers and glass blowers and East Liverpool potters, delayed the day of deskilling. Factory organization was delayed in Cincinatti, a result of strong Republican ideology and capital shortages and the staying power of the Cincinatti artisan was evident until the 1880s. Danbury and Boston hatters sustained work-control practices, unionized, and sacrificed monetary gains where necessary to defend their traditional skills. Cultural factors were also indispensable, claimed Winkpenny, to the persistence of skill in Lancaster, Pennsylvania – artisanal occupations expanded from 1820 to 1880 as a consequence both of German craft traditions, and of the innate conservatism of the community bonded through the generations. Against this pattern of artisanal resilience, Winkpenny placed the ante-bellum decline of skill in New York, Philadelphia and Newark. This was explained in terms of the countervailing power of merchant capital and master craftsmen. Merchants increasingly dominated and thus reorganized the businesses formerly controlled by artisans; merchants' facility with emerging transport and market organization provided the competitive edge. The creation of the wage-earning class resulted. Master craftsmen may have become employers in trades such as shoemaking, saddlery and iron-working, but most journeymen and apprentices were reduced to factory hand status. That the eastern coastal towns were reception points for immigrant labour, were the axis for burgeoning industrial know-how, and were released from dependency on power sources by the spread of steam technology, further inclined them towards factory organization while the inland towns enjoyed a temporary measure of insulation by their isolation.

Evidence of artisanal persistence was produced by Rodger in his paper 'Alternatives to mass production; industrial dualism and business structure in Victorian Scotland', although the focus was more directly concerned with the continuation of small workshops in the face of counter-pressures towards the formation of large-scale business units in the wake of economic modernization in mid-Victorian Scottish burghs. In one sector of the economy after another, and from the most unexpected quarters – chemicals, iron working, non-ferrous metals, shipbuilding – resistance to economies of scale was emphatically demonstrated. By pointing to the dominance of the small firm, Rodger did not wish to say that new forms of corporate organization did not exist, or that for significant numbers of the urban working class factory production or labour identity was not real. The intent was to identify and quantify the degree of reliance on small producers in the component parts of Scottish urban manufacturing in 1851, to avoid the former emphasis on the major industrial landmarks which are normally associated with Scottish industrialization, and to examine the characteristics of Scottish urban industrial structure by identifying the typical size and scale of operations for producers in a dozen manufacturing subdivisions.

In his paper, 'Germany and Britain: economic inequality', KENNETH BARKIN (University of California, Riverside) argued that in reality the historiographical interpretation as sustained by Veblen, Brentano and Gerschenkron of greater German inequality was false. It followed that to argue that the introduction of welfare provisions in Germany was a product of relative inequality was invalid, since judged by landownership concentration, or by the distribution of income, there was relatively less need in Germany than in Britain. Barkin then argued that the ideas behind welfare reforms in the Edwardian period were not a product of egalitarianism, or compassion, a conclusion which corresponds with recent writing in the United Kingdom on the political motives of the new or radical liberals in the twentieth century and their redefinition of policies on property, wealth and taxation. Indeed, Barkin produced some data to demonstrate increasing income inequality in Britain since 1946, which in rethinking the politics of the 1980s, the latest version of the Liberals might do well to contemplate.

Two further papers concerned with the scale of German industry were of significance to urban economic structure. CRAIG PATTON (University of Alabama, Birmingham) investigated two German cartels in 'War, inflation and international trade: sales and profits in the German chemical industry 1914–24'. Bayer/BASF/ AGFA and Hoechst were the two industrial conglomerates which produced 90 per cent of the world's dyestuffs in 1914. About 75–80 per cent of output was exported. During the First World War some internal reorganization of company structure and their ability to weather post-war difficulties, a fire, and uncertainties about the product range meant they participated in considerable expansion during hyperinflation and subsequent stabilization. ERIC WEITZ (St Olaf College) summarized the standard version of the proliferation of mergers and rationalization in German industry before the First World War. In his paper, 'Economic rationalization and Germany's industrial labour force 1890–1928', Weitz argued that between 1910 and 1923 the merger movement proceeded no further. But from 1923, cost cutting pressures associated with the generally collapsed state of business produced demands by employers for longer working days and piece work: the process fractured the German working class, created an unemployed urban underclass which developed support for the German communist movement, the first such mass movement and party organization outside the USSR. As a reaction, a significant element of support rallied around the National Socialists.

Though not explicitly conceived in an urban context, the sessions on artisan and workshop production, and on the nature of German business, addressed the underacknowledged importance of the interrelationships of business dynamics and urban structure. Of course, the conferees need not have attended the sessions to discover this since the proximity of Chinatown with its distinctive business practices and retailing patterns underscored the point – and probably more emphatically. And if they did linger around the conference sessions, there were offerings on Dillard Department Stores, Coca Cola Corporation, and 'Frozen fillets and French fries: the rise of the frozen food industry' to explore further the interconnections of business and spatial patterns. Alternatively some forsook the academic for the purely experiential – the box of urban delights. Didn't Dyos state that you ought to be able to 'smell the city'?

*The editorial board would like to acknowledge the assistance of Mary Daly, Kris Garrigan, Tim Harris, Stana Nenadic and Peter Read.*

# Review of periodical articles

It is always reassuring to find evidence in other journals that the *Yearbook* is carefully read. E. Bloomfield has subjected this periodical to critical scrutiny in 'The *Urban History Yearbook* – interdisciplinary forum or indispensable research tool?', *Urban History Rev.*, XVI (1987). Weighing recent volumes against the formidably ambitious goals outlined by the journal's founder, H. J. Dyos, Bloomfield inevitably finds shortfalls amid the successes. Having acknowledged the utility of the *Yearbook*'s methodological and survey articles, its reviews and its various research aids, she recommends greater attention to the perspectives of other disciplines and enhanced coverage of countries outside Britain, especially of Continental Europe.

Such advice is timely for the Review of Periodical Articles which this year adds contributors with particular expertise in medieval and early modern history to the incumbent modernist. Since the inception of the *Yearbook* various lone authors of the Review have drawn their selection of articles from all periods and countries and from various disciplines in addition to history. In continuing to pursue this approach, chronological specialization should enable the new 'collective' to broaden the Review's coverage as well as to deepen its expertise.

However, in this age of the market, evaluation of the 'new' Review, as of the *Yearbook* as a whole, must be left to the consumer. This process can commence with scrutiny of the following analyses of articles published (for the most part) during the 12 months beginning in July 1986.

## Pre-1500

by R. Malcolm Hogg, Saint David's University College, Lampeter

The interplay and relative importance of political and socio-economic factors in the origin and growth of towns can be seen in a number of articles this year. J. Haslam, 'Market and fortress in England in the reign of Offa', *World Archaeology*, XIX (1987), shows this vigorous Mercian king in the later eighth century constructing defensive enclosures at bridges to prevent the penetration of Viking warships up-river. At the same time, the increased trading (visible also in the Carolingian Empire) stimulated royal establishment of markets at these points, but often outside the defensive enclosures; living quarters were also mostly outside. On the other hand, T. Tatton-Brown, 'The topography of Anglo-Saxon London', *Antiquity*, LX (1986), shows markets outside the Roman city walls mostly in peaceful times, 'the age of the *wics*' in the early Anglo-Saxon period; at the time of the Viking attacks they retreated into the neglected old city, which was then vigorously developed. B. J. Graham, 'Urban genesis in early medieval Ireland', *J. Historical Geography*, XIII (1987), doubts whether towns arose around monasteries in more than a very few instances. Although Irish society was in principle capable of sustaining towns, most monastic settlements hardly displayed urban character-istics. The older theory that the Anglo-Norman conquest of 1169 brought towns to Ireland may be substantially right after all. R. Favreau, 'Les débuts de la ville de la Rochelle', *Cahiers de civilisation médiévale*, XXX (1987), surveys the fairly sudden appearance of a French town of great interest to English medieval historians because of its connections with the English kings. Growth from the salt pans of the tenth and eleventh centuries began in the first half of the twelfth century when the great family of the area lost their previous urban seat to rivals, and it expanded rapidly in the next hundred years, taking more than its fair share of the great economic and urban growth of western Europe in this period and linking its wine-producing hinterland to the Atlantic trade routes. D. Roffe and C. Mahany, 'Stamford and the Norman Conquest', *Lincolnshire History and Archaeology*, XXI (1986), briefly consider the impact on this town of the Norman castle and administrative change.

In evaluating Stratford-upon-Avon and Lichfield as new towns of the twelfth century, T. R. Slater, 'Ideal and reality in English episcopal medieval town planning', *Trans. Inst. British Geographers*, n.s., XII (1987), stresses the sophistication of this town planning, and argues for the adaptation of a notional regular plan (both at the level of streets and at the level of burgage plots) to allow irregularities. Thus, for example, earlier landscape features could be incorporated, and the wishes of the occupants could be met – perhaps often the initial occupants of the new town, who, in particular, sub-divided burgages and rented the portions out at a considerable profit. A. J. L. Winchester, 'Medieval Cockermouth', *Trans. Cumberland and Westmorland Antiq. and Archaeol. Soc.*, LXXXVI (1986), deals with, apparently, another planned town. Its fluctuating economic fortunes are briefly traced as far as the sixteenth century. Post-medieval sources are used to reconstruct the layout of the burgage plots, part of which may have been determined by a previously existing settlement. Similarly, J. Houghton, 'Burgage tenure and topography in Lewes, East Sussex', *Sussex Archaeol. Collns*, CXXIV (1986), attempts to work back from post-medieval rentals and other documents to reconstruct the layout of the burgage plots in another medieval planned town. D. Stroud, 'The site of the borough at Old Sarum 1066–1226: an examination of some documentary evidence', *Wiltshire Archaeol. and Nat. Hist. Mag.*, LXXX (1986), briefly suggests that it was mainly within the ramparts of the Iron Age fort, with a suburb outside. Some details of Carlisle's topography at a later date emerge in B. C. Jones, 'House building in Carlisle in the middle ages', *Trans. Cumberland and Westmorland Antiq. and Archaeol. Soc.*, LXXXVI (1986). B. Auzary, 'Le Petit Pont, la passerelle et les plaideurs', *Revue historique*, CCLXXVI (1986), shows that when bridges over the Seine at Paris were wrecked by flooding in the early fifteenth century a temporary footbridge was constructed. This may have been a common procedure.

In contrast to such mundane matters, J. M. Fritz and G. Michell, 'Interpreting the plan of a medieval Hindu capital, Vijayanagara', *World Archaeology*, XIX (1987), argue that its layout, which includes both royal and sacred centres, is an expression of Hindu kingship, linking the earthly order with the cosmic order and symbolizing the outward diffusion of divine power to the kingdom at large. Rather than the usual story of conflict between urban elite and rural feudal nobility, G. Dameron, 'Episcopal lordship in the diocese of Florence and the origins of the commune of San Casciano Val di Pesa, 1230–1247', *J. Medieval History*, XII (1986), shows the commune of Florence helping its bishops to enforce their feudal jurisdiction over a rural area. The commune thereby put itself in a position to establish its own later control of the surrounding countryside. In the same issue of this journal, J. M. Murray, 'Failure of corporation: notaries public in medieval Bruges', explores the nature of Flemish notaries public. A particular aspect of marketing regulations which affected English towns in the thirteenth and fourteenth centuries is elucidated in R. H. Britnell, 'Forstall, forestalling and the Statute of Forestallers', *English Hist. Rev.*, CII (1987). P. J. P. Goldberg, 'Female labour, service and marriage in the late medieval urban north', *Northern History*, XXII (1986), examines such towns as York and Hull. Women formed the majority of the population, many of them unmarried immigrants, and often supporting themselves economically in an independent role, but rarely with the degree of success achieved by the larger group of successful men. J.-P. Cuvillier, 'Economic change, taxation and social mobility in German towns in the late middle ages', *J.*

*European Economic History*, xv (1986), examines the fluid situation of the fourteenth and fifteenth centuries in Germany's major towns, when many of the previous economic and social controls gave way to allow greater social inequality but with considerable differences between individual towns. M. Asenjo-González, 'Clientélisme et ascension sociale à Ségovie à la fin du moyen-âge', *J. Medieval History*, xii (1986), explores in outline the social climbers of this Castilian city from the thirteenth century onwards, highlighting the help given to them by the nobility and, especially in the fifteenth century, the monarchy. In the face of Venice's reputation as a gerontocracy, S. Chojnacki, 'Political adulthood in fifteenth-century Venice', *American Hist. Rev.*, xci (1986), highlights the large proportion of young men who, despite their occasional escapades, were involved at the lower levels of the city's government. Indeed, their participation in councils and offices was a way for their elders to keep an eye on them and educate them into more responsible civic attitudes.

Finally, a group of brief articles in *Economic History Rev.*, 2nd ser., xxxix (1986), continues the long-running controversy over urban prosperity or decay in late medieval England, focusing especially on what some have seen as the crucial question, the interpretation of the 1334 and 1524 taxation evidence. S. H. Rigby in 'Late medieval urban prosperity: the evidence of the lay subsidies' criticizes A. R. Bridbury's use of this source in making the case that towns prospered. In 'Dr Rigby's comment: a reply', Bridbury defends his limited and tentative use of this evidence and in criticizing Rigby's argument mentions some of the other evidence and logic which point to prosperity. In 'From dissonance to harmony on the late medieval town?', J. F. Hadwin, the author of substantial work on the lay subsidies, arbitrates by emphasizing the degree of consensus obtainable when the participants' misunderstandings of one another's arguments are eliminated: the population of towns decreased, and in many cases decreased more than that of the countryside, but urban vigour and vitality remained.

## 1500–1800

by Peter Borsay, Saint David's University College, Lampeter

The constraints of present-day academic research and publication dictate that there is little time to read beyond the narrow confines of one's chosen field. Indeed, reading itself (as opposed to desultory scavenging for titbits of evidence) can appear a guilty pleasure, to be reserved for late evenings and holidays. Therefore, being asked to review the profuse periodical literature of the early modern town has been something of a liberating experience. It has also, for a contributor to this journal, been a rather unnerving one. It cannot be honestly be claimed that the majority of those whose pieces are reviewed below concentrate on the specifically urban element in their work. Towns are usually portrayed as simply containing rather than moulding events. On the other hand, early modern urban history's weakness is also its strength. Eclectic by nature, it attracts a steady (if sometimes unwitting) flow of academic talent, ensuring its freshness and vitality.

Historical demography has contributed considerably to our understanding of the basic features of urban living, and this tradition continues. Though broadly confirming received wisdom, G. J. Mayhew's 'Epidemic mortality in 16th-century Rye', *Sussex Archaeol. Collns.*, cxxiv (1986), is a nicely researched piece. It compares the impact of plague and influenza, assesses the measures employed (not always unsuccessfully) to prevent the spread of the former, and finds evidence to link the spread of major epidemic diseases with the return of wounded soldiers from the continent. More innovative and challenging are two articles by J. Landers, 'Mortality, weather and prices in London, 1675–1825: a study of short-term fluctuations', *J. Hist. Geography*, xii (1986), and 'Mortality and metropolis: the case of London 1675–1825', *Population Stus.*, XLI (1987). Using the bills of mortality as his major source, Landers discovers that the metropolis's mortality levels 'were at once markedly higher and noticeably more stable than in rural or smaller urban communities'. However, when substantial fluctuations did occur, he suggests that this was due not so much to the direct impact of biological, seasonal or economic factors on the indigenous population, as to changing patterns of migration. Thus a rise in rural food prices might stimulate an influx into the capital of subsistence migrants, whose comparatively high vulnerability to disease could then prompt a mortality crisis.

The movement of people and its significance are themes that recur in several papers. D. M. Palliser, 'A regional capital as magnet: immigrants to York, 1477–1566', *Yorkshire Archaeol. J.*, LVII (1985), shows that a high proportion of the city's freemen immigrants had travelled a relatively long distance (69 per cent from over 20km away), pointing to its economic pull as a regional capital. Most came from a north-westerly direction, reflecting the pattern of York's trade routes and the geographical distribution of other urban centres offering rival employment opportunities. Smaller towns depended more on short-distance migrants, as J. Dils demonstrates for Abingdon, Newbury and Reading between 1558 and 1620. Her 'Deposition books and the urban historian', *Local Historian*, XVII (1987), makes a strong case for the value of these church court records, with their brief biographies of witnesses, and verbatim accounts of evidence, as a source for both quantitative and qualitative investigation. International migrants are the subject of T. L. Purvis, 'The national origins of New Yorkers', *New York History*, LXVII (1986), which attempts a more refined surname analysis of the 1790 census than has been previously undertaken, so as to establish the national origins of the state's residents. Embedded in this are several references to New York City, including the fact that even at this date a quarter of its white population was of Irish origin. Immigrants of a rather superior kind feature in G. Behre's 'Scots in "Little London": Scots settlers and cultural development in Gothenburg in the eighteenth century', *Northern Scotland*, VII (1987), which explores the impact of the Scottish (largely bachelor) community on what was then Sweden's second largest town. Though the Scots supported their own charitable relief system and church, they mixed with the native bourgeoisie in societies and clubs, and helped Gothenburg to become 'a gateway for English language and literature during a period when French was the predominant language of the educated classes in Sweden'. Human movement on a microcosmic scale is investigated in J. Boulton's inventive 'Residential mobility in seventeenth-century Southwark', *Urban History Yearbook 1986*. Challenging the idea of the anonymous metropolis he finds that 'a significant number of householders spent a substantial proportion of their lives within a relatively small urban area', and concludes that 'rather than finding himself or herself marooned in the faceless impersonal city the rural immigrant may have been merely exchanging one restricted set of social horizons for another'. However, as Boulton acknowledges, his study concentrates on heads of households and on a relatively wealthy district in Southwark, both factors which could exaggerate the degree of stability.

The workings of an individual domestic unit are the subject of R. Jüte, 'Household and family life in late sixteenth-century Cologne: the Weinsberg family', *Sixteenth Century J.*, XVII (1986). Using one of those unique personal sources that can be such a revelation but leave one wondering how typical they are, Jüte reconstructs the 'material infrastructure of life' (income, living space, consumption, budget and diet) of a bourgeois multiple household built around the conjugal families of two brothers. Studies of towns during the Reformation era appear to be a booming industry at present. L. A. Smoller's fascinating 'Playing cards and popular culture in sixteenth-century Nuremburg', *ibid.*, XVII (1986), challenges the proposition that there existed a sharp divide between elite and popular idioms, and questions the extent to which the Reformation altered cultural attitudes. The impact of religious change is examined in B. L. Beer, 'London parish clergy and the Protestant Reformation, 1547–1559', *Albion*, XVIII (1986). This study of a group of 63 clergymen appointed to London benefices during the reign of Edward VI reveals the existence not only of zealous reformers but also of trimmers and careerists, providing ammunition both for those advocating the thesis of a rapid transition to Protestantism, and those supporting that of a slow one. The degree to which religious reform redefined the boundaries of acceptable behaviour and altered the way immorality was treated, is explored in *'Disciplina Nervus Ecclesiae*: the Calvinist reform of morals at Nîmes', *Sixteenth Century J.*, XVIII (1987). R. A. Mentzer Jr suggests that the Calvinist as opposed to Catholic approach to discipline focused on public offences rather than ones of personal conscience, and concludes that 'the consistory was itself a public institution designed to enforce a community morality'. The notion of community, carrying as it does consensual and inclusive connotations, needs to be used with considerable care, as T. F. Sea demonstrates in 'The Reformation and the restoration of civic authority in Heilbronn, 1525–32', *Central European History*, XIX (1986). He contends that 'the concept of community' in this particular city 'acquired a double meaning' (highlighted by the experiences of the Peasants' War), and was 'increasingly interpreted in an adversarial sense to distinguish those who needed to be controlled by the Council and who resented that control'. On a different tack, L. Roper's '"The common man", "the common good", "common women": gender and meaning in the German Reformation commune', *Social History*, XII (1987), shows that the contemporary idea of community did not embrace all equally, but 'had a built-in, intrinsic understanding of the political as male territory'.

A concern to reveal women's specific historical experience is one that now attracts a good deal of attention. A. M. Boylan's 'Timid girls, venerable widows and dignified matrons: life cycle patterns among organized women in New York and Boston, 1797–1840', *American Q.*, XXXVIII (1986), argues that whereas women's participation in benevolent societies reinforced the family orientation of their lives, joining groups pursuing reform (in the broadest sense) encouraged the development of 'a new set of priorities' centred on individual fulfilment, and led some directly into feminism. Though voluntary activities offered middle-class women an obvious sphere of achievement outside the home, the opportunities provided by business should not be dismissed. In '"To acquaint the ladies": women traders in Colchester c.1750–c.1800', *Local Historian*, XVII (1986), S. D'Cruze suggests that a significant proportion of the town's trading proprietors were female, and shows how they dominated the prestigious millinery business, the running of which was not incompatible with a prosperous genteel background, or even (in some cases) with marriage.

The way society defines and treats 'minority' and 'deviant' groups can be deeply revealing about its overall nature. L. Roper, 'Discipline and respectability: prostitution and the Reformation in Augsburg', *History Workshop*, XIX (1985), argues that the transformation of the whore from a professional group into a 'moral category' during the Reformation, reflected a 'new obsession with women's sexual experience' in general. Roper notes that in German cities both prostitutes and Jews were required to wear similar distinguishing attire. This is a point further developed in 'Distinguishing signs: ear-rings, Jews and Franciscan rhetoric in the Italian Renaissance city', *Past & Present*, CXII (1986). D. O. Hughes demonstrates how clothing and jewellery were used to isolate and marginalize prostitutes and Jews, thereby protecting the city from their presence, while at the same time preserving the essential sexual and economic services which they provided. She also shows how the meaning of personal effects could alter radically in response to changes in the political context. The subtleties of analysis present in the work of Roper and Hughes give way to a more straightforward account of 'The Jews of Bath', in *Bath History*, I (1986). M. Brown and J. Samuel chart the rise and fall of an active religious community, apparently in response to the changing economic fortunes of the Georgian and Victorian city. The first issue of this new journal reveals some of the tensions injected into the study of Bath's history by the work of

R. S. Neale. In 'English spas' B. Mitchell presents the traditional and relatively sanitized version of spa history (but also interestingly noting the special importance of watering-place society to women), while G. Davis's 'Entertainments in Georgian Bath: gambling and vice' self-consciously pursues the darker and hidden side of the city's past, largely through the perspective of early nineteenth-century prostitution.

As Davis makes clear, the supply of prostitutes owed much to the prevalence of poverty. The latter is a subject that has produced a number of valuable contributions. Potentially the most influential of these is T. Arkell's, 'The incidence of poverty in England in the later seventeenth century', *Social History*, XII (1987), which argues for greater sophistication in the definition and measurement of preindustrial poverty, stressing the need to see the poor as a multi-layered phenomenon (some of whom were scarcely poor at all by contemporary standards) rather than an undifferentiated mass. This point is developed by W. A. Champion in 'The Shrewsbury Lay Subsidy of 1525', *Trans. Shropshire Archaeol. Soc.*, LXIV (1985), which questions the assumption that those assessed at the lowest rates were among the poor, and therefore sees a need to modify the pyramid-shaped model often used to represent the social structure of pre-modern towns. P. Ripley, 'Poverty in Gloucester and its alleviation 1690–1740', *Trans. Bristol and Gloucestershire Archaeol. Soc.*, CIII (1985), suffers a little from the criticisms raised by Arkell, but provides a useful account of the causes and treatment of poverty in a neglected period, and hints at the conflict in towns between parochial and centralized control of poor relief. In 'From charity to welfare in Revolutionary Paris', *J. Modern History*, LVIII (1986), I. Woloch trenchantly defends the Revolution's record in the field of social welfare, emphasizing the degree of order and local fraternity that underpinned the system introduced, and blaming the serious weaknesses that it developed on economic rather than political factors. Poverty is the human reality behind the detailed statistical analysis in J. Söderberg, 'Real wage trends in urban Europe, 1730–1850: Stockholm in a comparative perspective', *Social History*, XII (1987). This focuses on the eighteenth century, but adopts a genuinely European perspective, arguing for an almost universal fall in real wages for much of the century, and with it 'a triple process of pauperization, polarization, and income redistribution towards the agrarian sector'. The first two of these processes feature strongly in G. B. Nash's lively survey article, 'The social evolution of pre-industrial American cities, 1700–1820: reflections and new directions', *J. Urban History*, XIII (1987). But in addition to the presence of 'deepening social inequalities', he also stresses the 'diversifying of urban populaces' under the impact of immigration, and the contribution of voluntary organizations in helping 'stitch together urban centres that sometimes seem, in historical perspective, to have been coming apart at the seams'.

Social polarization is one of the processes described in P. Kriedte's comprehensive 'Demographic and economic rhythms: the rise of the silk industry in Krefeld in the eighteenth century', *J. European Economic History*, XV (1986). However, in this case the 'emergence of a class society' may have had more to do with the loss of economic independence among the textile workers than any decline in living standards, particularly since the silk masters appear to have deliberately avoided laying off employees during economic crises so as to protect their supply of skilled labour. As Krefeld's textile industry expanded in the early eighteenth century, so broadcloth manufacture in Worcester declined. But, as G. Talbut makes clear in 'Worcester as an industrial and commercial centre, 1660–1750', *Trans. Worcestershire Archaeol. Soc.*, X (1986), compensation was found in the development of a more diversified economy based upon gloving, metalworking, building, and the food and luxury trades. Diversity was the most characteristic feature of early modern London's economy, one facet of which was the provision of financial services. In 'Deposit banking in London, 1700–90', *Business History*, XXVIII (1986), F. T. Melton investigates four of the city's banks, demonstrating the impact of the gentry season on their cash-flow position, and revealing the substantial business that they generated by arranging mortgage-based loans and acting as bankers to army regiments. The impression Melton conveys of a sophisticated financial sector is reinforced by L. Neal's 'The integration and efficiency of the London and Amsterdam Stock Markets in the eighteenth century', *J. Economic History*, XLVII (1987), which stresses the advances already made by the second quarter of the eighteenth century. The extent to which later Stuart and Georgian London increasingly displayed the organizational characteristics of a modern economy can be seen in P. G. E. Clemens and J. M. Price, 'A revolution of scale in overseas trade: British firms in the Chesapeake trade, 1675–1775', *ibid.*, XLVII (1987). The authors reveal a remarkable process of business concentration among the metropolis's tobacco traders, a development also to some extent discernible in the major provincial ports. Historians are well used to analysing the economic impact on towns of industry, commerce and finance, less so that of factors such as religion and piracy. J. R. I. Cole, '"Indian Money" and the Shi'i shrine cities of Iraq, 1786–1850', *Middle Eastern Stus.*, XXII (1986), and C. R. Pennell, 'Tripoli in the late seventeenth century: the economics of corsairing in a "Sterill Country"', *Libyan Stus.*, XVI (1985), might provide some food for thought. In both cases the sources of the cities' wealth had important political repercussions: in the former in sustaining the influence of the particular branch of Shi'ism that prevailed in the shrine cities, in the latter by injecting endemic instability into Tripoli's internal power structure.

Political activity, in the broadest sense, is a theme explored in many contributions. The politics of work is examined in M. Sonescher's thought-provoking 'Journeymen, the courts and the French trades, 1781–1791', *Past & Present*, CXIV (1987). Focusing largely on Paris, this shows how journeymen were able to use the legal system during economic conflicts with their masters (though with decreasing frequency in the later eighteenth century), and questions the idea that a deep fissure existed between elite and artisan culture. In a quite different vein, I. McCalman, 'Ultra-radicalism and convivial debating-clubs in London, 1795–1838', *English Hist. Rev.*, CII (1987), argues for the continuity of an ultra-radical tradition in the English metropolis between the mid-1790s and the rise of Chartism. The debate itself is a familiar one, but his emphasis on the role of clubs and his imaginative analysis of their political culture is stimulating. Dissenting congregations could act rather like clubs in fostering political attitudes: chapels were used in London as a front for radical debating societies. In 'Social sources of Denominationalism reconsidered: post-revolutionary Boston as a case study', *American Q.*, XXXVIII (1986), A. C. Rose shows how the various religious denominations displayed markedly different social and political characteristics, though over time there was a general tendency for their membership to become more prosperous and their organization bureaucratic. Specific studies of urban elites seem surprisingly few. J. W. Kirby's 'Restoration Leeds and the aldermen of the Corporation, 1661–1700', *Northern History*, XXII (1986), is a wide-ranging if rather diffuse investigation of a gerontocratic, 'close-knit, self-perpetuating oligarchy', among whom the key group were the town's merchants. However, with almost a third of the aldermen in office 1660–1700 dying without an heir, one wonders how much of a tightly-knit hereditary caste they were. M. Berlin demonstrates how the growing oligarchical element in London's government from the early fifteenth century led to an increasingly elitist and secularized form of civic ritual, epitomized in the decline of the Midsummer Watch and the rise of the Lord Mayor's Show. His 'Civic ceremony in early modern London', *Urban History Yearbook 1986*, also argues that this process was accompanied, particularly from the mid-1580s, by 'a policy of repression of the more disorderly aspects of popular customs'.

The differences between popular and elite forms of protest are explored in W. H. Beik, 'Urban factions and the social order during the minority of Louis XIV', *French Historical Stus.*, XV (1987). But more central to this study of public disturbances in three Languedoc towns is the thesis that local factional conflicts resulted from 'a crisis in the structure of absolutism', as the royal minority temporarily created a 'confusion of lines of authority'. The notion that urban politics can only be satisfactorily understood by reference to the external political framework finds equally strong support in 'Urban conflicts and the imperial constitution in seventeenth-century Germany', *J. Modern History*, LVIII (1986), supplement. C. R. Friedrichs shows that the political feuding in early seventeenth-century Wetzlar (an imperial free city) represented a three-cornered struggle between the town council, a dissident burgher party, and the local territorial prince: he goes so far as to argue that 'the imperial constitution may have played as important a role in sustaining and prolonging urban conflicts as it ever did in resolving them'. Relations between city and state also feature in M. D. Carroll's revealing study of 'Civic ideology and its subversion: Rembrandt's *Oath of Claudius Civilis*', *Art History*, IX (1986). She demonstrates how tensions between the burgomasters of Amsterdam and the House of Orange led the city fathers to reject a historical painting that they had commissioned from Rembrandt, because his treatment of the subject appeared to elevate unduly the political status of the Dutch royal house.

The importance of external political factors can also be seen in a number of studies of English towns. J. F. Quinn, 'York elections in the age of Walpole', *Northern History*, XXII (1986), reveals how between 1722 and 1741 the city was embroiled in a series of party battles, led by the county gentry, for the control of York's two parliamentary seats; with a large freemen electorate, fiercely contested elections and a predominantly Tory corporation, city and county politics were closely intertwined during these years. London's politics and that of the nation were inevitably welded together. In 1660 the city council understood the critical importance of affirming its loyalty to Charles II, and made him a handsome monetary gift, delivered even prior to his return. But, as C. A. Edie demonstrates in 'For "The Honour and Welfare of the City": London's gift to King Charles II on his coming into his kingdom, May 1660', *Huntington Library Q.*, L (1987), the collection of the money exposed the tensions that existed within the city's body politic, and raised fears that the gift might set an unfortunate precedent for future dealings with the king. Relations between monarch and metropolis are also central to T. Harris, 'The Bawdy House Riots of 1668', *Historical J.*, XXIX (1986). This sees the apprentices' attack on the city's brothels that year not simply as a piece of traditional prostitute-baiting, but also as an implied criticism of Charles's bawdy and Catholic court, and a reflection of the 'bitter disappointment' among some 'with the Restoration religious settlement', and of 'a widespread undercurrent of popular hostility towards episcopacy'. London's proximity to the organs of state may have introduced volatility into its public life, but it also ensured that the capital played a uniquely important role in the collection and distribution of news, and the moulding of provincial political attitudes, a point made by R. Cust in 'News and politics in early seventeenth-century England', *Past & Present*, CXII (1986). During the Civil Wars many English towns were drawn willy-nilly into the vortex of national politics. J. Binns, 'Scarborough and the Civil Wars, 1642–1651', *Northern History*, XXII (1986), is largely concerned with establishing the strategic significance of the town, but also briefly assesses the degree to which it suffered because of this.

One area where Scarborough did sustain damage was its physical fabric. This theme is addressed more specifically in S. Porter, 'Property destruction in the English Civil Wars', *History Today*, XXXVI (August 1986), which reveals that towns located in the war zone frequently incurred quite serious damage, both as a consequence of deliberate offensive and defensive action, and because of the greatly increased risk of accidental fires. In general, studies of the urban landscape appear rather thin on the ground at present, but an important recent contribution is F. E. Brown's 'Continuity and change in the urban house: developments in domestic space organization in seventeenth-century London', *Comparative Stus. in Society and History*, XXVIII (1986). The author detects a growing differentiation in room function, and notes the emergence of the front-room parlour, the latter prompting the suggestion that 'one may perhaps take the spatial shift of the parlour as witness to a changing social experience, and to changing social needs, within the middling stratum of society'. The reader may baulk a little at Brown's diagrammatic representations, but here is a serious attempt to link architectural and social history. Two contributions that add to our knowledge of the planning process are R. J. Cox, 'Trouble on the chain gang: city surveying, maps and the absence of urban planning in Baltimore, 1730–1823; with a checklist of maps of the period', *Maryland Historical Mag.*, LXXXI (1986), and P. Mitter, 'The early British port cities of India: their planning and architecture, *circa* 1640–1757', *J. Soc. Architectural Historians*, XLV (1986).The former sees a direct relationship between the extent and sophistication of town mapping, and the presence or otherwise of urban planning. Mitter challenges the thesis that European cities on the subcontinent were uniform and planned and Indian ones ill-focused and organic. Nonetheless, the author notes that in the British port cities a good deal of attention was paid to specific features of the urban environment. Among the latter were public walks and gardens, which are the subject of P. Borsay's 'The rise of the promenade: the social and cultural use of space in the English provincial town c. 1660–1800', *British J. for Eighteenth-Century Stus.*, IX (1986). Anyone studying the landscape of smaller to medium-sized eighteenth-century British towns might consult T. V. Jackson, 'The Sun Fire Office and the local historian', *Local Historian*, XVII (1986), which discusses the usefulness of the fire insurance policy registers lodged at London's Guildhall Library.

For those seeking pieces covering a broad geographical canvas, there is little to offer. The majority of contributions focus on a particular town, and few stray beyond national boundaries. One exception is P. Spierenburg's 'From Amsterdam to Auburn: an explanation for the rise of the prison in seventeenth-century Holland and nineteenth-century America', *J. Social History*, XX (1986). This stresses 'the role of state formation processes in the development of penal systems', and argues that prisons emerge in Holland and North-East America at a point in time when both societies 'had recently emerged as relatively pacified entities'. Such comparative studies though difficult to research and vulnerable to the disease of over-generalization, can reveal a great deal about fundamental urban patterns and processes, and offer a potentially rewarding avenue for investigation.

## Post-1800

by Richard Trainor, University of Glasgow

Long preoccupied with questions of definition, modern urban historians are diverting their introspective energies to the problems and opportunities of various types of sources, especially those applicable to British towns. M. Jubb exposes some of the pitfalls awaiting analysts of income tax records and statistics in 'Income, class and the taxman: a note on the distribution of wealth in nineteenth-century Britain'. *Historical Research*, LX (1987). E. Higgs is also alarmed by historians' neglect of the idiosyncratic and variable ways in which sources were often compiled. In 'Women, occupations and work in the nineteenth-century censuses', *History Workshop*, XXIII (1987), Higgs warns particularly about the tabulation of domestic servants in the printed census; only systematic local and regional studies can probe the historical reality lying behind such cultural constructs. Yet just such a study can be found in the careful article by N. Vickers, 'The structure of the Whitby jet industry in 1871', *Local Population Studies*, XXXVIII (1987), which shows how the census enumerators' returns can be used to reconstruct a major urban occupation by relating it to topics such as age, family and migration. Likewise, M. J. Lewis and R. Lloyd-Jones demonstrate the reliability and flexibility of another key source in 'Rate books: a technique for reconstructing the local economy', *Local Historian*, XVII (1987). In contrast to a complementary source, trade directories, rate books provide evidence of manufacturing capacity and output, as the authors prove through analyses of early nineteenth-century Manchester and late nineteenth-century Sheffield. Admittedly many towns and cities have huge gaps in their collections of rate books, a source which future historians will lack altogether for studies of the poll tax era. Fortunately, unexpected gaps in sources are often offset by surprising survivals, as in the rich household investigations which K. Bales discusses in 'Reclaiming antique data: Charles Booth's poverty survey', *Urban History Yearbook 1986*. Computer-assisted investigation of Booth's notebooks allows historians to assess both standards of living and policy responses to them. Urban historians should not be discouraged even by massive, inconsistent, problematical runs of statistics such as those relating to crime. True, some writers *are* discouraged. R. S. Sindall is gloomy in 'The criminal statistics of nineteenth-century cities: a new approach', *Urban History Yearbook 1986*. Abandoning hope of employing the figures as a 'direct measure of criminality', Sindall contents himself with using the statistics as phenomena which shaped contemporary perceptions of crime. While such attitudes deserve scholarly scrutiny, dismissing the figures even as measures of criminal prosecutions seems unduly negative. By contrast, S. J. Stevenson, having recognized the limitations of the statistics, reveals important regional contrasts and local variations in his careful study of 'The "habitual criminal" in nineteenth-century cities: a new approach', *ibid*. Thus, while urban historians should approach sources with some wariness, they should avoid a pessimism over records which, if taken to excess, would paralyse or trivialize research.

Urban systems are far from trivial, though at times they seem very abstract. P. Bairoch and G. Goertz provide an intelligently quantitative treatment of a huge subject in their 'Factors of urbanization in the nineteenth-century developed countries: a descriptive and econometric analysis', *Urban Stus.*, XXIII (1986). In Europe, industrialization was the key promoter of urbanization, while in European-settled countries overseas agricultural productivity was paramount. Although trade, population, topography and industrial type also help to explain varying degrees of urbanization, the extent of the various railway networks surprisingly does not. In the Third World, differences in urban and rural productivity are major causes of urban growth, as K. N. Pribadi and B. J. L. Berry point out in 'Urbanization in Indonesia: application and extension of a model suggested by Tolley', *Urban Geography*, VII (1986). Yet the particular theory employed, like all such models, must be adapted to the case in question, in this instance to migration among the country's islands.

One of the many healthy aspects of modern urban history today is its increasing concern with the economic bases of towns. A superficial example of this trend can be found in T. F. Kinsella, 'Traditional manufacturing cities in transition to human-centred cities', *J. Urban History*, XIII (1986). Ignoring problems of economic transition and political adjustment, Kinsella foresees a rosy future for defunct industrial cities trading on their 'knowledge functions' – provided they enjoy a 'strong advanced service base'. Britain's 'Midland Metropolis' enjoyed this asset throughout its industrialization, as E. Hopkins demonstrates in 'The trading and service sectors of the Birmingham economy', *Business History*, XXVIII (1986). Trading and services expanded alongside metal manufactures, in part because Birmingham was a regional capital as well as a centre of production. Hopkins posits a contrast to cotton towns which were based on new spinning technology, but Manchester, like Birmingham, had a highly diversified economic structure. R. Lloyd-Jones and M. J. Lewis's ratebook-based exploration of 'The economic structure of "Cottonopolis": Manchester in 1815', *Textile History*, XVII (1986), finds warehouses far more valuable than factories, though the two types of building were closely linked. Factories remained the major stimulants to urban expansion, in part because Manchester's manufacturing was not limited to cotton, as S. Levitt shows in 'Manchester mackintoshes: a history of the rubberized garment trade in Manchester', *ibid*. The timely supply of capital, the availability of rubber through the port of Liverpool, plentiful cotton, an appropriately skilled labour force, and the drive of mainly Jewish entrepreneurs allowed Manchester to capture the trade from Glasgow, where the 'mac' had been invented. Meanwhile, in the French capital, the demand for fashions more refined than the raincoat entailed production methods less advanced than those found in Manchester. As W. Walton proves in '"To triumph before feminine taste": bourgeois women's consumption and hand methods of production in mid-nineteenth century Paris', *Business History Rev.*, LX (1986), the female demand for art and originality fostered the persistence of less skilled handicraft methods in a variety of trades.

The final two economic studies reveal more about national and international markets than about urban context. R. C. Michie's valuable investigation of 'The London and New York stock exchanges, 1850–1914', in *J. Economic History*, XLVI (1986), reveals the more restrictive structure of the American market, an important factor in the mergers and deep financial panics of the United States' economy. London was surrendering its superior stock flexibility on the eve of the First World War; yet the preceding period had also featured considerable London-based success in the gem market, where the strong link with Kimberley was crucial. C. Newbury's 'The origins and function of the London diamond syndicate, 1889–1914', *Business History*, XXIX (1987), shows that 'periodic crises were contained within the arrangements between the mining company and its sales outlet in a market susceptible to rumour, over-production, and organized to promote a good which was only considered to be worth buying if its price was artificially supported and raised.'

Construction was a major urban business as well as the source of each city's 'shapes on the ground'. The tallest urban buildings are the subject of G. Gad and D. W. Holdsworth's Toronto-based 'Corporate capitalism and the emergence of the high-rise office building', *Urban Geography*, VIII (1987). In contrast to most historical accounts of the skyscraper, Gad and Holdsworth's article emphasizes changes in the demand for office space as corporate capitalism emerged. At first, the proliferation of small interdependent firms was critical; then, from the 1920s, the emergence of large companies with hundreds of white-collar employees proved more important. C. Hamnett and B. Randolph descend one echelon in the building hierarchy to investigate 'The rise and fall of London's purpose-built blocks of privately rented flats: 1853–1983', *London J.*, XI (1985). These structures, which house large numbers in central and inner London, have recently passed from the care of residential investment companies into the hands of speculative landlords. The blocks' clientele has also shifted upward, helping to cause the rise in London's social profile which, however, as Hamnett notes in 'The changing socio-economic structure of London and the South-East, 1961–1981', *Regional Stus.*, XX (1986), has been especially marked outside inner London. In the house sector, M. J. Vill's 'Building enterprise in late nineteenth-century Baltimore', *J. Historical Geography*, XII (1986), indicates that American, like British, house builders were usually small-scale businessmen who had to depend on small amounts of credit from diverse sources. The public and private determinants of the styles such builders used are investigated in M. Horsey, 'London speculative housebuilding of the 1930s: official control and popular taste', *London J.*, XI (1985). Municipal bye-laws produced less monotonous layouts, but consumer preferences mandated anachronistic building styles distinct from the more avant-garde modes found in council housing.

Such government-built housing is the subject of a special number of *J. Urban History*, XII (1986) surveying half a century of the New York Housing Authority. Studies by R. Genevro, P. Marcuse, A. L. Buttenweiser and J. Schwartz show that powerful economic and political interests produced housing projects ill-suited to the needs of tenants, whose values were also in conflict with the authoritarian attitudes of administrators in central and local government. Public housing proved inadequate for other reasons in inter-war Liverpool, as C. G. Pooley and S. Irish observe in 'Access to housing on Merseyside, 1919–39', *Trans. Inst. British*

*Geographers*, n.s. XII (1987). In the local context of generally low and unstable wages, council housing, like the private ownership sector, was available only to the minority on high, regular incomes. Thus '[t]he distinctive nature of housing sub-markets on inter-war Merseyside led to great variations in housing quality for different households.' By contrast, municipal housing emerges as the inevitable, if inadequate, solution to the previously unchecked rigours of the housing market in R. Rodger's provocative study, 'Political economy, ideology and the persistence of working-class housing problems in Britain, 1850–1914', *International Rev. Social History*, XXXII (1987). Reasserting a pessimistic view of the housing question, Rodger finds housing and public health improvements limited to artisans and those even higher in the social scale.

Yet most recent writing about urban public health measures is enthusiastic. In an important article, 'Mortality in Victorian England: models and patterns', *J. Interdisciplinary History*, XVIII (1987) R. Woods and P. R. A. Hinde take issue with McKeown's emphasis on improved nutrition as the principal explanation for falls in death rates. Given the large discrepancy between urban and rural mortality in 1861, they argue, the subsequent major fall in death rates presupposed significant urban improvement caused by reforms in water supply. Whatever the outcome of this long-running general debate, detailed local studies are required to illuminate significant variations both in life expectancy and in relevant factors such as the supply of doctors. Effective public health measures are not confined either to industrial or to Western cities, as S. Hanley demonstrates in her intriguing investigation, 'Urban sanitation in pre-industrial Japan', *J . Interdisciplinary History*, XVIII (1987), which focuses on Edo (later Tokyo) prior to the Restoration of 1868. Edo's pure water supply and efficient waste disposal allowed its citizens life expectancies comparable to those in the West despite inferior living standards. Once Japan began to experience industrialization its sanitation record became less impressive. Even worse conditions prevailed in rapidly changing Indian cities, as I. Klein shows in 'Urban development and death: Bombay City, 1870–1914', *Modern Asian Stus.*, XX (1986). Countering the fashionably optimistic outlook toward modernization, Klein argues that worsening death rates for the masses stemmed directly from the city's development, which increased inequality and produced severe overcrowding. Bombay's native elite had much better health, of course. Such urban leaders also used cultural flexibility to strike acceptable bargains with 'modernization', as D. E. Haynes shows in his study of Surat, 'From tribute to philanthropy: the politics of gift-giving in a Western Indian city', *J. Asian Stus.*, XLVI (1987). Changing modes of generosity allowed local businessmen to foster ties with political superiors, drawn at first from the Raj and later from the Indian National Congress.

The internal structure of cities continues to preoccupy many urban historians. Shop location forms the subject of S. Brown's 'The complex model of city centre retailing: an historical application', *Trans. Inst. British Geographers*, n.s. XII (1987), which focuses on Belfast. Brown finds that shop types vary between core and periphery in a complex pattern best explained by the impact, in a free market system, of retailers' desires for accessibility. An even more fundamental aspect of urban structure, the distinction between the central city and its suburbs, attracts several authors in *J. Urban History*, XIII (1987), who respond to Kenneth Jackson's study of American suburbanization, *The Crabgrass Frontier*. Analysing 'The suburban Sunbelt', C. Abbott emphasizes its similarity to suburbs elsewhere in the United States; even the Sunbelt's less fragmented government resembles the municipalities of the Frostbelt in the latter's great period of suburban expansion. Having noted French and British as well as American influences on Canadian suburbs, P-A. Linteau provides an ambiguous answer to the question, 'Canadian suburbanization in a North-American context: does the Border make a difference?'. The international context dominates R. L. Fishman's lively discussion, 'American suburbs/English suburbs: a transatlantic comparison'. Since the Second World War American suburbs have become semi-autonomous 'metrolands', whereas

British planning restrictions have kept suburbia subordinate to the core. Fishman's conclusion that 'England remains *the* suburban nation' is challenged in Jackson's 'Suburbanization in England and North America..... Noting that both Britain and the United States devalue cities while praising a semi-rural lifestyle, Jackson gives America pride of suburban place because of Britain's relatively high land costs and its allegedly slow and inefficient transport system. The final point finds some echoes in R. H. Morgan's 'The development of an urban transport system: the case of Cardiff', *Welsh History Rev.*, XIII (1986), which argues that municipalization of the trams was a pragmatic response to the inability of private enterprise to produce a profitable, expanding network.

More ambitious attempts by local authorities to alter cities have received at best mixed reviews this year. Remarkably, two articles have appeared on the then Brazilian capital's early twentieth-century improvement plans: T. Meade, '"Civilizing Rio de Janeiro": the public health campaign and the riot of 1904', *J. Social History*, XX (1986), and J. D. Needell, 'The *Revolta contra Vacina* of 1904: the revolt against "modernization" in Belle-Époque Rio de Janeiro', *Hispanic American Historical Rev.*, LXVII (1987). In both studies, the dispute's apparent focus on vaccination is related to a more general clash between rival social ideals. Meade's article, the more urban-minded of the two, convincingly depicts the riots as a futile revolt against measures that the urban oligarchy promoted in order to make Rio fit for investment and comfortable middle-class life. As she notes, the elite's successful attempt to segregate the poor from urban services foreshadowed the extreme inequalities of late twentieth-century cities in the Third World. Such conflicts between popular needs and urban renewal have by no means disappeared, as N. Kleniewski demonstrates in 'Triage and urban planning: a case study of Philadelphia', *International J. Urban and Regional Research*, X (1986). 'Triage', which assumes that some areas will be developed while others are deliberately neglected, has permeated the urban renewal policies of the City of Brotherly Love since the late 1940s, penalizing the black residents of Philadelphia's poorest neighbourhoods. Underlying this paradoxical policy is the need of urban governments to seek private sector investment as well as political support in a fiscal setting starved of suburban wealth. The imbalance between resources and the demand for services hamstrings all the activities of urban government, as D. Hum and F. M. Strain note in 'Fiscal imbalance and Winnipeg: a century of response', *Urban History Rev.* XV, (1986). Technical as well as political obstacles block reform of urban revenue-raising. The latter's occasionally 'progressive' elements are more accidental than intentional, as R. White shows in 'Urban history and the politics of the property tax: the case of single residential property in the city of Toronto 1920s–1970s', *ibid.*

Urban renewal and more general planning policies may have had greater success in the Orient. This suggestion arises from K. P-H. Ying, 'District population change in Hong Kong, 1961–1981: some policy implications', *Urban Geography*, VIII (1987). Quantitative analysis indicates that the colony's policies have succeeded in spreading population from the old core to the new periphery of the city. Yet the effect of such measures on community life remains unexplored. This neglect is remedied, for early twentieth-century Continental Europe, by a special number of *Oral History* (XIII.2, Autumn 1985) concerned with 'City space and order'. Studies of Madrid, Turin and Vienna suggest the vitality of community life. They also reveal the latter's complex interaction both with physical space and with the impersonal forces of public planning and the market.

The stylistic aspects of planning have been studied in four recent articles. In a two-part investigation in *Town Planning Rev.*, LIII (1986) and LVIII (1987), J. Punter attempts 'A history of aesthetic control: the control of the external appearance of development in England and Wales'. The twists and turns of policy make for confusing and gloomy reading, especially given continual disputes concerning the aims and execution of such measures. A more incisive analysis of urban design appears in G. Wright's 'Tradition in the service of modernity: architecture and urbanism in French colonial policy 1900–1930', *J. Modern History*, LIX (1987). French administrators in Indochina, Madagascar and Morocco used urban design to enhance colonialism among Europeans while making it tolerable to the colonized. This ultimately unsuccessful policy tried to synthesize modernity and tradition. Those strategies were starkly juxtaposed in Palestine, as Y. Katz shows in 'Ideology and urban development: Zionism and the origins of Tel-Aviv, 1906–1914', *J. Historical Geography*, XII (1986). The Jewish new town contrasted markedly with its traditional Arab surroundings and differed even from Arab garden suburbs in its social heterogeneity and community functions. A secular Zionism 'influenced the choice of site for the garden suburb, its planning, its selection of population and inspired its development as the Hebrew national centre in Palestine.'

The mechanisms and consequences of the migration process which underlies so much urbanization continue to fascinate historians. D. F. Doeppers systematically applies the micro-techniques of North Atlantic migration studies to the Far East in 'Destination, selection and turnover among Chinese migrants to Philippine cities in the nineteenth-century', *ibid.* Doeppers finds stable chains of migration coexisting with high turnover rates within the immigrant communities. By contrast to the Philippines and also to Thernstrom's Newburyport, T. Dublin discerns a high degree of stability among immigrants in 'Rural-urban migrants in industrial New England: the case of Lynn, Massachusetts, in the mid-nineteenth-century', *J. American History*, LXXIII (1986). Relatively good economic and marriage opportunities explain this persistence, which also contributed to Lynn's emergence as a centre of the labour movement. Dublin argues that his methodology, which includes collective biography and the examination of sources beyond the city of destination, is especially important for studying the migration of women. His view that females often migrated as individuals is shared by J. Meyerowitz in 'Women and migration: autonomous female migrants to Chicago, 1880–1930', *J. Urban History*, XIII (1987). Female migration had special causes, especially the paucity of paid work opportunities in rural areas and small towns, and the stigma of unmarried sexual activity in such settings. Yet solo women migrants were highly vulnerable in cities, as the female leaders of women's voluntary societies realized. Attempts to provide facilities for unattached women had to appeal to the economic goals of male entrepreneurs, as D. Pedersen shows in '"Building today for the womanhood of tomorrow": businessmen, boosters and the YWCA, 1890–1930', *Urban History Rev.*, XV (1987), which focuses on Canadian cities but has wider ramifications for the analysis of urban charities and women's movements.

How far does migration to a distant urban setting affect reproductive behaviour? J. W. Briggs moves beyond speculation by reconstructing the marriage and childbirth 'cultures' of emigrants from an Italian village to Rochester, New York. His 'Fertility and cultural change among families in Italy and America', *American Historical Rev.*, XCI (1986), shows no linear change toward 'modern' patterns; the New Yorkers were more 'traditional' with regard to premarital conception than were the Italian villagers, for example. Profiting from enhanced economic power and a more favourable sex ratio, immigrant women were better able to insist on congenial reproductive strategies than they had been in Italy. R. G. Fuchs concentrates on women who found child-raising impossible in 'Legislation, poverty, and child-abandonment in nineteenth-century Paris', *J. Interdisciplinary History*, XVIII (1987). As the century progressed married women were less likely to abandon children. Demographic and economic factors became less useful predictors of abandonment rates as more complex public policy emerged. D. S. Reher provides useful methodological enhancements for the study of more stable domestic units in 'Old issues and new perspectives: household and family within an urban context in nineteenth-century Spain', *Change and Continuity*, II (1987). Applying analysis over time and nominative record linkage to the small provincial capital of Cuenca, Reher detects continual changes in family structure despite apparent stability. For example, although nuclear families predominated at any given moment, at some point most individuals would live in an extended or multiple structure. Reher illuminates the urban dimension of family life both by noting the circulation of kin which linked urban and rural areas and by speculating that in rural areas less intense mobility was balanced by stronger family networks.

Long-distance migration often resulted in urban ethnic minorities of substantial size. V. A. Shepherd provides a morose example in 'From rural plantations to urban slums: the economic status and problems of East Indians in Kingston, Jamaica, in the late nineteenth and early twentieth-centuries', *Immigrants and Minorities*, v (1986). The minority who sought urban opportunities were disadvantaged by black domination of good jobs, by high rents, and by discriminatory legislation; unlike the Jews, Lebanese and Chinese they failed to secure stable footholds in retailing. Merely establishing the size of minorities can be difficult, especially once assimilation has begun, as B. A. Kosmin, S. Waterman and N. Grizzard demonstrate in 'The Jewish dead in the Great War as an indicator for the location, size and social structure of Anglo-Jewry in 1914', *ibid.* Rejecting the usual reliance on the *Jewish Year Book* in favour of *The British Jewry Book of Honour*, the authors conclude that London's Jewish population has been greatly underestimated. The political complexion of London Jewry is H. Srebrnik's subject in 'Communism and pro-Soviet feeling among the Jews of East London, 1935-45', *ibid.* The Communist victory in Stepney in the general election of 1945 is explained in part by the political events of the preceding 12 years, in part by the political affiliations of working-class Eastern European Jews in other countries. A similarly urban-based study of the marked subsequent swing to the Conservative Party among British Jews would make a useful counterpoint to this study. Such complexity is emphasized in R. Swift's survey of 'The outcast Irish in the British Victorian city: problems and perspectives', *Irish Historical Stus.*, xxv (1987). Recent research has suggested that this group's increasing social and political adaptation occurred within an Irish framework more 'in' than 'of' its British location. It has also questioned the depressive effect of the Irish on urban wages, the extent of the immigrants' Catholicism and the depth of the 'racial' prejudice directed against them.

Prejudice is usually too mild a term for the discrimination which prevails when, as in the United States, the urban group in question differs by colour from the 'host' population. This is not to say that the dominant group has an untroubled existence. For example, city slaves caused Southern leaders considerable anxiety before the Civil War. In 'Quantitative sources for studying urban industrial slavery in the antebellum US South', *Immigrants and Minorities*, v (1986), R. D. Green uses a manufacturing census to prove that these elites had cause for worry: the especially volatile category of hired slave formed a majority of Richmond's tobacco workers. Yet the subsequent 'War Between the States' brought remarkably little alteration to the social structure of the urban South, as C. A. Haulman points out in 'Changes in wealth holding in Richmond, Virginia, 1860–1870', *J. Urban History*, xiii (1986). Despite a rate of turnover in top economic families much more rapid than before the Civil War, the 'nobs' of 1870 closely resembled their counterparts of a decade earlier in origins, occupations and economic interests.

By the turn of the century the urban as well as the rural South had countered emancipation with segregation. Its origins are illuminated by J. Roback, 'The political economy of segregation: the case of segregated streetcars', *J. Economic History*, xlvi (1986), a study of various Southern cities. Segregation laws went well beyond existing practice and were not the result of agitation either by the streetcar companies or by the average white passenger. Yet frequently such statutes preempted even more drastic forms of white supremacy. In this unpromising setting blacks sometimes managed to launch successful businesses. A. B. Henderson chronicles a notable example in 'Herman E. Perry and black enterprise in Atlanta, 1905–1925', *Business History Rev.*, lxi (1987). Perry ultimately went bankrupt, but his achievements in sectors such as insurance and banking helped lay the foundations for a large black business community in Atlanta. Still, the social and political as well as the racial structures of Southern cities proved surprisingly durable. Despite claims for the 'modernizing' impact of the New Deal, its effects remained 'essentially ... cosmetic', according to R. Biles, 'The persistence of the past: Memphis in the Great Depression', *J. Southern History*, LII (1986), which notes the survival of the city's 'rural' character. Further evidence of social backwardness in Southern cities is provided by R. J. Norrell's 'Caste in steel: Jim Crow careers in Birmingham, Alabama', *J. American History*, LXXIII (1986). In Birmingham, as in other cities, white workers used trade unions to push black workers out of desirable jobs.

The partially economic roots of such segregation link America to South Africa, as Norrell notes. A special number (XII.1) of *J. Historical Geography* (1986) success-fully relates South Africa's racially skewed urban structure to its economic and social development. In 'Labour, capital, class struggle and the origins of residential segregation in Kimberley, 1880–1920', A. Mabin argues that strict separation between white and black workers at home as well as on the job resulted from the capital-labour struggle. J. Crush notes in 'Swazi migrant workers and the Witwatersrand gold mines 1886–1920' that the mining revolution brought an 'irreversible fusion of town and countryside'. G. H. Pirie observes in 'Johannesburg transport 1905–1945: African capitulation and resistance' that poor and expensive travel facilities imposed a heavy burden on blacks while making viable both residential segregation and secure control of the workforce. Such unequal cities even neglected the most basic services for their racially-defined underclass, as C. M. Rogerson points out in 'Feeding the common people of Johannesburg, 1930–1962', an account of the white city government's successful war against coffee cart traders.

For many urban historians, 'segregation' continues to refer mainly to the geographical separation of urban social groups in a largely homogeneous ethnic context. B. Sanford usefully injects class into discussions of social segregation while challenging ecological assumptions about urban growth in her neo-Marxian study, 'The political economy of land development in nineteenth-century Toronto', *Urban History Rev.*, XVI (1987). Focusing on the period to 1881, Sanford is on the whole convincing, if monocausal, in concluding that 'Toronto's social geography has historically been shaped by those with the power, wealth and position to protect and to promote their own class interests.' Using several indirect quantitative measures, D. R. Green provides an unusually early date for sharp residential polarization of rich and poor in Britain's metropolis in 'A map for Mayhew's London: the geography of poverty in the mid-nineteenth century', *London J.*, XI (1985). Residential stability was especially marked in well-off areas. The better-known social separation of the late nineteenth century is the subject of W. E. Marsden's 'Residential segregation and the hierarchy of elementary schooling from Charles Booth's London surveys', *ibid*. Displaying much subtlety in classi-fication, Booth's surveys showed great variations in need within London and indicated 'the links between residentially segregated communities and the hierarchical system of elementary schooling which faithfully reflected the social divisions'.

The extent to which poverty varied by locality and period has drawn the attention of several recent studies. E. P. Hennock traces the evolution of the methodology underlying modern investigations in 'The measurement of urban poverty: from the metropolis to the nation, 1880–1920', *Economic History Rev.*, 2nd ser., XL (1987). Whereas Booth shifted attention from the East End to London as a whole, Rowntree reflected a prevailing change of focus in his desire to measure poverty in urban Britain generally. While Rowntree's methods were inadequate to the task, early this century the Board of Trade (through the systematic study of many communities) and A. L. Bowley (through sampling) developed techniques which illuminated both general patterns of poverty and variations within them.

Poverty often stemmed from unemployment, but measuring the latter has proved very difficult for historians. H. Southall uses the previously underexploited records of the Amalgamated Society of Engineers in 'Regional unemployment patterns among skilled engineers in Britain, 1851–1914', *J. Historical Geography*, XII (1986). Southall's use of such proxies for general unemployment at the level of the individual town may be problematical, but his regional maps seem more soundly based. They are also very interesting, suggesting that the industrial north and west had relatively high unemployment even before the First World War despite the (admittedly diminishing) superiority in wages they enjoyed, according to E. H. Hunt's 'Industrialization and regional inequality: wages in Britain, 1760–1914', *J. Economic History*, XLVIII (1986). B. Eichengreen attempts to throw light on national patterns by studying the metropolis in 'Unemployment in inter-war Britain: new evidence from London', *J. Interdisciplinary History*, XVII (1986). He discovers that joblessness was concentrated among those least able to cope: the very young, the old, the low-waged, the low-skilled, renters and families with children. Paid work for women was a common response to inter-war unemployment in London. In Glasgow, such workers were often relegated to very poorly paid and insecure jobs, as J. H. Treble notes in 'The characteristics of the female unskilled labour market and the formation of the female casual labour market in Glasgow, 1891–1914', *Scottish Economic and Social History*, VI (1986). On Clydeside the more general employment problems of women were exacerbated by the assumption that they would leave work when they married, an expectation that propelled many married women into the casual sector.

For the destitute there was, of course, poor relief. This year two studies illustrate the counterproductive obsessions of the urban British Poor Law. R. H. Crocker's 'The Victorian Poor Law in crisis and change: Southampton, 1870–1895', *Albion*, XIX (1987) indicates that the renewed attempt at strict enforcement had begun to collapse by the mid-1890s. For Crocker, this episode was 'the swan song of a Victorian Poor Law whose premises were already widely admitted to be obsolete'. Likewise, in Worcestershire, which had several urban Unions, attempts to establish a uniform system for treating vagrancy failed. As G. Matthews points out in 'The search for a cure for vagrancy in Worcestershire, 1870–1920', *Midland History*, XI (1986), the authorities were obsessed with symptoms rather than causes and at best diverted problems to neighbouring jurisdictions.

Scrutiny of attitudes to vagrancy allows J. S. Adler to observe the relationship between the pattern of urban growth and the nature of urban anxieties in 'Vagging the demons and scoundrels: vagrancy and the growth of St Louis, 1830–1861', *J. Urban History*, XIII (1986). Variations in rates of urban expansion altered the nature and perception of the 'dangerous class': in good times, urban worthies feared threats to economic vitality; in bad times they worried about disorder. Similarly, R. Tombs, 'Paris and the rural hordes: an exploration of myth and reality in the French civil war of 1871', *Historical J.*, XXIX (1986), shows how collective urban delusions (in this case the mistaken view that the Commune was besieged by rural Catholic reactionaries but would soon be relieved by allies representing the true allegiances of the provinces) can defuse class tensions within a city.

Can the actions and attitudes of urban elites promote social cohesion? C. Behagg attempts to remove a case frequently cited in the affirmative in 'Myths of cohesion: capital and compromise in the historiography of nineteenth-century Birmingham', *Social History*, XI (1986). Although both labour and capital projected images of social consensus, these were elements of their respective self-justifications; in fact their notions of reciprocity were in conflict. Behagg may well be correct that the 'consensus' interpretation of Birmingham's social history has unduly dominated the historical literature, but his own interpretation finds little support in C. Dellheim, 'The creation of a company culture: Cadbury's, 1861–1931', *American Historical Rev.*, XCII (1987). Although the firm had its social and economic problems, the Cadburys' Quaker-inspired worker benefits, company rituals and beautiful site promoted much labour-management co-operation. K. Burgess prefers to stress market forces rather than the specific strategies of employers in

'Authority relations and the division of labour in British industry, with special reference to Clydeside, c.1860–1930', *Social History*, XI (1986). Like Dellheim he has little time for M. J. Wiener's 'decline of the industrial spirit', preferring a regional perspective grounded in detailed social and economic research.

In recent years many writers have shown that Clydeside was not nearly so 'red' as was previously supposed. Such revisionism has not yet affected the home of Bolshevism, to judge from W. G. Rosenberg and D. P. Koenker's 'The limits of formal protest: worker activism and social polarization in Petrograd and Moscow, March to October, 1917', *American Historical Rev.*, XCII (1987). As the economy weakened, strikes evolved from ways of resolving labour-management conflict to methods of expressing deep alienation from the existing order. The American company town seems remote from such turbulence, but two recent studies suggest points of similarity. In Carnegie's industrial base, domination of the workplace did not produce secure control of the town, where radical political revolts occurred periodically, according to I. W. Marcus, J. Bullard and R. Moore's 'Change and continuity: steel workers in Homestead, Pennsylvania, 1889–1895', *Pennsylvania Mag. History and Biography*, CXI (1987). A similar locality elected a socialist mayor during a time of labour strife, as W. Scheuerman indicates in 'The politics of protest: the great steel strike of 1919–20 in Lackawanna, New York', *International Rev. Social History*, XXXI (1986). Ethnic divisions within the workforce handicapped but did not prevent political agitation.

California's cities long had especially united and radical labour movements, which were based on citywide labour federations relatively unaffected by ethnic and industrial divisions. Yet M. Kazin's 'The great exception revisited: organized labour and politics in San Francisco and Los Angeles, 1870–1940', *Pacific Historical Rev.*, LV (1986) shows that the emergence of large, multiracial industrial unions in the 1930s dictated dependence on the Democratic party and the end of united craft-centred radicalism. Since the Second World War organized labour in California has suffered more than its counterparts elsewhere from the mushrooming growth of the clerical and service sectors. The weakness of organized labour has been especially severe south of Los Angeles where even manufacturing industry, organized in small informal units, has had little unionization, as A. J. Scott points out in 'High technology industry and territorial development: the rise of the Orange County Complex, 1955–1984', *Urban Geography*, VII (1986). E. J. Malecki's partly critical 'Comments . . .', *ibid.*, VIII (1987), question whether Orange County is a discrete urban entity whose 'vertical disintegration' is the wave of the future. Yet the area's pattern of weak unions in the midst of sophisticated urban infrastructure has echoes across the Sunbelt.

Urban politics with significant social echoes both preceded and survived the classic age of trade unions. F. O'Gorman makes a major contribution to this topic in 'The unreformed electorate of Hanoverian England: the mid-eighteenth century to the Reform Act of 1832', *Social History*, XI (1986). Reminding his readers of the consensus regarding the moderate change wrought by the Great Reform Act, O'Gorman delineates a pre-1832 political system which had reasonably broad electorates, frequent contests, lively campaigns and issues involving local hierarchies if not national questions. O'Gorman acknowledges considerable local variation, a theme related to the uneven development of cities by M. C. Brown and C. N. Halaby in 'Machine politics in America, 1870–1945', *J. Interdisciplinary History*, XVII (1987), which attempts to systematize the mainly qualitative relevant work on 30 cities. Brown and Halaby make an important distinction between 'factional' and 'dominant' machines. They note that the conventional periodization of a late nineteenth-century rise and an early twentieth-century fall applies more to the former than the latter, which declined only from the 1930s.

The structures and styles of urban politics proved remarkably durable even in the ashes of Nazism, according to B. Marshall's study of 'The democratization of local politics in the British Zone of Germany: Hanover 1945–47', *J. Contemporary History*, XXI (1986). The occupiers concentrated on security rather than denazification; the Hanoverian Left was preoccupied with food and jobs in a devastated city which Allied bombing had reduced to less than half its pre-war population. In the Soviet Zone, considerable attention was subsequently devoted to urban symbolism, as M. Azaryahu shows in 'Street names and political identity: the case of East Berlin', *ibid.* The East German authorities continued the pre-1945 tradition of renaming roads, but some old names survived, reflecting the ambiguous identity of the GDR itself. A third investigation of the impact of central authoritarianism on urban local government emerges from B. O'Leary's 'Why was the GLC abolished?', *International J. Urban and Regional Research*, XI (1987). O'Leary provides little historical perspective in reaching his convincing conclusion that 'the government embarked upon a major initiative as an unintended and ill-considered byproduct of its other policies.' Yet his modes of policy analysis, which supplement standard administrative, political, ideological and class perspectives with social psychological insights, have much urban historical potential.

Central–local relations also pertain to that lively urban subject, law and order, as E. G. Spencer observes in 'State power and local interests in Prussian cities: police in the Düsseldorf District, 1848–1914', *Central European History*, XIX (1986). Prussia's desire to prevent disorder proved the key spur to the emergence of professional policing, and the state gave local elites little voice in police affairs. Local worthies eventually adjusted to this impotence. So too did the people of the City of Brotherly Love to the demise of a remarkably populist system of criminal justice which relied primarily on private prosecutions until the mid-nineteenth century. As A. Steinberg points out in 'The spirit of litigation: private prosecution and criminal justice in nineteenth-century Philadelphia', *J. Social History*, XX (1987), this system 'incorporated' citizens in law enforcement, presumably defusing many potential social conflicts. Far more controversy often surrounded professional judges, notably the man investigated by J. Eaton in '"Union smasher of the boss class"? The judgeship of John Bryn Roberts in Glamorgan, 1906–18', *Welsh History Rev.*, XIII (1986). This innovative examination of the origins and impact of judicial judgments in an urban context emphasizes the inherent difficulty of making well-received decisions in such a field. It also shows the extent to which the judge's unpopularity was a smokescreen for the weakness of local conciliation machinery. Over time Judge Roberts became more equitable; the same cannot be said for the Berlin police, as C. Bowlby demonstrates in 'Blutmai 1929: police, parties and proletarians in a Berlin confrontation', *Historical J.*, XXIX (1986). Police violence defied political control, yet the SPD was forced to defend this notable bloodletting, thereby further dividing the Left and weakening the Republic.

Another crucial urban service, education, has attracted three diverse recent studies. The progressive role of central and state rather than local government emerges from M. K. Vaughan's surprisingly upbeat 'Primary schooling in the city of Puebla, 1821–60', *Hispanic American Historical Rev.*, LXVII (1987), which notes the relatively good records of Mexico's larger cities. Yet the remarkable importation of the Lancaster teaching method into Mexico had mixed results. J. L. Tropea probes behind regulations to trace the 'backstage rules that guided urban school authorities in dealing with difficult pupils' in 'Bureaucratic order and special children: urban schools, 1890s–1940s', *History of Education Q.*, XXVII (1987). Focusing on Detroit, Tropea finds that rigid attendance laws forced the authorities to abandon expulsion of troublemakers in favour of lowered standards and segregation. Meanwhile, E. W. Jenkins discovers a high-quality but underfunded sphere of urban education in a case study with general implications, 'Junior technical schools, 1905–1945: the case of Leeds', *History of Education*, XVI (1987).

To judge from recent articles, religion may have meant more to nineteenth-century urban Britons than historians have often supposed. Admittedly C. G. Brown emphasizes social divisions and the decline of inner city churches in his trenchant analysis of 'The cost of pew-renting: church management, church-going and social class in nineteenth-century Glasgow', *J. Ecclesiastical History*, XXXVIII (1987). In the early nineteenth century the rapid rise in population and strong middle-class demand for sittings shattered durable arrangements for pan-class churchgoing. P. Hillis is more optimistic in 'Education and evangelisation: Presbyterian missions in mid-nineteenth century Glasgow', *Scottish Historical Rev.*, LXVI (1987). Although he acknowledges that many working-class members had at most a loose connection to their churches, his emphasis on the significant proportion of working-class members in some congregations accords well with H. McLeod's important general study, 'New perspectives on Victorian working class religion: the oral evidence', *Oral History*, XIV (1986). Focusing on major urban areas, McLeod argues that the churchgoing minority was larger, the impact of Christianity on occasional churchgoers greater, and the decline of the churches more gradual than has usually been argued.

Nevertheless, even the full acceptance of such revisionism could not obscure the increasing importance of secular leisure for Britain's urban working class. S. Farrant suggests that an altering relationship with London dominated changes in Sussex seaside towns in her 'London by the sea: resort development on the South coast of England 1880–1939', *J. Contemporary History*, XXII (1987). Local government began to take a larger role as populist and informal, as well as exclusive and planned, resorts proliferated. S. G. Jones places leisure firmly in a general social and economic context in 'Work, leisure and the political economy of the cotton districts between the wars', *Textile History*, XVIII (1987). The state of the cotton trade dictated the amount of holiday savings; hours reductions made more holiday time available; and the mills continued to play a large role in providing and shaping leisure activities.

Jones concludes with a call for town-based studies of leisure. This advice would not please L. Colley, who laments the 'scholarly pointillism' of urban history in her magisterial article, 'Whose nation? Class and national consciousness in Britain 1750–1830', *Past & Present*, CXIII (1986). In Britain, she argues persuasively, class and nation were 'two sides of the same historical process': the working and middle classes used patriotism for their own ends. This is historical writing at its best. Yet Colley's equation of urban history with local studies of the powerless ignores the recent tendency (represented in medieval and early modern as well as modern articles) to analyse elites, wealth and power. Likewise, her assumption that studies of small units are devoid of wider implications is belied by much of the recent writing in urban history surveyed above, even in a year perhaps less sparkling than usual.

Yet this defence of urban history is special pleading. An objective verdict on the current state of the field, as on the present condition of the Review of Periodical Articles, must be left to the reader.

# Research in urban history: a review of recent theses

compiled by David Reeder

The annual number of completed theses which can be reasonably described as having urban themes has remained quite steady in recent years. In the lists of the Institute of Historical Research, for example, it is possible to identify 58 theses as having urban themes in the return for 1985, 41 theses in the 1986 return and 50 theses in that for 1987. It is true that in many cases such theses are not written as contributions to urban history specifically, but nevertheless they can provide much useful information and new insights on urban processes and town life even when the urban aspect of the study is incidental to the main theme. This is especially true of the selection made for this year's review which focuses more than usually on theses concerned directly or indirectly with aspects of urban society and politics in the past, and with a particular emphasis on the history of the urban working class. The review covers mostly theses completed in 1986–7 with some late additions from earlier years. It is based necessarily on the abstracts except for about a third of the theses noticed where it has been possible to examine the text. However, the aim of the review is to indicate the interest which a thesis might have for urban historians rather than to give a comprehensive assessment – which is probably inappropriate for unpublished work.

The review starts by noting two very different approaches to studying the physical development of towns in the past before going on to the social and political themes. It begins with a carefully controlled but rather narrowly devised study of the topography of an industrial landscape which may provide useful illustrative material for urban historical geographers. This is N. MUSTO, 'The role of the "company town" in urban settlement in Britain. An investigation into the influence of entrepreneurial provision of housing and amenities on the evolution of urban morphology. A case study of Halifax parish in the nineteenth century' (Ph. D., University of Southampton, 1985). The thesis is concerned essentially with explaining the patterns of development in a parish characterized by the number and diversity of industrial settlements in the nineteenth century, and proceeds by testing out some quite specific hypotheses about this type of urban development, including the significance of the investment in housing of surplus business capital. It discusses the pattern of settlement in terms of nucleated centres of growth, despite the influence and importance of Halifax, considers the road and street layout, examines the quality and type of housing provided and looks at the spatial relations between houses and mills. Among other points made, the author finds that the availability of business capital was associated with attempts by developers to raise housing standards, and in several cases the developers showed interesting design concepts. However, the intense individualism of entrepreneurs made for heterogeneity. The topography of the land and its availability for purchase were decisive in explaining the housing patterns and there was little intermingling of houses of different sizes.

In contrast to the latter's single parish study, MICHAEL TURNER's thesis, 'The nature of urban renewal after fires in seven English provincial towns, c.1675–1810' (Ph.D., University of Exeter, 1985), is dependent on a series of case studies. He thereby contributes substantially to the growing recognition of the importance in this period of changes transforming older town centres as well as the rise of new towns. Turner sees the outbreak of fire as a major, almost structural feature of urban society in the seventeenth and eighteenth centuries, not merely a one-off event of importance chiefly in the London context, but as something which repeatedly ravaged almost all towns in the early-modern period. His well-documented and thoroughgoing thesis is concerned centrally with asking how towns managed to contain the problem eventually and channel its impact to positive ends. Thus he is concerned not simply with the incidence of fires but with the timing and nature of rebuilding acts, the use of new materials and other building innovations, street improvements, and related matters, ending up with some thoughts on the relations between fire renewal and urban renewal, including the development of a model to account for these.

Another thesis rooted in the urban world of the country towns, and which provides an entrée into it, is not a town study as such but a carefully edited version of the diary of a prosperous Suffolk yarn-maker turned banker complete with explanatory notes and appendices. This is P. J. FISKE, 'The diary of a country banker: James Oakes 1778–1827' (Ph.D., University of East Anglia, 1987). Presented in three volumes, the first of these is represented simply as an introduction to the diary but in fact could stand on its own as an examination of the business and social world in which Oakes operated. It is meticulously documented, using a wide range of primary material in addition to the voluminous diary to build up a picture of Oakes's life and to place his activities in a national context. Indeed the combination of firmly analytical, academic context with the vigorous individuality of James Oakes himself is one of this study's greatest strengths. Chapter 2, for example, relates Oakes's career as a yarn-merchant to the general prosperity of the Suffolk yarn industry at this time and suggests reasons for its rapid decline after the 1780s. Chapters 3 and 4, which cover his activities in banking and in local politics, adopt an equally comprehensive approach. The most striking elements of both thesis and diary, however, relate to their detailed depiction of the world of Bury's social elite, both inside and outside the immediate family circle. Bury 'society' is revealed as a relaxed and open elite, a harmonious mixture of local nobility and urban tradesmen, who nevertheless exhibited a passion for maintaining the fine distinctions of social life. As Joyce Ellis asks in her report on this thesis, a classic case of English compromise?

The role of dissent in the social and cultural world of English urban life is now well understood, but in Belfast, the capital of Presbyterianism in Ireland, a process of social aggrandizement can be traced back to the seventeenth-century when the Presbyterians first achieved a decisive majority in the local population. J. NESON's concern in 'The Belfast Presbyterians, 1670–1830: an analysis of their political and social interests' (Ph.D., Queen's University, 1985) is essentially to explain the coherence of this community over so many years. His answer provides some clues to the Protestant outlook in Northern Ireland. He points out that strength and unity had to be recreated after a period of adversity when Protestants were excluded from the corporation and beset with theological disputes. This was done interestingly through charitable activity, social work and the volunteer movement, and despite some faltering over theological matters, the sense of unity proved greater than the many divisive factors

RUTH WATTS remedies a neglected aspect of English urban dissent in 'The Unitarian contribution to education in England from the late eighteenth century to 1853' (Ph.D., University of Leicester, 1987). This is a balanced account noteworthy for the way she traces the interconnections between Unitarian families and groups and uncovers their influence in a wide range of educational ventures from infant schools through to higher education. She demonstrates the centrality of education to the moral and religious outlook of Unitarians, noting the consistent and determinedly aggressive propagation for both male and female of a modern, liberal, rational and scientific education. However, despite much remarkable work it seems that the success of the Unitarians was limited by external factors and internal contradictions. They could not solve the problems of middle-class education on their own and their efforts to provide for the education of the poor were influenced by their own economic and class position as well as a generally humanitarian outlook.

Historians of rescue work in Victorian Britain have focused on the reclamation of prostitutes as an area which illustrates particularly well the tensions between middle-class ideology, as exhibited by the rescue workers and their organizations, and the experience of working-class women. GILLIAN BALL contributes to the historiographical development of this subject in 'Practical religion: a study of the Salvation Army's social services for women 1884–1914' (Ph.D., University of Leicester, 1987). She identifies the two principal themes of recent work as being the appropriateness of viewing rescue work as a form of social control, or as an inspiration for feminism. However, the justification for her approach in this thesis is that no rescue society has been studied in depth, and consequently the relationship between theory and practice has not been documented. Her carefully worked out and perceptive study of one of the largest and most prominent rescue work agencies in late-Victorian London adds to our understanding both of the development of a theory of social service, bringing out the way in which it redefined gender and class relationships, and of the social and practical significance of this kind of city social work for women and girls. In addition to the account of Booth's ideas and the organizational development of the Army's Social Services for Women, she deals also with the problematical relationship between rescue work and the social purity movement. But perhaps the most interesting feature of her study is the investigation of the 'rescued' – their social and economic support networks and their progress in the rescue homes – through an analysis of 1,500 case histories drawn from three different periods. This enables her to highlight a contrast between the limitations of the religious perspective and the practical context of the social programme which Booth embarked upon, in assessing its role and value in late-Victorian Britain.

This last attempt to focus on those who were the subjects of middle-class ministrations as people in their own right characterizes recent work also in the history of education. ALYSON ANDREW, for example, is concerned with bringing out the active and positive involvement of working-class people in education and schooling rather than seeing them as people for whom provision had to be made. Her locally based study, 'The working class and education in Preston 1830–1870: a study in social relations (Ph.D., University of Leicester, 1987), explores the attitudes and perceptions of working-class people. It marks an important change of direction from the older history of working-class relations to education which was concerned largely with the history of labour movements. A noteworthy feature of the thesis is the extended treatment of what A. E. Dobbs once called 'an education by collision' whereby she not only explores how education was defined in and through labour organizations and movements but how in a broad sense these movements provided educational experiences themselves. She also explores the quality of children's schooling in the period and tries to probe the ambiguities and tensions in parental attitudes in so far as this is possible to do. A final chapter draws attention to the complications of gender relations in a discussion of the attitudes of working-class women towards education both for themselves and for their own children.

Social historians are beginning to recognize that the history of school attendance can provide a significant indicator of class and community relations in various localities – thanks to the efforts of new research of which that by CATHERINE G. ELLIOTT on 'The school and the family: patterns of educational interaction in four communities, 1861–1891' (D.Phil., University of Oxford, 1986) is a thoroughgoing and innovative example. The thesis is concerned with the nature of the public response to the provision of elementary schools, mainly in the crucial decade for school attendance of the 1870s, and in respect of the experience of four contrasting communities – three villages and a small town in Oxfordshire, the northern industrial town of Northwich, and the London district of Lisson Grove. The assessment is based on trying to understand the reality of the school experience, utilizing a range of quantitative and qualitative research methods. It takes the view as a starting point that for the majority of people, public elementary education entailed a continuing compromise between the values and interests of the family and the school, with the latter representing in many cases disputed territory between parents and teachers. The core of the work is a set of sample statistics drawn from the censuses of 1871 and 1881 and 'matched' against school attendance records. These inform the account of the demographic and socio-economic characteristics of the local case studies and the discussion of restraints on family choice. Children's work and career prospects are also examined. Further chapters identify and explore areas of contention between school and family, and the reasons for friction – paying attention to the perceptions and characteristics of teachers – and also areas of negotiation – taking account of what is described as the 'common ground' and assessing parental responses to local school initiatives. The picture that emerges, needless to say, is one of great variation and complexity throughout the period in all these respects.

Another thesis to draw on family history in what seems to be a rewarding way, in so far as one can tell from the abstract, based in this instance on a single case study and concerned essentially with a demographic argument, is KARL ERIC ILLMAN, '"The Manufactory of Men"; work, society and family life in Bradford, West Yorkshire, 1851–1881' (Ph.D., University of Pennsylvania, 1987). This thesis is concerned with the so-called 'demographic revolution', namely the timing and reasons for the decline of marital fertility among the working-class. The place chosen for this study is not merely a convenient location, but as it turns out, forms a crucial social context for demographic change. Part of the thesis is taken up with reconstructing overall and age-specific patterns of marital fertility based on samples taken from the four censuses between 1851 and 1881. These serve to show that a decline in marital fertility did indeed begin in Bradford in the nineteenth century, as early as the decade of the 1870s, and that decline began among women above the age of 30. However, the wider interest of the thesis derives from the attempt to document the social context of fertility decline, focusing on the interaction between the family economy, the socio-economic structure and the new working-class culture that began to emerge after 1850. This approach is predicated on the view that a need for security had coloured the development of social life in Bradford over the mid-Victorian period but this became more acute with the depression in the worsted trade after 1873 leading to new pressures, economic and psychological, on the working-class family. Fertility control, it is argued, was one of a number of strategies to survive in an increasingly hostile environment.

It is a bit unnerving, nevertheless, that in this last thesis, as in other social history, quite basic assumptions have to be made about patterns of working-class family life when there are still so few detailed studies available for comparing the impact of change in a more all-round way. Michael Anderson's work on family and kinship in mid-Victorian Preston has been virtually all we have had to go on and as Anderson recognized, there are questions to be answered about how far his findings and interpretation were representative only of the impact of a specific kind of factory-based industrialization. Fortunately this situation is beginning to be remedied with Marguerite Dupree's recent work on the Potteries and now by another challenging thesis, from MARTIN A. CLARKE, 'Household and family in Bethnal Green, 1851–71: the effects of social and economic change' (D.Phil., University of Oxford, 1986). The location of Bethnal Green is intriguing given its importance in the historiography of working-class urban culture and the seeming paradox, as Clarke maintains, of a district whose community relations in the 1940s as represented in Young and Willmott's well-known survey appear at least superficially to be the antithesis of that calculative instrumentality which Anderson regarded as forming the basic of relationships in mid-Victorian Preston. Did this represent a genuine shift in the pattern of urban working-class family life since the 1850s, or was post-war Bethnal Green a legacy of a very different type of community from the factory town of Preston? Clarke goes back to the census enumerators' books for sample data on the district as a whole for 1851 and 1871 and also constructs family histories for a smaller area. These sources, along with other contemporary materials of a qualitative kind, form a basis for his discussion of the socio-economic characteristics of the district, migration and mobility patterns, the structures of household and family at the two census dates, and residential stability. There is also a chapter of a rather different kind on what he calls the content of relationships. It turns out that Bethnal Green at this time was indeed a distinctive type of urban community in which the effects of economic and social change on family forms and behaviour were rather muted. However, Clarke's ambition to make sense of these findings in relation to the wider historical debate about the impact of urbanization on family and community life leads him into further comparisons based on the analysis of sample census statistics. Thus he replicates Anderson's study of rural villages, adds to it with a study of the town of Sudbury in Suffolk, and deals more directly with the influence of occupation in respect of silk-weavers in both Bethnal Green and Sudbury. All of which leads to the conclusion that Bethnal Green had little in common with Preston in this period and more in common with the more proletarianized parts of mid-Victorian Suffolk. He does not hesitate to point up the wider significance of this finding in emphasizing that the interrelationship of family and social change was much more complex than any simple antithesis of urban/industrial versus rural/agrarian allows. He is not the first historian of the family to be critical of the urban/rural dichotomy but there can be little doubt that his research and arguments merit serious attention.

Another thesis dealing with the East End can be rather belatedly noticed at this point as offering a new geographically-based analysis of the more familiar themes of poverty and the emergence of two Londons. This is DAVID R. GREEN, 'From artisans to paupers: the manufacture of poverty in mid-nineteenth-century London' (Ph.D., University of Cambridge, 1984). The title gives a clue to the nature of this study which is concerned with analysing the longer-term processes that lay behind the deepening in East End poverty during the key formative period of the first half of the nineteenth century. Thus the thesis starts by examining the material basis for the emergence of East London as a poverty district with an analysis of how changes in the metropolitan economy affected the London trades. This analysis deals with the relations between economic imperatives and labour organization and discusses how far workers in different trades were able to defend customary practices and maintain levels of skill in the face of various cost-cutting strategies on the part of manufacturers. From this the author is able to underline the emergence of a crucial distinction between 'honourable' and 'dishonourable' sectors in the London trades, a distinction which is then shown to be 'eminently geographical' in the sense of underlying the development of what is described as two distinctive regional economies in London associated with the East and West ends. The long-term conditions, David Green goes on to explain, help also to account for the dimensions of the crisis of pauperism as economic and geographical developments undermined the fiscal ability of the poor law authorities to cope with cyclical and seasonal distress. More importantly, these conditions account for the geographical stability of poverty over the nineteenth century such that the patterns evinced by Booth later on showed a remarkable congruence with those established for mid-century by the author of this thesis. Whilst there is nothing in the findings of this work that will surprise, it does offer a more precise analysis than has been attempted before of the geographical pattern of poverty in mid-Victorian London based on a range of social indicators, and in the context of an elegantly constructed argument relating this pattern to structural changes in the metropolitan economy in the context of economic power and cultural traditions. This brief summary may serve to indicate, therefore, how this thesis illustrates the widening horizons of historical geographers by seeking to develop a wide-ranging explanation of the inequality in the distribution of resources so characteristic of Victorian London.

As if that were not enough to digest, we also now have available new studies on the cultural life of the English urban working-class. CARL CHINN dissects the alleged cultural schism in working-class urban society in the late-Victorian and

Edwardian period in 'The anatomy of a working-class neighbourhood: West Sparkbrook 1870–1914' (Ph.D., University of Birmingham, 1987). The thesis starts from the premise that during this period a significant and influential division opened up within the working-class in this district as elsewhere in urban England, based initially on economic differences, allied with residential segregation, whose members pursued in many ways quite different ways of life. The thesis is structured so as to explore this proposition in terms of the institutions, habits and behaviour of the working-class people of the district, utilizing documentary, archival and oral evidence to examine differences in housing, schooling, working and shopping, and attitudes to drink, gambling and fighting. There are also chapters dealing with family life and the role of women, residential stability, leisure behaviour, and the work of religious and charitable institutions in the neighbourhood. Although mainly descriptive, the study contains some useful statistical evidence and interesting comparative analyses, as for example, the extended treatment of the incidence and regularity of attendance at the local board schools in terms of catchment areas and with comparisons between children from different streets and social groups, including shopkeepers. It would require, however, a much closer inspection of this thesis than has been possible to judge how successfully it identifies and deals with cultural differences in terms of two broad categories. The author's claim is that his study enables us to have a clearer idea of the limits imposed on behaviour by notions of 'rough' and 'respectable', and the extent to which these were developed by each group within its specific social, economic and cultural environment.

London's immigrant Jewish workers have represented a rather awkward element within the historiography of the working-class. The reason for this is made clear in a new and revealing scrutiny of Jewish East End workers in DAVID M. FELDMAN, 'Immigrants and workers. Englishmen and Jews: Jewish migration to the East End of London, 1880–1906' (Ph.D., University of Cambridge, 1987). Despite the historical attention lavished on the Jewish East End this new study seems entirely justified by reason of its revisionist and broadly based approach. David Feldman does not find any of the existing accounts entirely satisfactory and some he regards as being misguided. Hence the underlying aim of this ambitious thesis is to investigate and conceptualize the methodological problems of writing the history of the Jewish working class. He is determined moreover that the Jewish worker should not be relegated to a ghetto of Jewish history and works hard to show how the complexities he sets out to reveal have a significance to the wider history of the working class, and above all to an understanding of the unorganized majority within it. What he provides in effect is a study of the politics of cultural change, focusing on the characteristics of Jewish working-class settlement in the East End, particularly in regard to political developments, before going on to examine how attitudes towards the settlers as workers and Jews were formed and implemented in social and cultural policies. A feature of the thesis is the way it probes English attitudes towards Jewish workers: the author tries to understand the stereotypes and get rid of the demonology associated with the history of anti-alien sentiment, which at the level of popular politics and culture is regarded as having been the occasion for an assertion of Englishness that crossed class boundaries – a manifestation of a patriotism that was one facet of an independent working-class culture in London. This view of the social background to immigration policy forms a bridge for entering on a study of the process of cultural change in terms of different programmes of Anglicanization, involving competing ideals, on the part of groups with greatly unequal financial and political resources. On the one hand, Feldman provides a dynamic picture of a powerful Anglo-Jewish elite mediating relations between immigrants, the state, public opinion in general and social policy in particular; and, on the other hand, he shows how revolutionary socialism in the Jewish East End became a force for the progressive reform of Jewish migrant habits and patterns of thought, while also rejecting capitalist relations. The point being, as the author explains, that Anglicanization did not follow a pre-determined course of adaptation but involved a resistance on the part of the Jewish East End to the attempts by Anglo-Jewry to mould its cultural and political development. Even on a brief reading, it is possible to recognize the interest and wider relevance of a thesis that seems to be offering an alternative to those views of the process of cultural change which, in the authors's terms, are needlessly deterministic or dependent on assumptions about a unity of culture which in fact did not exist.

At first sight, the next thesis – a study of the new service industry and leisure-time pursuit of boxing in late-Victorian and Edwardian London – seems likely to offer but an oblique light on working-class cultural development. But for S. A. SHIPLEY, boxing not only provides a way into some of the larger themes of the social history of sport but directly illuminates several aspects of working-class life in London in this period. The key argument in 'The boxer as hero: a study of social class, community and the professionalization of sport in London 1890–1905' (Ph.D., University of London, 1987), is that boxing became a central and creative part of working-class culture. With the demise of prize fighting and the disappearance of the gentleman amateur, the locus of the sport moved from the National Sporting Club in the West End to the Wonderland and other centres in the East End, and in no time at all a boxing culture was flourishing and extending into working-class life. The study begins therefore with a discussion of the reasons for this transformation, traces out the ways that boxing was professionalized and promoted in London's working-class districts and shows how boxing as a popular pastime was encouraged and facilitated in polytechnics, workingmen's clubs and above all the boys' clubs of the period. There is in truth more to this rather sprawling thesis than a disquisition on boxing and digressions are made to comment on various aspects of working-class leisure institutions and behaviour and an argument emerges about the role of popular boxing in the small halls of East London in the community life of the working-class, leading on to a discussion of the connections between boxing and the labour movement. While the thesis is concerned to explore what went on outside the ring, there is also much evocative oral evidence to recall the excitements and rituals of the Edwardian boxing scene.

Compared with this foray into the interstices of working-class cultural life, JOHN W. MARRIOTT's local study of urban political development in London seems almost traditional despite its fashionable intellectual theme. This is 'London over the border: a study of West Ham during rapid growth, 1840–1910' (Ph.D., University of Cambridge, 1984) which shares with Feldman's study the laudable aim of overcoming the theoretical difficulties of historians of working-class movements influenced by overly reductionist or determinist approaches. What Marriott suggests, however, is that the potential of an alternative, broadly Gramscian approach to ideology and politics should be more deliberately explored than hitherto in this kind of historical analysis. This is not the place to assess the generalized structural arguments of his thesis or indeed to make any judgements about how far the theoretical rationale has been carried through, which would demand a more careful reading than can be given. But it is worth noting that the thesis is organized in quite a straightforward descriptive way despite its theoretical ambitions. After a preliminary section on aspects of growth, with detailed chapters on industry and population, it goes into a narrative account of historical phases in working-class political activity (or in the author's phrase, the growth of political culture) – the pre-industrial environment, the prolonged period of political passivity during the first stage of growth, and the emergence and subsequent decline of an oppositional working-class political culture. Historians of labour will be especially interested in the account of the growth of labour organization in a district which was probably the site for the birth of modern trade unionism, as also in his thoroughgoing analysis of the problems of labour in municipal power and the way they were ousted.

Another way of bringing out the complexities in the history of labour movements is by means of a comparative approach and it may be worth noting, albeit belatedly, the work done on urban working-class movements in Europe by KARL JAMES

STRIKWERDA, 'Urban structure, religion and language: Belgian workers, 1880–1914' (Doct. Diss., University of Michigan, 1983). Despite common concerns, socialists in the three cities examined adopted very different tactics. Thus in Ghent socialist textile workers drew together unskilled and skilled workers in a network of co-operatives, unions and insurance societies, but in Brussels, by contrast, socialist craft unions refused to organize unskilled workers, and in Liège, socialist miners' and metallurgists' unions remained weak and fragmented. The position was further complicated by the way that democratic Catholicism emerged along with socialism, and often antagonistically, as new kinds of working-class movements. Catholics in Ghent and Brussels organized a progressive workers' movement to compete with the socialists with Catholic unions drawing heavily upon Flemish linguistic nationalism to recruit workers. Just before the First World War, in part responding to the Catholics, socialists in Brussels transformed their craft unions into much larger industrial unions. In Liège, however, Catholic paternalism prevented a true Catholic workers' movement from emerging, leading eventually to the gap being filled with the emergence of large socialist unions, in part inspired by syndicalist ideas. The thesis demonstrates therefore that although labour history has often focused on the creation of working-class solidarity, the Belgian experience shows how regional and national movements were built up out of the competing economic, linguistic, and religious interests of workers.

Returning to England and the municipal history of labour in late-Victorian and Edwardian England, reference should be made to a thesis which takes up the labour question in a fresh way as a touchstone for an evaluation of the London County Council as a progressive force in pre-1914 London. In 'The "Labour Question" and the London County Council' (D.Phil., University of Oxford, (1986), SUSAN D. PENNYBACKER examines the perceptions of those principally involved with the LCC through the avenue of employment, explores the Council's response to challenges to becoming a force for enlightenment and social transformation through a model approach to labour policy and analyses this and other projects undertaken by the LCC in relation to the problems of administration and the changing political scene. As the abstract makes clear, this results in three subjects or themes being studied, each of them dealt with in relation to the relevant social context. The first of these concerns the clerical workers employed by the LCC, presented as a study of the problem of the lower middle class in labour history, with material on conditions of work and labour organization. Secondly there is the account of the experiment in direct labour undertaken in the creation of the LCC Works Dept. under the Progressives. This experiment is placed in the context of a contemporary debate about fair wages and public employment, and the reasons for the political animosity which it generated are examined, a subject linked to the wider issue of the controversial nature and divisive effect of the Council's 'cultural programme'. A point is also made of how the representatives of the LCC staff became increasingly militant in their response to Council labour policy during the First World War. This links in with the subject of the changing mood and tone of Council politics, with the author showing how the optimistic pre-war spirit of Progressivism and the municipal socialist vision for labour tended to be superseded by a more moderate and 'realistic' perspective.

Finally, a belated report on a thesis about the nature of local government in the Medway towns, in marked contrast to the pragmatic character of the previous thesis, but one which can be picked out for the way it brings history to the service of theory rather than vice versa. This is S. SIMON, 'A political economy of urbanization and state structure: urban and industrial change in two selected areas' (Ph.D., University of Kent, 1984). The thesis is concerned to examine critically the proposition that the provision of urban goods and services, and the day-to-day contemporary power relationship between business enterprises and local government, is 'functional to capital'. To put it bluntly the author finds this to be something of a myth for recent times. In any case the proposition begs a series of historical questions, he argues, over the development of local government, the arbitration of capitalist interests and indeed about the evolution of urban sociological theory itself. This is his justification for attempting to elaborate a three-stage political economy of urban politics and service provision. The period-ization involves (1) early domination of local authorities by essentially reactionary oligarchies of 'competitive' capitalists, (2) a struggle for ascendancy by a distinct group of progressive 'monopoly' capitalists, leading to (3) the eclipse of local business elites and the 'advanced' consolidation of the powers of local government over all social interests in urban politics. The transition to the autonomous state in urban planning is then studied more empirically in relation to the history of local government in the Medway towns, ending up with the conclusion that urban planning today often bears no relationship to locally observable business interests and articulated demands. Whatever may be thought of this somewhat provocative argument, or of the model of changing relations between local government and local business interests, it is encouraging to find history accorded such an emphatic place in modern political economy, As the author's abstract concludes, the tendency amongst local authorities to 'plough their own fields' is best understood by reference to transformations in urban politics at between 50 and 110 years ago.

# Current bibliography of urban history

compiled by Diana Dixon and Nicholas Wilson

This bibliography is a continuation of and a complement to those published in *UHY* 1974–87. It aims to provide as comprehensive a coverage of recently published British books as possible. The material is augmented by scanning a wide range of periodicals and by the selections of material sent by our foreign correspondents. We are extremely grateful to them all for the valuable contribution they make. This year we are particularly indebted to Monsieur Pierre Costa (France), Dr Elizabeth Bloomfield (Canada), Dr G–M Van der Waal (South Africa), Dr Alan Mayne (Australia), Dr David Reeder (periodicals) and Mrs Jill Voyce. We are aware that every year some relevant items are overlooked and wherever possible we try to incorporate them in later years. We hope that the compilers will be notified of omissions so that deficiencies in coverage can be remedied.

The arrangement and format follows that of previous years. Cross-references are provided wherever necessary and there is an index of towns on pp 168–70.

**Outline of the classification**

**I GENERAL**
RESEARCH METHODS, AIDS AND MATERIALS
URBAN HISTORY – DEFINITIONS AND HISTORIOGRAPHY
URBANIZATION AND THE GROWTH AND FORTUNES OF TOWNS
EMPIRICAL STUDIES OF TOWN GROWTH
HISTORY AND FORTUNES OF INDIVIDUAL TOWNS
PORTRAITS OF TOWNS – LITERARY, PHOTOGRAPHIC AND GRAPHIC

**II POPULATION**
RESEARCH METHODS, AIDS AND MATERIALS
GENERAL FEATURES OF URBAN POPULATIONS
NATALITY AND MORTALITY
DISEASE
MEDICINE
MIGRATION TO, FROM AND BETWEEN TOWNS
FAMILY AND HOUSEHOLD STRUCTURE

**III PHYSICAL STRUCTURE**
RESEARCH METHODS, AIDS AND MATERIALS
PHYSICAL AND STRUCTURAL CHARACTERISTICS OF TOWNS
PHYSICAL AND STRUCTURAL CHARACTERISTICS OF AREAS WITHIN TOWNS
SITES AND BUILDINGS
HOUSING
ENVIRONMENTAL CONDITIONS

**IV SOCIAL STRUCTURE**
RESEARCH METHODS, AIDS AND MATERIALS
SOCIAL STRUCTURE AND CHARACTERISTICS OF TOWNS
SOCIAL STRUCTURE AND CHARACTERISTICS OF AREAS WITHIN TOWNS
SOCIAL ORGANIZATIONS, CLUBS AND SOCIETIES
CLASS STRUCTURE
SOCIAL LIFE
SOCIAL PROBLEMS AND DEVIANCE
SOCIAL REFORM AND IMPROVEMENT
MINORITY GROUPS
WOMEN

# V ECONOMIC ACTIVITY
**RESEARCH METHODS, AIDS AND MATERIALS**
**URBAN ECONOMIC ACTIVITY**
**INDUSTRY**
**EXTERNAL TRADE**
**INTERNAL TRADE AND SERVICES**
**CONSUMPTION**
**WORKING CONDITIONS**
**LABOUR ORGANIZATION**

# VI COMMUNICATIONS
**MODES OF INTER-URBAN COMMUNICATIONS**
**MODES OF INTRA-URBAN COMMUNICATIONS**

# VII POLITICS AND ADMINISTRATION
**RESEARCH METHODS, AIDS AND MATERIALS**
**URBAN POLITICS AND ADMINISTRATION**
**URBAN POLITICS AT NATIONAL LEVEL**
**ASPECTS OF URBAN ADMINISTRATION**
**PUBLIC UTILITIES**

# VIII SHAPING THE URBAN ENVIRONMENT
**RESEARCH METHODS, AIDS AND MATERIALS**
**TOWN PLANNING AND ENVIRONMENTAL CONTROL**
**HOUSING IMPROVEMENT**
**NEW AND EXPANDED TOWNS**

# IX URBAN CULTURE
**URBAN CULTURE AND ENTERTAINMENT**
**ENTERTAINMENT**
**FINE ARTS**
**EXCHANGE OF INFORMATION**
**EDUCATION**
**URBAN INFLUENCE ON RURAL AREAS AND THE WIDER WORLD**

# X ATTITUDES TO CITIES
**VIEWS OF THE CITY IN LITERATURE, GRAPHIC AND DRAMATIC ART**

## Journal abbreviations

| | | | |
|---|---|---|---|
| A | *Antiquity* | AE | *Annales de l'Est* |
| Aa | *Archaeologica* | AEHR | *Australian Economic History Review* |
| AA | *Archaeogica Aeliana* | | |
| AAG | *Annals of the Association of American Geographers* | AESC | *Annales, Economies, Sociétés, Civilisations* |
| AAn | *American Antiquity* | AgH | *Agricultural History* |
| AAnth | *American Anthropologist* | AG | *Annales de Geographie* |
| AAQ | *Architectural Association Quarterly* | AGS | *Australian Geographical Studies* |
| ABo | *Annales de Bourgogne* | AHQ | *Australian Historical Quarterly* |
| ABS | *American Behavioral Science* | | |
| Acad | *Acadiensis* | AHR | *American Historical Review* |
| AcIBL | *Académie des Inscriptions et Belles-Lettres* | AHRF | *Annales Historique de la Révolution Française* |
| AcG | *Acta Geographica* | AI | *Annals of Iowa* |
| AC | *Archaeologica Cantiana* | AJ | *Archaeological Journal* |
| ACa | *Archaeologia Cambrensis* | AJA | *American Journal of Archaeology* |
| AdB | *Annales de Bretagne* | | |
| AdM | *Annales du Midi* | AJC | *Anthropological Journal of Canada* |
| AdN | *Annales de Normandie* | | |
| AD | *Architectural Design* | AJES | *American Journal of Economics and Society* |
| ADH | *Annales de Démographie Historique* | | |
| AeJ | *Antiquaries Journal* | AJewHQ | *American Jewish Historical Quarterly* |

| | |
|---|---|
| AJH | American Jewish History |
| AJo | Architects Journal |
| AJPH | American Journal of Political History |
| AJPS | American Journal of Political Science |
| AJS | American Journal of Sociology |
| AIH | Alberta History |
| AIHR | Alberta Historical Review |
| AIR | Alabama Review |
| AmA | American Antiquity |
| AmAr | American Archivest |
| AmLibJ | American Library Journal |
| AmQ | American Quarterly |
| AMS | Ancient Monuments Society |
| An | Annales |
| AnJ | Antiquaries Journal |
| AnS | Annals of Science |
| Ant | Anthropologie et Sociétés |
| Ap | Apollo |
| APS | American Philosophical Society Proceedings |
| APSR | American Political Science Review |
| APSS | Annals of the American Academy of Political and Social Science |
| AQ | American Quarterly |
| Arc | Archives |
| Arch | Archaeology |
| ArH | Architectural History |
| ArtH | Art History |
| Arts | Arts Canada |
| AR | Architectural Review |
| ARCS | American Review of Canadian Studies |
| AsS | Asian Survey |
| AS | Acta Sociologica |
| ASI | Archivio Storico Italiano |
| ASR | American Sociological Review |
| AtEcR | Atlanta Economic Review |
| AuG | Australian Geographical Studies |
| AuGe | Australian Geographer |
| AuHAB | Australian Historical Society Bulletin |
| Au1888 | Australia 1888 |
| AuJPH | Australian Journal of Politics and History |
| Au1938 | Australia 1938–1988; a bicentennial history |
| AW | Arizona and the West |
| BA | Business Archives |
| BAn | Bradford Antiquary |
| BAJ | Berkshire Archaeological Journal |
| BAS | Birmingham Archaeological Society Transactions |
| BCHESRL | Bulletin de Centre d'Histoire Economique et Sociale de la Région Lyonnaise |
| BCS | British Columbia Studies |
| BE | Built Environment |
| BedA | Bedfordshire Archaeology |
| BER | Bulletin of Economic Research |
| BGAS | Bristol and Gloucestershire Archaeological Society Proceedings |
| BIHTP | Bulletin de l'Institut du Temps Présent |
| BJRL | Bulletin of John Rylands Library |
| BJS | British Journal of Sociology |
| Bl | Blackcountryman |
| BLHEMR | Bulletin of Local History East Midland Region |
| BMHS | Bulletin of Missouri Historical Society |
| BMQ | British Museum Quarterly |
| Brig | Brigantian |
| Brit | Britannia |
| BSHM | Bulletin de la Société d'Histoire Moderne |
| BSLH | Bulletin for the Study of Labour History |
| BSLHR | Bourne Society and Leatherhead Historical Record |
| Bu | The Builder |
| BuH | Business History |
| BuHR | Business History Review |
| BurM | Burlington Magazine |
| CalH | California History |
| CalHQ | California Historical Quarterly |
| CanEthS | Canadian Ethnic Studies |
| CanGeog | Canadian Geographer |
| CarmH | Carmarthen History |
| CathHR | Catholic Historical Review |
| CA | Current Archaeology |
| CAS | Cambridge Antiquarian Society Proceedings |
| CASP | Cambridge Archaeological Society Proceedings |
| CC | Cake and Cockhorse |
| CColl | Canadian Collector |
| CdH | Cahiers d'Histoire |
| Cer | Ceredigion |
| CEA | Cahiers d'Etudes Africaines |
| CEH | Central European History |
| CEthS | Canadian Ethnic Studies |
| ChH | Church History |
| CHA | Canadian Historical Association |
| ChesH | Cheshire History |
| ChiH | Chicago History |
| CHQ | California Historical Quarterly |
| CHR | Canadian Historical Review |
| CHST | Caernarvonshire Historical Society Transactions |
| CinHSB | Cincinnati Historical Society Bulletin |
| CIS | Cahiers et Internationaux de Sociologie |
| CIUAR | Cahiers de l'Institut d'Urbanisme et d'Aménagement Régional Université des Sciences Humaines de Strasbourg |

| | | | |
|---|---|---|---|
| City | City Magazine | EEH | Explorations in Entre- |
| CJ | Classical Journal | | preneurial History |
| CJPS | Canadian Journal of Political | EEQ | East European Quarterly |
| | Science | EG | Estudios Geographicos |
| CL | Country Life | EHR | English Historical Review |
| CLHSB | Cambridgeshire Local | EJ | Essex Journal |
| | History Society Bulletin | EMG | East Midlands Geographer |
| CLHSJ | Cheltenham Local History | En | Encounter |
| | Society Journal | EN | Environment |
| CoH | Connecticut History | Er | Erdekunde |
| CoHS | Connecticut Historical Society | ERA | East Riding Archaeology |
| | Bulletin | ESR | Economic and Social Review |
| Comm | Communiqué: Canadian | Eth | Ethnicity |
| | Studies | EthRS | Ethnic and Racial Studies |
| Con C | Continuity and Change | EUJ | Edinburgh University |
| CONT | Contact | | Journal |
| CQ | Classical Quarterly | EuSR | European Studies Review |
| CQR | Church Quarterly Review | EW | Epworth Witness |
| CS | Canadian Studies | F | Folklore |
| CSP | Canadian Studies in | FCHQ | Filson Club Historical |
| | Population | | Quarterly |
| CSSH | Comparative Studies in | FHS | French Historical Studies |
| | Society and History | FlaHQ | Florida Historical Quarterly |
| CTLHSB | Cleveland and Teeside Local | FL | Folk Life |
| | History Society Bulletin | G | Geography |
| CWAAS | Cumberland and Westmor- | GaHQ | Georgia Historical Quarterly |
| | land Antiquarian and | GA | Geografiska Annaler |
| | Archaeological Society | GB | Geographical Bulletin |
| | Transactions | Ge | Geography |
| D | Daedalus | Geo | Geoforum |
| DAJ | Derbyshire Archaeological | GJ | Geographical Journal |
| | Journal | GlHB | Gloucestershire Community |
| DAr | Deutsches Archiv | | Council Local History |
| DART | Devonshire Association | | Bulletin |
| | Research Transactions | GLRQB | Greater London Research |
| DCLHSB | Durham County Local | | Quarterly Bulletin |
| | History Society Bulletin | GM | Geographical Magazine |
| De | Demography | GR | Geographical Review |
| DE | Die Erde | GRBS | Greek, Roman and Byzantine |
| Del | Delta | | Studies |
| DevA | Devon Archaeology | GRI | Geographical Review of India |
| DevH | Devon Historian | GUM | Guildhall Studies in London |
| DGNH | Dumfries and Galloway | | History |
| | Natural History and Anti- | GV | Geographical Viewpoint |
| | quarian Society Proceedings | GZ | Geographische Zeitschrift |
| DHST | Denbighshire Historical | H | History |
| | Society Transactions | HaST | Halifax Antiquarian Society |
| DL | Dorset Life | | Transactions |
| DM | Derbyshire Miscellany | HatR | Hatcher Review |
| DNHS | Dorset Natural History and | HAHR | Hispanic American Historical |
| | Archaeological Society | | Review |
| | Transactions | HEJ | History of Education Journal |
| DurA | Durham Archaeology | HEdQ | Higher Education Quarterly |
| DUJ | Durham University Journal | HerA | Hertfordshire Archaeology |
| E | Ekistics | HES | Histoire, Economie et Société |
| EAH | Essex Archaeology and | HFCAS | Hampshire Field Club and |
| | History | | Archaeological Society |
| EAM | East Anglian Magazine | | Transactions |
| EAS | Essex Archaeological Society | HGN | Historical Geography News- |
| | Transactions | | letter |
| Ec | Economica | HHB | Hornsey Historical Bulletin |
| EcG | Economic Geography | Hist | Historian |
| EcHR | Economic History Review | HJ | Historical Journal |
| EcSoc | Economy and Society | HLQ | Huntington Library |
| EDCC | Economic Development and | | Quarterly |
| | Cultural Change | HMMCHS | Historical Messenger of |

| | | | |
|---|---|---|---|
| | Milwaukee City History Society | JDA | Journal of Developing Areas |
| HMN | Historical Methods News- | JEcH | Journal of Economic History |
| | letter | JEtHS | Journal of Ethnic Studies |
| HO | Human Organization | JEEH | Journal of European |
| HPP | Hertfordshire Past and Present | | Economic History |
| HQ | Historical Quarterly | JEH | Journal of Ecclesiastical |
| HS | Historical Studies | | History |
| HSC | Honourable Society of | JESHO | Journal of Economic and |
| | Cymrodorian Transactions | | Social History of the Orient |
| HS/SH | Histoire Sociale/Social | JFamH | Journal of Family History |
| | History | JG | Journal of Geography |
| HSLC | Historic Society of Lancashire | JGH | Journal of Garden History |
| | and Cheshire | JHES | Jewish Historical Society of |
| HT | History Today | | England |
| HTh | History and Theory | JHG | Journal of Historical |
| HTN | Hommes et Terres du Nord | | Geography |
| HuAS | Hunter Archaeological | JICH | Journal of Imperial and |
| | Society Transactions | | Commonwealth History |
| HW | History Workshop | JIllSHS | Journal of Illinois State |
| HZ | Historische Zeitschrift | | History Society |
| IA | Industrial Archaeology | JInH | Journal of Interdisciplinary |
| IBG | Institute of British | | History |
| | Geographers Transactions | JITP | Journal of the Institute of |
| IESHR | Indian Economic and Social | | Town Planners |
| | History Review | JJS | Journal of Jewish Studies |
| IG | L'Information Géographique | JJSoc | Jewish Journal of Sociology |
| IHR | Bulletin of the Institute of | JLAS | Journal of Latin American |
| | Historical Research | | Studies |
| IHS | Irish Historical Studies | JLibH | Journal of Library History |
| IJAHS | International Journal of | JLCBWHS | Journal of the Lancashire and |
| | African Historical Studies | | Cheshire Branch of |
| IJCS | International Journal of | | the Wesley Historical |
| | Comparative Sociology | | Society |
| IJURS | International Journal of | JMedH | Journal of Medical History |
| | Urban and Regional | JMisH | Journal of Mississippi |
| | Research | | History |
| IM | International Migration | JMH | Journal of Modern History |
| IMin | Immigrants and Minorities | JMRS | Journal of Medieval and |
| IMR | International Migration | | Renaissance Studies |
| | Review | JNH | Journal of Negro History |
| IMS | Informationen zur modernen | JNPH | Journal of Newspaper and |
| | Stadtgeschichte | | Periodical History |
| InMH | Indiana Magazine of History | JOrS | Journal of Oriental Studies |
| IESH | Irish Economic and Social | JP | Journal of Politics |
| | History | JQ | Japan Quarterly |
| IrG | Irish Geographer | JReS | Journal of Regional Science |
| IRSH | International Review of Social | JRelH | Journal of Religious History |
| | History | JRIC | Journal of Royal Institution of |
| JAdH | Journal of Advertising | | Cornwall |
| | History | JRPE | Journal of Radical Political |
| JAfH | Journal of African History | | Economics |
| JAsH | Journal of Asian History | JSA | Journal of Society of Archivists |
| JAH | Journal of American History | JSAH | Journal of Society of Archi- |
| JAIP | Journal of American Institute | | tectural Historians |
| | of Planners | JSDH | Journal of San Diego History |
| JAsS | Journal of Asian Studies | JSEAS | Journal of South-East Asian |
| JAS | Journal of American Studies | | Studies |
| JAusS | Journal of Australian Studies | JSH | Journal of Southern History |
| JBAS | Journal of the British | JSocH | Journal of Social History |
| | Archaeological Association | JSportH | Journal of Sporting History |
| JBS | Journal of British Studies | JSS | Jewish Social Studies |
| JBlS | Journal of Black Studies | JTH | Journal of Transport History |
| JCH | Journal of Contemporary | JUA | Journal of Urban Affairs |
| | History | JUE | Journal of Urban Economics |
| JCanS | Journal of Canadian Studies | JUH | Journal of Urban History |
| | | JW | Journal of the West |

| | | | |
|---|---|---|---|
| JWG | Jahrbuch für Wirtschaft-weschichte | MoA | Moyen Age |
| | | MS | Manchester School of Economic and Social Studies |
| JWH | Journal of World History | | |
| KanH | Kansas History | MunJ | Municipal Journal |
| KAR | Kent Archaeological Record | NArch | Northamptonshire Archaeology |
| LancsLH | Lancashire Local History | | |
| LabH | Labour Historian | NebH | Nebraska History |
| LakUR | Lakehead University Review | NCTR | Nineteenth Century Theatre Research |
| LaS | Louisiana Studies | | |
| LAHS | Leicestershire Archaeological and Historical Society Transactions | NDQ | North Dakota Quarterly |
| | | NEQ | New England Quarterly |
| | | NH | Northern History |
| LARR | Latin American Research Review | NiaF | Niagara Frontier |
| | | NJH | New Jersey History |
| LauUR | Laurentian University Review | NLWJ | National Library of Wales Journal |
| LBI | Leo Baeck Institute Yearbook | NMS | Nottingham Medieval Studies |
| LDLHS | Leatherhead and Dorking Local History Society Proceedings | NoA | Norfolk Archaeology |
| | | NovSHR | Nova Scotia Historical Review |
| LE | Land Economics | NPP | Northamptonshire Past and Present |
| LGS | Local Government Studies | | |
| LeiH | Leicestershire Historian | NQ | Notes and Queries |
| LH | Labor History | NS | Northern Scotland |
| LHA | Lincolnshire History and Archaeology | NSFJ | North Staffordshire Journal of Field Studies |
| Lib | The Library | NYH | New York History |
| LibH | Library History | NYHSQ | New York, Historical Society Quarterly |
| LitH | Literature and History | | |
| L–J | London Journal | NZG | New Zealand Geographer |
| Ll | Llafur | NZJG | New Zealand Journal of Geography |
| LocH | Local History | | |
| LoH | Local Historian | NZJH | New Zealand Journal of History |
| LoMAS | London and Middlesex Archaeological Society Transactions | | |
| | | O | Oxoniensa |
| | | ODU | ODU: a Journal of West African Studies |
| LonA | London Archaeologist | | |
| LPLS | Leeds Philosophical and Literary Society Transactions | OEP | Oxford Economic Papers |
| | | OhH | Ohio History |
| LPS | Local Population Studies | OH | Oral History |
| LSJ | London Society Journal | Ontgeog | Ontario Geography |
| L/T | Labor/Le Travailleur | OntH | Ontario History |
| LouH | Louisiana History | OrHQ | Oregon Historical Quarterly |
| M | Morgannwgw | PaP | Past and Present |
| MA | Medieval Archaeology | PA | Public Administration |
| MAA | Monmouthshire Archaeological Association | PAH | Perspectives in American History |
| MaM | Mariners Mirror | PenH | Pennsylvania History |
| MAsS | Modern Asian Studies | PenMHB | Pennsylvania Magazine of History and Biography |
| MC | Montgomeryshire Collections | | |
| MdHM | Maryland Historical Magazine | PennGeog | Pennsylvania Geographer |
| | | PGM | Petermanns Geographische Mitteilungen |
| Mean | Meanjin | | |
| MeA | Medium Aevum | PGR | Pakistan Geographical Review |
| MedH | Medical History | | |
| MES | Middle Eastern Studies | Phy | Phylon |
| MH | Maritime History | PHB | Planning History Bulletin |
| MHSB | Missouri Historical Society Bulletin | PHR | Pacific Historical Review |
| | | PiAm | Pioneer America |
| MicQR | Michigan QR | Pl | The Planner |
| MidAm | Mid-America | PlC | Plan Canada |
| MidH | Midland History | PMA | Post Medieval Archaeology |
| MisHR | Missouri Historical Review | PNW | Pacific North West Quarterly |
| MissQ | Mississippi Quarterly | PolP | Policy and Politics |
| MM | Marxist Miscellany (Delhi) | Pop | Population |
| Mnem | Mnemosyne | PP | Patterns of Prejudice |

| | | | |
|---|---|---|---|
| PQ | Political Quarterly | SAUS | South Atlantic Urban Studies |
| PH | Provence Historique | SCalQ | Southern California |
| PS | Population Studies | | Quarterly |
| PSJ | Policy Studies Journal | SCHM | South Carolina Historical |
| PSQ | Political Science Quarterly | | Magazine |
| PWHSE | Public Works Historical | SCI | Bolletino de Societa |
| | Society Essays | | Geographica Italiana |
| QJLC | Quarterly Journal of Library | SCJ | Sixteenth Century Journal |
| | of Congress | SCLG | Studies in Comparative Local |
| QS | Quaderni Storico | | Government |
| Ra | Race and Class | ScM | Scripta Mercaturae |
| RadS | Radnorshire Society | SCM | South Carolina Magazine |
| | Transactions | ScS | Scottish Studies |
| RA | Revue d'Alsace | ScSo | Science and Society |
| RAH | Reviews in American History | SEA | Social and Economic |
| RBPS | Review of Black Political | | Administration |
| | Studies | SEcHR | Scandinavian Economic |
| RCHST | Railway and Canal Historical | | History Review |
| | Society Transactions | SEER | Slavonic and East European |
| RecH | Recusant History | | Review |
| ReO | Revista de Occident | SEHR | Socio Economic History |
| ReS | Regional Studies | | Review |
| REH | Review of Economic History | SEG | South Eastern Geographer |
| REJ | Revue des Etudes Juives | SES | Social and Economic Studies |
| RHAF | Revue Historique Americaine | SF | Social Forces |
| | Française | SG | Soviet Geography |
| RFHL | Revue Française d'Histoire du | SGM | Scottish Geographical |
| | Livre | | Magazine |
| RH | Revue Historique | SH | Social History |
| RHEF | Revue d'Histoire de l'Eglise de | SHP | Studies in History and |
| | France | | Politics |
| RHES | Revue d'Histoire Economique | SHR | Scottish History Review |
| | et Sociale | SIAH | Suffolk Institute of |
| RHiH | Rhode Island History | | Archaeology and History |
| RHMC | Revue d'Histoire Moderne et | SIH | Sussex Industrial History |
| | Contemporaine | SJPE | Scottish Journal of Political |
| RHS | Royal Historical Society | | History |
| | Transactions | SJS | Scottish Journal of Sociology |
| RIBA | Royal Institute of British | SlR | Slavic Review |
| | Architects Journal | Soc | Societas |
| RicH | Rickmansworth Historian | SocQ | Sociological Quarterly |
| RKHS | Register of the Kentucky | SouH | Southern History |
| | Historical Society | Sp | Speculum |
| RM | Railway Magazine | SPA | Social Policy and |
| RMSSR | Rocky Mountain Social | | Administration |
| | Science Review | SR | Socialist Review |
| RN | Revue du Nord | SS | Soviet Studies |
| RocH | Rochester History | SSAHS | South Staffordshire |
| RQ | Renaissance Quarterly | | Archaeological and Histor- |
| RR | Russian Review | | ical Society |
| RS | Rural Sociology | SSH | Social Science History |
| RSAI | Royal Society of Antiquaries | SSJ | Social Science Journal |
| | of Ireland | SuAC | Surrey Archaeological |
| RSI | Revista Storica Italiana | | Collections |
| RussH | Russian History | SulHRN | Suffolk Local History Review |
| RutR | Rutland Record | | and Newsletter |
| SAC | Sussex Archaeological | SuR | Suffolk Review |
| | Collections | TCLAS | Transactions of Lancashire |
| SANHS | Somerset Archaeology and | | and Cheshire Archae- |
| | Natural History Society | | ological Society |
| | Proceedings | TexH | Textile History |
| SAQ | South Atlantic Quarterly | ThS | Thoroton Society |
| SaskH | Saskatchewan History | Thunder Bay | Thunder Bay Historical |
| SAS | Society of Antiquaries of | HS | Society |
| | Scotland Proceedings | UHR | Urban History Review |
| SAST | Shropshire Archaeological | UHY | Urban History Yearbook |
| | Society Proceedings | | |

| | | | |
|---|---|---|---|
| VerH | Vermont History | WHR | Welsh History Review |
| VS | Victorian Studies | WHS | Wesleyan Historical Studies |
| WANSM | Wiltshire Archaeological and Natural History Society Magazine | WMS | West Midlands Studies |
| | | WPennHM | West Pennsylvania Historical Magazine |
| WANHS | Worcestershire Archeaological and Natural History Society | WQ | Wilson Quarterly |
| | | YH | York History |

## 1 GENERAL

### RESEARCH METHODS, AIDS AND MATERIALS

#### Printed documentary sources
1 *Index to 1851 census [Doncaster]*. Doncaster: Doncaster Society for Family History 1986. pp 35.
2 *Parish registers in the Birmingham Reference Library*. Birmingham: Birmingham Public Libraries 1985. pp viii + 82.

#### Statistical publications
3 DAHMS FA, Regional urban history: a statistical and cartographic survey of Huron and southern Bruce counties. *UHR* 15 (1987) 254–68.
4 HERCULE P, *Paroisses et communes de France: dictionnaire d'histoire administrative et démographique: Charente-Maritime*. Paris: CNRS 1985. pp 632.

#### Maps and plans
5 MILLER ST, Rain's Eye Plan: unique historical source. [Sunderland and Bishopwearmouth]. *LoH* 17 (1987) 417–22.
6 MOORE JN, *The mapping of Scotland: a guide to the literature of Scottish cartography prior to Ordnance Survey*. Aberdeen: University of Aberdeen 1983. pp iv + 73.

#### Bibliographies and guides to the literature
7 BLOOMFIELD E, Bibliography: recent publications relating to Canada's urban past. *UHR* 14 (1985).
8 BLOOMFIELD E, International urban history bibliography: recent publications in urban history. *UHR* 16 (1987) 78–118.
9 CASPAR DE, *City profiles in periodical literature, a checklist 1974–1984*. Monticello, Il: Vance Bibliographies 1985.
10 RAY BJ, *Global urbanisation and urbanism, cause and effect: a bibliography*. Monticello, Il: Vance Bibliographies 1986.
11 WALTON H, The Hunter collection in the Sheffield Central Library. *HuAS* 13 (1985) 47–64.

#### Archives
12 COSS PR ed, *The early records of medieval Coventry*. British Academy & Oxford UP 1986. pp xiii + 450.
13 DILS J, Deposition books and the urban historian. *LoH* 17 (1987) 269–76.
14 *Index to Cornish probate records*. Cornwall County and Diocescan Record Office 1984. pp 72.
15 *London local archives: a directory of local authority record offices and libraries*. Guildhall Library 1985. pp 28, il.
16 WALSH M, Municipal records and local history in Windsor [Ont]. *Families* 24 (1985) 209–15.

### URBAN HISTORY–DEFINITIONS AND HISTORIOGRAPHY

#### Historiography
17 BUCK DD, The study of urban history in the People's Republic of China. *UHY* (1987) 61–75.
18 EBNER MH, The comparative tradition in American urban history. *JInH* 17 (1987) 639–43.
19 HAWKINS DJ, Plymouth: histories and historians. *DevH* 83 (1986) 11–14.
20 HOHENBERG PM, *The making of urban Europe 1000–1950*. Harvard UP 1985. pp xiv + 395.
21 JEAN M, Le père Etienne Isnard, premier historiographe de Toulon (1591–1656). *PH* 139 (1985) 47–51.

**URBANIZATION AND THE GROWTH AND FORTUNES OF TOWNS**
22  CARVER M, *Underneath English towns*. Batsford 1987. pp 176.
23  MARGUERAT Y, *L'armature urbaine du Togo*. Paris: ORSTOM 1985. pp 166.
24  WHITEHAND JWR, Urban geography within the city. *PHG* 10 (1986) 103–17.


**Theory of urbanization**
25  CAUVIN C & REYMOND H, *L'espacement des villes: théorie des lieux centrale et analyse spectrale*. Paris: CRNS 1985. pp 188.
26  FAIR TJD, The urbanization process in South Africa. *RSA 2000* 1 (1985) 1–6.
27  LADD EC, *Ideology in America: change and response in a city, a suburb and a small town*. University P of America 1986. pp 404.
28  MCKEOWN K, *Marxist political economy and Marxist urban sociology: a review and elaboration of recent developments*. Basingstoke: Macmillan 1987. pp 256.
29  MARTI M, *No place to hide: crisis and future of American habitats*. Greenwood 1984. pp xviii + 245.
30  SAUNDERS P, *Social theory and the urban question*. Hutchinson Education 1986. pp 348.


**EMPIRICAL STUDIES OF TOWN GROWTH**
31  The anatomy of cities. *Economist* (Dec 20 1986) 73–81.
32  ARMSTRONG W, *Theatres of accumulation: studies in Asian and Latin American urbanization*. Methuen 1985. pp xvi + 269.
33  ARMSTRONG WH & MCGEE TG, Les villes du tiers monde: théâtres d'accumulation, centres de diffusion, série dépendance alimentaire et urbanisation. *Revue Tiers-Monde* 26 (1986) 823–40.
34  BAIROCH P, *De Jericho à Mexico: villes et économie dans l'histoire*. Paris: Gallimard 1985.
35  BROWN K et al, eds, *Middle Eastern cities in comparative perspective*. Cornell UP 1986. pp 360.
36  HAARHOF EJ, *A spatial analysis of African urbanisation and informal settlement in Natal/Kwalzulu*. s.1.: s.n. 1985.
37  HAINES R & BUIJS G, *The struggle for social and economic space urbanization in twentieth century South Africa*. Durban: UD–W 1985. pp xx + 269.
38  JOLY R, *La ville et la civilisation urbaine: essai*. Paris: Messidor Editions Sociales 1985. pp 276.
39  KRAAYENBRINK EA ed, *Studies on urbanisation in South Africa*. Johannesburg: South African Institute on Race Relations 1984. pp vi + 96.
40  LE GOFF & GUIEYSSE L eds, *Crise de l'urbain, futur de la ville*. Paris: Economica 1985. pp 249.
41  PEIL M, *African urbanization in comparative perspective*. Birmingham: Birmingham UP 1984. pp 12.


**Ancient**
42  COLLIS J, *Oppida: earliest towns north of the Alps*. Sheffield: Sheffield U 1984. pp x + 250.
43  *Petra et les villes morts de Syrie*. Paris: Atlas 1985. pp 75.
44  STARR CG, *Individual and community: the rise of the polis 800–500 BC*. New York: Oxford UP 1986.


**Medieval and early modern**
45  CLARKE HB & SIMMS A eds, *The comparative history of urban origins in non-Roman Europe : Ireland, Wales, Denmark, Germany, Poland and Russia, 9th to 13th century*. Oxford: British Archaeological Association 1985. 748 pp.
46  Domesday heritage: towns and villages of Norman England through 900 years. Arrow 1986. pp 95.
47  DESPORTES P, Villes et paroisses en France du Nord au moyen âge. *HES* (1985) 163–78.
48  DIVORNE F, LAVERGNE B & PANERAI P, *Les bastides d'Aquitaine, du Bas Languedoc et du Bearn*. Paris: Archives d'architecture moderne 1985. pp 132, il.
49  FAUCHERRE N, *Places fortes: bastion du pouvoir*. Paris: Rempart 1986. pp 112, il.
50  GOTTMANN J, *Orbits: the ancient Mediterranean tradition of urban networks: a lecture delivered at New College, Oxford*. Leopard's Head P 1984. pp 15.

51  GRAHAM B, Urbanization in medieval Ireland, ca. AD 900 to ca. AD 1300. *JUH* 13 (1987) 169–96.

52  HALL R, The Vikings as town dwellers. *HT* 37 (Jan 1987) 29–34.

53  HILL R, Parish life in Hertfordshire in the thirteenth century. *HPP* 22 (1987) 3–5.

54  HOBERMAN LS & SOCOLOW SM eds, *Cities and society in colonial Latin America.* Albuquerque: New Mexico UP 1986. pp 400.

55  HOLMES G, *Florence, Rome and the origins of the Renaissance.* Oxford: Clarendon P 1986. pp xiv + 273, il.

56  HOPE KE, *Urbanization in the Commonwealth Caribbean.* Boulder: Westview P 1986. pp 400.

57  NASH GB, *The urban crucible: the North American seaports and the origins of the American Revolution.* Cambridge, Mass: Harvard UP 1986. pp xv + 281.

58  NOBLE M, Growth and development in a regional urban system: the country towns of eastern Yorkshire 1700–1850. *UHY* (1987) 1–21.

59  RAYMOND A, *The great Arab cities in the sixteenth to eighteenth centuries: an introduction.* New York: New York UP 1984. pp 155.

**Modern**

60  BRADLEY J, *Muzhik and Muscovite: urbanization in late Imperial Russia.* California UP 1985. pp xvi + 422.

61  CONZEN MP, *World patterns of modern urban change: essays in honour of Chancy D. Harris.* Chicago: Dept Geography, Chicago U 1985. pp 479

62  DAHMS FA, Regional urban history: a statistical and cartographic survey of Huron and Southern Bruce counties. *UHR* 15 (1987) 254–68.

63  DRAKAKIS-SMITH D eD, *The third world city.* Methuen 1987. pp 80.

64  DUBY G ed, *Histoire de la France urbaine. V La ville aujourd'hiu.* Paris: Seuil 1985. pp 668, il.

65  ECHENIQUE M, *Urban systems: towards an explorative model.* Centre for Environmental Studies 1987. pp 87.

66  ELAZAR DJ, *Building cities in America: urbanization and suburbanization in a frontier society.* U of America P 1987.

67  GILBERT A, *The political economy of land: urban development in an oil economy.* Aldershot: Gower 1985. pp xv + 170.

68  HALLSWORTH G, Towns in northern Ontario: some aspects of their municipal history. *LauUR* 17 (1985) 103–12.

69  HUDSON JC, *Plains country towns.* Minneapolis: Minnesota UP 1985. pp 189.

70  LINTEAU P–A, Canadian urbanization in a North American context: does the border make a difference. *JUH* 13 (1987) 252–74.

71  LOWDER S, *Inside third world cities.* Croom Helm 1986. pp 288.

72  MCCANN LD, *People and place: studies of small town life in the Maritimes.* Fredericton: Acadiensis P 1987.

73  MORTON HW & STUART RC, *The contemporary Soviet city.* Basingstoke: Macmillan 1984. pp xiv + 262.

74  OBUDHO RA, *Demography, urbanisation and spatial planning in Kenya: a bibliographical survey.* Greenwood 1985. pp xix + 285.

75  POLLARD M, *Cities of the world.* Basingstoke: Macmillan Educational 1986. pp 48.

76  ROBSON R, Ontario Hydro colonies: a study of frontier settlement. *LauUR* 17 (1985) 113–39.

77  SIT VFS, *Chinese cities: the growth of the metropolis since 1949.* Oxford: Oxford UP 1985. pp xvi + 239, il.

78  THRIFT N, *The prize of war: urbanization in Vietnam 1954–85.* Allen & Unwin 1986. pp xiv + 188.

79  WRIGLEY EA, *People, cities and wealth: the transformation of traditional society.* Oxford: Basil Blackwell 1987. pp 400.

**HISTORY AND FORTUNES OF INDIVIDUAL TOWNS**

This section is arranged alphabetically by the name of the town

80  EARDMANN C, *Aachen im jahre 1812. Wirtschafts-und sozialraum Differenzuerung einer fruhindustriellen Stadt.* Stuttgart: Franz Steiner Verlag 1986.

81  FRASER GM, *Aberdeen street names: their history, meaning and personal associations.* Aberdeen: Bisset 1986. pp xvii + 214.

82  SMITH JS ed, *New light on medieval Aberdeen.* Aberdeen: Aberdeen UP 1985. pp xi + 66.

83  STEVENSON D ed, *From lairds to louns: country and burgh life in Aberdeen 1600–1800.* Aberdeen: Aberdeen UP 1986. pp 100.

84 WHITELOCK D, *Adelaide from colony to jubilee: a sense of difference*. Adelaide: Savvas Publishing 1985.
85 HORN P, Alresford and Mary Russell Mitford. *HatR* 3 (1986) 86–94.
86 HUBSCHER R ed, *Histoire d'Amiens*. Toulouse: Privat 1986. pp 334, il.
87 GUICHONNET P ed, *Histoire d'Annecy*. Toulouse: Privat 1987. pp 320.
88 ROHRBURGH MJ, *Aspen: the history of a silver-mining town, 1879–1893*. New York: Oxford UP 1986.
89 STRAUSS B, *Athens after the Peloponnesian war: class, faction and policy 403–386 BC*. Croom Helm 1986. pp 325.
90 WARREN ME & M, *Baltimore: when she was what she used to be, 1850–1930*. Baltimore: Johns Hopkins UP 1983. pp 148.
91 BONDAR B, *Banff chronicles: the story and the sights*. North Vancouver: Whitecap Books 1986.
92 SMITH D, Barry: a town out of time. *M* 29 (1985) 80–5.
93 HAIGH MH, *The history of Batley 1800–1974*. Batley: MM Haigh 1985. pp 223, il.
94 WOODS C, *Beechworth: a titan's field*. Beechworth: Hargreen Pub Co 1985.
95 BARDON J, *Belfast 1000 years*. Belfast: Blackstaff 1985. pp 36.
96 MIKA N & H, *Belleville: the seat of Hastings county*. Belleville: Mika 1986. pp 96.
97 WILLIAMS M, *Berkeley: an appreciation of its buildings and history*. Berkeley: author 1987.
98 SAGNES J ed, *Historie de Béziers*. Toulouse: Privat 1986. pp 351, il.
99 PENDLEBURY G, *Aspects of the English Civil War in Bolton and its neighbourhood 1640–1660*. Manchester: Richardson 1983. pp 20, il.
100 KOSAMBI M, *Bombay in transition: the growth and social ecology of a colonial city, 1880–1980*. Almquist & Wiksell 1986. pp 204.
101 MUIR GW & KEMPSTER J, *Brantford: Grand River crossing*. Burlington: Windsor Pubs 1986.
102 FLYNN A, *History of Bray*. Cork: Mercier 1986. pp 150, il.
103 FLOWER R, *The old ship: a prospect of Brighton*. Croom Helm 1986. pp 176.
104 BELSEY J et al, *Bristol: the growing city*. Bristol: Redcliffe P 1986. pp 126.
105 BELSEY J, *The forgotten front*. Bristol: Redcliffe P 1986. pp 77.
106 *Historic Bristol*. Norwich: Jarrold 1985. pp 32, il.
107 LOVERING J, *The success of Bristol: the failure of South Wales*. Cardiff: UWIST 1984. pp ii + 37.
108 SALUSSOLIA B, The city of Burlington and municipal incorporation in Vermont. *VerH* 54 (1986) 5–19.
109 NIBBI A, *Ancient Byblos reconsidered*. Oxford: DE Publications 1985. pp 125.
110 DERVILLE A & VIONA A eds, *Histoire de Calais*. Lille: Beffrois 1985. pp 350, il.
111 RACINE J, *Calcutta: la ville, sa crise et le débat sur la planification et l'aménagement urbains*. Paris: Editions de la Maison des sciences de l'homme 1986.
112 PEGRUM R, *The bush capital: how Australia chose Canberra as its federal city*. Sydney: Hale & Iremonger 1983.
113 VOKATY HA, *Cape Town and Montreal: a tale of two cities: a study comparing the evolution of their urban environments*. s.l.: s.n. 1985. 2 vols. pp xvi + 378, il.
114 HILLIER BJ, *The story of Chandler's Ford*. Southampton: Paul Cave 1986. pp 88, il.
115 MOORE JH, Charleston in World War 1: seeds of change. *SCHM* 86 (1985) 39–49.
116 FOURNIAL E, *Charlieu, histoire de la ville et de ses habitants*. Charlieu: Association pour la connaissance de Charlieu 1985. pp 432, il.
117 WADE LC, *Chicago's pride: the Stockyards, Packington and environs in the nineteenth century*. Urbana: Illinois UP 1986.
118 GREEN K, *Chichester past and present*. Horndean: Milestone 1986. pp 96.
119 MOORE R, *Memories of Clun: Edwardian life in a small rural town*. Shrewsbury: Shropshire Libraries 1987. pp 120, il.
120 MANGO C, *Le développement urbain de Constantinople IV–VIIe siècles*. Paris: De Boccard 1985. pp 69, il.
121 COOKE RT, *Cook and Scanlon's guide to the history of Cork*. Cork: Modest Man P 1985. pp 96.
122 PAYNE MR, *Crowborough: the growth of a Wealden town*. Studley: KAJ Brewin 1985. pp xvi + 140.
123 AHMED SU, *Dacca: a study in urban history and development*. Curzon 1986. pp xii + 266, il.
124 IRVING D, *The destruction of Dresden*. Macmillan 1985. pp 255.
125 GOLDSTEIN L, Detroit an American city. *Michigan QR* 25 (1986) 151–48.
126 WARHURST RJ, *A view of Dulwich, Peckham and Camberwell around 1300*. Author 1985. pp 34.
127 CARTER JS, *The history of Dundas*. Belleville: Mika 1985. pp 463.

128 BONDAR B, *Edmonton chronicles: the story and the sights*. North Vancouver: Whitecap Books 1986.

129 SHINN PL, Eugene in the depression. *OrHQ* 86 (1985) 341–69.

130 CURTIS E, *Fleetwood: a town is born*. Lavenham: T Dalton 1986. pp 128.

131 BLACK A, *Old Fort William*. Thunder Bay: Singing Shield Productions 1984. [Thunder Bay]

132 MOHL R & BETTEN N, *Steel city: urban and ethnic patterns in Gary, Indiana, 1906–1950*. Chicago: Holmes & Meier 1986.

133 PIUZ AM, *Genève et canton de Genève aux XVIIe et XVIIIe siècles*. Lausannne: Payot 1985. pp 304, il.

134 MARZAROLI O, *Glasgow 1956–86: shades of grey and some light too*. Edinburgh: Mainstream 1986. pp 196.

135 COOMBS D, *Godalming 400*. Godalming Trust 1984. pp 36, il.

136 HENNING CG, Die kultuurontwikkeling van Graaff Reinet [The cultural development of Graaf Reinet]. *Lantern* 2 (1986) 35–160.

137 PEACOCK T, *Hagley, Worcestershire from the sixteenth to the nineteenth century: some aspects of Hagley's history based on the documents from the parish chest*. Hagley: Hagley Parish Records Research Group 1985. pp vi + 88, il.

138 KROLL RE ed, *Intimate fragments: an irreverent chronicle of early Halifax*. Halifax: Nimbus Books 1985. pp 135.

139 PAYZANT JW, *Halifax: cornerstone of Canada*. Burlington: Windsor Pubs 1985. pp 222.

140 *Around and about Hamilton*. Hamilton: Head of the Lake Historical Society 1986.

141 DEAR MJ et al, eds, *Steel city: Hamilton and region*. Toronto: Toronto UP 1987.

142 SLEIGHTHOLM S, *Hamilton: a community in symphony*. Burlington: Windsor Publications 1986. pp 168.

143 *Hanover remembers: sketches of the past*. Hanover: Hanover Historical Society 1985. pp 46.

144 MCINTOSH MK, *Autonomy and community: the Royal Manor of Havering 1200–1500*. Cambridge: Cambridge UP 1986. pp 460.

145 GARDENER C, *From acorn to oak: a history of Headingley*. Leeds: Thornton 1985. pp 32, il.

146 CHENG JYS, ed, *Hong Kong in transition*. Oxford: Oxford UP 1986. pp xvi + 480, il.

147 ROBERTS C, *Victorian Hoylake: recollections of Hoylake 1865–1915*. Hoylake: Ceehjay Publishing 1986. pp 40, il.

148 STRAWHORN J, *The history of Irvine: royal burgh and new town*. Edinburgh: John Donald 1985. pp vii + 263.

149 BONDAR B, *Jasper chronicles: the story and the sights*. North Vancouver: Whitecap Books 1986.

150 ECKHARDT AL, *Jerusalem: city of the ages*. Lanham: U of America P 1987.

151 VAN DER WAAL G–M & GRUTER W, *Early Johannesburg*. Cape Town: Human & Rousseau 1986. pp 143, il.

152 OLIVIER-MARTIN F, *Notes historiques sur la ville et la châtellerie du Jugnon: des origines à 1789*. Paris: Rue des Scribes 1985. pp 272, il.

153 DE LA PRYME A, *A history of Kingston-upon-Hull*. Hull: Hull City Council 1986. pp 118.

154 RICE HAJ, *Kirby Lonsdale and its neighbourhood*. Kendal: Westmorland Gazette 1983. pp 30 il.

155 BLOOMFIELD E, Berlin's last bonus: or how Kitchener became the rubber capital of Canada. *Waterloo Historical Society* 74 (1986) 6–22.

156 DELAFOSSE M, ed, *Histoire de La Rochelle*. Toulouse: Privat 1985. pp 312.

157 GILL R, *The book of Leicester*. Buckingham: Barracuda 1985. pp 128, il.

158 MARSHALL JS, *The life and times of Leith*. Edinburgh: Donald 1986. pp ix + 204.

159 ROSSER AG, The town and guild of Lichfield in the late middle ages. *SSAHS* 27 (1987) 39–47.

160 *Glimpses of the town of Listowel, Ontario, Canada*. Stratford: Stratford-Perth Archives 1985.

161 BATES LM, *The Thames on fire: the battle of London river 1939–1945*. Terence Dalton 1985. pp ix + 189.

162 BEIER AL & FINLAY R eds, *London 1500–1700: the making of the metropolis*. Longmans 1986. pp x + 283.

163 HIBBERT C, *Royal London*. Macmillan 1987. pp 224.

164 MACK J, *London at war: the making of Victorian London 1939–1945*. Sidgwick & Jackson 1985. pp 176.

165 RAWCLIFFE M, *Victorian London*. Batsford 1985. pp 48.

166 THORNBURY W, *Old London: Charterhouse to Holborn*. Alderman 1987. pp 196, il.

167 THORNBURY W, *Old London: Cheapside and St Paul's*. Alderman 1986. pp 192.

168 THORNBURY W, *Old London: Shoreditch to Smithfield*. Alderman 1987. pp 196, il.

169 THORNBURY W, *Old London: the Tower and the East End*. Alderman 1986. pp 192.

170 *The village London atlas: the changing face of greater London 1822–1903*. Alderman 1986. pp 208.

171 WALFORD E, *London recollected: its history, lore and legend*. Vol 5. Alderman 1987. pp 576, il.

172 WALFORD E, *Old London: Covent Garden and the Thames to Whitehall*. Alderman 1987. pp 196, il.

173 WALFORD E, *Old London: Strand to Soho*. Alderman 1987. pp 196, il.

174 SPEROU A`& LAMPEN J eds, *If stones could speak: glimpses of a city over three hundred years*. Derry: North West Centre for Learning and Devlopment 1985. pp 60. [Londonderry]

175 WALL BL, *Long Melford through the ages: a guide to the buildings and streets*. Ipswich: EAM 1986. pp 130, il.

176 MURLE P & WINSOR J, *Portrait of Malvern*. Chichester: Phillimore 1986.

177 CROOK D, The community of Mansfield from Domesday book to the reign of Edward III. Pt 2. *ThS* 89 (1985) 16–29.

178 CLAVEL-LEVEQUE M, *Marseille grecque*. Paris: J Lafitte 1985. pp 211, il.

179 GEORGE PS, Brokers, binders and builders: greater Miami's boom of the mid-1920s. *F1HQ* (1986) 27–51.

180 LEVINE BB, Miami: the capital of Latin America. *WQ* 9 (1985) 47–69.

181 NICHOLSON JA, *Middle River: past and present history of a Cape Breton community, 1806–1985*. Middle River: Middle River Hist Soc 1985. pp 308.

182 LEROUX E, *Histoire d'une ville et de ses habitants, Nantes*. Vol 2 de 1914 à 1939. Paris: ACL 1985. pp 330.

183 PEARSON J, *Neston and Parkgate*. Birkenhead: Countywise 1985. pp 80, il.

184 DOCHERTY JC, *Newcastle: the making of an Australian city*. Sydney: Hale & Iremonger 1983.

185 MCGOWRAN T, *Newhaven on Forth: port of grace*. Edinburgh: John Donald 1985. pp ix + 252.

186 GERBOD P, Niederbronn, station thermale d'alsacienne de 1800 à 1939. *RA* 111 (1985) 99–110.

187 MCKEON C, *Oakville: a place of some importance*. Burlington: Windsor Pubs 1986. pp 134.

188 CAMPBELL EC, *Oromocto in view*. Oromocto: Roger's Pubs. 1984.

189 CHEVALLIER R, *Ostie antique: ville et port*. Paris: Belles lettres 1986. pp 289.

190 HILL H, *Before and after Colonel By*. Ottawa: Ottawa Historical Society of Ottawa 1983. pp 13. [reprint of lecture on early history of Ottawa 1923]

191 LAMOUREUX G, *Ottawa 1900–1926 et sa population canadienne-française*. Ottawa: Author 1984. pp 321.

192 TAYLOR J, *Ottawa: an illustrated history*. Toronto: Lorrimer 1986.

193 *Paris: des origines à nos jours*. Paris: Bordessoules 1985. pp 700, il.

194 RICHAR G, *Parry Sound: historical minatures*. Nobel: Morsel P 1987.

195 JOHNSTON M, *Around the banks of Pimlico*. Dublin: Attic 1985. pp 135.

196 WOODWARD FW, *Citadel: the story of the Royal Citadel, Plymouth*. Exeter: Devon Books 1987. pp 160, il.

197 FAVREAU R ed, *Histoire de Poitiers*. Toulouse: Privat 1985. pp 480, il.

198 TURCOTTE D, *Port Dalhousie: shoes, and ships and sealing wax*. Erin: Boston Mills P 1986.

199 NORTON D, *A history of Port Moody*. Surrey BC: Hancock House 1986.

200 OLIVIER JJ & HATTING PS, Die Suid-Afrikaanse stad as funksioneel-ruimtelike sisteem, met besondere verwysing na Pretoria [The South African city as a functional spatial system with special reference to Pretoria]. *RSA 2000* 1 (1985) 7–18.

201 BUSSON C, *The book of Ramsgate*. Buckingham: Barracuda 1985. pp 148.

202 MICHELL F, *Annals of an ancient Cornish town: being notes on the history of Redruth*. Redruth: Dyllansow Truran 1985. pp 247, il.

203 ALLEN R & DINE D, *Ringwood seen and remembered*. Winchester: Hampshire County Library 1985. pp 53, il.

204 GABET C, *La naissance de Rochefort sous Louis XIV 1665–1715*. Rochefort: Centre d'animation lyrique et cultural de Rochefort 1985. pp 267, il.

205 PURLE B, *A chronology of Rochester to 1899*. Rainham: Meresborough 1984. pp 24.

206 VERHULST A, Saint Baron et les origines de Gand. *RN* 69 (1986) 455–70.

207 WRIGHT HE & O'LEARY BE, *Fortress Saint John: an illustrated military history 1640–1985*. St John: Partridge Island Research Project 1985. pp 131.

208 LAURENT C, *Atlas historique des villes de France: Saint Malo*. Paris: CNRS 1987.

209 LEVESQUE B, *Saint Quentin: déjà trois quarts de siècle*. St Quentin 1986. pp 446.

210 DURAND R, GUY-VARC'H D & MACE F, *Du village a la cité-Jardin: Saint Sebastian sur Loire depuis les origines*. Paris: ACL 1986. pp 386, il.

211 FONTAINE J & A, *Senlis, berceau de la France*. Paris: Zodiaque 1985. pp 92, il.

212 HOLMES MJ ed, *Somers Town: a record of change [London]*. London: Camden Libraries 1985. pp 36.

213 MURRAY E & WHITE K, *The golden years of Stawell*. Melbourne: Town of Stawell & Lothian Pub 1984.

214 JENKINS JG, *Stoke-on-Trent: federation and after*. Stafford: Staffordshire County Libraries 1985. pp 252–71.

215 DAVIDSON J ed, *The Sydney Melbourne book*. Sydney: Allen & Unwin 1986.

216 LIVET E & RAPP F eds, *Historie de Strasbourg*. Toulouse: Privat 1987. pp 512.

217 PETTIGREW J & PORTMAN J, *Stratford: the first thirty years*. Toronto: Macmillan 1985. pp 76.

218 ISAAC ICA, *Vale Vistas: the story of Streatham Vale and its parish church 1900–82*. Victoria 1982. pp 55.

219 SYMEONOGLOU S, *The topography of Thebes: from the bronze age to modern times*. Guildford: Princeton UP 1985. pp xxii + 335.

220 LECKIE SA, Toledo in 1890: a time of great expectations. *Northwest Ohio Quarterly* 57 (1985) 119–31.

221 LECKIE S, Toledo, Ohio: a study in the process and problems of nineteenth-century urbanization. *Old Northwest* 10 (1984) 319–37.

222 MACDONALD D, *The Tolsta townships*. Tolsta: Tolsta Community Association 1984. pp 181.

223 ARTHUR E, *Toronto, no mean city*. Toronto: Toronto UP 1986.

224 FILEY M, *Not a one horse town: 125 years of Toronto and its streetcars*. Willowdale: Toronto of Old 1986. pp 144.

225 NAYLOR J, Toronto 1919. *CHA Hist Papers* (1986) 33–55.

226 CHEVALIER B ed, *Histoire de Tours*. Toulouse: Privat 1985. pp 423, il.

227 CARRE G, *Histoire populaire de Troyes et de département de l'Aube*. Paris: Sedepols 1986. pp 482.

228 GUIRAL HADZIIOSSIF J, *Valence, port méditerranéen au XVe siècle*. Paris: Publication de la Sorbonne 1987. pp 555.

229 MALESTROT J de & LAURE E, *Histoire de Vallet*. Montpellier: Herault Imprimerie 1986. pp 336.

230 KELLER B, *On the shady side: Vancouver 1886 to 1914*. Ganges, BC: Horsdal & Schubart 1986.

231 LANE FC, *Studies in Venetian social and economic history*. Variorum 1987. pp 350, il.

232 BASKERVILLE PA, *Beyond the island: an illustrated history of Victoria*. Burlington: Windsor Pubs 1986. pp 144.

233 BONDAR B, *Victoria chronicles: the story and the sights*. North Vancouver: Whitecap Books 1986.

234 REKSTEN T, *More English than the English: a very social history of Victoria*. Victoria: Orca Book Pubs 1986.

235 AUDIGIE C & BERTON M, *Histoire de Villemoisson sur Orge*. Paris: Amattis 1986. pp 264, il.

236 KINGSTON WJ, *The story of West Carberry*. Waterford: Friendly 1985. pp vi + 133.

237 SHERLOCK B, *The Winchester story*. Horndean: Milestone 1986, pp 96.

238 RICHARDSON L, *The bitter years: Wollongong during the great depression*. Sydney: Hale & Iremonger 1984.

239 BARNSBY GW, *The origins of Wolverhampton to 1085: towards a people's history of Wolverhampton*. Wolverhampton: Wolverhampton Borough Council 1985. pp 22.

240 FARISH HC, *Yarmouth, 1821*. Yarmouth: Yarmouth County Hist Soc 1986. pp 47.

241 WHITEHEAD B, York and the Jacobite rebels: some events and people in the York of 1745 to 1747. *YH* (1985) 59–71.

**PORTRAITS OF TOWNS – LITERARY, PHOTOGRAPHIC AND GRAPHIC**
This section is arranged alphabetically by the name of the town

**Graphic and photographic portrayals**

242 BALLEN R, *Dorps: small towns of South Africa*. Cape Town: Clifton 1986.

243 *Figures de la ville*. Paris: Aubier Montaigne 1985. pp 208.

244 *Views of Alloa*. Alloa: Clackmannan District Libraries 1986. pp 16.

245 ALIQUOT H, *Avignon pas à pas, ses rues, ses monuments, ses hommes célèbres*. Paris: Horvath 1985. pp 207, il.

246 DEBBAS F, *Beyrouth, nôtre mémoire: promenade guidée à travers une collection d'images de 1880 à 1930.* Beyrouth: Nanfal 1986. pp 256, il.
247 ROUSSEAU A, *Bourges autrefois.* Paris: Horvath 1985. pp 143, il.
248 FRYER MB & TENCATE A eds, *Brocksville: a pictorial history.* Brocksville: Besancourt 1986. pp 256.
249 WHITING R, *Cheltenham in old photographs.* A Sutton 1986. pp 160.
250 CLARIDGE A & WILLIAMSON B, *Clifton not so long ago: photographs from the Tozer collection.* 1986.
251 HAMMOND A, *Crystal Palace, Norwood Heights; a pictorial record.* Royce 1986. pp 80.
252 CONLIN S, *Historic Dublin: a portfolio.* Dublin: O'Brien 1986, pp 208, il.
253 WILSON A & EVANS D, *Around Dursley in old photographs.* A Sutton 1986. pp 160.
254 GOODING M, *Ealing in the 1930s and 1940s: old photographs of the London borough of Ealing.* Nelson: Hendon Publishing 1985. pp 44, il.
255 STEVENSON RL, *Picturesque old Edinburgh.* Edinburgh: Albyn P 1986. pp 32, il.
256 MORGAN G, *Fishguard in old photographs.* Swansea: C Davies 1986. pp 55.
257 PIERRE DU THAU J, *Grasse.* Paris: Serre 1985. pp 128, il.
258 ULYATT ME, *Old Hull remembered.* Clapham: Dalesman 1986. pp 62, il.
259 *Huntsville's heyday.* Erin: Boston Mills P 1986. pp 80.
260 *Huntsville: pictures from the past: lake of bays.* Erin: Boston Mills P 1986. pp 159.
261 NORWICH OI, *A Johannesburg album.* Johannesburg: Donker 1986. pp 116, il.
262 *Kettering: a noonsday book.* Kettering: Rotary Club Kettering 1985. pp 310, il.
263 *Old Kilpatrick in pictures.* Clydebank: Clydebank District Libraries 1984. pp 30, il.
264 ARMSTRONG FH, *The forest city: an illustrated history of London, Ontario.* Burlington: Windsor Pubs 1986.
265 PELLETIER J, *Lyon pas à pas: son histoire à travers ses rues.* Paris: Horvath 1985. pp 236, il.
266 *Newcastle between the wars.* Newcastle: Newcastle City Libraries 1985, pp 24.
267 WRIGHT HB, *Paris as it was.* Nelson: Hendon 1985. pp 75, il.
268 MILLER FM et al, *Still Philadelphia: a photographic history 1890–1940.* Philadelphia: Temple UP 1983. pp 290.
269 MATHIEU P, *Pontoise: 300 cartes postales anciennes en 1900.* Paris: Val d'Oise 1985. pp 184, il.
270 HILLIER J, *A portfolio of old Poole.* Poole: Historical Trust 1985. pp 176.
271 CRAMER J, *The book of Portsmouth.* Buckingham: Barracuda Books 1985. pp 44, il.
272 PEAKE N ed, *City at war: a pictorial memento of Portsmouth, Gosport, Fareham, Havant and Chichester during World War 2.* Horndean: Milestone 1986. pp 160.
273 CANT C, *Saint Etienne autrefois.* Paris: Horvath 1985. pp 183, il.
274 HILLAIRET J, *L'île Saint Louis: rue par rue, maison par maison.* Paris: Minuil: Plaisir du Texte 1985. pp 285.
275 RIONDET A & MIRISKI P, *Senlis: entre la pierre et l'arbre.* Senlis: Editions de la Pommeraise 1985. pp 110, il.
276 RANCE AB, *Southhampton: an illustrated history.* Horndean: Milestone 1986. pp 192.
277 MOUNT GS, *The Sudbury region: an illustrated history.* Burlington: Windsor Pubs 1986. pp 160.
278 DALE R, *Toronto past and present.* Toronto: Toronto Public Library 1984, pp 31.
279 LINNEMER J, *Toulon autrefois: images retrouvées.* Paris: Horvath 1985, pp 144, il.
280 VIALLES H, *Tours pas à pas: ses rues, ses monuments, ses hommes célèbres.* Paris: Horvath 1985. pp 206, il.
281 LLOYD E & ORTON I, *Tower Hamlets at war.* Tower Hamlets Libraries 1986. pp 42.
282 LLOYD E & ORTON I, *Tower Hamlets past and present.* Tower Hamlets Libraries 1986. pp 42.
283 ALLEN RE, *Vancouver yesterday and today: a pictorial history.* Vancouver: Gordon Soule 1986. pp 160.
284 DAVIS C & MOONEY S, *Vancouver: an illustrated chronology.* Burlington: Windsor Pubs 1986. pp 288.
285 KLUCKNER M, *Victoria the way it was.* Vancouver: Whitecap Books 1986.
286 WATSON J, *Woolwich reviewed.* Greenwich Libraries 1986. pp 32.

**Literary portrayals and personal reminiscences**
287 DAYUS K, *Where there's life.* [Birmingham 1914–30]. Bath: Chivers 1986. pp x+ 369.
288 RETTER F, *An Exeter boyhood.* Exeter: Obelisk 1984. pp 96, il.
289 GLASSER R, *Growing up in the Gorbals.* [Glasgow] Chatto & Windus 1986. pp 207.
290 *Hastings voices: local people talking about their lives in Hastings and St Leonards before the second world war.* Brighton: Hastings Modern History Workshop 1982. pp 74, il.
291 FORSBERG R, *Means test kid: childhood in a Yorkshire fishing port during the hungry thirties.* [Hull] Beverley: Hutton 1985. pp 95, il.

292 POTTER I, *Tales from old Kenilworth: short stories based on historical fact*. Kenilworth: author 1985. pp 48, il.

293 *Visages urbains de Liège depuis 1830*. Liège: Crédit Communuel de Belgique 1985. pp 199, il.

294 FINN AL, *Grief forgotten: the tale of an East End Jewish boyhood*. Macdonald 1985. pp 208.

295 FINN AL, *Time remembered: the tale of an East End Jewish boyhood*. Macdonald 1985. pp 189.

296 MCCARTHY T, *Boysie* [Islington]. Braunton: Merlin Books 1986. pp 200.

297 RODAWAY A, *A London childhood*. Bath: Chivers 1986. pp xxiii + 239, il.

298 WATKIN H, *From Hulme all blessings flow: a collection of Manchester memories*. Manchester: N Richardson 1985. pp 99.

299 WHARTON MH, *Marlborough revisited and the war remembered*. Gloucester: A Sutton 1987. pp 128, il.

300 PADIN LC & GARDINER SJ, *Stroud and the five valleys in old photographs*. Alan Sutton 1986. pp 16.

301 HUTSON K, *Recollections of Uxbridge 1830–1940: a portrait of an English county town written about the year 1884 and descriptive of Uxbridge fifty years earlier*. Beaumaris: Uxbridge Local History Group 1985. pp 61.

**Statistical portrayals**

302 DAUZATS A & SERULLAZ M eds, *Bordeaux en 1832: carnet du musée du Louvre*. Paris: Hermann 1986. pp 96, il.

## II POPULATION

### RESEARCH METHODS, AIDS AND MATERIALS

303 BERENT IM, The east European Jewish immigrant in America: an index to the 1900 Baltimore census. *MdHM* 80 (1985) 280–306.

304 EDGINGTON SB, *Micro-history: local history and computing projects*. Hodder & Stoughton 1985. pp xii + 64.

305 NUSTELING HPH, La population d'Amsterdam de la fin du XVIe siècle au début du XIXe siècle. Une méthode de reconstitution. *Pop* 41 (1986) 961–77.

### GENERAL FEATURES OF URBAN POPULATIONS

see also 4, 74, 979

306 BLUM A & HOUDAILLE J, 12000 Parisiens en 1793. Sondage dans les cartes de civisme. *Pop* 41 (1986) 259–302.

307 BONVALET C, Les parisiens dans leur maturité: origine, parcours, intégration. *Pop* (1987) 225–47.

308 EBNER MH, Re-reading suburban America: urban population deconcentration, 1810–1890. *AmQ* 37 (1985) 368–81.

309 FAIR D, Population and urban growth in South Africa and sub-Saharan Africa. *Africa Institute of SA Bulletin* 8 (1985) 96–8.

310 FONSECA C, Valeur merchande, amour maternel et survie: aspects de la circulation des enfants dans un bidonville brésilien. *AESC* 40 (1985) 991–1022.

311 HORVATH R, La France en 1618 vue un statisticien hongrois, Maiton Szepsi Csombor. *Pop* 40 (1985) 335–46.

312 HOUDAILLE J, La nuptialité dans un faubourg de Manille à la fin du XIXe siècle. *Pop* 41 (1986) 163–4.

313 KLEPP SE, The demographic characteristics of Philadelphia 1788–1801: Zachariah Poulsen's bills of mortality. *PennH* 53 (1986) 201–21.

314 LAMOUREUX G, *Ottawa 1855–1876 et sa population canadienne-française*. Ottawa: author 1980.

315 LAMOUREUX G, *Ottawa 1876–1899 et sa population canadienne-française*. Ottawa: author 1982.

316 LAMOUREUX G, *Ottawa 1900–1926 et sa population canadienne-française*. Ottawa: author 1984.

317 LAPERCHE FOURNEL MS, *La population du duché du Lorraine de 1580 à 1720*. Nancy: Presse Universitaire de Nancy 1985. pp 236.

318 MATHEWS G, *Le choc démographique*. Montreal: Boreal Express 1984.

319 OBERLE R, La démographie mulhousienne sous Louis XIV.2. *RA* 111 (1985) 79–98.

320 RADEFF A, Espace et différenciation urbaine: une analyse factorielle de la population de Lausanne à la fin du XVIIIe siècle. *HEI* 7 (1986) 401–6.

321 STALS ELP ed, *Afrikaners in die Goudstad* (Afrikaners in the City of Gold) Vol 2. Pretoria: HAUM 1986. pp 220, il.


## NATALITY AND MORTALITY

322 COBB R, *La mort dans Paris: enquête sur le suicide, le meutre et autres morts subités à Paris au lendemain de la Terreur, octobre 1795–septembre 1801*. Paris: Chemin Vert 1985. pp 192.

323 DYE NS & SMITH NB, Mother love and infant death, 1750–1920. *JAH* 73 (1986) 329–53.

324 GINSBURG CA & SWEDLUND AC, Vox-specific mortality and economic opportunities: Massachusetts 1860–1899. *ConC* 1 (1986) 415–44.

325 MOSS D, Death in fifteenth century Tottenham. *LPC* 38 (1986) 36–44.


## DISEASE

326 CARMICHAEL AG, *Plague and reform in Renaissance Florence*. Cambridge: Cambridge UP 1986. pp 180.

327 CURSON PH, *Times of crisis. Epidemics in Sydney 1788–1900*. Sydney: Sydney UP 1985.

328 MAYNE AJC, *Fever, squalor and vice: sanitation and social policy in Victorian Sydney*. St Lucia: Queensland UP 1982.

329 WHITE KA, Pittsburgh in the great epidemic of 1918. *WPennHM* 68 (1985) 221–42.


## MEDICINE

see also 749, 1119–24,

330 BATER JH, Modernisation and public health in St Petersburg 1890–1914, *Forschungen zur Osteuropäischen Geschichte* 37 (1984) 253–69.

331 CLARKE C, *Bristol infirmary ... 250 years*. Portshead P 1985. pp 32, il.

332 DIGBY A, *From York Lunatic Asylum to Bootham Park hospital*. York: Borthwick Institute 1986.

333 DINET-LECOMTE MC, Recherche sur la clientèle hospitaliers aux XVIIe et XVIIIe siècles: l'exemple de Blois. *RHMC* 33 (1986) 345–73.

334 DINET-LECOMTE MC, La vie des personnes âgées à l'hôpital de Blois au XVIIIe siècle. *ADH* (1985) 311–21.

335 DINET-LECOMTE MC, Viellir et mourir à l'hôpital de Blois au XVIIIe siècle. *ADH* (1985) 85–101.

336 GRANSHAW L, *St Mark's Hospital: a social history of a specialist hospital*. King Edward's Hospital Fund 1985. pp xvi + 526, il.

337 *Histoire de l'école médicale de Montpellier*. Paris: Comité de travaux historiques et scientifiques 1985. pp 370.

338 LEWIS J, The prevention of diptheria in Canada and Britain 1914–1945. *JSocH* 20 (1986) 163–76.

339 MARLAND H, *Medicine and society in Wakefield and Huddersfield, 1780–1870*. Cambridge: Cambridge UP 1987.

340 RIVETT G, *The development of the London hospital system 1823–1982*. King Edward's Hospital Fund 1986, pp 423.

341 ROSS EC, *Public virtue, public love: the early years of the Dublin lying-in hospital*. Dublin: O'Brien 1987. pp 176, il.

342 SIMON N, *La pitie salpêtrière*. Paris: Arbres à image 1986. pp 126, il.

343 SULLIVAN JR & BALL NR, *Growing to serve: a history of Victoria Hospital, London, Ontario*. London: Victoria Hospital 1985. pp 198.


## MIGRATION TO, FROM AND BETWEEN TOWNS

see also 714, 822

344 BARMAN J, Ethnicity in search of status: British middle and upper class migration to British Columbia in the late nineteenth and early twentieth centuries. *CanEthS* 18 (1986) 32–51.

345 BEAFLEURY F de, *L'établissement des juifs à Bordeaux et à Bayonne*. Paris: Harriet 1986. pp 256, il.

346 BRIGGS ER, Une évasion de protestants nimois: la fortune de la famille Vernedi. *XVII* 17 (1985) 161–77.

347 COSSE DURLING J, Le droit d'asile à Valenciennes aux XIVe et XVe siècles d'après les listes entrée en franchise. *RN* 267 (1985) 905–21.

348 DOLAN C, Famille et intégration des étrangers à Aix en Provence au XVIe siècle. *PH* 142 (1985) 401–11.

349 DUBLIN T, Rural-urban migrants in industrial New England: the case of Lynn, Massachusetts in the mid-nineteenth century. *JAH* 73 (1986) 623–44.

350 FRANCOIS E ed, *Immigration et société urbaine en Europe occidentale: XVIe–XXe siècles.* Paris: Recherches sur les civilisations 1985. pp 156.

351 GOTTLIEB P, *Making their own way: southern blacks migration to Pittsburgh 1916–1930.* Champaign: Illinois UP 1987.

352 HOCHSTADT S, Urban migration in Imperial Germany: towards a quantitive model. *CHA Hist Papers* (1986) 197–210.

353 NICHOLAS S & SHERGOLD JPR, Internal migration in England 1818–1839. *JHG* 13 (1987) 155–68.

354 PARTON A, Poor law settlement certificates and migration to and from Birmingham. *LPS* 38 (1987) 23–9.

355 POULAIN M, *Urbanisation et migration en Belgique: une vue d'ensemble de 1800 à nos jours.* Louvain: Dept de Démographie 1984.

356 POULAIN M, *Urbanisation, migrations et problèmes démographiques urbains en Belgique.* Brussels: Fondation Roi Baudouin 1984.

357 ROSE GS, The origins of Canadian settlers in southern Michigan. *OntH* 79 (1987) 31–52.

358 STREIFFELIER F & MUDIMBA M, *Village, ville et migration au Zaire: enquête psycho-sociologique sur mouvement des populations de la sous-région de la Tshopo à la ville de Kisangani.* Paris: l'Harmattan 1987. pp 178.

**FAMILY AND HOUSEHOLD STRUCTURE**
see also 828

359 BENERIA L & ROLDAN M, *The crossroads of class and gender: industrial homework, subcontracting and household dynamics in Mexico city.* Chicago: Chicago UP 1987. pp 224.

360 BRUCKER J, *Giovanni and Lusanna: love and marriage in Renaissance Florence.* Weidenfeld & Nicolson 1986. pp x + 138, il.

361 BULLEN J, Hidden workers: child labour and the family economy in late nineteenth century urban Ontario. *Labour/Le Travail* 18 (1986) 163–78.

362 COURGEAU D, Constitution de la famille et urbanisation. *Pop* (1987) 57–81.

363 DONNELLY FK, *Family and household in mid-nineteenth century New Brunswick.* Saint John: U of New Brunswick 1986. pp 106.

364 GERRISH M, Household structure and status: the case of textile workers in nineteenth century Nottingham. *BLHEMR* 21 (1986) 1–16.

365 FAUVE CHAMOUX A, Innovation et comportement parental en milieu urbain (XV–XIXe siècles). *AESC* 40 (1985) 1023–39.

366 GERRISH M, Household structure and status: the case of textile workers in nineteenth century Nottingham. *BLHEMR* 21 (1986) 1–16.

367 MATOVIC MR, the Stockholm marriage: extra-legal family formation in Stockholm 1860–1890. *ConC* 1 (1986) 385–414.

368 REHER DS, Old issues and new perspectives: household and family within an urban context in nineteenth century Spain. *ConC* 2 (1987) 103–44.

369 WALL R, Leaving home and the process of household formation in pre-industrial England. *ConC* 2 (1987) 77–102.

370 YOUNG M & WILMOTT P, *Family and kinship in East London.* Routledge & Kegan Paul 1986. pp xxxi + 234, il.

**III PHYSICAL STRUCTURE**

**RESEARCH METHODS, AIDS AND MATERIALS**

371 BRONER K, *New York face à son patrimoiné: préservation de patrimoiné architectural urbain à New York, analyse de méthodologie étude de cas sen le secteur historique de Soho.* Paris: Mardaga 1986. pp 272, il.

372 BURNBY J, John Conyers, London's first archaeologist. *LoMAS* 35 (1984) 63–80.

**Archives**

373 FOULAR J, *Protocol book of John Foular.* Edinburgh: Scottish Record Society 1985. pp xxviii + 223.

374 GEERE J, *Index to Oxfordshire hearth tax 1665.* Oxford: Oxfordshire Family History Society 1985. pp 64.

375 KAIN R, *An atlas and index of the tithe files of mid-nineteenth century England and Wales*. Cambridge: Cambridge UP 1986. pp xxvii + 651.
376 TURNER M & MILLS D eds, *Land and property: the English land tax 1692–1832*. Gloucester: Alan Sutton 1986. pp xiii + 239, il.

## Printed documentary sources and bibliographies
377 DIXON N, *An archaeological bibliography of Bristol*. City of Bristol Museum 1987. pp 58.

## PHYSICAL AND STRUCTURAL CHARACTERISTICS OF TOWNS
378 ATKIN M, Excavation in Gloucester: an interim report. *Glenevis* (1986) 3–12.
379 BARFOOT J, Machynlleth town hall excavations, 1983. *MC* 74 (1986) 79–84.
380 BEAUSSART P, Valenciennes: première évaluation d'un patrimoiné archaeologique urbain. *RN* 264 (1985) 103–19.
381 BEDWIN O, Excavations at the Mount House, Braintree. *EAH* 16 (1983–4) 28–39.
382 BIDEAU D, *Les lieux disparus de Lyon*. Lyon: Manufacture 1985. pp 172, il.
383 BRIMBLECOMBE P, *The big smoke: a history of air pollution in London since medieval times*. Methuen 1986. pp 220.
384 BLIECK G, Les fouilles de l'îlot des tanneurs à Lille. *RN* 264 (1985) 121–40.
385 BURNS LS et al, eds, *Spatial cycles*. Aldershot: Gower 1986. pp 200.
386 ELLIS P, Excavations at Friarn St and West Quay, Bridgwater 1983/4. *SANHS* 127 (1985) 69–80.
387 FEVRIER PA, FIXOT M & RIVET L, Les fouilles des abords de la cathédrale de Fréjus. Apport à la connaissance de la topographie urbaine. *PH* 141 (1985) 267–77.
388 FINK DPJ, *Walsall guildhall: past, present and future*. Walsall: Walsall Local History Soc 1984. pp 29, il.
389 GRICOURT D, Les fouilles de quartier Baudimont en 1985 – les monnaies. *RN* 268 (1986) 101–20.
390 GRIFFITHS D & GRIFFITH FM, An excavation at 39 Fore Street, Totnes. *DevA* 42 (1984) 77–100.
391 GRUBER K, *Forme et caractère de la ville allemande*. Bruxelles: Archives de l'architecture moderne 1985. pp 336, il.
392 HANOUNE R & MULLER A, Recherches archaeologiques à Cassel (Nord) Castellum Manapiorum 111. *RN* 264 (1985) 177–87; 268 (1986) 65–74.
393 HUNT PE, Excavations at the Old High Pavement School, Nottingham. *ThS* 89 (1985) 143–44.
394 JACQUES A et al, Les fouilles de la rue Baudimont à Arras en 1985. *RN* 268 (1986) 75–97.
395 LOMBARD JOURDAN A, *Aux origines de Paris*. Paris: CNRS 1985. pp 248.
396 MASSON PHILLIPS EN, The bounds of the borough of Totnes. *DART* 118 (1986) 13–24.
397 MILTON BH, Excavations at the White Hart hotel, George St, Harwich 1979. *EAH* 16 (1983–4) 23–7.
398 MURPHY K & O'MAHONEY C, Excavation and survey at Cardigan Castle. *Cer* 10 (1985) 189–218.
399 PELLETIER A, Archaeologie et histoire à Lyon de 1974 à 1986. *CdH* 32 (1987) 3–25.
400 ROBLIN M, *Quand Paris était à la campagne: origine, rurales et urbaines de vingt arrondissements*. Paris: Picard 1985. pp 256, il.
401 SHOESMITH R, St Guthlac's priory, Hereford. *WNHFC* 94 (1984) 321–51.
402 THOMAS EN, JE Pritchard and the archaeology of Bristol. *BGAS* 104 (1986) 7–25.

Ancient
see also 538
403 JAMES T, Excavation at the Augustinian priory of St John and St Teulyddog, Carmarthen, 1979. *ACa* 134 (1985) 53–105.
404 Roman Derby excavations 1968–1983. *DAJ* 105 (1985) 7–345.
405 WICKENDEN NP, Prehistoric settlement and the Romano-British small town at Heybridge, Essex. *EAH* 17 (1986) 7–60.

Medieval and early modern
406 ASHTON N & BARWOOD P, The excavations of post-medieval structures at Plas Du, Montgomery 1980–82. *ACa* 134 (1985) 190–209.

407 BAKER E, Three excavations in Bedford, 1979–84. *BedA* 17 (1984) 51–71.

408 BLIECK G eds, Les fouilles de la collègiale Saint Pierre de Lille. Les fouilles 1985. *RN* 268 (1986) 121–52.

409 DANIELS R, The medieval defences of Hartlepool, Cleveland: the results of excavation and survey. *DurA* 1 (1984) 67–71; 2 (1986) 63–72.

410 EDDY MR, Excavations in medieval Rochford. *EAH* 16 (1983–4) 7–22.

411 EVISON VI, *Dover: the Buckland Anglo-Saxon cemetery*. Historic Buildings and Monuments Commission for England 1987. pp 350, il.

412 GADD D, The London inn of the abbots of Waltham: a revised reconstruction of a medieval town house in Lovat Lane. *LoMAS* 33 (1982) 171–7.

413 HASLAM J, The ecclesiastical topography of early medieval Bedford. *BedA* 17 (1984) 41–51.

414 PORTER S, Property destruction in civil war London. *LoMAS* 35 (1984) 59–62.

415 ROUSSEAU X, Les fouilles de l'église Saint Etienne à Lille, 1983–84. *RN* 264 (1985) 141–7.

416 SLATER TR, The topography and planning of medieval Lichfield: a critique. *SSAHS* 26 (1986) 36–43.

417 STROUD D, The site of the borough at Old Sarum 1066–1226: an examination of some documentary evidence. *WANSM* 80 (1986) 120–6.

418 TRINGHAM NJ, The chantry priest's house in Lichfield cathedral close. *SSAHS* 26 (1986) 36–43.

419 WARD S, Recent work on the medieval wall of Chester. *JCAS* 68 (1985) 59–70.

420 WEDDELL PJ, The excavation of medieval and later houses at Wolborough St, Newton Abbot. *DevA* 43 (1985) 77–131.

421 WHITE R, Excavations in Caernarvon 1976–77. *ACa* 134 (1985) 53–105.

## Modern

422 BRUNET JP, Constitution d'un espace urbain: Paris et sa banlieu de la fin du XIXe siècle à 1940. *AESC* 40 (1985) 641–659.

423 DIETZ P, *Garrison: 10 British military towns*. Brasseys Defence 1986. pp 225.

424 KELLY I, *Hong Kong: a political-geographic analysis*. Macmillan 1986. pp 192.

425 RELPH E, *The modern urban landscape 1880 to the present*. Beckenham: Croom Helm 1987. pp 288.

## PHYSICAL AND STRUCTURAL CHARACTERISTICS OF AREAS WITHIN TOWNS

426 BRAUMAN A & LE DEMANET M, *Le 200, la cité scientifique et la ville*. Paris: Archives d'architecture moderne 1985. pp 180, il.

427 BRULET R et al, Le quartier Saint Brice de Tournai à l'époque mérovingienne. *RN* 69 (1986) 361–9.

428 CHERVALIER J, *Dictionnaire historique illustré des rues de Puy en Velay*. Paris: Lafitte 1985. pp 230, il.

429 GARETTA JC, *L'Ile de la Cité*. Paris: Manufacture 1987. pp 192, il.

430 GENTY YN, *Le domaine de la ville de Paris au XVIIIe siècle*. Paris: Presse Universitaire de France 1985. pp 104.

431 HARDOY J E & SATTERTHWAITE D, *Small and intermediate urban centres: their role in regional and national development in the Third World*. Hodder & Stoughton 1986. pp 416.

432 MOUSNIER J, *Paris, 18e arrondissement: historique et pittoresque*. Paris: M Dansel 1985. pp 212.

433 PORT ZAMPARC C de, *La cité de la musique: Paris-Villette*. Paris: Champ Vallon 1986. pp 48, il.

## The central business district

434 BLOCK EJ, *Macmillan guide to the City*. Macmillan 1986. pp 180.

435 CLARKE M, *Regulating the city: competition, scandal and reform*. Milton Keynes: Open UP 1986. pp 192.

436 PLENDER J, *The square mile: a guide to the new City of London*: Century 1985. pp 246.

## Industrial areas

437 NEVEUX H, Entreprise et residence: le cas des fabricants de bas caennais, (1714–1716). *AdN* 37 (1987) 13–22.

**Working-class areas**

438 FREY JP, *La ville industrielle et ses urbanités: la destruction ouvriers, employés. Le Creuset 1870–1930*. Paris: Mandaga 1986. pp 386, il.

439 MELVERN L, *The end of the street*. Methuen 1986. [London]

**Suburbs**

see also 422, 480, 524

440 ABBOTT C, The suburban sunbelt. *JUH* 13 (1987) 275–301.

441 ADAMOWICZ S, *Paris, 17e arrondissement*. Paris: M Dansel 1985. pp 200, il.

442 COUTRAS J, *Des villes traditionnelles aux nouvelles banlieues*. Paris: Sedes 1987. pp 176.

443 FARANT S, *Changes in Brighton and Hove's suburbs: Preston and Patcham 1841–1871*. Hove: author 1985. pp 86.

444 FISHMAN RL, American suburbs? English suburbs: a transatlantic comparison. *JUH* 13 (1987) 237–51.

445 HALL J & R, Suburbanisation in metropolitan Essex: the interrupted development of a Repton Park at Highams. *LJ* 12 (1986) 89–99.

446 JACKSON KT, *Crabgrass frontier: the suburbanization of the United States*. Oxford UP 1985. pp.x + 396.

447 JACKSON KT, Suburbanization in England and North America: a response. *JUH* 13 (1987) 312–16.

448 LEMOINE M, *Les cités interdites*. Paris: Encre 1987. pp 430.

449 PARASTEAU J, *Voyage insolite dans la banlieu de Paris: itinéraire historique et sentimental des banlieux de Paris*. Paris: Perrin 1985. pp 704, il.

450 ROULEAU B, *Villages et faubourgs de l'ancien Paris*. Paris: Seuil 1985. pp 380.

451 THORNE R, The White Hart Lane estate: an LCC venture in suburban development. *LJ* 12 (1986) 80–8.

452 WRIGHT G, Tradition in the service of modernity: architecture and urbanism in French colonial policy, 1900–1930. *JMH* 59 (1987) 291–316.

453 BROWEN MB, *Richmond Park: the history of a royal deer park*. Hale 1985. pp 208.

454 COUTTS S, Easeful death in Toronto: a history of Mount Pleasant cemetery. *SSSAB* 11 (12986) 8–10.

455 EDGAR D, *The Royal Parks*. WH Allen 1986. pp 216.

456 LAMONDE Y & MONTPETIT R, *Le parc Sohmer de Montreal 1889–1919. Un lieu de culture urbaine*. Québec: Institute québecois de recherche sur la culture 1986. pp 231.

457 LYTH P, The deer parks of the archbishops of York at Southwell. *ThS* 90 (1986) 14–29.

458 SMITH H, Down (town) on the farm: Ottawa's central experimental farm. *CanHeritage* 12 (1986) 14–17.

459 SOPRANI A, *Jardins de Paris*. Paris: MA 1986. pp 288, il.

460 TONKA H & AURICOSTE I eds, *Parc ville Villette*. Paris: Champ Vallon 1987. pp 124, il.

461 TSCHOMI B, *Cinégramme folie: le parc de la Villette: Paris dixneuvième arrondissement*. Paris: Champvallon 1987. pp 60, il.

**SITES AND BUILDINGS**

462 CRAWFORD P, Of grounds tastefuly laid out: the landscaping of public buildings in nineteenth century Ontario. *Society for the Study of Architecture in Canada Bulletin* 11 (1986) 1–7.

463 GONTHIER N, *Sites et monuments historiques de Lyon*. Paris: L'Hermes 1985. pp 172, il.

**Building industry**

464 DOUGHTY M, *Building the industrial city*. Leicester: Leicester UP 1986. pp xii + 212.

465 GRISLAN J & LE BLAN M, L'ait de bâtir chez les Roubaisiens: la filature Motte Bossut (1853–1985). *RN* 265 (1985) 485–516.

**Building methods**

466 PORTER S, Thatching in early modern Norwich. *NoA* 38 (1986) 310–12.

467 TRINGHAM NJ, Bishop's Palace, Lichfield cathedral close: its construction 1686–87. *SSAHS* 27 (1987) 57–63.

468 WOODGER A, The building history of St John the Baptist Church Peterborough. *NPP* (1986–7) 235–40.

## Architecture

469 BEHAR M & SALAMA M, *Paris nouvelle architecture*. Paris: Regirex-France 1985. pp 175, il.

470 BELLAN G & RIVIERE R, *Architectures parisiennes: la rue Réaumur*. Paris: Parage 1986. pp 32, il.

471 BLANC A, *La cathédrale de Valence*. Valence: Peuple libre 1985. pp 212, il.

472 BORSI F & GOLODI E, *Vienne architecture 1900*. Paris: Flammarion 1985. pp 288, il.

473 BOUCHAT M, Contribution à l'etude de loeuvre de l'architecte liègeois Bartholémy Dignelle (1724–1784). *RN* 68 (1986) 877–92.

474 CHARBONNEL N & EVEN P, *L'hôpital de la Rochelle*. Paris: l'arbre à images 1986.

475 CHASLIN F, *Le Paris de François Mitterand: histoire des grands projects architecturaux*. Paris: Gallimand 1985. pp 254, il.

476 COCLANIS PA. The sociology of architecture in colonial Charleston: pattern and process in an eighteenth century southern city. *JSocH* 10 (1985) 607–23.

477 COLVIN H, Inigo Jones and the Church of St Michael le Querne. *LJ* 12 (1986) 36–9.

478 DEMOUY P, *Nôtre Dame de Reims: la cathédrale royale*. Paris: Centurion Nôtre histoire 1986. pp 117, il.

479 DURLIAT M, *Saint Sernin de Toulouse*. Toulouse: Eche 1986. pp 221, il.

480 ETIENNE P, *Le Faubourg Poissonière: architecture, élégance et décor*. Paris: Délégation à l'action artistique de la ville de Paris 1986. pp 312, il.

481 FOUCART-BONRVILLE J, Les débuts du neoclassicisme à Amiens (1761–1778). *RN* 68 (1986) 791–808.

482 Le Grand siècle de l'architecture genevoise 1800–1914: un guide de douze promenades. Paris: Georg 1985. pp 231, il.

483 GLIBOTA A & EDELMANN F, *Chicago 150 ans d'architecture, 1833–1933*. Paris: Paris Art Centre 1985. pp 384.

484 GOWANS A, *The comfortable house: North American suburban architecture, 1890–1930*. Cambridge, Ma: MIT P 1986.

485 GREEN EM, On change, grandeur and designs: the early history of the Middlesbrough Exchange. *CTLHS* 50 (1986) 71–80.

486 HARVEY AD, Pioneering classical barbarism. [Milner Sq, London] *LoMAS* 35 (1984) 271–4.

487 HEERS J ed, *Fortification, portes de villes, places publiques dans le monde méditerranéen*. Paris: Presse de l'universitaire de Paris-Sorbonne 1985. pp 340.

488 HIBBERT C, Carlton House. *LJ* 12 (1986) 51–5.

489 JOUDIOU G, Saint Wasnon et Saint Veast: deux remarquables églises de Contant d'Ivry. *RN* 68 (1986) 835–58.

490 KEARNEY BT, Inspiration and appropriateness? Sub-tropical Deco and the Berea style. *Planning and Building Developments* 74 (1985) 43–9.

491 LEIGHTON JM, South Africa house in the making. *Lantern* 2 (1985) 3–20.

492 LESAFFRE O, Les projets de Jacques François Joseph Lesaffre pour le parlement de Douai. *RN* 68 (1986) 809–26.

493 MACDONALD WL *The architecture of the Roman Empire. Vol 2 An urban appraisal*. New Haven: Yale UP 1986. pp 328.

494 MCTEAGUE M, In the spirit of a new epoch. *Planning and Building Developments* 73 (1985) 13–21.

495 MARE EA, Die Alhambra (The Alhambra). *De Arte* 32 (1985) 20–32.

496 MERCIER G & LECLERC M, *La place Stanislas*. Nancy: L'est republicain 1986. pp 37, il.

497 MORRIS GCR, Surgeons Hall, Old Bailey designed by William Jones. *LoMAS* 35 (1984) 91–9.

498 PEYREFITTE A & BIGAL F, *L'Hôtel de ville de Paris*. Paris: Vilo 1985, pp 160, il.

499 PILLON-CAILLOL V, Un foyer négligé de Néoclassisme en Provence: Toulon dans l'année 1780. *PH* 140 (1985) 179–93.

500 PONSAR A. *Nôtre Dame de Paris: le mystère devoilé*. Paris: Centurion Nôtre Histoire 1986. pp 117, il.

501 PORT MH, An aedile for London. *LJ* 12 (1986) 58–64.

502 PORT MH, An aedification of architects. *LJ* 12 (1986) 100–8.

503 PROUDFOOT OR, The development of architectural education in Sydney 1880–1930. *HS* 21 (1984) 197–211.

504 SABATINE-LECRET V & GLOTON JJ, Un chef d'oeuvre inédit à l'aube du baroque en Provence: L'hôtel de Grimaldi Regusse à la Ciotat. *PH* 140 (1985) 123–33.

505 SAINT A, Whatever happened to Jonathan Carr. *LJ* 12 (1986) 65–79.

506 SAINT FARE GARNOT PN, *L'hôpital Saint Louis*. Paris: l'arbre à images 1986.

507 SAUNDERS A. Westminster Hall: a sixteenth century drawing. *LJ* 12 (1986) 29–35.

508 STERN R et al, *New York 1900: metropolitan architecture and urbanism, 1890–1915*. New York: Rizzoli International 1984. pp 520.

509 STIENNON P, Contradiction à l'étude des églises de Liège (XVIe XVIIIe siècles). *RN* 68 (1986) 893–928.
510 VAN DER WAAL G–M & GRUTER W, *From mining camp to metropolis. The architecture of Johannesburg 1886–1940*. Johannesburg: Van Rensburg 1986. pp xv + 294, il.
511 WESTFALL W & THURLBY M, The church in the town: the adoption of sacred architecture to urban settings in Ontario. *EC/CS* 20 (1986) 49–60.
512 WILLIAMS M, *Berkeley: an appreciation of its buildings and history*. Berkeley: author 1987. pp 24.

**Building surveys**
513 Francis Sheppard and the survey of London. *LJ* 12 (1986) 3–10.

## HOUSING

**Housebuilding**
514 BAXTER JH, *Settlement examination 1720–1844: Rawreth and Rayleigh, Essex.* Benfleet: Essex Society for Family History 1985. pp 48.
515 BOTT O, The growth of Macclesfield in the 1820s. 1 A suburb for silk workers in Macclesfield. *ChesH* 18 (1986) 31–4.
516 BOTT O, The growth of Macclesfield in the 1820s. 2 The reasons for and the development of progress of the housing development. *ChesH* 19 (1987) 19–24.
517 BOUDRIOT PD, Un source pour l'étude de l'habitat parisien au début du XVIIe siècle: Pierre le Muet. *HES* (1985) 29–41.
518 CAYEZ P. Les petits logements dans les grandes villes. *MS* 137 (1986) 280–53.
519 DAVIES RJ & MCCARTHY JJ, *Residential growth in the Durban-Pietermaritzburg metropolitan region during the 1960s*. Pietermaritzburg: Natal Town and Regional Planning Commission 1984. pp 78.
520 DEWAR D, Housing policy in South Africa: an evaluatory overview. *RSA 2000* (1985) 19–34.
521 GROVES R, *A review of recent housing research in England and Wales*. Birmingham: Centre for Urban and Regional Studies, U of Birmingham 1984. pp 46.
522 HORSEY M, London speculative housebuilding of the 1830s: official control and popular taste. *LJ* 11 (1985) 147–59.
523 MAASDORP G & HAARHOFF E, *Housing policy in conditions of rapid urbanisation*. Durban: UN 1984.
524 MAGAIS S, Le mouvement de locataires à Paris et dans le banlieu 1919–1925. *MS* 137 (1986) 55–76.
525 MIRON J, *Housing in postwar Canada: demographic change, household formation and housing demand*. Montreal & Kingston: McGill-Queens UP 1987. pp 416.
526 ORSON WE, The making of a Baltimore row house community: the Edmondson Avenue area. *MdHM* 80 (1985) 203–27.
527 PENANT T, Housing the urban labor force in Malawi: an historical overview 1930–1980. *African Urban Studies* 16 (1983) 1–22.
528 VILL MJ, *Building enterprise in late nineteenth century Baltimore*. *JHG* 12 (1986) 162–81.
529 WEIR C, The growth of an inner urban housing development, Forest Fields, Nottingham 1883–1914. *ThS* 89 (1985) 122–31.

**House types**
see also 412, 418, 420, 484, 491
530 BROWN AB, A medieval stone house in Chester. *ChesH* 68 (1985) 143–53.
531 BUTTENWIESER AL, Shelter for what and for whom on the route towards Vladeck houses 1930 to 1940. *JUH* 12 (1986) 391–413.
532 CHAGNY R, Le logement social à Grenoble dans l'entre deux guerres. L'Office publique des habitations à bon marché de 1921 à 1938. *MS* 137 (1986) 77–108.
533 DAWSON D et al, *The cheaper end of the owner occupied housing market: an analysis for the city of Glasgow 1971–1977*. Edinburgh: Scottish Economic Planning Dept 1982. pp 125.
534 Entry deleted
535 HAMNETT C & RANDOLPH B, The rise and fall of London's purpose-built blocks of privately rented flats 1853–1983. *LJ* 11 (1985) 160–75.
536 HANNA DB, *The layered city: a revolution in housing in nineteenth century Montreal*. Montreal: Dept Geography McGill University 1986.

537 JEFFREY S, John James and Carpenter's buildings. *LoMAS* 33 (1982) 187–95.

538 MCWHIRR A, *Houses in Roman Cirencester. Cirencester Excavations 3*. Cirencester: Cirencester Excavation Committee 1986. pp 272.

539 MURTON B, Colonial cottage to state house: one century of housing styles in Gisborne, New Zealand. *JCultG* 5 (1984) 103–22.

540 PETOUT P, *Hotels et maisons de Saint Malo: XVIe–XVIIe siècles*. Paris: Picaud 1985. pp 256, il.

541 RADFORD DJC, A postscript on the stoepkamer. *Lantern* 3 (1985) 44–8.

542 RADFORD D, The detached kitchen: its occurrence in South African architecture. *Restorica* 16 (1984) 18–27.

543 RADFORD D, The stoepkamer tradition in South African architecture. *Lantern* 1 (1984) 26–34.

544 REVAULT J, GOLVIN L & AMAHAN A, *Palais et demeures de Fes. 1 L'époque mézinide et saadienne XIV–XVIIe siècles*. pp 352.

545 WESSELS C, Die kultuurhistoriese beland van die hardebieshuise van Hopefield (The cultural historical significance of the hardebies' houses at Hopefield. *Kronos* 10 (1985) 3–22.

## Homeownership

see also 599

546 HARRIS R, Boom and bust: the effects of house price inflation on homeownership patterns in Montreal, Toronto and Vancouver. *Cangeog* 30 (1986) 302–15.

547 HARRIS R, Class differences in urban home ownership: an analysis of recent Canadian changes. *Housing Studies* 1 (1986) 133–46.

548 HARRIS R & HAMMETT C, The myth of the promised land: the social diffusion of homeownership in Britain and North America. *AAAG* 77 (1987) 176–85.

549 KARN VA, *Home ownership in the inner city: salvation or despair?* Aldershot: Gower 1986. pp ix + 162.

550 LAWSON R & NAISON M, *From tenant rebellion to tenant management: housing protest and community change in New York city 1904–1984*. New Brunswick; Rutgers UP 1986.

551 PEEL M, On the margins: lodgers and boarders in Boston 1860–1900. *JAH* 72 (1986) 813–34.

552 SCHWARTZ J, The Consolidated Tenants League of Harlem: black self-help vs. white liberal intervention in ghetto housing 1939–1944, *Afro-Americans in New York Life and History* 10 (1986) 31–51.

553 SCHWARTZ J, Tenant unions in New York City's low rent housing 1933–1949. *JUH* 12 (1986) 414–43.

## Housing conditions

see also 606, 680

554 BURNETT J, *A social history of housing 1815–1985*. Methuen 1986. pp 387.

555 LATREMOUILLE J, *Pride of home: the working class housing tradition in Nova Scotia 1749–1949*. Hantsport, NS: Lancelot P 1986. pp 96.

556 NERDON MORTON C, Black housing patterns in Baltimore City 1885–1953. *MdH* 26 (1986) 25–39.

557 SZUCHMAN MD, Household structure and political crisis: Buenos Aires 1810–1860. *LARR* 21 (1986) 55–94.

## IV SOCIAL STRUCTURE

### RESEARCH METHODS, AIDS AND MATERIALS

see also 748

558 BURSTIN H, Pour un histoire sociopolitique du Paris révolutionnaires: réflexions méthodologiques. *AHRF* 263 (1986) 22–34.

559 DUCOUDRAY E, La bourgeousie parisienne et la Révolution remarques méthodoloques pour de nouvelles recherches. *AHRF* 263 (1986) 7–21.

560 *Registres de la Compagnie des pasteurs de Genève au temps de Calvin*. Paris: Droz 1986. pp xxiv + 528.

## SOCIAL STRUCTURE AND CHARACTERISTICS OF TOWNS

Ancient
561 GAUTHIER N & PICARD JC eds, *Topographie chrétienne des cités de la Gaule des origines au milieu du VIIIe siècle.* 4 vols. Paris: de Boccard 1986. pp 65, 105, 146, 80.

Medieval and early modern
562 NASH GB, The social evolution of pre-industrial American cities, 1700–1800. *JUH* 13 (1986) 115–46.
563 UNDERDOWN D, *Revel, riot and rebellion: popular politics and culture in England 1603–1660.* Oxford: Oxford UP 1987. pp xii + 336, il.

Modern
see also 100, 875
564 BARNES ST, *Patrons and power: creating a political economy in metropolitan Lagos.* Manchester: Manchester UP 1986. pp 336, il.
565 BAZIN JF, *Vivre à Dijon en 1900.* Paris: Horvath 1985. pp 199, il.
566 ELLIOT M, *Heartbeat London: the anatomy of a super city.* Firethorn 1986. pp 224.
567 EWART P, *A poor man's Rye: the daily life of a labouring family 1847–1983.* Canterbury: author 1985. pp 36, il.
568 FAURE D et al, *From village to city: studies in the traditional roots of Hong Kong society.* Hong Kong: Centre of Asian Studies, Hong Kong U 1987.
569 FITZGERALD S, *Rising damp. Life and work in Sydney 1870–90.* Melbourne: Oxford UP 1987.
570 GARDINER M, *The other side of the counter: the life of a shop girl 1925–45.* Brighton: Queenspark 1985. pp 39, il.
571 GARRIOCH D, *Neighbourhood and community in Paris, 1740–1790.* Cambridge: Cambridge UP 1986. pp ix + 404, il.
572 GIRFFEN C, Towards an urban social history of New Zealand. *NZJH* 20 (1986) 111–32.
573 INGHAM GK, *Capitalism divided?: the city and industry in British social development.* Basingstoke: Macmillan 1984. pp viii + 304.
574 LINTEAU P–A, Rapport de pouvoir et emergence d'une nouvelle élite canadienne-française à Montreal. *EC/CS* 21 (1986) 163–72.
575 MCCALMAN J, *Struggletown: public and private life in Richmond 1900–1965.* Melbourne: Melbourne UP 1984.
576 MAYERM RENAUD M, *La distribution de la pauvreté et de la richesse dans les régions urbaines du Québec: portrait de la région de Montréal.* Montréal: Centre du services sociaux du Montréal métropolitan 1986. pp 109.
577 MITCHELL JC, *Cities, society and social perception: a central African perspective.* Oxford: Clarendon 1987. pp 298.
578 MORRIS RJ, *Class, power and social structure in nineteenth century British towns.* Leicester: Leicester UP 1986. pp 240 (Themes in urban history)
579 OSBORN B & DUBOURG T, *Maryborough: a social history 1854–1904.* Maryborough: Maryborough City Council 1985.
580 PEAK S, *Fishermen of Hastings: two hundred years of the fishing community.* St Leonards: New Books 1985. pp 160.
581 ROOS JP & SICINSKI A, *Ways and styles of life in Finland and Poland: comparative studies on urban populations.* Gower 1987. pp 212, il.
582 *Saint Nazaire et le mouvement ouvrier de 1939 à 1945.* Saint Nazaire: Aremor 1986. pp 288.
583 SCWARZ L, London apprentices in the seventeenth century: some problems. *LPS* 37 (1986) 18–22.
584 SIGOULES A & GIRAUD R, *Vivre à Bédarieux de 1870 à 1940.* Bédarieux: Société archaeologique et historique des hauts cantons de l'Hérault 1985. pp 179, il.
585 STEPHENSON J, 'Emancipation' and its problems: war and society in Wurtemberg 1939–45. *EHQ* 17 (1987) 345–66.
586 TREPANIER P, La société canadienne d'économie sociale de Montréal 1888–1911: sa fondation, ses buts et ses activités. *CHR* 67 (1986) 343–67.

## SOCIAL STRUCTURE AND CHARACTERISTICS OF AREAS WITHIN TOWNS
587 HEINRITZ G & LICHTGENBERGER E, *The take off of suburbia and the crisis of the central city.* Stuttgart: Franz Steiner Verlag 1986.
588 MATHEWS, G, *L'évolution de l'occupation du parc residential plus ancien de Montréal de 1951 à 1979.* Montréal: Institut National de la Recherche scientifique 1986. pp 240.

## Inner city
see also 587

589  HALL P ed, *The inner city in context: the final report of the SSRC Inner Cities working party*. Aldershot: Gower 1986. pp viii + 175.
590  HAUSNER V, *Changing cities: an introduction to the ESRC Inner Cities Research Programme*. ESRC 1985. pp 38.
591  KENNEDY C, *Mayfair: a social history*. Hutchinson 1986. pp xvi + 300, il.


## Slums
see also 1156–7

592  GODWIN G, *London shadows: a glance at the homes of the thousands*. Garland 1985. pp viii + 79.
593  REES C, *Miracles in the slums* [Chicago and Illinois]. Garland 1985. pp 301.
594  WHITE J, *The worst street in north London, Campbell Bank, Islington between the wars*. Routledge & Kegan Paul 1986. pp 312.
595  WILLIAMS R, *London rookeries and colliers' slums*. Garland 1985. pp viii + 82, il.


## Suburbs
see also 312, 587, 1094

596  *Actes colloqués d'Angers 6–7 décembre 1984: les périphéries urbaines: quelles sociétés? quels espaces? quel dynamisme?* Caen: centre de publication de l'université de Caen 1985. pp 270, il.
597  BINFORD HG, *The first suburbs: residential communities on the Boston periphery 1815–1860*. Chicago: Chicago UP 1985. pp xiv + 304 il.
598  BOULTON J, *Neighbourhood and society: a London suburb in the seventeenth century*. [Southwark] Cambridge UP 1986. pp 432, il.
599  EDEL M et al, *Shaky palaces: home ownership and social mobility in Boston's suburbanization*. New York: Columbia UP 1985. pp 334.
600  KARR RD, Brookline and the making of an elite suburb. *CHiH* 13 (1984) 36–47.
601  LIS C, *Social change and the labouring poor, Antwerp 1770–1860*. New Haven: Yale UP 1986.
602  MOLLET A ed, *Droit de cité: à la recontre des habitants des banlieux delaissées*. Paris: l'Harmattan 1987. pp 158.
603  ROTHBLATT DN, *Suburbia: an international assessment*. Croom Helm 1986. pp xv + 336.
604  VAUCHERET E, Un faubourg de Montréal dans Bonheur d'Occasion de Gabrielle Roy. *EC/CS* 19 91985) 189–98.


## SOCIAL ORGANIZATIONS, CLUBS AND SOCIETIES
see also 827

605  BLANVILLAIN B, La franc-maconnaire en Anjou pendant la deuxième moitié du XVIIIe siècle. *AdB* (1985) 411–18.
606  CUBELLS M, Franc-maconneue et société de recruitement des loges à Aix en Provence dans la deuxième moitié du XVIIIe siècle. *RHMC* 33 (1986) 463–84.
607  FAUQUET JM, *Les sociétés de musique de chambre à Paris de la Restauration à 1870*. Paris: Aux Amateurs des livres 1986. pp 448.
608  GUILLERAND CHAMPENIER MC, Histoire d'une congrégation feminine saumuroise à la fin de l'Ancien Régime et sous la Révolution 'Les Servantes des Pauvres de Saumur' (1736–1816). *AdB* (1985) 355–66.
609  LECOQ B, Les cercles parisiens au début de la Troisième République: de l'apogée au déclin. *RHMC* 32 (1985) 591–616.
610  MCCALMAN I, Ultra-radicalism and convivial debating clubs in London, 1795–1838. *EHR* 102 (1986) 309–33.
611  MARTIN M, 'La grande famille': l'Association des journalistes parisiens (1885–1939). *RH* 557 (1986) 129–57.
612  RAMSDEN JW, *Who comes here? a history of the Freemasons at Keith 1750–1985*. Keith: Lodge St James No 713, 1985. pp 103.
613  TEAGUE SJ, An intelligent interest and a public spirit. *LSJ* 412 (1986) 3–8.


## CLASS STRUCTURE
see also 800

## Occupational structure
see also 578

614  BORDIER JC, Quelques renseignements et réflexions sur les luthiers et la lutherie au XVIIIe siècle à Caen. *AdN* 35 (1985) 39–47.

615  BRAULT LERCH S, *Le Orfèvres de Troyes*. Paris: Droz 1986. pp 372.

616  CHARLE C, *Les professeurs de la faculté des lettres de Paris. 2 Dictionnaire biographique 1909–1939*. Paris: Editions du CNRS 1986. pp 216.

617  CHARPIN D. *Le clergé d' Uz au siècle d'Hanemurabi XIXe–XVIIIe siècle avant JC*. Genève: Droz 1986. pp 520.

618  DOUMERC B, Les marchands du Midi à Alexandrie au XVe siècle. *AdM* 171 (1985) 269–84.

619  GAYOT F, Les entrepreneurs au bon temps des privileges: la draperie royale de Sedan au XVIIIe siècle. *RN* 265 (1985) 413–45.

620  GILIOMEE HB & SCHLEMMER L eds, *Up against the fences. Poverty, passes and privilege in South Africa*. Cape Town: Philip 1985.

621  HAINE M, *Les facteurs d'instruments de musique à Paris au XIXe siècle*. Bruxelles: Bruxelles UP 1985. pp 422, il.

622  OESTREICHER R, *Solidarity and fragmentation: working people and class consciousness in Detroit 1875–1900*. Urbana: Illinois UP 1986.

623  PAPAYANIS N, La prolétarisation des cachers de fiacres à Paris (1878–1889). *MS* 132 (1985) 59–82.

624  POMIAN K, *Collectionneurs, amateurs et curieux. Paris-Veune XVIe–XVIIe siècle*. Paris: Gallimard 1987. pp 376.

625  PYTHON F, *Mgr Etienne Marilley et son clergé à Fribourg au temps du Sondenbund: 1848–1856: intervention politique et defense religieuse*. Fribourg: Ed Universitaire de Fribourg 1987. pp 616.

626  RICALENS H, Statut et revenues de metayers de Moissac au début du XVIIIe siècle. *AdM* 169 (1985) 39–51.

627  ROCK HB, *Artisans of the new republic and tradesmen of New York City in the age of Jefferson*. New York: New York UP 1984. pp 340.

628  TERRIER D, Une famille de marchands au début du règne de Louis XV: les Charpentier de Saint Quentin. *RN* 265 (1985) 381–412.


## Class composition and interaction
see also 555, 567,

629  BENSON J, Penny capitalism: a task for the local historian. *LoH* 17 (1986) 26–35.

630  BERGERE MC et al, Essai de prosapographique des élites shangaiennes à l'époque républicaine 1911–1949. *AESC* 40 (1985) 901–29.

631  CAGE RA ed, *The working class in Glasgow 1750–1914*. Croom Helm 1986. pp 224.

632  COLLIN JC, Le patronat fertois du textile. Contribution a l'étude de la Bourgeoisie bas normande aux XIXe et XXe siècles. *AdN* 35 (1985) 349–70.

633  CORFIELD PJ, Class by name and number in eighteenth century Britain. *H* 72 (1987) 38–68.

634  CORFIELD P, From rank to class: innovation in Georgian England. *HT* 37 (Mar 1987) 29–35.

635  CROSSICK G, Classes and the masses in Victorian England. *HT* 37 (Mar 87) 36–42.

636  DAVIES EJ, *The anthracite aristocracy: the evolution of urban leadership in the hard coal fields of northeastern Pennsylvania*. Dekalb: Northern Illinois UP 1985.

637  FIGEAC M, La noblesse bordelaise au lendemain de la Restauration. *HES* 5 (1986) 381–405.

638  GAUDENET J, *Le gouvernants à Rome*. Paris: Jovene 1985. pp 195.

639  GILKESON JS, *Middle class Providence 1820–1940*. Princeton: Princeton UP 1986. pp 368.

640  GINSWICK J ed, *Labour and the poor in England and Wales 1849–1851: the letters to the 'Morning Chronicle' from the correspondents in the manufacturing and mining districts, the towns of Liverpool and Birmingham, and the rural districts*, Vol 4 *Liverpool and Birkenhead*; Vol 5 *Birmingham*. Cass 1987. pp 283, 269, il.

641  GREISSLER R, *La classe politique dirigeante à Strasbourg, 1650–1750*. Strasbourg: Quai 1987. pp 302.

642  HILLS P, Division and cohesion in the nineteenth century middle class: the case of Ipswich 1830–1870. *UHY* (1987) 42–50.

643  JONES P, Perspective, sources and methodology in a comparative study of the middle class in nineteenth century Leicester and Peterborough. *UHY* (1987) 22–31.

644  LACORDAIRE S, *Les inconnus de la Seine*. Paris: Hachette 1985. pp 305.

645  LEONARD JW ed, *Local history experienced* [Middlesbrough] Middlesbrough: Teesside Polytechnic 1985. pp 96.

646 LIS C, *Social change and the labouring poor: Antwerp 1770–1860*. Yale UP 1986. pp 224.

647 LOGAN WS, *The gentrification of inner Melbourne: a political geography of inner city housing*. U Queensland P 1985. pp xxxiii + 328.

648 LOUPES P, Milieu capitalaire et carrières canoniales en Guyenne aux XVIIe et XVIIIe siècles. *HES* (1985) 61–89.

649 LUBECK PM, *Islam and urban labour in Northern Nigeria: the making of a Muslim working class*. Cambridge: Cambridge UP 1986. pp 368, il.

650 MAKAHONUK G, Class conflict in a prairie city: the Saskatoon working class. *Labour/Le Travail* 19 (1987) 89–123.

651 MARTIN G, *Les petits métiers d'autrefois*. Nimes: Librairie Lacour 1985. pp 215, il.

652 MUNCK R, Cycles of class struggle and the making of the working class in Argentina, 1890–1920. *JLAS* 19 (1987) 19–39.

653 NENADIC S, Record linkage and the exploration of nineteenth century social groups: a methodological perspective on the Glasgow middle class in 1861. *UHY* (1987) 32–41.

654 RAMDIN R, *The making of the black working class in Britain*. Aldershot: Gower 1986. pp 628.

655 RULE J, *The labouring classes in early industrial England 1750–1850*. Longman 1986. pp x + 408.

656 SCHAFFER R & SMITH N, The gentrification of Harlem. *AAAG* 76 (1986) 347–65.

657 SMITH N & WILLIAMS P, *Gentrification of the city*. Allen & Unwin 1986. pp xiii + 257.

**Protests and disorders**
see also 550, 563, 801, 810–11

658 JONES D, *The last rising: the Newport insurrection of 1839*. Oxford: Clarendon 1985. pp 273.

659 LAPIED M, Les mouvements populaires à Avignon et dans le Comtat Venaissin au XVIIIe siècle. *PH* 36 (1986) 325–38.

660 MCDONALD P, *Hotheads and heroes: the Bristol riots 1831*. Swansea: Sketty 1986. pp 185.

661 PEARCE J, *Promised land: peasant rebellion in Chalatenango, El Salvador*. Latin American Bureau 1986. pp viii + 324.

662 ROYLE E, *Chartism*. Longman 1986. pp v + 153.

663 SHOEMAKER RB, The London 'mob' in the early eighteenth century. *JBritS* (1986) 273–304.

664 THOMPSON D, *The Chartists: popular politics in the industrial revolution*. Aldershot: Wildwood House 1986. pp 399.

665 VIRLOUVET C, *Famines et éments à Rome des origines de la république à la mort de Nerou*. Rome: Ecole Française de Rome 1985. pp viii + 133.

**SOCIAL LIFE**

**Social life, customs and traditions**
see also 825, 963, 1030

666 ASPIN C, *Surprising Rossendale*. Helmshore: Helmshore Local History Society 1986. pp 57, il.

667 BAILEY P, *Leisure and class in Victorian England: rational recreation and the contest for control, 1830–1855*. Methuen 1987. pp 288, il.

668 BENJAMIN EA, *Footprints on the sands of time: Aberystwyth 1800–1900*. Carmarthen: Dyfed County Council Cultural Services Dept 1986. pp 230.

669 BULMER M, *Neighbours: the work of Philip Adrams*. Cambridge: Cambridge UP 1986. pp xviii + 282.

670 CHAGNIOT J, *Paris et l'armée au XVIIIe siècle*. Paris: Economica 1985. pp 678.

671 CUBELLS M, Franc-macconneue et société: le recruitement des loges à Aix en Provence dans le deuxième moitié du XVIIIe siècle. *RHMC* 33 (1986) 463–84.

672 CUZZI JC, *San Francisco: la ville ou s'invente l'avenir*. Paris: Rochevignes 1985. pp 200, il.

673 DENIS MN, Usage de l'alsacien en milieu urbain: évolution et perspective. *RA* 111 (1985) 149–56.

674 GRUSSI O, *La vie quotidienne des jouers sous l'ancien régime à Paris et la cour*. Paris: Hachette 1985. pp 257.

675 HERMAN G, *Ritualised friendship and the Greek city*. Cambridge: Cambridge: Cambridge UP 1986. pp 220.

676 MAGNUSSON L, Drinking and the Verlag system 1820–1850: the significance of taverns and drink in Eskilstuna before industrialisation. *SEcHR* 24 (1986) 1–19.

677 *One hundred years of Nottingham life: the centenary lectures delivered at Nottingham University.* Nottingham: Nottingham U 1987. pp 83, il.

678 ROPER M, Inventing traditions in colonial society: Bendigo's Easter fair 1871–1885. *JAuS* 17 (1985) 31–40.

679 SACKETT L, Marching into the past: ANZAC day celebrations in Adelaide. *JAuS* 17 (1985) 18–30.

680 SYKES CS, *Private places: life in the great London houses.* Chatto & Windus 1985. pp 352.

681 WALDEN K, Respectable hooligans: male Toronto college students celebrate Hallow'een 1884–1910. *CHR* 1 (1987) 1–34.

## Religious activity
see also 779

682 BARTON R & TORODE B, Gloucester and its Catholics during the reign of James II. *GLHB* 54 (1987) 7–12.

683 BEER BL, London parish clergy and the Protestant reformation, 1547–1559. *Albion* 18 (1986) 375–94.

684 BUKOWCZYK JJ, The church in the immigrant city. (Review essay) *JUH* 13 (1987) 207–17.

685 CASSAN M, Les multiples visages des confrières de dération: l'exemple de Limoges au XVIe siècle. *AdM* 177 (1987) 35–52.

686 CONNOLLY GP, The Catholic church and the first Manchester and Salford Trade Unions in the age of the industrial revolution. *TLCAS* 83 (1985) 125–60.

687 CROSSLEY EVANS MJ, The clergy of the city of Chester, 1630–1672. *JCAS* 68 (1985) 97–124.

688 DAMERON G, The cult of St Minias and the struggle for power in the diocese of Florence 1011–1018. *JMeH* 13 (1987) 125–42.

689 ELLIOTT BE. Ritualism and the beginnings of the reformed episcopal movement in Ottawa. *CCHSJ* 27 (1985) 18–47.

690 FROSTIN C, Lyon place jesuite, et l'ouverture sur la mission lointaine (fin XVIe – début XVIIe siècle). *CdH* 30 (1985) 231–62.

691 GANTER E, *L'église catholique de Genève: seize siècles d'histoire.* Geneve: Slatkine 1987. pp 515, il.

692 GLASS P, Hugh Price Hughes and the West London mission. *WHS* 45 (1986) 129–46.

693 GODFROY MF, Le médicateur franciscain Thomas Illyricus à Toulouse (novembre 1518–mai 1519). *AdM* 179 (1985) 101–14.

694 HANLON G, Pieté populaire et intervention des moines dans les miracles et les sanctuaires miraculeux en Agenais-Condomais au XVIIe siècle. *AdM* 170 (1985) 115–27.

695 HILLIS P, Education and evangelisation, Presbyterian missions in mid-nineteenth century Glasgow. *SHR* 66 (1987) 46–62.

696 HOGG J, *To those in need: the story of the Hull Methodist Mission, 1847–1946.* Hull: Hull City Council 1987.

697 JAY E, *Faith and doubt in Victorian Britain.* Macmillan 1986. pp 144.

698 LA HOUBLONNIERE R de & BENRIOU N, *La Prédication de Ranulphe de la Houblonnier, sermons au clercs et au simples gens à Paris au XIIIe siècle.* Paris: Etudes Augustiniennes 1986. 2 vols. pp 224, 416.

699 MCLEOD H, New perspectives on Victorian class religion: the oral evidence. *OH* 14 (1986) 31–49.

700 MCROBERTS D, *The catholic directory for Scotland 1829–1975.* Glasgow: Burns 1976. pp 32.

701 MALFROY M, OLIVIER B & GUIRAUD J, *Histoire religieuse de Pontailier et du Haut Doubs.* Paris: Cetre 1985. pp 376.

702 MARTIN O, *La conversion protestante à Lyon: 1659–1687.* Geneva: Droz 1987. pp 312.

703 MERLE R, De la pre-révolution à la restauration. Aix foyer original d'expression provencale. *PH* 36 (1986) 463–72.

704 MONTAGNES B, Marseille avec sans miracle la polémique autour des murales attribués à Mgr. J B Gault. *PH* 36 (1986) 435–62.

705 NICHOLLS M, *Some trends in theological education in London 1830–1890.* Leicester: UCCF Associates 1981. pp 31.

706 O'BRIEN S, A transatlantic community of saints: the great awakening and the first evangelical network, 1735–1755. *AHR* 91 (1986) 811–32.

707 POWER EG, *St John's Chapel, Belper: the life of a church and a community.* Cromford: Scarthia 1985. pp iv + 40, il.

708 ROYLE E, *Nonconformity in nineteenth century York.* York: St Anthony P 1985. pp 39.

709 SWANSON RN, *A calendar of the register of Richard Scrope, Archbishop of York 1398–1405*. York: Borthwick Institute of Historical Research 1985. pp xvii + 160.

710 TROUBNIKOFF A, *Les martyrs de Lyon et leur temps*. Lyon: OEIL 1986. pp 167.

711 VIGUERIE J de, *Nôtre Dame des Ardilliers à Saumur: le pèlerinage de Loire*. Paris: Oeil 1986. pp 249, il.

712 WILDING J, *Brentford and Isleworth Friends' Meeting House: a local Quaker history*. Isleworth: Brentford & Isleworth Preparative Meeting 1985. pp 73, il.

**Holidays and resorts**

713 FARRANT S, London by the sea: resort development on the south coast of England, 1880–1939. *JCH* 22 (1987) 137–62.

714 HEWSON JE, Who were the Skegness pioneers: a study of the people who settled in the new town of Skegness 1871–1881. *LHA* 21 (1986) 63–5.

715 HUGGINS M, The rise and decline of the seaside resort of Seaton Carew 1790–1902. Pt 2 Failure to expand as a resort. *DCLHSB* 35 (1985) 35–54.

716 OWEN AEB, Mablethorpe, St Peters and the sea. *LHA* 21 (1986) 61–2.

717 SKUDDER J, The seaside resort as a business venture: Clacton-on-Sea 1864–1901. *EAH* 17 91986) 65–82.

718 STAFFORD F & YATES N, *Kentish sources. 9 The later Kentish seaside (1840–1974): selected documents*. Gloucester: A Sutton for Kent Archives Office 1985. pp x+194.

719 WHYMAN J, *Kentish sources. 8 The early Kentish seaside (1736–1840): selected documents*. Gloucester: A Sutton for Kent Archives Office 1985. pp ix + 405.

## SOCIAL PROBLEMS AND DEVIANCE

**Delinquency**
see also 818

720 BURFORD EJ, *Wits, wenches and wantons: London's low life: Covent garden in the eighteenth century*. Hale 1986. pp 224.

721 CHAMPLAIN P de, *Crime organisé à Montréal (1940–1980)*. Hull: Editions Asticou 1986. pp 288.

722 CHIFFOLEAU J, Les mendiants, le prince et l'hérésie à Marseille vers 1260. *PH* 36 (1986) 3–19.

723 Correctional reform in New York: the Rockefeller years and beyond. UP of America 1986. pp 184.

724 DAVIES S, Aborigines, murder and the criminal law in early Port Phillip, 1841–1851. *HS* 22 (1987) 313–35.

725 GUTTON AM, La culte du Sacré Coeur en Lyonnais au XVIIe et XVIIIe siècles. *CdH* 32 (1987) 27–42.

726 HENRY P, *Crime, justice et société dans la principauté de Neuchatelan XVIIIe siècle*. Paris: Baconniere 1985. pp 808.

727 HENWOOD P, *Bagnards à Brest*. Paris: Ouest France 1986. pp 208, il.

728 KELLAND G, *Crime in London*. Bodley Head 1986.

729 O'RIORDAN C, Civil war squatters in the Middlewich house of correction. *ChesH* 19 (1987) 21–3.

730 PINNOCK D, *The brotherhood: street gangs and state control in Cape Town*. Gobal 1984. pp 116.

731 PRETORIUS R, Verstedeliking en misdaad (urbanization and crime). *RSA 2000* 1 (1985) 47–53.

732 SMITH, S, *Crime, space and society*. Cambridge: Cambridge UP 1986. pp 365.

733 TOURET C, Douai au XVIe siècle: une sociabilité de l'agression. *RHMC* 34 (1987) 3–30.

734 WEISS RP, Humanitarianism, labour exploitation, or social control? A critical survey of theory and research on the origin and development of prisons. *SH* 12 (1987) 331–51.

735 WOODS DC, Customary rights and popular legitimation: industrial stealing in the Black Country. *WMS* 17 (1984) 7–20.

736 YOUNG J, *Crime in the inner city*. Aldershot: Wildwood 1986. pp 176.

**Poverty and poor relief**
see also 576, 601, 640, 646

737 BRYANT WN, Plymouth workhouse in the census returns of 1861. *DevH* 33 (1986) 26–8.

738 CLEMENT PF, *Welfare and the poor in the nineteenth century city: Philadelphia 1800–1854*. Cranbury, NJ: Fairleigh Dickenson 1985. pp 223.

739 CROCKER RH, The Victorian poor law in crisis and change: Southampton 1870–1895. *Albion* 19 (1987) 19–44.

740 DEWAR D, *Urban policy and city development.* Cape Town: SA Labour & Development Research Unit 1984.

741 DURAND-LASSERVE A, *L'exclusion de pauvres dans les villes du tiers monde: accés au sol et au logement.* Paris: L'Harmattan 1986. pp 198.

742 FALLOWFIELD M & WATSON I, *The New Poor Law in Humberside.* Hull: Humberside College of Education 1987.

743 FLAME MJ, The politics of poor law administration in the Borough of Poole 1835–c.1845. *DNHS* 108 (1986) 19–25.

744 GREEN DR, A map for Mayhew's London: the geography of poverty in the mid-nineteenth century. *LJ* 11 (1985) 115–26.

745 HENNOCK EP, The measurement of urban poverty: from the metropolis to the nation, 1880–1920. *EcHR* 40 (1987) 208–27.

746 MACKINNON M, Poor law policy, unemployment and pauperism. *EEH* 23 (1986) 299–336.

747 MAYNE AJC, 'The question of the poor' in the nineteenth century city. *HS* 20 (1983) 557–73.

748 PAGE SJ, A new source for the historian of urban poverty: a note on the use of charity records in Leicester 1904–29. *UHY* (1987) 51–60.

749 PROCHASKA FK, Body and soul: bible nurses and the poor in Victorian London. *BIHR* 60 (1987) 336–48.

## Other social problems
see also 818

750 ADLER JS, Vagging the demons and scoundrels: vagrancy and the growth of St Louis, 1830–1861. *JUH* 13 (1986) 3–30.

751 BACKHOUSE C, Nineteenth century prostitution law: reflections of a discriminating society. *HS/SH* 18 (1985) 387–424.

752 CARLISLE M, Disorderly city, disorderly women: prostitution in antebellum Philadelphia. *PMBH* 110 (1985) 549–68.

753 DAVIDSON G, DUNSTAN D & MCCONVILLE C eds, *The outcasts of Melbourne: essays in social history.* Sydney: Allen & Unwin 1985.

754 FUCHS RG, Legislation, poverty and child abandonment in 19th century Paris. *JIH* 18 (1987) 55–80.

755 RONSIN F, Les 'prostituées' de Rambervilliers. *RHMC* 34 (1987) 138–53.

## SOCIAL REFORM AND IMPROVEMENT

## Social reform movements and improvements
see also 738, 809, 820

756 BENNETT PW, Turning 'bad boys' into 'good citizens': the reforming impulse of Toronto's industrial schools movement, 1883 to the 1920s. *OntH* 78 (1986) 209–32.

757 KERRIGAN C, Father Mathew and teetotalism in London, 1843. *LJ* 11 (1985) 107–14.

758 LOWE S, *Urban social movements: the city after Castells.* Basingstoke: Macmillan 1986, pp xii + 206.

## Charities

759 CLEMENT PF, Children and charity: orphanages in New Orleans 1817–1914. *LouH* 27 (1986) 337–52.

760 DRAPER M, Thomas Arneway's charity. *LJ* 12 (1986) 25–8.

761 HARVEY RP, Black beans, banners and banquets: the Charitable Irish Society of Halifax at two hundred years. *Nova Scotia HR* 6 (1986) 16–35.

762 KENNEDY R, *Charity warfare. The Charity Organisation Society in colonial Melbourne.* Melbourne: Hyland House 1985.

763 MAREC Y, De la dame patronnesse à l'institutrice. La petit enfance entre la charité et l'instruction à Rouen au XIXe siècle. *AdN* 35 (1985) 121–50.

764 RUBIN M, *Charity and community in medieval Cambridge.* Cambridge: Cambridge UP 1986. pp 425.

765 SPENCELEY GFR, Social control, the Charity Organization Society and the evolution of unemployment relief policy in Melbourne during the depression of the 1930s. *HS* 22 (1986) 232–51.

766 WOLOCH I, From charity to welfare in revolutionary Paris. *JModH* 58 (1986) 779–812.

**MINORITY GROUPS**

**Racial and ethnic minorities**
see also 303, 345, 351, 552, 556, 826, 1098, 1103, 1131, 1259

767 BECKERMANN R, *Vienne, rue de temple: le quartier juif 1918–1938*. Paris: F Hazan 1986. pp 144, il.

768 CLARKE CG, *East Indians in a West Indian town: San Fernando, Trinidad 1920–1970*. Allen & Unwin 1986. pp 192.

769 COWAN RA ed, *Victorian Jews through British eyes*. Oxford: Oxford UP 1986. pp 244.

770 HENRIQUES U, The Jews and crime in South Wales before World War 1. *MM* 29 (1985) 59–73.

771 HILLABY J, Hereford gold, Welsh and English land: the Jewish community at Hereford and its clients 1179–1253. *WNNHFC* 94 (1984) 321–51.

772 HUBBARD S, *William Peyton Hubbard, municipal reformer: the story of a nineteenth century black politician*. Toronto: Dundurn P 1986.

773 HUGHES DO, Distinguishing signs: ear-rings, Jews and Franciscan rhetoric in the Italian renaissance city. *PaP* 112 (1986) 3–59.

774 JOHNSON M, *Class and client in Beirut: the Sunni Muslim community and the Lebanese state, 1840–1985*: Ithaca UP 1986.

775 LANE R, *Roots of violence in black Philadelphia 1860–1900*. Cambridge, MA: Harvard UP 1986.

776 LANGLAIS J & ROME D, *Juifs et québecois, 200 ans d'histoire commune*. Montreal: Fides 1986. pp 285.

777 MORAWSKA E, 'For bread with butter': life worlds of east central Europeans in Johnstown, Pensylvania 1800–1940. New York: Cambridge UP 1984. pp 429.

778 MORMINO GR & POZZETTA GE, *The Immigrant world of Ybor city: Italians and their Latin American neighbours in Tampa 1885–1985*. Urbana: Illinois UP 1987.

779 ORSI RA, *The madonna of 115th street: faith and community in Italian Harlem* [New York]. Yale UP 1985. pp xxiii + 287.

780 PETTEGREE A, *Foreign Protestant communities in sixteenth century London*. Oxford: Clarendon P 1986. pp ix + 329.

781 PLACE GW, The repatriation of Irish vagrants from Cheshire 1750–1815. *JCAS* 68 (1985) 59–70.

782 PRIDE RA & Woodard JD, *The burden of busing: the politics of desegregation in Nashville, Tennessee*. Knoxville: Tennessee UP 1985.

783 ROCKAWAY RA, *The Jews of Detroit from the beginning 1762–1914*. Detroit: Wayne State UP 1986.

784 SACKETT RE, Images of the Jew: popular joketelling in Munich on the eve of World War 1. *T&S* 16 (1987) 527–64.

785 SETO W & SHYU LN, *The Chinese experience in New Brunswick: a historical perspective*. Fredericton: Chinese Cultural Association of New Brunswick 1986. pp 113.

786 SHERIDAN TE, *Los Tusonses: the Mexican community in Tucson 1854–1941*. Tucson: Arizonia UP 1986. pp 327.

787 SIMON L, *Les juifs à Nimes et dans le Gard durant la deuxième guerre mondiale de 1939 à 1945*. Nimes: Librarie Lacour 1985. pp 53.

788 STEPHENSON D, Colchester: a smaller medieval jewry. *EAH* 16 (1983–4) 48–52.

789 STURINO F, Post World War Two Canadian immigration policy towards Italians. *Polyphony* 7 (1985) 67–72.

790 SWIFT R & GILLEY S, *The Irish in the Victorian city*. Croom Helm 1985. pp 312.

791 TAYLOR HL, On slavery's fringe: city building and black community development in Cincinnati 1800–1850. *OhH* 95 (1986) 5–33.

792 TELL W, Ethnicity and stability: the Italians and Jews of South Portland 1900–1940. *PacHR* 54 (1985) 161–89.

793 WILLIAMSON JG, The impact of the Irish on British labour markets during the industrial revolution. *JEcH* 46 (1986) 693–720.

794 WRIGHT GC, *Life behind the veil: blacks in Louisville, Kentucky 1865–1930*. Baton Rouge: Louisiana UP 1985.

795 ZUCCHI JE, Mining, railway building and street construction: Italians in Toronto before World War One. *Polyphony* 7 (1985) 7–14.

**WOMEN**
see also 945, 959, 983

796 ARROM SM, *The women of Mexico city 1790–1857*. Stanford: Stanford UP 1985. pp 384.

797 BERNSTEIN D. *The struggle for equality: urban women workers in prestate Israeli society*. Praeger 1986. pp 224.

798  BLACKWELDER JK, *Women of the Depression: caste and culture in San Antonio.* College Station: Texas A&M UP 1984.

799  BUDNICK C, The performing arts as a field of labour for Winnipeg women 1870–1930. *Manitoba History* 11 (1986) 15–21.

800  CAPLAN P, *Class and gender in India: women and their organizations in a south Indian city.* Tavistock 1985. pp xiii + 258.

801  CROSS G & SHERGOLD P, 'We think we are oppressed:' gender white collar work and grievances of late nineteenth century women. *LabH* 28 (1987) 23–53.

802  CRUZE SD, 'To acquaint the ladies': women traders in Colchester c. 1750–c.1800. *LoH* 17 (1986) 158–62.

803  DENIEL R, *Femmes des villes africains.* Paris: Imades 1985. pp 220.

804  DUBOIS EC, Working women, class relations and suffrage militance: Harriet Stanton Blatch and the New York women's suffrage movement, 1894–1909. *JAH* 74 (1987) 34–59.

805  EWEN E, *Immigrant women in the land of dollars: life and culture on the lower east side.* New York: Monthly Review P 1985.

806  FRANCIS R, 'No more Amazons': gender and work process in the Victorian clothing trades, 1890–1939. *LabH* 50 (1986) 95–112.

807  FRAZOI B, *At the very least she pays the rent: women and German industrialization 1871–1914.* Greenwood 1985. pp xii + 206.

808  GAUDETTE J, Les réfugiés acadiens à Québec en 1757. *CSHA* 17 (1986) 144–9.

809  GOLDSTEIN JH, *The effects of the adoption of woman suffrage: sex differences in voting behaviour: Illinois 1914–1921.* Eastbourne: Praeger 1984. pp 252.

810  GODDEN J, British models and colonial experience: women's philanthropy in late nineteenth century Sydney. *JAuS* 19 (1986) 40–55.

810a GORDON E, Women, work and collective action: Dundee jute workers 1870–1906. *JSocH* (1987) 27–48.

811  HALL JD, Disorderly women: gender and labour militancy in the Appalachian south. *JAH* 73 (1986) 354–82.

812  HEATHER J, *How long is a piece of elastic?: the measurement of female activity rates in British censuses 1951–1981.* Centre for Economic Policy Research 1984. pp 21.

813  HEWITT NA, *Women's activism and social change: the case of Rochester, New York 1822–1872.* Rochester: Cornell UP 1984.

814  HIGGS E, Women, occupations and work in the nineteenth century censuses. *HW* 22 (1986) 59–80.

815  JOHN AV, *Unequal opportunities: women's employment in England, 1800–1918.* Oxford: Basil Blackwell 1986. pp xiii + 297.

816  LEBSOCK S, *The free women of Petersburg: status and culture in a southern town, 1784–1860.* New York: WW Norton 1984.

817  LOPATA HZ, *City women in America: work, jobs, occupations and careers.* Praeger 1986.

818  MCCREERY D, 'This life of misery and shame': female prostitution in Guatamala city 1880–1920. *JLAS* 22 (1987) 155–76.

819  MAGEE J, *A Belgian inheritance: 200 years of Belgian presence in Ontario.* Toronto: Dundurn 1987.

820  MALDONADO L & MOORE J, *Urban ethnicity in the United States: new immigrants and old minorities.* Sage 1985. pp 304.

821  MEDJUCK S, Women's response to economic and social change in the nineteenth century: Moncton parish, 1851–1951. *Atlantis* 11 (1985) 7–21.

822  MEYEROWITZ J, Women and migration: autonomous female migrants to Chicago 1880–1930. *JUH* 13 (1987) 147–68.

823  MORIN R et al, *Développement urbain et marché immobilier en périphéré du centre-ville: le cas du quartier centre-sud à Montréal.* Montréal: Département d'études urbaines, U de Quebec à Montréal 1986. pp 85.

824  PEDERSEN D, Building today for the womanhood of tomorrow: boosters and the YWCA, 1890–1930. *UHR* 15 (1987) 225–43.

825  PREISS K, *Cheap amusements, working women and leisure in turn of the century New York.* Philadelphia: Temple UP 1986.

826  RAMIREZ B, Brief encounters: Italian immigrant workers and the CPR 1900–30. *Labour/Le Travail* 17 (1986) 9–28.

827  REEKIE G, War, sexuality and feminism: Perth women's organizations, 1938–1945. *HS* 21 (1986) 576–91.

828  SHARMA U, *Women's work, class and the urban household.* Tavistock 1987. pp 240.

829  ST ANSELL C, *City of women: sex and class in New York 1789–1860.* New York: Knopf 1986.

830  TREPANIER P, Les peintres juifs à Montreal dans l'entre deux guerres. *EC/CS* 21 (1986) 133–40.

831 WEIER L, In a nation of immigrants, whose house is home? *Canadian Heritage* 12 (1986) 29–35.

832 WHIPP R, Women and the social organization of work in the Staffordshire pottery industry 1900–1930. *MidH* 12 (1987) 103–21.


## V ECONOMIC ACTIVITY

### RESEARCH METHODS, AIDS AND MATERIALS

833 CHILDS WR et al. *The customs accounts of Hull 1453–1490.* York Archaeological Society 1986.

834 GRENIER JY, *Répertoire des séries économies françaises à la periode moderne XVIe–XVIIe siècles.* Oaris: Ecole pratique des hautes études en sciences sociales 1985. pp 685.

835 JACKSON TV, The Sun fire office and the local historian. *LoH* 17 (1986) 141–9.

836 LEWIS MJ & LLOYD JONES R, Rate books: a technique for reconstructing the local economy. *LoH* 17 (1987) 277–80.

837 MARESCOE C, *Markets and merchants in the late seventeenth century: the Marescoe–David letters, 1668–1680.* Oxford: Oxford UP 1987. pp 616.

838 STEVENS KF ed, *The brokerage books of Southampton for 1477–8 and 1527–8.* Southampton: Southampton UP 1985. pp xxi + 230.

839 WALTON JR, Trades and professions in late eighteenth century England: assessing the evidence of directories. *LoH* 17 (1987) 343–50.


### URBAN ECONOMIC ACTIVITY
see also 67, 179, 191, 564

#### General

840 BRUCE G, *A family and a fortune: Bournemouth and the Cooper Deans.* Bridport: Laverstock Books 1987. pp 190.

841 JACOBS J, *Cities and the wealth of nations.* Harmondsworth: Penguin 1986. pp ix + 257.


#### Medieval

842 BRIDBURY AR, Dr Rigby's comment on late medieval urban prosperity. *EcHR* 39 (1986) 417–22.

843 MCGRAIL D, Economic activity and economic aspects of urban change in the borough of Plympton 1500–1780. *DevH* 33 (1986) 28–34.

844 RIGBY SH, Late medieval urban prosperity: the evidence of lay subsidies. *EcHR* 29 91986) 411–16.


#### Modern

845 *L'action économique des grandes villes en France et à l'étranger.* Paris: Economica 1987. pp 316.

846 BEHAGG C, Myths of cohesion: capital and compromise in the historiography of nineteenth century Birmingham. *SH* 11 (1986) 375–84.

847 HAUSNER VA, *Critical issues in urban economic development.* Oxford: Clarendon 1986. pp 240.

848 KEATING M, *Remaking urban Scotland: strategies for local economic development.* Edinburgh: Edinburgh UP 1986. pp viii + 176.

849 LEVER W & MOORE C eds, *The city in transition: policies and agencies for the economic regeneration of Clydeside.* Oxford: Clarendon 1986. pp xvi + 173.

850 WORGER WH, *South Africa's city of diamonds: mine workers and monopoly capitalism in Kimberley 1867–1895.* New York: Yale UP 1987. pp 352.


### INDUSTRY
see also 155, 806, 832

851 AMOURIC H & LANDURE C, Archives et archéologie: l'exemple de l'artisanat céramique à Fréjus. *PH* 141 (1985) 299–308.

852 BEATTY B, Lowells of the South: northern influences on the nineteenth century Carolina textile industry. *JSouH* 53 (1987) 37–62.

853 BLOOMFIELD E, Industry in Ontario urban centres 1870. *UHR* 15 (1987) 279–83.

854 BLOOMFIELD E et al, *Industry in Ontario urban centres 1870: accessing the manuscript census.* Guelph: Dept Geog U of Guelph 1986. pp 60.

855 BLOOMFIELD E, *Urban industrial growth processes in southern Ontario 1870–1930*. Winnipeg: Institute of Urban Studies U of Winnipeg 1986. pp 31.

856 BLOOMFIELD GT, Shaping the character of a city: the automobile industry and Detroit. *MichQR* 25 (1986) 167–81.

857 BLUM JA, South San Francisco: the making of an industrial city. *CalH* (1984) 114–34.

858 BONNET C, La savonnerie marseillaise de 1800 à 1815. *PH* 147 (1987) 69–88.

859 BOWLING R et al, *Cotton town: Bollington and the Swindells family in the nineteenth century*. Wilmslow: Wilmslow Historical Society 1986.

860 CABAL M & THOEN H, L'industrie du sel à Ardres à l'époque romaine. *RN* 264 (1985) 193–206.

861 CAMPION P, *Matches from Gloucester: the story of William Taylor and the other matchmakers of the Island of 1870 including a chapter on Gloucester Fire Brigades*. Cheltenham: author 1987. pp 40.

862 CONWAY-JONES H, Price Walker and company: 250 years of timber trading in Gloucester. Gloucester: the company 1986. pp 24.

863 COSSON A, L'industrie textile à Nimes: la fin d'une hégomonie (1790–1850). *MS* 133 (1985) 5–24.

864 DUBOIS J, L'usine de Fives-Lille et la construction ferroviaire française au XIXe siècle. *RN* 265 (1985) 517–25.

865 DUNLEAVY J, Industrial revolution and religious change. *LancsLH* 4 (1984) 19–24.

866 EVANS M, *In the beginning: the Manchester origins of Rolls Royce*. Derby: Rolls Royce 1984. pp 169.

867 FAURE A, Petit atelier modernisme économique. La production en mietles au XIXe siècle. *HES* (1986) 531–57.

868 FERNS JL, Missing canons: the Walker Company of Rotherham. *LoH* 17 (1986) 236–41.

869 *Gold on the green: Glaxo years at Greenford*. Glaxo Pharmaceuticals Ltd 1986.

870 GREENMAN D, *75 years of Bristol aerospace*. Bristol: Royal Aeronautical Society 1985. pp 48.

871 GREENWOOD HM, A model Victorian mill for making wire products, John Pring and Son, Ltd. *ChesH* 18 (1986) 38–40.

872 GRIFFIN C, Conciliation in the coal mining industry before 1914: the experience of the Leicestershire coalfield. *MidH* 12 (1987) 67–84.

873 HAMMOND D ed, *Steelchest, nail in the boot and the barking dog: the Belfast shipyard: a story of the people, told by the people*. Belfast: Flying Fox Films 1986. pp 128.

874 HAMMOND PJ, The clay tobacco pipe making industry of Newark. *ThS* 89 (1985) 86–107.

875 HANAGAN M, Industrialization and urban society in nineteenth century France [review essay]. *JUH* 13 (1987) 218–29.

876 HIRSH JP, La région lilloise: foyer industriel au place de negoce? *MS* 132 (1985) 27–41.

877 HOBBS JT, History of Fielding and Platt Ltd. *Stationery Engine* (1986) 5–7.

878 HUBERMAN M, Invisible handshakes in Lancashire cotton spinning in the first half of the nineteenth century. *JEH* 46 (1986) 987–98.

879 JENKINS AP, Cuthbert Watkinson, Liverpool gunsmith. *LancsLH* 4 (1986) 42–6.

880 JONES SG, Work, leisure and the political economy of the cotton districts between the wars. *TexH* 18 (1987) 33–58.

881 LEVITT S, Manchester mackintoshes: a history of the rubberised garment trade in Manchester. *TexH* 18 (1987) 51–70.

882 LLOYD-JONES R & LEWIS MJ, The economic structure of cottonopolis. *TexH* 18 (1987) 71–90.

883 MALDEN RJ, Elusive virtuosi: Thomas and Joshua Man [engravers]. *YH* (1985) 43–55.

884 NELSON J, The demand for silk and the waste silk industry in eighteenth century Lancaster 1711–80. *LancsLH* 3 (1985) 24–31.

885 PERRETT W, Three centuries of Wilton's carpet trade. *HatR* 3 (1987) 159–65.

886 ROSS SJ, Industrialization and the changing images of progress in nineteenth century Cincinnati. *Queen City Heritage* 43 (1985) 2–24.

887 SAXTON WA, *Singer: the sewing machine and Paignton*. Brixham: Brixham Museum & Historical Society 1983. pp 13, il.

888 SCRANTON P & LICHT W, *Work sights, industrial Philadelphia, 1890–1950*. Philadelphia: Temple UP 1986.

889 SMITH LD, *Carpet weavers and carpet masters: the hand loom carpet industry of Kidderminster 1780–1850*. K Tomkinson 1986. pp 316, il.

890 STEARN B, *Croydon cars: the history of car manufacturing in the London Borough of Croydon 1896–1985*. Croydon: author 1985. pp 24.

891 SUTTON AF, William Shore: merchant of London and Derby. *DAJ* 106 (1986) 127–39.
892 TOMLIN D, A note on the iron works of the Stockton area. *CTLHS* 51 (1986) 21–5.
893 TWEEDALE G, *Giants of Sheffield steel: a century of commercial and technological independence, 1830–1930.* Sheffield: Sheffield Libraries 1986. pp 92, il.
894 VICKERS N, The structure of the Whitby jet industry in 1871. *LPS* 37 (1986) 8–17.
895 WALLACE W, *Some notes on the coal industry in Hamilton.* Hamilton: Bell College 1985.

### EXTERNAL TRADE

896 ASHTOR E, *East-West trade in the medieval Mediterranean.* Variorum Reprints 1986. pp 344.
897 CAIN PJ & HOPKINS AG, Gentlemanly capitalism and British expansion overseas II: new imperialism 1850–1945. *EcHR* 40 (1987) 1–26 [role of City of London]
898 CIRIACONO S, Venise et ses villes. Structuration et destruction d'un marché regional (XVI–XVIIIe siècles) *RH* 560 (1986) 273–307.
899 DOUMERC B, La crise structurelle de la marine vénitienne au XVe siècle: le problème du retard des Mude. *AESC* 40 (1985) 605–23.
900 HEFFER J, *Le port du New York et le commerce exterieur americain 1860–1900.* Paris: publication de la Sorbonne 1986. pp 568.
901 JELIC R, The Latin American market for Birmingham and Black country metal manufacturers 1871–1913. *WMS* 17 (1984) 21–8.
902 ORIGO I, *The merchant of Prato.* Folio Society 1984. pp vi + 371.
903 PRICE JM, Sheffield v. Starke: institutional experimentation in the London Maryland trade *c.* 1696–1706. *BuH* 28 (1986) 19–39.
904 SONENSCHER M, Journeymen, the courts and the French trades 1781–1791. *PaP* 114 (1987) 72–109.
905 STONE RCJ, *Young Logan Campbell [Auckland].* Auckland: Auckland UP 1982. pp 287.

### INTERNAL TRADE AND SERVICES

#### Food supply
see also 665

906 DEVAUX O, L'alimentation de lycéens toulousains au début du XIXe siècle. *RH* 553 (1986) 165–72.
907 DUROUX R, La boulangerie cantalienne à Madrid au XIXe siècle. *CdH* 30 (1985) 139–60.
908 FRANCIS JONES G, *Cows, cardis and cockneys.* Borth: author 1984. pp 143.
909 HORII T, La crise alimentaire de la 1853 à 1856 et la caisse de la boulangerie de Paris. *RH* 552 (1984) 375–401.
910 HOULIHAN M, 'A most excellent dish': a study of the tripe trade in the north west. *LancsLH* 3 (1985) 18–23.
911 JEHANNO C, Boire à Paris au XVe siècle: le vin à Hôtel-Dieu. *RH* 559 (1986) 3–28.
912 *The house that William Greensmith built: some historical observations on Britain's first retail outfitters.* D King 1985.
913 LAWRENCE R, An early nineteenth century malting business in East Suffolk [Halesworth, Beccles, Southwold]. *SuR* 36 (1986) 115–29.
914 MACKEITH M, *History and conservation of shopping arcades.* Mansell 1986. pp 100, il.
915 POSTLES D, Markets for rural produce in Oxfordshire 1086–1350. *Mid H* 12 (1987) 14–25.
916 TERRELL-NEILD CE, The caves under York house, Mansfield Rd: history and present invertebrate fauna. [brewing] *ThS* 90 (1986) 69–78.

#### Finance, banking and insurance
see also 835

917 BALDWIN DO, The growth and decline of the Charlottetown banks 1854–1906. *Acad* 15 (1986) 28–52.
918 BALDWIN DO & GILL HM, The Savings bank of Prince Edward Island: philanthropy and self interest in the nineteenth century. *JCanS* 20 (1985/6) 115–25.
919 CHECKLAND SG, *The city and the businessman viewed historically: an aspect of the performance of capitalism.* Leicester: Leicester U, Victorian Studies Centre 1986. pp 25.
920 CLARKE WM, *How the city of London works: an introduction to its financial markets.* Waterlow 1986. pp 112.

921 COURTNEY P, The first Welsh mints and the origins of Cardiff. *M* 29 (1985) 65–9.
922 CUSHMAN JW, The Khaw group: Chinese business in early twentieth century Penang. *JSEAS* 17 (1986) 58–79.
923 DAVIS M, *Every man is his own landlord: a history of the Coventry Building Society*. Coventry: the Society 1985.
924 GOLDTHWAITE RA, The Medici bank and the world of Florentine capitalism. *PaP* 114 (1987) 3–31.
925 HEWLETT N, *All change in the city: a report on recent change and future prospects in London's financial markets*. Economist Pubs 1985. pp 101.
926 INGHAM GK, *Capitalism divided?: the city and industry in British social development*. Basingstoke: Macmillan 1984. pp viii + 304.
927 LA FAURIE J, Les monnaies emises à Cambrai aux VIe à IXe siècles. *RN* 69 (1986) 393–404.
928 LLOYD-JONES D, *Manchester and the age of the factory: the business structure of 'cottonopolis' in the industrial revolution*. Beckenham: Croom Helm 1987. pp. 272.
929 MELTON FT, Deposit banking in London 1700–90. *BuH* 28 (1986) 40–50.
930 NEAL L, The integration and efficiency of the London and Amsterdam Stock markets in the eighteenth century. *JEH* 47 (1987) 97–116.
931 NEWBURY C, The origins and functions of the London Diamond Syndicate 1889–1914. *ThS* 29 (1987) 5–26.
932 O'NEILL J, Self help in Nottinghamshire: the Woodborough Male Friendly Society. *ThS* 90 (1986) 57–63.
933 PARKER J, *'Nothing for nothing for nobody': a history of Hertfordshire banks and banking*. Hertford: Hertfordshire Publications 1986.
934 POUCHAIN P, Banque et credit à Lille de 1800 à 1939. *RN* 68 (1986) 635–61.
935 TURNER JJ, Early friendly societies in North Yorkshire and South Durham. *CTLHS* 50 (1986) 65–70.
936 TREBILCOCK C, *Phoenix Assurance and the development of British insurance*. Vol 1 *1782–1870*. Cambridge: Cambridge UP 1985.
937 WIDLAKE B, *In the city*. Faber 1986. pp 327.

**Retailing**
see also 802, 837
938 ANDERSON BL & LATHAM AJH ed, *The market in history*. Croom Helm 1986. pp 230.
939 *Builders and boosters: Kitchener Chamber of Commerce 100th anniversary*. Kitchener: Book Committee 1986.
940 CROSSICK G & HEINZ GERHARD H, *Shopkeepers and master artisans in nineteenth century Europe*. Methuen 1984. pp 282.
941 DAY J, *The medieval market economy*. Basil Blackwell 1987. pp 288.
942 DOERFLINGER TM, *A vigorous spirit of enterprise: merchants and economic development in revolutionary Philadelphia*. Chapel Hill: N Carolina UP 1986.
943 GALENSON DW, *Traders, planters and slaves: market behaviour in early English America*. Cambridge UP 1986. pp xiv + 530, il.
944 GERRARD CM, Taunton fair in the seventeenth century: an archaeological approach to historical data. *SANHS* 128 (1984) 65–82.
945 LAI A et al, Chinatown Annie: the East End opium trade 1920–35: the story of a woman opium dealer. *OH* 14 (1986) 18–30.
946 MASTORIS SN, Regulating the Nottingham markets: new evidence from a mid-thirteenth century manuscript. *ThS* 90 (1986) 79–83.
947 MONOD D, Bad days: the managerial revolution and the Hudson's Bay Company department stores. *CHA Hist Papers* (1986) 173–96.
948 THWAITES W, Banbury horse fairs in the eighteenth century. *CC* 10 (1987) 120–4.
949 WHITE DL, Parsis in the commercial world of western India, 1700–1750. *IESH* 183–204.

**Other non-municipal services**
950 BELCHER V, A London attorney of the eighteenth century: Robert Andrews. *LJ* 12 (1986) 36–9.
951 CORFIELD JL, Cockett and Nash architects and auctioneers of Royston. *HP* 23 (1987) 15–19.
952 HOPKINS E, The trading and service sectors of the Birmingham economy. *BuH* 27 (1986) 77–97.
953 ROTH LOCHNER B, L'évolution de l'activité notarialé à Genève aux XVIIe et XVIIIe siècles. *RHMC* 33 (1986) 96–113.

954 WHITTET TD, Hertfordshire apothecaries' tokens and their issuers. *HP* 20 (1986) 3–9.

## CONSUMPTION

955 CHAABABE K, *Transformation du complexe agro-alimentaire et évolution de la consommation dans les grandes villes de Tunisie.* Montpellier: Institut agronomique méditerranéen de Montpellier 1985. pp 28.

956 PINCH S, *Cities and services: the geography of collective consumption.* Routledge & Kegan Paul 1985. pp xi + 213.

### Earnings

957 BLACKBURN S, Employers and social policy: the Black Country chain masters, the minimum wage campaign and the Cradley Heath strike of 1910. *MidH* 12 (1987) 85–102.

958 COURTINE R, *La vie parisienne. 2. Le Ventre de Paris: de la Bastille à l'étoile ... des siècles d'appetit.* Paris: Perrin 1985. pp 406.

959 CROSS G & SHERGOLD P, The family economy and the market: wages and the residence of Pennsylvania women in the 1980s. *JFamH* 11 (1986) 245–66.

960 SOBERBERG J, Real wage trends in urban Europe 1730–1850: Stockholm in a comparative perspective. *SocH* 12 (1987) 155–76.

### WORKING CONDITIONS

961 ARNESEN E, To rule or ruin: New Orleans dock workers struggle for control 1902–1903. *LabH* 28 (1987) 139–66.

962 GODINEAU D, Travail et politique à Paris pendant la Révolution: l'exemples des Ateliers Municipaux. *AHRF* 263 (1986) 35–49.

963 JONES SG, Work, leisure and the political economy of the cotton districts between the wars. *TexH* 18 (1987) 33–58.

964 LANDES DS, The ordering of the urban environment: time, work and the occurrence of crowds 1790–1835. *PaP* 116 (1987) 192–2. HARRISON M, A rejoinder. 199–205.

### LABOUR ORGANIZATION
see also 583, 636, 649

965 FULLER K, *Radical aristocrats: London busworkers from the 1880s to the 1890s.* Lawrence & Wishart 1985. pp 256.

966 MILLS H & WELLMAN D, Contractually sanctioned job action and workers' control: the case of the San Francisco longshoremen. *LabH* 28 (1987) 167–95.

967 PALLADINO G, When militancy isn't enough: the impact of automation on New York city building service workers, 1934–1970. *LabH* 28 (1987) 196–220.

968 PREVO K, Voronezh in 1905: workers and politics in a provincial city. *RussH* 12 (1985) 48–70.

969 SIBALIS MD, Parisian labour during the French Revolution. *CHA Hist papers* (1986) 11–32.

### Gilds
see also 159

970 BRAY RGW, The Worshipful Company of Makers of Playing Cards. *LSJ* 411 (1986) 3–10.

971 DELECLUSE J, *Les consuls de Rouen: marchands d'hier, entrepreneurs d'aujourd'hui: histoire de la chambre du commerce et d'industrie de Rouen des origines à nos jours.* Rouen: Ed du P'tit Normand 1985. pp 414, il.

972 LARS E, Crafts in transformation? Masters, journeymen and apprentices in a Swedish town 1800–1850. *ConC* 1 (1986) 363–84.

973 MACKENNEY R, *Tradesmen and traders: the world of the guilds in Venice and Europe c.1250–c.1650.* Beckenham: Croom Helm 1986. pp 256.

### Trade unions
see also 686

974 BELLUSH J, *Union power and New York: Victor Gotbaum and District Council 37.* Eastbourne: Praeger 1984. pp xxii + 473.

975 KAZIN M, *Barons of Labor. The San Francisco building trades and union power in the progressive era.* Chicago: Illinois UP 1986.

976 TAPLIN E, *The dockers' union: a study of the National Union of Dock Labourers 1889–1922*. Leicester: Leicester UP 1986. pp xviii + 198.

## Strikes and lockouts
see also 957

977 CORNFORTH W, *The long hard road: (the story of Darlington railwaymen and the struggle for social justice). Darlington:* 1985. pp 120.

978 GRAY J, *Cities in revolt: James Larkin and the Belfast dock strike of 1907*. Belfast: Blackstaff 1985. pp xii + 225.

979 HAIMSON L, Changements démographiques et grèves ouvrières à Saint Petersbourg, 1905–1914. *AESC* 40 (1985) 781–803.

980 HALL B, Luddite riots in Middleton. *LancsLH* 3 (1985) 8–11.

981 LEVY C, *A very hard year: the 1984–85 miners' strike in Mauchline*. Glasgow WEA 1985. pp 34.

982 ROSE AG, Trucking magistrates of Lancashire in 1842. *TLCAS* 83 (1985) 40–70.

983 SMART J, Feminists, food and the fair price: the cost of living demonstrations in Melbourne, August–September 1917. *LabH* 50 (1986) 113–31.

## Redundancy
see also 747

984 BUCK NH et al, *The London employment problem*. Oxford: Clarendon 1986. pp xvi + 213.

985 DAVIDSON A et al, *Leith loves – memories at work: a look at unemployment between the wars*. HMSO 1987. pp 32.

986 HENDERSON RA, *The employment performance of established manufacturing industry in the Scottish new towns*. Edinburgh: Economics and Statistical Unit: Scottish Economic Planning Dept 1982. pp 26.

987 Entry deleted.

988 PHILLIPS G, *Casual labour: the unemployment question in the port transport industry 1880–1970*. Oxford: Clarendon 1985. pp ix + 324.

989 *Redundancies in Dundee: summary of a study conducted with the Dept of Economics Dundee University*. Edinburgh: Scottish Economic Planning Dept 1980. pp 101.

990 *Unemployment in Strathclyde: June 1985*. Glasgow: Strathclyde Regional Council Economic and Industrial Development Committee 1985. pp 11.

# VI COMMUNICATIONS

## MODES OF INTER-URBAN COMMUNICATIONS

## Roads and streets

991 BUTLER DJ, A plan so replete with advantages to the traveller: the building of Durham's North Rd 1828–1830. *DCLHSB* 35 (1985) 22–34.

992 HILTON A, *Mexborough and Swinton: a route history*. Sheffield: author 1985. pp 16.

993 PHILLIPS ADM & TURTON BJ, Staffordshire turnpike trusts and traffic in the early nineteenth century. *JTH* 8 (1987) 126–46.

## Shipping
see also 57

994 FARR EJ et al, *Bristol city docks remembered 1900–1973*. Bristol: Bristol Shiplovers Society 1986. pp 40.

995 HANNAH GW, The evolution of Bridport harbour. *DNHS* 108 (1986) 27–31.

996 PERKINS KS, Early steampower links with Devonport and Torpoint. *DevH* 33 (1986) 20–7.

997 PROUD JH, *Seahorses of the Tees: the story of the Tees Towing Company Limited*. Middlesborough: the company 1985. pp 189.

## Railways

998 BODY G, *Oxford Hereford line: a description of the history, route and operation of a rail artery through the Cotswold and Malvern countryside*. Weston-super-Mare: British Rail 1985. pp 31.

999 BONAVIA M, *A history of Southam railway*. Allen & Unwin 1987. pp 256.

1000 COX JG, *Castleman's corkscrew: the Southampton and Dorchester railway, 1844–1848*. Southampton: City of Southampton 1986. pp 39.
1001 ELLIOTT PH, *Rugby's railway heritage*. Blaby: Anderson 1985. pp 72.
1002 GLADWIN TW, *Welwyn's railways: a history of the Great Northern line from 1850–1986*. Ware: Castlemead 1986. pp 120, il.
1003 JACKSON AA, *London's metropolitan railway*. Newton Abbot: David & Charles 1986. pp 416, il.
1004 MAGGS CG, *The Birmingham Gloucester line*. Cheltenham: Line One 1986.
1005 MICHEL S, *Chemins de fer en lyonnais: 1827–1957*. Lyon: Presses Universitaire de Lyon 1986. pp 250.
1006 MITCHELL V, *Chichester to Portsmouth*. Midhurst: Middleton 1984. pp 96.
1007 PIRIE GH, South African railways and the South African state 1902–1963. *JHG* 13 (1987) 283–95.
1008 POPPLEWELL L, *Against the grain: the Manchester and Southampton railway dream*. Bournemouth: Melledgen 1986. pp 44, il.
1009 ROBBINS M, Railway development in south west London. *LoMAS* 34 (1983) 259–69.
1010 SIMMONS J, *The railway in town and country, 1830–1914*. Newton Abbot: David & Charles 1986.
1011 THOMAS RHG, *London's first railway – the London and Greenwich*. Batsford 1986. pp 270, il.

**MODES OF INTRA-URBAN COMMUNICATIONS**
1012 WEBBER M, Urban growth and transport. *Energos* 11 (1985) 75–8.

**Public transport**
1013 CAMWELL WA, *Birmingham in the electric tramway era*. Solihull: Birmingham Transport Historical Group 1983. pp 72.
1014 DENTON AS, *Coventry transport 1884–1940*. Birmingham: Birmingham Transport Historical Group 1985. pp 64, il.
1015 *Evolution des transports urbaines*. Bruxelles: Conference Européenne des Ministres des Transports 1985. pp 90.
1016 GANDY K, *Sheffield Corporation tramways: an illustrated history*. Sheffield: Sheffield City Libraries 1985. pp ii + 186.
1017 JOYCE J, *Roads and rails of Tyne and Wear 1900–1980*. I Allan 1985. pp 143.
1018 LUCKING JH, *The Weymouth harbour tramway*. Poole: Oxford Publishing 1986. pp 128.
1019 MORGAN RH, The development of an urban transport system: the case of Cardiff. *WHR* 13 (1986) 178–93.
1020 PAPAYANIS N, The development of the Paris cab trade 1855–1914. *JTH* 8 (1987) 52–65.
1021 PAPAYANIS N, Un secteur des transports parisiens: le fiacre de la libre entreprise au monopole (1790–1855). *HES* (1986) 559–72.
1022 PEASGOOD A, *The horse buses of Brighton and Hove*. Falmer: Sussex U 1985. pp 54.
1023 ROBUCK J, The political economy of segregation: the case of segregated streetcars. *JEH* 46 (1986) 893–918.
1024 STONEBANKS JA, *Public transport in and through Walton on Thames: the station bus service*. Walton & Weybridge Local History Society 1985.

**Telephone, telegraph, post**
1025 DODD A, *History of the telephone service in Gloucester 1887–1987*. Gloucester: British Telecom 1987. pp 62.
1026 EARL RAJ, *The development of the telephone in Oxford*. British Telecom Museum 1985. pp ix + 158.
1027 LECOUTURIER Y, Genèse du reseau téléphonique dans le Calvados. *RH* 555 (1985) 143–58.

**VII POLITICS AND ADMINISTRATION**

**RESEARCH METHODS, AIDS AND MATERIALS**
1028 *Catalogue des coutumes d'Orléans et de Lozzi-Montargis*. Orléans: ville d'Orleans 1986. pp xii + 71, il.
1029 STEVENSON M, *Toronto and its metropolitan government: a bibliography*. Monticello: Vance Bibliographies 1986.

**URBAN POLITICS AND ADMINISTRATION**

1030 DAWSON WH, *Municipal life and government in Germany.* Garland 1985. pp xvi + 507.

1031 MCDONALD TJ & WARD SK, *The politics of urban fiscal policy.* Sage 1984. pp 176.

1032 The pocket boroughs of the Eliot family at St Germans, Liskeard and Grampound. *JRIC* 9 (1985) 321–49.

**Ancient**

1033 GAUTHIER P, *Les cités grecques et leur bienfaituers IVe–Ie siècles avant JC.* Paris: Ecoles Françaises d'Athenes 1985. pp x + 236.

**Medieval and early modern**

1034 ATTREED LC, Medieval bureaucracy and York's fee farm. *YH* (1985) 24–31.

1035 BRITNELL RH, Colchester courts and court records 1310–1525. *EAH* 17 (1986) 1333–40.

1036 BUTTERS HC, *Governors and government in early sixteenth-century Florence 1502–1519.* Oxford: Clarendon 1985. pp xviii + 350.

1037 CHOJNACKI S, Political adulthood in fifteenth century Venice. *AHR* 91 (1986) 791–810.

1038 GASPARRI F, *La principauté d'Orange au Moyen Age fin XIIIe–XVe siècles.* Paris, Leopard d'Or 1986. pp 280.

1039 GILKES RK, The chamberlain and his role in local government 1544–1835 [Banbury]. *CC* 10 (1986) 41–6; 54–66.

1040 HEERS J, *A la cour pontificale au temps des Borgia et des Medicis: 1420–1520.* Paris: Hachette 1986. pp 282.

1041 MIEVRAY JM, Failure of corporation: notaries public in medieval Bruges. *JMedH* 12 (1986) 155–66.

1042 MURRAY H, The mayor's esquires. *YH* (1985) 3–23.

1043 RACK HD, The Manchester corporation project of 1763: legend or history. *TLCAS* 84 (1987) 118–42.

1044 SEA TF, The reformation and the restoration of civic authority in Heilbronn 1525–32. *CEH* 19 (1986) 235–61.

1045 WILLIAMS JH, The forty men of Northampton's first customal and the development of borough government in late twelfth century Northampton. *NPP* (1986–7) 215–33.

1046 ZELIN M, *The magistrates tael: rationalising fiscal reform in eighteenth century Ching China.* California UP 1984. pp xviii + 385.

**Modern**

see also 772, 809, 968

1047 ABBOTT J, Sault Ste Marie explorations in the origins and evolution of municipal government. *LauUR* 17 (1985) 57–68.

1048 *L'Administration des grandes villes dans le monde.* Paris: Presses Universitaires de France 1987. pp 368.

1049 ALEXANDER R, The Federes of Dijon in 1815. *HJ* 30 (1987) 367–90.

1050 AYCOBERRY P, Les luttes pour le pouvoir dans les grandes villes d'Allemagne imperiale. *MS* 136 (1986) 83–102.

1051 AZARYAHU M, Street names and political identity: the case of East Berlin. *JCH* 21 (1986) 581–604.

1052 BARNES ST, *Patrons and power: creating a political community in metropolitan Lagos.* Manchester: Manchester UP 1986. pp 336.

1053 BERNARD MP, A propos de la situation à Marseille à la veille de la Libération. *PH* 36 (1986) 183–95.

1054 BILES R, *Big city boss in depression and war: Mayor Edward J Kelly of Chicago.* Dekalb: Northern Illinois UP 194. pp 219.

1055 BOND S, *Taking over the city: threats to the future of services and jobs in Sheffield.* Sheffield 1985. pp 37.

1056 BOOTH A, The United Englishman and radical politics in the industrial north west of England, 1795–1803. *IRSS* 31 (1986) 271–97.

1057 BRAHAM M, *Southport Liberal Association: the first 100 years.* Southport: The Association 1985. pp 82.

1058 BROWN MC & HABABY CN, Machine politics in America 1870–1945. *JInH* 17 (1987) 587–612.

1059 BROZOWSKI R, Development of municipal government in North Bay. *LauUR* 17 (1985) 27–41.

1060 CARTER LB, *The quiet Athenian*. Oxford: Clarendon P 1986. pp ix + 224.

1061 COOK R, *Portsmouth at the polls: one hundred and fifty years of reformed elections in a naval dockyard borough 1832–1982*. Studley: Brewin 1982. pp 72.

1062 CRAIG FWS, *Chronology of British parliamentary by-elections, 1833–1986*. Chichester: Parliamentary Research Services 1987. pp 300.

1063 DOYLE JK, Maury Maverick and racial politics in San Antonio, Texas 1938–1941. *JSouH* 53 (1987) 194–224.

1064 FINLAYSON KA, A national urban policy for South Africa. *Planning and building developments* 80 (1986) 48–54.

1065 FOX K, *Metropolitan America: urban life and urban policy in the United States 1940–1980*. Macmillan 1985. pp xiii + 274

1066 HARRIS J, *The town reeves of Bungay, 1725–1986: a study of a unique and ancient office and those who have occupied it*. Kings Lynn: Roseland 1986. pp 80.

1067 JOHNSON C, *The city in conflict*. Mansell 1985. pp 123.

1068 JONES PE, *Bangor 1883–1983: a study in municipal government*. Cardiff: Wales UP 1986. pp ix + 281.

1069 KELIKAN AA, *Town and country under fascism: the transformation of Brescia 1915–1926*. Oxford: Clarendon P 1986. pp xi + 228.

1070 LANCASTER B, Towards the socialist commonwealth: cooperation in Leicester in the late nineteenth century. *MidH* 12 (1987) 48–66.

1071 LAURENT J, Tom Mann, R S Ross and evolutionary socialism in Broken Hill, 1902–1912: alternative social Darwinism in the Australian Labour movement. *LabH* 51 (1986) 54–69.

1072 LINEBERRY RL & MASOTTI LH eds, *Urban problems and public policy*. UP of America 1986. pp 240.

1073 MORRIS N, *Eastleigh: an illustrated history of the Council, 1895–1986*. Horndean: Milestone 1986. pp 64.

1074 MOWBRAY M, The red shire of Kearsley, 1944–1947; communists in local government. *LabH* 51 (1986) 83–94.

1075 *Municipal Glasgow: its evolution and enterprises*. Garland 1985. pp iv + 340.

1076 PAGE H, *Local authority borrowing: past, present and future*. Allen & Unwin 1985. pp 360.

1077 REES G & LAMBERT J, *Cities in crisis: the political economy of urban development in postwar Britain*. E Arnold 1985. pp vii + 224.

1078 REINTGES CM, *Rents and urban political geography*. Durban: Natal U 1986. pp ix + 148, il.

1079 SAARINEN O, Municipal government in northern Ontario: an overview. *LauUR* 17 (1985) 5–25.

1080 SOUTH R, *Heights and depths: Labour in Windsor*. Windsor 1985. pp 72.

1081 WAGSTAFF J & PULLEN D eds, *Beckenham: an anthology of local history to celebrate the golden jubilee of Beckenham's charter of incorporation*. Historical Ass. 1984. pp 76, il.

1082 WALLACE C, Sudbury: the northern experiment with regional government. *LauUR* 17 (1985) 87–101.

1083 WESSELS E, *Urbanisation in Africa*. Pretoria: African Institute of South Africa 1984.

**URBAN POLITICS AT NATIONAL LEVEL**

1084 ANTIER JJ, *Le Sabordage de la flotte française à Toulon*. Paris: Ed de la cité 1986. pp 144, il.

1085 BRYANT LM, La cérémonie de l'entrée à Paris au moyen age. *AESC* 41 (1986) 513–42.

1086 CAILLE J, Les seigneurs de Narbonne dans le conflit Toulouse–Barcelone au XIIe siècle. *AdM* 171 (1985) 227–44.

1087 CHAMPDOR A, *Les rois de France à Lyon: de Charles VI à Louis XIV*. Lyon: Librarie des Terreaux 1986. pp 160.

1088 DEWAR D et al, *Urbanisation and settlement policy in South Africa*. Cape Town: UCT 1986. pp v + 53.

1089 DEWAR D & WAWTSON V, *An urbanisation strategy for South Africa*. Cape Town: UCT 1986. pp 43.

1090 ESTERHUYSE WP, *Swart verstedeliking (black urbanisation)*. Potchefstroom: IRS 1986. pp 20.

1091 FEJTO F, *1956 Budapest l'insurrection: la première révolution anti-totalitaire*. Paris: Complex 1986. pp 224.

1092 FINLAYSON KA, A national urban policy for South Africa. *Planning and building developments* 80 (1986) 48–54.

1093 FORREST R, *An unreasonable act?: central–local government conflict and the Housing Act 1980*. Bristol: Bristol U 1985. pp 170.

1094 FOURCAUT A, *Bobigny banlieue rouge*. Paris: Éditions ouevrées: Presses de la Fondation nationale des sciences politiques 1986. pp 215.

1095 GODECHOT J, *La Révolution française dans le Midi Toulousiain*. Toulouse: Privat 1986. pp 320, il.

1096 *Grenoble et les Vercors de la résistance a la libération 1940–1944*. Grenoble: la Manufacture 1985. pp 337.

1097 GUTTON JP ed, *Les lyonnais dans l'histoire*. Toulouse: Privat 1985. pp 420, il.

1098 HUMPHRIES R, The evolution of black politics. *Energos* 11 (1985) 87–91.

1099 ISSEL W & CHERNY RW, *San Francisco 1865–1932: politics, power and urban development*. Berkeley: California UP 1984.

1100 LE COUTURIER Y, Le groupe collaboration de Caen. *AdN* 35 (1985) 49–66.

1101 MOISSONIER M, Le parti communiste français dans la région Lyonnaise (fin 1938–fin 1941). *CdH* 30 (1985) 3–31.

1102 MONNIER R, L'évolution du personnal politique de la section de Marat et la rupture de germinal an 11. *AHRF* 263 (1986) 50–73.

1103 MOSTERT JPC, Black urbanization. *JCH* 1 (1986) 115–21.

1104 MOULINAS R, *Histoire de la Révolution d'Avignon*. Avignon: Aubanel 1986. pp 392, il.

1105 MULLER N, The future of constrained urbanization and African rural welfare. *RSA 2000* 1 (1985) 54–61.

1106 OLIVIESI A, Notes sur le T.S.O. à Marseille. *PH* 147 (1987) 3–15.

1107 PANICACCI JL, La Libération à Nice, seulevement patriotique à l'année révolutionnaire. *PH* 36 (1986) 213–23.

1108 PERAULT G, *Paris sous l'occupation*. Paris: Belfond 1987. pp 352, il.

1109 ROMMELSPACHER EE, *Conflict over urban land use and change in Cape Town*. Stellenbosch: U Stellenbosch 1984. pp iii + 163, il.

1110 SIMKINS CEW, *Patterns of urbanisation in South Africa: past, present and possible future*. Cape Town: Cape Town U 1985.

1111 THOMAS WH, Projecting urbanisation. *Energos* 11 (1985) 22–7.

1112 THORNHILL C, Regerings-en administratiewe reelings vir 'n stedelike gemeenskp (government and administrative arrangements for an urban community). *RSA 2000* 1 (1985) 35–40.

1113 VAN DER WESTHUIZEN GL, Swart verstedeliking (black urbanisation). *Oenskou* 9 (1985) 339–46.

1114 VAN JAARSVELD FA, *Verstedeliking in Suid Afrika (urbanisation in South Africa)*. Pretoria: U Pretoria 1985. pp 160.

1115 VAN VUUREN CJ, Westerse en tradisionele norme by dorpsuitleg in KwaNdebele (western and traditional norms in urban planning in Kwandabele). *RSA 2000* 1 (1985) 62–73.

1116 VISSIERE JL, Marseille à Leipzig. Chronique du STO. *PH* 147 (1987) 17–56.

1117 VULLIEZ A, *L'enfer de Brest*. Paris: France-Empire 1985. pp 273.

1118 *White paper on urbanisation*. Pretoria: Dept Constitutional Development and Planning 1986. pp 73.


**ASPECTS OF URBAN ADMINISTRATION**

**Public health**
see also 326–43

1119 BORSA S & MICHE CR, *La vie quotidienne des hôpitaux en France au XIXe siècle*. Paris: Hachette 1985. pp 246.

1120 BOUDRIOT PD, Essai sur l'ordure en milieu urbain a l'époque pré-industrielle, Beues, immodices et gadone à Paris au XVIIIe siècle. *HES* (1986) 515–28.

1121 CORAJOUD G, *Pouvoirs, ville et santé*. Presses polytechiques romandes 1985. pp 265, il.

1122 EMMS M, Swanage local board of health. *DNHS* 108 (1986) 11–18.

1123 MAYNE AJC, *Fever, squalor and vice: sanitation and social policy in Victorian Sydney*. St Lucia: Queensland UP 1982.

1124 MEADE T, Civilising Rio de Janeiro: the public health campaign and the riot of 1904. *JSocH* 20 (1986) 301–22.


**Police**

1125 BOWLBY C, Blatmai 1929: police, parties and proletarians in a Berlin confrontation. *HJ* 29 (1986) 137–58.

1126 CHRISTIE P, Bideford's first policeman. *DART* 118 (1986) 123–40.

1127 CRANFIELD R, Durham prisons in an age of change 3: 1837–1867. *DCLHSB* 37 (1986) 24–37.

1128 HUGHES S, Fear and loathing in Bologna and Rome: the papal police in perspective. *JSocH* (1987) 97–116.
1129 SPENCER EG, State power and local interests in Prussian cities: police in the Dusseldorf district 1848–1914. *CEH* 19 (1986) 293–313.
1130 TAYLOR D, The birth of the blues: preliminary observations on the early Middlesbrough police force. *CTLHS* 52 (1987) 45–57.

**PUBLIC UTILITIES**

**General public utilities**
1131 *Les équipements des villes.* Paris: INSEE 1985. pp 173.
1132 RIGAUDIERE A, Le financement des fortifications urbaines en France du milieu du XIVe siècle à la fin du XVe siècle. *RH* 553 (1985) 19–95.

**Power**
1133 BARLEY R, Sources of energy in Rochester's history. *RocH* 46 (1984) 1–24.
1134 BELTRAN A, La difficulté conquête d'une capitale: l'énergie électrique à Paris entre 1878 et 1907. *HES* (1985) 369–95.
1135 BUTLER D, Street lighting in Durham before the advent of gas. *DCLHSB* 38 (1987) 23–33.

**VIII SHAPING THE URBAN ENVIRONMENT**

**RESEARCH METHODS, AIDS AND MATERIALS**
1136 CHADWICK G, *Models of urban regional systems in developing counties: some theories and their application in physical planning.* Pergamon 1986. pp xv + 353.
1137 HULS ME, *The history of the garden city idea: a bibliography.* Monticello: Vance Bibliographies 1986.

**TOWN PLANNING AND ENVIRONMENTAL CONTROL**

Medieval
1138 CLIER J, Les projets d'agrandissement pour l'arsenal de Marseille à la fin du XVIIIe siècle et l'apport de Vauban. *PH* 140 (1985) 147–61.
1139 SLATER TR, Ideal and reality in English medieval town planning. *IBG* 12 (1987) 191–203.

Modern
1140 BATEY PWJ, *The history of planning methodology: a framework for the assessment of Anglo-American theory and practice.* Reading: Dept Geography Reading U 1982.
1141 BETTS D, Planned industrial settlement in the Netherlands 1813–1920. *PHB* 8 (1986) 35–44.
1142 FAINSTEIN NI & S, Economic restructuring and the politics of land use planning in New York City. *JAPA* 53 (1987) 237–43.
1143 FREDERIC J, Osborn 1885–1978. *TCP* 54 (1985).
1144 GOLDFIELD DR, Metropolitan planning in Sweden: the European context. *HEI* 7 (1986) 335–57.
1145 GOLDSMITH E & HILDYARD N, *Green Britain or industrial wasteland? a critique of Britain's evnironmental record.* Basil Blackwell 1986. pp 280.
1146 HALL T, *Planning Europïscher Hauptstäde zur Entwicklung des Städtebaues im 19 Jahrhundert.* Stockholm: Almquist & Wicksell 1986.
1147 HUTCHINGS A & BUNKER R, *With conscious purpose: a history of town planning in South Australia.* Adelaide: Wakefield P 1986.
1148 JOHNSON DL & LANGMEAD D, *The Adelaide city plan: fiction and fact.* Adelaide: Wakefield P 1986.
1149 MURET JP et al, *Les espaces urbains; conservoir, réaliser Geres.* Paris: Moniteur 1987. pp 320.
1150 RENAUD B, *Politique d'urbanisation nationale dans Pes pays en développement.* Paris: Economica 1985. pp 191.
1151 TILLIETTE B ed, *Un nouvel art des villes.* Paris: Autrement 1985. pp 186.
1152 *Urbanisation et enjeux quotiediens: terrains ethnologiques dans la France actuelle.* Paris: Anthropes 1985. pp 200.
1153 VON BAEYER E, The battle against disfiguring things: an overview of the response by

non-professionals to the city beautiful movement in Ontario from 1880 to 1920. *Society for the study of architecture in Canada bulletin* 11 (1986) 3–9.

## HOUSING IMPROVEMENT

### Public housing
see also 451
1154  HOLE J, *The homes of the working classes: with suggestions for their improvement.* Garland 1985. pp xiv + 214.
1155  ROOME KM, *Styleman's almshouses.* Bexley: author 1985.

### Slum clearance
1156  BRADLEY J, 'Once you've eaten Khitrov soup, you'll never leave': slum clearance in late Imperial Russia. *RussH* 11 (1984) 1–28.
1157  YELLING JA, *Slums and slum clearance in Victorian London.* Allen & Unwin 1986.

### Urban renewal
1158  CONWAY J, *Capital decay: an analysis of London's housing.* SHAC 1985. pp 89.
1159  THOMAS A, *Housing and urban renewal: residential decay and revitalisation in the private sector.* Allen & Unwin 1986. pp x + 225.

### NEW AND EXPANDED TOWNS
1160  CHALINE C, *Les villes nouvelles dans le monde.* Paris: Presse Universitaire de France 1985. pp 128.

## IX URBAN CULTURE

### URBAN CULTURE AND ENTERTAINMENT

#### Medieval and early modern
1161  BLACK R, *Benedetto Accolt: and the Florentine Renaissance.* Cambridge: Cambridge UP 1985. pp xv + 367.
1162  CHRISMAN MU, L'imprimerie et l'évolution de la culture laïque a Strasbourg (1480–1599). *RA* 111 (1985) 57–77.
1163  MOUREAU F, Les entrées royals ou le plaisir du prince. *XVIII* 17 (1985) 195–208.

#### Modern
1164  *Beaubourg, les dix premières années du Centre Georges Pompidou 1877–1987.* Paris: Beaux Arts 1987. pp 130.
1165  CHAMBERS I, *Popular culture: the metropolitan experience.* Methuen 1986. pp 256.
1166  GADILLE J, Jean-Baptiste Vanel et l'histoire ecclésiastique à Lyon au début de ce siècle. *RHEF* 186 (1985) 73–83.
1167  MABRO J, *I ban everything: free speech and censorship in Oxford between the wars.* Oxford: Ruskin college Library 1985. pp 42.
1168  PARINAUD A, *Les arts de la rue: l'animation des villes, la communication, responsibilité des élus, l'enfant dans las ville, l'avenu de l'affiche.* Paris: Monituer 1985. pp 524.

### ENTERTAINMENT
see also 799
1169  BLAU JR & HALL RH, The supply of performing arts in metropolitan places. *UAQ* 22 (1986) 42–65.

#### Theatre
1170  BOUQUET BOYER MT, Public et répértoire au théâtres Regio et Canignano de Turin. *XVIII* 17 (1985) 229–40.
1171  BUTT V, Banbury theatre and the Jackamans. *CC* 10 (1986/7) 12–15; 32–35; 106–7.
1172  DUPONT F, *L'Acteur-roi ou le théâtre dans le Rome antique.* Paris: Belles Lettres 1985. pp 350.

1173 LAGRAVE J & ROUYER P, *La vie théâtrale à Bordeaux*. Paris: CNRS 1985. pp 504.
1174 LINDSAY J, *The Royal Alex/the Old Vic*. Erin: Boston Mills P 1986. pp 64.
1175 RANGER P, The rivals: two Georgian theatre managers [Portsmouth Gosport]. *HFCAS* 43 (1987) 219–35.
1176 USIN LV, A history of Ottawa's town theatre. *Canadian Drama* 12

### Cinema
1177 OLIVO G, Aux origines du spectacle cinématographique en France. La cinéma forain: l'exemple des villes du midi méditerranéen. *RHMC* 33 (1986) 210–28.

### Opera, ballet and music
1178 GOURRET J, *Histoire des salles de l'Opera de Paris*. Maisme Tredamet 1985. pp 255, il.
1179 *Hamilton Philharmonic orchestra celebrating 100 years of music, 1884–1984*. Hamilton: Wentworth 1984. pp 80, il.

### Spectator sports
1180 ADELMAN ML, *A sporting time: New York City and the rise of modern athletics 1820–1870*. Urbana: Illinois UP 1986.
1181 ANDRAULT M, PARAT P & GUVAN A, *Palais omnisports de Paris Bercy*. Paris: Moniteur 1985. pp 68, il.
1182 BROWN GRANT E, The Banbury horse races. *CC* 10 (1986/7) 26–31; 68–78; 110–19.
1183 FLOOD B, *Saint John: a sporting tradition 1785–1985*. St John: Neptune Publishing 1985. pp 256.
1184 HUGGINS M, The glory years: an early northeast football club 1878–1887. *CTLHSB* 51 (1987) 28–40.

### FINE ARTS
1185 TAILLEFER M, Une fête maconnique à Gaillac en 1781. *AdM* 97 (1985) 435–40.

### Painting
1186 ALBRICHT T, *Art in the San Francisco bay area 1945–1980: an illustrated history*. Berkeley: California UP 1985.
1187 BELOT E, Peintures murales romaines fragmentaires à Bavay. *RN* 268 (1986) 5–17.
1188 BOTTINEAU-FUCHS Y, A propos de quelques représentations du tombeau des cardinaux d' Amboise. *AdN* 35 (1985) 17–37.
1189 BRESC-BAUTIER G & PINGEOT A, *Sculptures des jardins du Louvre du Carrousell et des Tuileries*. Paris: Musees Nationaux 1986. Vol 1 pp 203; vol 2 pp 454, il.
1190 *Le dessin à Gênes du XVIe au XVIIIe siècles*. Paris: Musées nationaux 1985. pp 123, il.
1191 LINANT DE BELLEFOND P, *Sarcophages antiques de la nécropole de Tyz: une étude iconographique*. Paris: Recherche sur les civilisations 1985. pp 186.
1192 PINCEMAILLE C, La guerre de Hollande dans le programme iconographique de la grande gallerie de Versailles. *HES* (1985) 313–33.
1193 SETTIS S, *La colonne Trajane: invention, composition, desposition*. *AESC* 40 (1985) 1151–96.
1194 WOLFF J & ARSCOTT C, Patronage and art in nineteenth century Manchester and Leeds. *HT* 37 (Mar 1987) 22–8.

### Other arts
1195 BARRALIALTET X, *Les mosaiques de pavement médiévales de Venise, Murano, Torcello*. Paris: Picaud 1985. pp 200, il.
1196 VILLELONGUE M, Un exemple de 'programme historique': les verrieres de la chapelle de la Charité de Lyons par Lucien Begule. *AdB* 93 (1986) 395–9.

### EXCHANGE OF INFORMATION
1197 DESGRAVES L, Le 450e anniversaire de l'imprimerie Neuchateloise. *RFHL* 43 (1984) 401–3.
1198 SHAW G, Les débuts de l'imprimerie gouvernmentale et commerciale en Jede. *RFHL* 43 (1984) 371–80.

**Newspapers**

1199  BENBASSA E, Presse d'istanbul et Salonique au service du Sionisme (1908–1904): les motifs d'une allégeance. *RH* 560 (1986) 337–66.

1200  BLACK J, Heavenly streamers, coal disputes and an attempted jail break: Durham and the press in the eighteenth century. *SCLHSB* 38 (1987) 11–12.

1201  BROWN L, London's knowledge of the provinces in the early nineteenth century. *JNPH* 3 (1986–7) 10–16.

1202  CHALLEN C, *The quarrelsome quill: Hull's radical press from 1830*. Hull: Voice 1984. pp 51.

1203  CLARK T, The Potts family and the 'Banbury Guardian'. *CC* 10 (1987) 1543–4.

1204  ELLISON S, *Bibliography of Newfoundland newspapers*. St Johns: Memorial University of Newfoundland Library 1985. pp 32.

1205  FEYEL F, La presse provinciale du XVIIIe siècle: géographie d'un réseau. *RH* 552 (1984) 353–74.

1206  HESP PA & ROBINSON PH, *Pages from the past: thirty years of Victorian life in the Beverley Guardian*. Highgate Publications 1986.

1207  HOWARD PITNEY D, Calvin Chase's Washington *Bee* and black middle class ideology 1882–1900. *JQ* (1986) 89–97.

1208  KLASSEN TC & JOHNSON OV, Sharpening of the *Blade*: black consciousness in Kansas 1892–97. *JQ* (1986) 298–304.

1209  MACDONALD C, *Historical directory of Saskatchewan newspapers 1878–1983*. Regina: Saskatchewan Archives Board 1984. pp 87.

1210  MARCH W, Newspaper competition in Halifax 1875–1900. *NS Hist Soc Colls* 42 (1986) 71–80.

1211  MUNRO D, 175 years of the *Montrose Review*: Scotland's second oldest weekly newspaper. *JNPH* 2 (1986) 14–21.

1212  RENOLD P, From the early *Banbury Guardian*. *CC* 10 (1986) 37–40.

1213  SINCLAIR A, *Madrid newspapers 1661–1870: a computerized handbook based on the work of Eugenio Hartzenbusch*. W S Maney 1985.

1214  TUDOR BA, Retail trade advertising in the *Leicester Journal* and the *Leicester Chronicle* 1855–71. *JAdH* 9 (1986)

1215  WOOLRICH AP, '*Ferner's Journal*' 1759/1760: an industrial spy in Bath and Bristol. 1986 pp 55.

**Other publications**

1216  BARBIER F, Une librairie 'internationale' Treutlel et Wuntz à Strasbourg, Paris et Londres. *RA* 111 (1985) 111–23.

1217  BERGER G, Littérature et lecteurs à Grenoble aux XVIIe–XVIIIe siècles: le public litteraire dans une capitale provinciale. *RHMC* 33 (1986) 114–32.

1218  DEBERGH M, Les oeuvres imprimées des mission européennes au Japon à Goa, Macao, Manille: 1588–1630. *RFHL* 42 (1984) 187–205.

1219  DENNING M, Cheap stories: notes on popular fiction and working class culture in nineteenth century America. *HW* 22 (1986) 1–17.

1220  ELDER C, W. J. Coates: an early 19th century Toronto printer. *York Pioneer* 81 (1986) 44–54.

1221  FAVIER R, Les 'Affiches' et la diffusion de l'innovation en Dauphine à la fin du XVIIIe siècle. *AdM* 170 (1985) 157–67.

1222  FOLLIE MM, De quelques bibliothèques metatrices au temps de la Papauté d'Avignon. *RFHL* 42 (1984) 247–56.

1223  SALMO N, L'édition chinoise dans le mond insulindien (fin XIXe siècle – début du XXe siècle) *RFHL* 43 (1984) 111–35.

1224  WICKLEN SJ, The growth and development of printing in the Wrexham area. *DHST* 35 (1986) 39–60.

**Libraries**

1225  BENEDICT P, Bibliothèques protestantes et catholiques à Metz au XVIIe siècle. *AESC* 40 (1985) 343–70.

1226  CARLEY JP, John Leland at Somerset libraries. *SANHS* 128 (1984) 141–54.

1227  COHOE M, Kingston's Mechanics Institute to free public library. *Historic Kingston* 33 (1985) 42–55.

1228  HOFFMANN S, Kitchener Public Library 1884–1984. *Waterloo HS* 72 (1984) 34–9.

1229 RAKOVSKY I, The Sailor's Institute in Thunder Bay. *Thunder Bay HMSPR* 14 (1986) 32–7.

1230 YEATMAN JL, Literary culture and the role of libraries in democratic America: Baltimore 1815–1840. *JLibH* 20 (1985) 345–67.

**EDUCATION**
see also 696, 757

1231 ALLSOBROOK D, Oundle before Sanderson: an episode in the history of a great school. *NPP* (1986–7) 271–84.

1232 BALL J&W, *Stockport Grammar School 1487–1987*. Congleton: Old vicarage 1987. pp 128.

1233 BASSARGETTE E, Une imagerie éducature: le mouchoir illustré rouennais. *HE* 30 (1986) 61–6.

1234 BLUM A & HOUDAILLE J, L'alphabétisation aux XVIIIe et XIXe siècles: l'illusion parisienne. *Pop* 40 (1985) 944–51.

1235 BRYANT ME, *The London experience of secondary education*. Athlone 1986. pp 540

1236 CHARLE C, *Dictionnaire biographique des universitaires au XIXe XXe siècles. 1: La Faculté des lettres de Paris 1809–1908*. Paris: CNRS 1986 pp 179.

1237 CONQUEST R, Ragged schools and others: the education of the poor of St Pancras before the Education Act of 1870. *LoMAS* 34 (1983) 245–58.

1238 COSTABEL P, *L'enseignement classique au XVIIIe siècle, collèges et universités*. Paris: Hermann 1986. pp 168.

1239 DEREGNAUCOURT G, Deux documents sur le seminaire et le seminariste du diocese de Cambrai au XVIIIe siècle: règlements de vie pratique et spirituelle. *RN* 266 (1985) 649–62.

1240 DEVAUX O, Les lycées imperiaux: des casienes: mythe ou realité? L'exemple de lycée de Toulouse. *RH* 553 (1985) 159–64.

1241 *East Boldon School centenary, 1885–1985*. East Boldon 1985. pp 20.

1242 EMMOTT DH, 150 years ago: the British and Foreign School Society in Doncaster. *HuAS* 13 (1985) 42–6.

1243 ENOCH DG, 'They that sow tears': a hindsight into Victorian education in Llantrisant. *M* 29 (1985) 80–5.

1244 EVANS M, *An early history of Queen Elizabeth Grammar School Carmarthen 1576–1800*. Carmarthen: Old Mandunians 1986. pp 95, il.

1245 GRACE G ed, *Education and the city: theory, history and contemporary practice*. Routledge & Kegan Paul 1984. pp 302.

1246 GRANDIERE M, L'éducation en France à la fin du XVIIIe siècle: quelques aspects d'un nouveau cadre éducatif, les maisons d'éducation 1760–1790. *RHMC* 33 (1986) 440–62.

1247 GREVET R, L'alphabétisation urbaine sous l'ancien règime: l'exemple de Saint Omer (fin XVIIe – début XIXe siècle) *RN* 266 (1985) 609–32.

1248 GRIFFIN P ed, *St Hugh's: one hundred years of women's education in Oxford*. Basingstoke: Macmillan 1986. pp 336.

1249 HOUSTON RA, *Scottish literacy and the Scottish identity: illiteracy and society in Scotland and northern England 1600–1800*. Cambridge: Cambridge UP 1985. pp x + 325.

1250 INGARFIELD LE & ALEXANDER MB, *Haberdashers' Aske's Boys' School: a short history*. Worshipful Company of Haberdashers 1985. pp vii + 56, il.

1251 JULIA D, REVEL J, CHARTIE R, *Les universités européennes du XVIe au XVIIIe siècles: histoire des populations étudiantes. 1 Bohème, Espagne, Etats italiens, pays germaniques, Pologne, Provinces-Unies*. Paris: Ecole des Hauts Etudes en Sciences Socials 1986. pp 264.

1252 LAISSUS Y & TORLAIS J, *Le Jardin du roi et le College royale dans l'ensiegnement des sciences au XVIIIe siècle*. Paris: Hermann 1986. pp 341.

1253 *Les sauvages dans la cité: auto-émancipation du peuple et instruction des prolétaires au XIXe siècle*. Paris: Champ Vallon 1985. pp 228.

1254 MABRO J, *I ban everything: free speech and censorship in Oxford between the wars*. Oxford: Ruskin College 1985. pp 45.

1255 MARCHAND P, Les petits soldats de demain. Les bataillons scolaires dans le département du Nord 1882–1892. *RN* 266 (1985) 769–803.

1256 MAINS B & TUCK A, *Royal Grammar School Newcastle upon Tyne: a history of the school in its community*. Stackfield: Oriel 1986. pp xii + 361, il.

1257 MARSDEN WE, Residential segregation and the hierarchy of elementary schooling from Charles Booth's London surveys. *LJ* 11 (1985) 127–46.

1258 MEROT C, Le recruitement des ècoles centrales sous la Révolution. *RH* 556 (1985) 357–85.

1259  PACAUT M, L'encadement pédagogique d'histoire et de géographie à la Faculté des lettres de Lyon (1883–1983). *CdH* 29 (1984) 265–84.
1260  PERLMANN J, *The schooling of blacks in a northern city: Providence, Rhode Island 1880–1925.* New York: Cambridge UP 1985.
1261  RATCLIFFE J, Roger Holland and the Farnworth and Jearsely Sunday School for children of all denominations. *LanLH* 3 (1985) 28–33.
1262  ROBERTS F, *A history of Sedgeley Park and Cotton College.* Author 1985. pp 267.
1263  RONNE G, *Histoire du lycée de jeunes filles de Reims.* Paris: Arers 1985. pp 147.
1264  SHATZMILLER J, Une expérience universitaire renouvelle: le studium de Manosque (1299–1300). *PH* 140 (1985) 195–203.
1265  SMITH AR, The Frodsham Grammar School. *ChesH* 18 (1986) 26–7.
1266  STEPHENS WB, *Education, literacy and society, 1830–1870: the geography of diversity in provincial England.* Manchester: Manchester UP 1986. pp 342.
1267  TRENARD L, Alphabétisation et scolarisation dans la région lilloise. Les effects de la crise révolutionnaire 1780–1802. *RN* 266 (1985) 633–48.
1268  VANACKER DHORME C, Les débuts de l'ensiegnement professionel dans le Nord: l'exemple de L'E.N.P. d'Armentières. *RN* 266 (1985) 749–68.
1269  WILSHERE J, *Evington School 1841–1957* [Leicester]. Leicester: Research Dept. Chamberlain Music and Books 1985. pp ii + 22.
1270  WINTERBURN JM, *A history of Arnold Lodge School, Royal Leamington Spa, Warwickshire 1864–1984.* Leamington: 1984. pp 38.
1271  YORK B, The Education Act of 1902 and the struggle for secondary schools [Kettering]. *NPP* (1986–7) 285–92.

**URBAN INFLUENCES ON RURAL AREAS AND THE WIDER WORLD**
1272  KIRKMAN K, Mid-nineteenth century rural change: the case of Pinner. *LoH* 17 (1986) 199–204.


# X ATTITUDES TO CITIES

**ATTITUDES TO CITIES**

**Medieval and early modern**
1273  AMELANG JS, *Honored citizens of Barcelona: patrician culture and class relations 1490–1714.* Princeton: Princeton UP 1986. pp 256.
1274  KING ML, *Venetian humanism in an age of patrician dominance.* Princeton: Princeton UP 1986. pp 575.


**Modern**
1275  BRADLEY J, The winter and the city in late imperial Russia. *SEER* 14 (1986) 321–38.
1276  COHEN GB, Society and culture in Prague, Vienna and Budapest in the late nineteenth century. *EEQ*-20 (1987) 467–84.
1277  FRASER D, Joseph Chamberlain and the municipal ideal. *HT* 37 (April 1987) 33–9.
1278  HALLEN H, Of dreams and cities. *Leadership* 4 (1985) 90–5.
1279  HARVEY D, *Consciousness and the urban experience.* Oxford: Blackwell 1985. pp xix + 293.
1280  MASHILE GG, Contained urbanization in South Africa: a study of Sowetans' attitudes towards their living space. *RSA 2000* 1 (1985) 80–3.


**VIEWS OF THE CITY IN LITERATURE, GRAPHIC AND DRAMATIC ART**

**Literature**
1281  GOLDSTEIN L, The image of Detroit in twentieth century literature. *MicQR* 25 (1986) 269–91.
1282  GREET M, Isaac Bell: Cheltenham's gardener rhymer. *LoH* 17 (1986) 163–8.
1283  THESING WB, Gerald Manley Hopkins's responses to the city: the composition of the crowd. *VS* 30 (1987) 385–408.


**Art**
1284  SLOWINSKI D, Detroit: sourcebook of images. *MicQR* 25 (1986) 213–32.

# Index of towns

Aachen 80
Aberdeen 81, 82, 83
Aberystwyth 668
Adelaide 84, 679, 1147
Agenais 694
Aix 703
Aix en Provence 606
Alloa 244
Alresford 85
Amboise 1188
Amiens 86, 481
Amsterdam 305
Ardres 860
Angers 596
Annecy 87
Antwerp 601, 646
Armentières 1268
Arras 394
Aspen 88
Athens 89
Auckland 905
Avignon 245, 659, 1104, 1222

Baltimore 90, 303, 528, 556, 1230
Banbury 948, 1039, 1182, 1203
Banff 91
Bangor 1068
Barcelona 1273
Barry 92
Bath 1215
Batley 93
Bayonne 345,
Beccles 913
Beckenham 1081
Bédarieux 584
Bedford 407, 413
Beechworth 94
Beirut 774
Belfast 95, 873, 978
Belleville 96
Belper 707
Bendigo 678
Berkeley 97, 512
Berlin 1051, 1125
Beverley 1206
Beyrouth 246
Béziers 98
Bideford 1126
Birmingham 287, 640, 846, 901, 952, 1004, 1013
Birkenhead 640

Bishopwearmouth 5
Blois 333, 334
Bobigny 1094
Bollington 859
Bologna 1128
Bolton 99
Bombay 100
Bordeaux 302, 345, 1173
Boston 551, 597, 599
Bourges 247
Bournemouth 840
Braintree 381
Brantford 101
Bray 102
Brentford 712
Brescia 1069
Brest 727, 1117
Bridport 995
Brighton 103, 1022
Bristol 104, 105, 106, 107, 331, 402, 660, 870, 994, 1215
Brocksville 248
Brookline 600
Bruges 1041
Budapest 1091, 1276
Buenos Aires 557
Bungay 1066
Burlington 108
Byblos 109

Caen 614, 1100
Caernarvon 421
Calais 110
Calcutta 111
Canberra 112
Camberwell 126
Cambrai 927, 1239
Cambridge 764
Cape Town 113, 730, 1109
Cardiff 921, 1019
Cardigan 398
Carmarthen 403, 1244
Cassel 392
Chalatenango 661
Chandler's Ford 114
Charleston 115, 476
Charlieu 116
Charlottetown 917
Cheltenham 249, 1282
Chester 419, 530, 687
Chicago 117, 483, 593, 822, 1054

Chichester 118, 1006
Cincinnati 886
Ciotat 504
Cirencester 538
Citadel 196
Clacton-on-Sea 717
Clifton 250
Clun 119
Colchester 788, 802, 1035
Condomais 694
Constantinople 120
Contant d'Ivry 489
Cork 121
Coventry 12, 923, 1014
Cradley Heath 957
Crowborough 122
Croydon 890
Crystal Palace 251

Dacca 123
Darlington 977
Derby 891
Detroit 125, 783, 856, 1281, 1284
Devonport 996
Dijon 565, 1049
Doncaster 1, 1242
Dorchester 1000
Douai 492, 733
Dover 411
Dresden 124
Dublin 252, 341
Dulwich 126
Dundas 127
Dundee 810a, 989
Durban 519
Durham 935, 991, 1127, 1135, 1200
Dusseldorf 1129

Ealing 254
East Boldon 1241
Eastleigh 1073
Edinburgh 255
Edmonton 128
Eskilstuna 676
Eugene 129
Evington 1269
Exeter 288

Fes 544
Fishguard 256
Fleetwood 130
Florence 326, 360, 688, 1036
Fort William 131
Fréjus 387, 851
Fribourg 625
Frodsham 1265

Gaillac 1185
Gary 132
Genève 133, 691, 953
Gisborne 539
Glasgow 134, 289, 533, 631, 653, 695, 1075
Gloucester 378, 682, 861, 862, 1004, 1025
Goa 1218
Godalming 135
Gosport 1175
Graaf Reinet 136
Grasse 257
Greenford 869
Greenwich 1011
Grenoble 1096, 1217
Guatamala 818

Hagley 137
Halesworth 913
Halifax 138, 139, 761, 1210
Hamilton 140, 141, 142, 895, 1179
Hanover 143
Harlem 552, 656, 779
Hartlepool 409
Hastings 290, 580
Havering 144
Headingly 145
Heilbronn 1044
Hereford 401, 771, 998
Heybridge 405
Hong Kong 146, 424, 568
Hopefield 545
Hove 1022
Hoylake 147
Huddersfield 339
Hull 258, 291, 696, 833, 1202
Huntsville 259, 260

Illinois 593
Ipswich 642
Irvine 148
Isleworth 72
Islington 296, 594

Jasper 149
Jerusalem 150
Johannesburg 151, 261, 510
Johnstown 777
Jugnon 152

Kansas 1208
Kearsley 1073
Keith 612
Kenilworth 292
Kettering 262, 1271
Kidderminster 889

Kilpatrick 263
Kingston upon Hull 153
Kimberley 850
Kirby Lonsdale 154
Kisangani 358
Kitchener 155, 939, 1228
Kwandabele 1115

Lagos 564, 1052
Lancaster 884
La Rochelle 156, 474
Lausanne 320
Leeds 1194
Leicester 157, 643, 748, 1070,
    1214
Liège 293, 473, 509
Leipzig 1116
Leith 158, 985
Leamington 1270
Lichfield 159, 416, 418, 467
Lille 384, 415, 934
Limoges 685
Listowel 160
Liverpool 640, 879
Llantrisant 1243
London 15, 161, 162, 163, 172, 173,
    264, 297, 340, 343, 372, 414, 436,
    501, 513, 522, 535, 566, 583, 592,
    595, 616, 663, 680, 683, 705, 720,
    728, 744, 749, 757, 780, 891, 897,
    903, 920, 929, 930, 931, 945, 950,
    965, 984, 1003, 1009, 1011, 1157,
    1158, 1235, 1257
Londonderry 174
Long Melford 175
Louisville 794
Lyon 265, 382, 399, 702, 710, 725,
    1005, 1087, 1096, 1101, 1166
Lynn 349

Mablethorpe 716
Macao 1218
Macclesfield 515, 516
Machynlleth 379
Madrid 907, 1213
Malvern 176
Manchester 298, 686, 866, 881, 928,
    1008, 1043, 1194
Manille 312
Mansfield 177
Marlborough 299
Marseille 178, 704, 722, 858, 1053,
    1106, 1116, 1138
Maryborough 579
Mauchline 981
Mayfair 591
Melbourne 647, 753, 762, 765, 983

Metz 1225
Mexborough 992
Mexico 359
Mexico City 796
Miami 179, 180
Middle River 181
Middlesborough 645, 1130
Middleton 980
Middlewich 729
Milton Keynes 435
Moncton Parish 821
Montgomery 406
Montpellier 337
Montreal 113, 456, 536, 546, 586, 588,
    604, 721, 823, 830
Montrose 1211
Munich 784

Nancy 496
Nantes 182
Narbonne 1086
Nashville 782
Neston 183
Newark 874
Newcastle 184, 266
Newcastle-upon-Tyne 1256
Newhaven on Forth 185
New Orleans 759, 961
Newport 658
Newton Abbot 420
New York 371, 508, 550, 553, 627, 723,
    779, 805, 825, 829, 900, 967, 974,
    1180
Nice 1107
Niederbronn 186
Nimes 787, 863
Northampton 1045
Nottingham 364, 393, 529, 677,
    946

Oakville 187
Old Sarum 417
Ontario 264, 343
Orange 1038
Orléans 1028
Oromocto 188
Ostie 189
Ottawa 190, 191, 192, 314, 315, 316,
    458, 689, 1176
Oundle 1231
Oxford 998, 1026, 1167, 1248

Paignton 887
Paris 193, 267, 306, 307, 322, 395, 400,
    422, 429, 430, 433, 459, 469, 470,
    475, 480, 498, 500, 525, 558, 559,
    571, 607, 611, 616, 621, 670, 674,

698, 754, 766, 909, 911, 958, 962, 969, 1019, 1020, 1084, 1108, 1119, 1134, 1164, 1178, 1181, 1189, 1195, 1236
Parkgate 183
Parry Sound 194
Peckham 126
Penang 922
Penn 329
Perth 827
Peterborough 643
Petersburg 816
Philadelphia 268, 313, 738, 752, 775, 888, 942
Pietermaritzburg 520
Pimlico 195
Pinner 1272
Pittsburgh 329, 351
Plymouth 19, 737
Plympton 843
Poitiers 197
Pontoise 269
Poole 270, 743
Port Delhousie 198
Portland 792
Port Moody 199
Port Phillip, 724
Portsmouth 271, 272, 1006, 1061, 1175
Prague 1276
Providence 639, 1260
Pretoria 200
Puy en Velay 428

Rambervilliers 755
Ramsgate 201
Redruth 202
Reims 478, 1263
Richmond 453
Ringwood 263
Rio de Janeiro 1124
Rochefort 204
Rochester 205, 813, 1133
Rochford 410
Rome 638, 665, 1128, 1172
Rossendale 666
Rotherham 868
Rouen 763, 971, 1233
Royston 951
Rugby 1001
Rye 567

St Louis 750
St Pancras 1237
St Peters 716
St Petersburg 330, 979
Saint Baron 206

Saint Etienne 273
Saint John 207, 1183
Saint Louis 274
Saint Malo 208, 540
Saint Nazaire 582
Saint Omer 1247
Saint Quentin 209, 628
Saint Sebastian sur Loire 210
Salford 686
San Antonio 798, 1063
San Fernando 768
San Francisco 672, 857, 966, 975, 1099, 1186
Saskatoon 650
Sault Ste Marie 1047
Saumur 711
Seaton Carew 715
Sedan 619
Senlis 211, 275
Sheffield 893, 1016, 1055
Skegness 714
Somers Town 212
Southam 999
Southampton 276, 739, 838, 1000, 1008
Southport 1057
Southwark 598
Southwell 457
Southwold 913
Stawell 213
Stockport 1232
Stockton 892
Stoke-on-Trent 214
Strasbourg 216, 641, 1162, 1216
Stratford 217
Streatham Vale 218
Stroud 300
Sudbury 277, 1082
Sunderland 5
Swanage 1122
Swinton 99
Sydney 215, 327, 328, 503, 569, 810, 1123

Tampa 778
Taunton 944
Thebes 219
Thunder Bay 1128
Toledo 220, 221
Tolsta 222
Toronto 223, 224, 225, 278, 454, 546, 681, 756, 795, 1029, 1220
Torpoint 995
Totnes 390, 396
Tottenham 325
Toulon 21, 279, 499, 1084
Toulouse 479, 693, 906, 1095, 1240

Tournai 427
Tours 226, 280
Tucson 786
Turin 1170
Tower Hamlets 281, 282
Troyes 227, 615

Uxbridge 301
Uz 617

Valence 228, 471
Valenciennes 347, 380
Vallet 229
Vancouver 230, 283, 284, 546
Venice 898, 899, 973, 1037
Victoria 233, 234, 285
Vienna 1276
Vienne 472, 767
Villemoisson sur Orge 235
Villette 460, 461
Voronezh 968

Wakefield 339
Walsall 388
Walton on Thames 1024
Washington 1207
Welwyn 1002
West Carberry 236
Westminster 507
Weymouth 1018
Whitby 894
Wilton 885
Windsor 16, 1080
Winnipeg 799
Wollongong 238
Wolverhampton 239
Woodborough 932
Woolwich 286
Wrexham 1224
Wurtemberg 585

Yarmouth 240
York, 241, 332, 708, 1034

# Reviews of books

Book review editors: Joyce Ellis and John Walton

## 1 GENERAL AND THEMATIC

P. R. Coss and S. D. Lloyd (eds), *Thirteenth-Century England I: Proceedings of the Newcastle-upon-Tyne Conference 1985*. Woodbridge: Boydell Press, 1986. vii + 196 pp. £29.50.

Anyone under the impression that the demise of the Powicke school has left the study of thirteenth-century England in the doldrums will be briskly disabused by this collection of sixteen papers, the first fruits of a conference that seems set fair to become an annual event. No unitary theme is invoked to impose an artificial homogeneity upon these diverse contributions. Ten of them are concerned with politics and government, three with urban history, two with literary questions and one with collective mentalities. Faced with such varied fare, the reviewer may perhaps be forgiven for selecting a few dishes that aroused his particular interest.

Five essays exemplify some of the new thinking about the reign of Henry III, of which the most notable, by David Carpenter, provides a corrective to the picture of Henry's financial plight as depicted by Treharne and Powicke. Using the enrolled Wardrobe accounts, Carpenter shows that a substantial gold reserve was accumulated in the Wardrobe under the Keepership of Chaceporc (described most unfairly by Tout as a period of profligate expenditure 'under foreign management'), and that even if his resources were insufficient to underwrite the pope's debts, Henry's government was by no means bankrupt in 1258. In another essay Clive Knowles draws attention to the surprisingly generous provision Henry made for the widows and dependants of the Montfortians who were disinherited after Evesham, a policy doubtless prompted as much by expediency as by compassion, for many of the victorious loyalists were connected to rebel families by ties of blood or marriage. Among four papers on aspects of Edward I's government, I found those by J. R. Maddicott and S. L. Waugh particularly interesting – the former for its penetrating investigation of the relations between the crown and the localities through the shrievalties, and the latter for the light it threw upon Edward's management of the crown's wards. It seems that until the crisis year of 1296 they were used as a form of patronage for the benefit of members of the court circle; thereafter, they were ruthlessly auctioned to maximize income.

Three of the essayists investigate the society and economy of four thirteenth-century towns. Edward Miller uses the records of York and Newcastle to test and broadly to endorse the current assumption that civic offices were virtually monopolized by a small group of magnate families, whose wealth was derived from the bourgeois vocations of trade, manufacture and finance. He shows, however, that these were not closed oligarchies: they were open to newcomers, and there was no sharp class demarcation between gentry and bourgeoisie, many of whom invested in rural properties. Henry Summerson uses the fragmentary evidence of the plea rolls of the justices in eyre to piece together the commercial links between the relatively sparsely populated town of Carlisle and Newcastle, York and Scotland. J. A. Watt writes about the collision of race and culture in thirteenth-century Dublin. He argues that the Hiberno-Norse – the *Ostmen* – were rapidly assimilated into the Anglo-Norman commune, but that the native Irish could only gain admission by express grants of English legal status, and that in this way their entry to the ranks of the colonists was controlled. An interesting but necessarily tentative essay, and one chapter in Watt's broader study of the two races in medieval Ireland.

**C. H. Lawrence**
Royal Holloway & Bedford New College, University of London

Maurice Garden and Yves Lequin (eds), *Habiter la Ville. XVe–XXe siècles*. Lyon: Presses Universitaires de Lyon, 1985. xvii + 315 pp. 95F.

This volume of essays forms a pair with *Construire la Ville*, published in 1983 and which I reviewed in the *Urban History Yearbook 1986*. They emerge from a series of round tables organized at the lively Centre Pierre Léon at Lyon. The project was an imaginative one which sought to relate to each other themes all too frequently compartmentalized in urban historical research: the construction of the town as the result (not merely the determinant) of its economic and social relations, and the way the space of the town was populated and then lived. The successful if uneven first volume focussed on the former theme, this sequel on the latter.

The good articles in the present collection are somewhat swamped by briefer or less substantial pieces which cannot really survive in the cooler air away from the round tables at which they were presented. The growing practice of automatically publishing conference and colloquium papers is an unhappy development, for its consequence will be either to suppress lively but insubstantial discussion papers whose authors would never wish to see them published, or to proliferate fairly lightweight books of essays. This collection is more substantial than that, but amongst its twenty essays are many pieces that amount to no more than brief, and often preliminary, research reports.

The substance of the volume should not be lost sight of, however, and it is a concentration of attention on the fashionable concept of *territoire*, a term that lacks in English an equivalent which embraces the multiple senses of urban space as physically, socially and culturally defined and contested. The book attempts to pin these down by approaching from three directions. The first is that of population mobility and the peopling of urban space. Olivier Zeller uses a 1597 census of Savoyards resident in Lyon (21 per cent of household heads) to explore their uneven distribution through the town's neighbourhoods, while Etienne François takes the same theme of migration into early-modern towns to contrast the policies of differing types of German town. He shows how the apparently strong differences between the classic model regulating entry to privileges and turning in upon itself as the period advanced, and the newer open free towns whose looser structure sought to attract mobile bourgeois and artisans, recede as we see how much these towns had in common, and how vulnerability induced the latter to behave increasingly like the former. Finally, Louise Tilly explores labour mobility and capital concentration in nineteenth-century Milan and Lyon to show the necessity of examining urban economic development as a regional phenomenon.

French urban historians have been turning increasingly to the neighbourhood (*quartier*) as a unit of social analysis, and if such a focus runs the danger of losing a sense of the urban whole, it nonetheless instructively compels us to think about the urban framework within which daily life was lived, and the economic forces and social relations that determine that framework. The best of the essays in the book's second section are concerned with identifying and exploring the neighbourhood. Herman Diederiks examines the *quartiers* of early nineteenth-century Amsterdam, but his attempt to discover whether or not there was a Jewish ghetto in the town loses its way and ends up offering little more than a demographic history of Amsterdam's Jews. Jean-Claude Robert takes two old neighbourhoods strongly affected by immigration in early-nineteenth-century Montreal, and tackles the awkward problem of seeking the sources of neighbourhood stability at a time of high rates of population movement. His suggestion that patterns of occupational structure and of property ownership provided the bases of stability over time sounds plausible, but his concentration on underlying structures diverts him from exploring the subsequent personal and cultural continuities. Paul-André

Linteau's well-researched study of the same town later in the century, showing property in the hands of a local petite bourgeoisie in new industrial suburbs, fails to pick up these themes of lived space and social relations (indeed it would have been better placed in the first volume).

The most substantial studies of neighbourhoods are provided by Antoine Prost on Orléans on the eve of the First World War and Gabriel Désert on mid-nineteenth-century Caen. The tight spatial social segregation in stagnating Caen comes as some surprise – Désert relates it to the tying of the locally-born to the older and declining sectors of the town's economy – but far more striking is Prost's analysis by *quartier* of Orléanais workers which shows a marked difference between quartiers on certain variables (marriage, women's work and others) even when the occupation of household head is held constant. His suggestion of a 'neighbourhood effect' is worth exploring further, for, as he writes, 'the town exists before its citizens'.

The remaining section of the book contains some stimulating essays – with Peter Clark summarizing arguments about the changing social role of early-modern English alehouses which he has presented at greater length elsewhere, and Daniel Roche offering a typically rich and elegant evocation of the world and the half-world of the bars of late-eighteenth-century Paris – but only Maurizio Gribaudi's provocative and overelaborate study of a neighbourhood in twentieth-century Turin draws us back to the theme of lived space and neighbourhood relations. He contrasts the *quartier* in its socialist (1900–20) years with its character in the Fascist period that followed. There is an interesting argument in his analysis about how sociability and language create a neighbourhood discourse that becomes a norm to which others have to conform, but his conviction that only through the reconstruction of individual life trajectories, ambitions and relations to others can we begin to talk about social cohesion and culture leads him into a level of personal detail that threatens an impossible disintegration of historical generalization.

As Gribaudi's attempt to challenge historical generalization suggests, there is much that is fashionable in this book, even though its originating round tables were held several years ago. There is also much in this collection that is either lightweight or – like John Merriman's picture of neighbourhood rivalries in Perpignan or Jean-Luc Pinol's reconstruction of mobility patterns in twentieth-century Lyon – preliminary reports on work in progress. However, in seeking to direct our attention to the internal organization of the town, the way it was populated and the way it was lived, the best of the essays make good and profitable reading.

**Geoffrey Crossick**
Department of History, University of Essex

J. A. Sharpe, *Early Modern England: A Social History 1550–1760*. London: Edward Arnold, 1987. x + 379 pp. Bibliography. £28.00 (hardback) and £9.95 (paperback).

Recently the assumption that 'social history' was rooted in economic analysis, with 'Whiggish' or Marxist connotations, has been vigorously challenged, most notoriously by J. C. D. Clark's *English Society*. Sharpe's textbook is much more level-headed and comprehensive than Clark's, but it shares the avowed aim to 'explore what emerges when simplistic models of socio-economic development are abandoned' (p.352), and its allocation of space reflects this. With 58 pages of background political chronology, a section on the nation-state and 100 pages on cultural history, only half the book is left for standard 'social history' issues, with only 24 pages directly discussing the economy. When analysing social structure, Sharpe is always keen to stress non-economic factors, such as demography, life-style or political influence, while he emphasizes consumption rather than production. He consistently deplores Marxist explanations, and largely ignores alternative suggestions linking different social structures to varied means of production, such as 'chalk' and 'cheese' communities. Indeed he suggests (p.300) that 'the most important changes in the period covered by this book came not in the realm of economic or social structures, but rather in the intellectual field'. There is greater vigour in his writing on political and cultural subjects than in the other sections, where Sharpe suffers rhetorically from arguing a negative case. He demolishes Stone on changes in the family and in affections, and he insists that we cannot simply analyse the economy as 'pre-industrial', but spends too long knocking down Aunt Sallies to build up an independent explanation. Keith Wrightson's *English Society 1580–1680* is much more satisfactory in these areas.

Sharpe criticizes Wrightson's book for neglecting the elite, and his own emphasis throughout is on continued aristocratic dominance of the 'English Ancien Regime'. He writes sympathetically and effectively, if briefly, on the attitudes of the poor, but he is clearly more interested in the relationship between the middling sort and the elite. Ironically, his conclusions here tie in very closely with Wrightson's, and indeed Thompson's, in stressing the fusion of middling and upper classes under aristocratic hegemony, and the absence of a bourgeois challenge to the status quo. He also shares their belief that the period falls into two very different halves, breaking *c.*1640–60. Before then he stresses crisis, pressure (especially demographic) and the 'shaking' of the social order, while thereafter he finds stability, the easing of pressures and 'equilibrium'. Echoing his revisionist approach to politics, he sees society before 1640 as reacting conservatively to the pressures for change and emerging after 1660 with a renewed commitment to order and property. Growing prosperity for the haves, together with poor relief for the have-nots, then allowed a luxurious flowering of elite sociability and culture.

Sharpe devotes 13 pages to urban life as such, while there is a brief discussion of 'urban masters', but almost nothing on the urban poor. There is a whole chapter on 'non-landed elites' but significantly, after 5 pages on 'merchants and industrialists', this concentrates on the professions. There will be little new to urban historians familiar with the publications of Peter Clark. This is hardly surprising, since the pattern of town history which Clark has laid down fits very closely with Sharpe's view of social change generally. So we have towns under threat before 1650, producing greater oligarchy and a decline in wider communal solidarity, followed by 'urban renaissance' after the Restoration on the Clark–Borsay model, with emphasis on the role of landed gentry, professions and the 'pseudo-gentry', and the revival of an exclusive urban culture and ritual. There are hints of towns generating broader political interests and new forms of mass culture, but these are played down, in favour of the integration of urban into landed society.

Sharpe has produced a careful synthesis of current thinking, which nevertheless conveys a distinctive message by its balance and organization. His insistence on the reintegration of politics and culture is praiseworthy and often well done. Where he failed, for this reviewer, was in evoking a sense of 'real people trying to get through life', seen in their own terms, certainly in relation to urban communities. Curiously, 'Whig' historians still appear better at this, in practice, than their revisionist critics.

**Jonathan Barry**
Department of History, University of Exeter.

Jeremy Black, *The English Press in the Eighteenth Century*. London: Croom Helm, 1987. xv + 321pp. Bibliography. Index of titles. £30.00.

This wide-ranging examination of the development of English newspapers in the eighteenth century seeks to provide the first general introduction to the growth and influence of the press on a national scale. Previous studies have been overwhelmingly metropolitan in their coverage and have concentrated on limited specialist areas, usually politics, printing or ownership. In contrast, Dr Black seeks to use his probably unrivalled knowledge of the fragmentary collections of newspapers that survive in archive offices across the country to build a picture of the whole spectrum of press activity, from the mechanics of editing, production and distribution to the vexed question of newspapers' influence and content.

Dr Black's main thesis is that the nature and influence of the eighteenth-century press have been overestimated in previous studies. Proliferating numbers of titles did not produce a marked rise in the numbers of papers operating at any one time: instead cut-throat competition for a limited readership required ceaseless efforts to attract and maintain circulation and few papers survived the pressure for long. Not surprisingly, Black claims, they were in no position to lead political opinion and instead wooed the political nation by appealing to the conservative, pious and loyalist sentiments that flourished as robustly in 1800 as they had in 1700. This analysis is sure to provoke controversy. Much less controversial is the vivid presentation on the other, more mundane, problems of content facing hard-pressed editors. Modern readers will appreciate the difficult balance to be struck between providing 'intelligence' in the form of hard political news and 'entertainment' in the form of crime, accident, scandal and human interest stories: could a paper maximize its readership by attracting the more frivolous without repelling the more serious? In a similar way eighteenth-century editors searched constantly for the optimum balance between advertising and 'legitimate' copy. Profitability depended on maximizing advertising revenue but circulation suffered if the balance swung too far in this direction, and falling circulation deterrred potential advertisers. Many an editor came to grief in the face of this age-old dilemma, while some papers survived only because their proprietors used them to publicize their own wares – sometimes infiltrating the news columns in the process.

Readers with a particular interest in political or press history will therefore find some interesting material in this study. However, there are signs that in trying to cover the entire newspaper press Dr Black has attempted too ambitious a task, with the multifarious subject producing a somewhat miscellaneous book. The reader is in effect confronted with a series of discrete chapters, some much better than others. Black's handling of the press and Europe, for example, is superb in both content and style, revealing the author's mastery of his own specialist field. Elsewhere his touch is much less sure and his method of building up blocks of text by the multiplication of examples palls after a few chapters. Moreover, the apparently comprehensive coverage turns out to be much more limited in practice: it clings to the traditional ground of press history, concentrating on the production and political content of the papers and relegating their role as purveyors of social news and values to a minor place. This problem is compounded by the inclusion of an index of titles rather than a subject index. On balance, despite the well-recognized value of eighteenth-century provincial papers as a historical source, readers interested in eighteenth-century society and in urban history will find the book disappointing.

**Joyce Ellis**
Department of History, University of Nottingham

Alain Corbin, *The Foul and the Fragrant: Odor and the French Social Imagination.* Leamington Spa: Berg, 1986. vii + 307pp.
British urban and social historians are well acquainted with the period between about 1800 and 1870 when scientists, medical men and sanitarians were obsessed with the relations between decay, stench and disease. One can hardly resist, in the light of their voluminous writings on these unsavoury topics, sometimes wanting to know precisely what a slum court in Leeds or a tanner's in Whitechapel in the 1840s may have smelt like. As it is, we have volume upon volume of parliamentary and other reports, listing numbers of inhabitants per room, mode (or absence of mode) of disposal of human waste, and the state of sewers and rivers. But the very plethora of words and statistics expressing appalled middle-class disgust and fear seems at times to mask rather than lay bare what was actually experienced by the senses in the great 'shock cities' of the early nineteenth century. Might it not be possible to gain some more direct historical access to smells, and the meaning of smells, in the past?

The answer which Alain Corbin gives in this densely argued book is a confident 'yes'. Like so many *Annales* and *Annales*-influenced scholars, he is determined to restore yet another of the most basic elements of everyday life to the mainstream of social history. Although the reader of *The Foul and the Fragrant* is not taken on any over-literalistic sensorama tour of the olfactory texture of working-class farts, vaginal fluid and semen, or brought within nosing distance of eighteenth-century musk or civet, he or she will undoubtedly finish this book convinced that odours are replete with sets of historical meanings which are distinctly more social than biologically or naturally 'given'. Having said that, one must enter the *caveat* that Corbin's ruminations on, for example, links between the growing privatization of human bowel evacuation and the emergence of modern individualism are speculative and reminiscent of analogous relationships in neighbouring fields proposed by Alan Macfarlane and Lawrence Stone.

What we emphatically do not have here are the worst theoretical excesses of psychohistory: extrapolations, rather, from a dizzying range of literary sources and a conviction that smells, and the changing social contexts in which smells have been produced and experienced, have played a central role in the making of modern French bourgeois culture. Corbin's book might, in that respect, be accused of the very reductiveness deplored in a number of the historical commentators – scientific, medical, 'olfactory' – that he discusses. Odour, in other words, tends to be abstracted from other human senses and is at times presented in the guise of historical actor, cause, even. One final general criticism needs to be made and it relates to chronology. The author is principally concerned with the fragrant and foul in French civilization between about 1750 and 1880, but within that span, he traces in several cycles relating to the balance between the public and the private, the 'animalistic' and the 'virginal' in perfumery, and working-class acceptance of and opposition to olfactory norms laid down by the social and political elite. A recurring difficulty is that the duration of each of these phases is never made explicit. (One is tempted to blame the translation: but that would be unfair to Miriam Kochan, Roy Porter and Christopher Prendergast – they have combined their skills to produce a very readable English version of a book whose style is simultaneously literary, declamatory and droll.)

Beginning with the accounts of 'air' most widely accepted by post-Enlightenment men of science, Corbin goes on to describe the late-eighteenth-century obsession with the escape of vile smells from town swamps, mud, ooze and long-decayed corpses. The attempt to 'lock up' these intolerable odours gradually gave way, in the author's view, to the necessity to police public space, and to project environmental noxiousness onto working people *en masse*. This phase was followed, during the second quarter of the nineteenth century, by an era in which the poor were disaggregated in terms of smell and the distinctive odours of ragman, sailors, factory workers and many others scrupulously and, indeed, pathologically investigated and recorded. Controls – in terms of sewage projects which would have improved the external environment and institutional training which sought to cleanse, deodorize and re-educate the poor – were strenuously applied. But, Corbin contends, sanitary engineering proved to be much weaker in France than in Britain and utilitarian commitment to the profitable agricultural disposal of human waste correspondingly stronger. (There is a serious underestimation here of the extent to which the idea, though not the reality, of the sale of sewage to farmers continued to co-exist with post-Chadwickian engineering projects in Britain in the late nineteenth century.) Corbin concludes that drastic reform of the urban environment was long delayed – a Parisian 'Great Stink' paralysed social life as late as 1880 – but that bourgeois definitions of what was acceptable in olfactory terms in the domestic sphere were already being universalized. Here, indeed, were the beginnings of a late-twentieth-century 'absence of smell in a deodorized environment'.

This review has been concerned more with Corbin's account of the collective assault on the foul than with his examination of the fragrant and its meanings and mediations in French social life. This is because readers of this *Yearbook* are more likely to be professionally interested in, and provoked by, the author's interpretation of programmes of urban purification in the eighteenth and nineteenth centuries, than in his analysis of the role of body odour and perfumery in social life. But the two themes are in fact intertwined and this demanding, though flawed, book should be read by anyone concerned with comparative social history.

**Bill Luckin**
Department of Humanities, Bolton Institute of Higher Education

Martin Doughty (ed.), *Building the Industrial City*. Leicester: Leicester University Press, 1986. xii + 212 pp. 23 figures. Tables. £27.50

Here is a book which fails to live up either to its title (its various subjects are town, region, and city), or to meet its clearly stated objective, namely to concentrate on 'the people ... who possessed the skills, personnel and equipment physically to build houses', and in particular the houses of the working classes. The publication of this volume clearly represents an understandable desire on the part of the editors of the *Themes in Urban History* series to present the core of recent postgraduate research into the building industry to a wider audience. In the absence of sufficient doctoral work in the chosen field (only one contribution really qualifies, and much of that author's work is already well known through extensive publication) the editor of this volume has instead had to deal with work in which the building industry is frequently (as in so much urban history) at the periphery. As a consequence either of editorial or authorial intransigence the introduction and the subsequent contributions are grossly mismatched, the one promising what the others patently fail to deliver. None, it should be stressed, are of poor quality; they simply seem for the most part to be in the wrong book.

The first essay, by Jane Springett, concentrates on land ownership and property development in the Ramsden Estate in Huddersfield, a bastion of middle-class housing brought to heel by 'the collective will of the petty bourgeoisie', in which only one builder, Lewis Starkey, appears as a real person. The second, by M. H. Yeadell, observes the impact of building societies on the provision of housing in the West Riding ('they did not exert a positive influence in exciting or encouraging house building activity'). The third is a curious study of a distinctive group of Welsh builders and builders' suppliers in Liverpool by Thomas A. Roberts. Here, we are told, the majority of the 100,000 houses built during the nineteenth century owed their construction to 'Welsh initiative and enterprise using materials imported from North Wales'. This same initiative and enterprise is credited with the production of 'a house plan which matched the criteria upon which the first mass market for cheap housing could be supplied' – a six-roomed terrace cottage or house looking remarkably similar to that which could be found in most English towns and cities in the nineteenth century. Based extensively on an existing corpus of materials relating to the Welsh community in Liverpool, notably J. R. Jones's *The Welsh Builders on Merseyside: annals and lives* (1946), the essay suggests that not only Liverpool, but possibly the Midlands 'where strong commercial links with the principality were in evidence as far back as the eighteenth century' owed their urban growth less to indigenous factors than to Cambrian immigrants.

Less nationalist but more national in its scope is the final contribution to the volume, Richard Rodger on the building industry and the housing of the Scottish working class. This is by far the most impressive chapter, in its grasp of the breadth of the urban process, and the scope of its consequences. Nonetheless for this reviewer at least its considerable virtues are vitiated by the pessimistic framework in which it is set. Drawing largely on qualitative sources of a type ranging from Glasgow's James Burn Russell, prince of the propagandists of the sanitary reformers (Scottish urban historians note – no more bodies on the dresser please!), to the 1917 report of the Royal Commission on the Housing of the Industrial Population of Scotland (a document whose anti-tenement stance was largely fashioned by its role as a vehicle for the imposition of an alien and socially divisive building form – the cottage – on the Scottish urban working classes), Rodger presents us with a picture of the Scottish city that rested more in the minds of the respondents to the various parliamentary papers he cites than in reality. He fails to sustain his contentions that the Scottish city was a failure of civil and social engineering, or that Scottish building regulations and an innately conservative building industry failed to adopt new materials or methods of construction to reduce the cost of tenement building. Moreover Rodger's essay comes largely in the form which the editor says he seeks to eschew, namely that which 'concentrate on the impact of the product rather than on the process of production itself'. For here we have only a handful of builders whose careers are sketched out from Rodger's extensive researches into Dean of Guild Court planning applications. They occupy only half a page of a 54-page essay and fail to command a place in the index. So much for the people who built the industrial city.

At £27.50 this book, although handsomely produced with useful and well-chosen plans (as opposed to the more usual gratuitous inclusions) and illustrations, is too expensive to reach the wide readership for which the *Themes* series was originally intended. Moreover, despite the undoubted relevance of all its contents to the general urban historian, it will do little to advance the knowledge of those interested in the building of the Victorian city, industrial or otherwise.

**Nicholas J. Morgan**
Department of Scottish History, University of Glasgow

Andrew Lees, *Cities Perceived. Urban Society and European and American Thought 1820–1940*. Manchester: Manchester University Press, 1985. xi + 360 pp. 30 plates. Bibliography. £35.00.

This is an ambitious work – no less than an attempt at an analytical coverage of the attitudes towards the growing cities expressed in published works in the United States and three major European countries during more than a century of urban growth and political change. The scope may indeed be too ambitious. At times the book reads like a critical catalogue, with only sketchy contextual information, linkage and analysis, of what are claimed to be 'well over a thousand books and essays, written by close to a thousand individuals', rather than an analysis-in-depth of cultural attitudes and social comment. Any historian who has studied seriously any of the thinkers covered here is likely to find Lees's treatment of them less than satisfying. This reviewer, for example, found the attention accorded some of the English thinkers early in the author's period – Southey, Cobbett and Carlyle amongst them – so cursory as to verge on the dismissive as well as sometimes misleading. (There is, too, nothing at all on Pugin and the early Gothic revivalists.) Even the fuller consideration given to Chadwick scarcely brings out the full significance of his work on public health and of its impact on contemporaries, not least on Dickens. Indeed, the influence (whether positive or negative) of certain thinkers on others is something for which the often breakneck pace of the coverage leaves little time. More pause for reflection, analysis and comparison would have helped. Another weakness of the sections on Britain is that the political dimension of the cities debate is scarcely developed. In this respect, as in others, it is sometimes hard to see why certain thinkers have been included and others excluded.

Yet the scope and pace of the treatment have considerable merits too. There is information and interest in every chapter and few, if any, readers will have themselves ranged anything like as widely among the sources as the author does. The present reviewer learnt most from the discussions of French and, particularly, of German attitudes. Admittedly, though the treatment of Germany is generous, that of France is modest except for one section on 'Paris in the eyes of the French' and there is scarcely a mention of any other country of continental Europe. This is not 'European thought' (whatever that is) but rather a series of vignettes of the perceptions of cities among the intelligentsia in three separate European countries with different cultural, political and economic experiences. Germany repays the treatment, though, and Lees's evidence lends some weight to his conclusion that

'Germany produced the most extreme polarization of opinion. It was also the country in which anti-urban hatreds were most pervasive.' If true, this conclusion works strongly against the thesis advanced by Martin J. Wiener and others that Britain's culture (and economy) suffered to a unique extent from its resistance to urban values and endeavours. Yet he admits that the writers he selects were not always typical in their predominant anti-urbanism. He concludes that 'below the higher levels of intellectual sophistication ... one encounters a widespread belief during most of the period that the cities were places of promise and opportunity.' Perhaps this divergence between the highest and the more modest levels of cultural debate in the four countries needs more investigation than it receives here. As for the comparative element in the analysis – the comparing and contrasting of the respective experiences and responses of Britain, France, Germany and the United States – it is the most ambitious and difficult of the book's aims and perhaps the least satisfactory in the realization. It is certainly not helped by the rather cataloguey structure and method adopted for large parts of the book.

It would be unfair, though, to characterize the work as an heroic failure. Even as a critical catalogue, it would have considerable merit and utility. Even knowledge-able readers are likely to find themselves informed and intrigued by some of the less familiar authors and works considered here. Few historians would care to attempt anything on this scale and so the cavils of other specialists ought to be appropriately cautious and respectful in tone. Considering the scale of the project he set himself, Andrew Lees has done enough to merit the gratitude of those of us who rest content with a lower setting of our sights.

**Bruce Coleman**
Department of History and Archaeology, University of Exeter

W. B. Stephens, *Education, Literacy and Society 1830–1870*. Manchester: Manchester University Press. 1987. xii + 386 pp. 13 maps. 18 Tables. 17 Appendices. Index. £35.00.

The subtitle of this book, 'The geography of diversity in provincial England', explains the problem W. B. Stephens has set himself. The smooth graph of rising literacy from the 1830s onwards, which culminates in the virtual disappearance of marks from the marriage registers in 1914, is in many respects profoundly misleading. Until late in the century there were immense variations in the levels of nominal literacy within and between the regions of the industrializing society. Adjacent registration districts could be separated by as many as 50 points, and inside the individual communities, age, gender and occupation were further agencies of differentiation. After exploring aspects of this problem in a series of articles over the last 15 years, Dr Stephens has now attempted to encompass it in its entirety.

The obstacles facing the enterprise are substantial. While the principal source material – census and Registrar General reports and a range of parliamentary enquiries – is easily identifiable, its exploitation is full of danger. If the tables of marks and signatures are reliable (even if their significance is open to debate), the remaining categories of statistical evidence, particularly school attendance, are fraught with difficulty. Moreover the range of explanatory variables extends into areas such as parental behaviour and the perceived material and cultural value of reading and writing which are not susceptible to any form of quantification. The diversity cannot be reduced to a series of tables and correlation exercises; the only solution is a painstaking study of the complex factors which shaped the profiles of the contrasting areas of the country. It is greatly to Dr Stephens's credit that he possesses the experience to avoid the facile solutions, and the patience to follow the alternative path to its distant destination. His book is both modest and ambitious. It attempts to come to terms with the diversity of nineteenth-century England on a scale rarely if ever matched in this or any other aspect of historical experience. At the same time the analysis is informed by a caution and a sense of proportion not always to be found in studies of literacy and education in past societies.

The book proceeds by way of a general survey of the patterns of literacy and their implications, and then tours the country region by region, surveying for each area the economic and social background, the demand for child labour, the attitudes of suppliers and consumers of schooling and the relationship between education and literacy. Inevitably there is an element of repetition in the exercise, but the achievements of the analysis more than compensate for the absence of a narrative drive. On their own terms, the studies of the regional economies and child labour provide comprehensive and accessible introductions to the subjects, and when brought to bear on the central issue of literacy, a clear picture begins to emerge.

The principal negative conclusion is that no single factor will explain the distribution of literacy. Provision of schools is clearly relevant, but decisions by parents to use non-inspected and frequently uncounted private establishments, or to use no schools at all, make it impossible to regard the fluctuations in the marriage registers as a direct function of the activities of the church societies. In any given area, attention has also to be paid to the occupational structure, to the demand for children's employment, to demographic factors such as migration and localized population explosions, to the changing economic relevance of literacy, and to traditions and ambitions amongst both the working class and their worried but uncertain superiors. On the whole Stephens is inclined to acquit parents of deliberate neglect, drawing attention instead to the pervasive influence of the occupational fortunes of the father and the work opportunities of the children. Where schooling was affordable and seen to be of material value, it was usually obtained by one means or another. The striking variations in the rates of brides and grooms, with women outperforming men in an increasing number of districts as the century wore on, is also explained in economic terms, with a falling demand for girl labour and a compensating rise in domestic service where a functional literacy was desired by employers. Finally Stephens insists that by 1870 the combination of voluntary provision and voluntary attendance had exhausted its capacity to push the rates up any further. The introduction of a comprehensive and then compulsory system was the only means of mopping up the still sizeable pockets of illiteracy to be found amongst unskilled labourers in many parts of the country.

**David Vincent**
Department of History, University of Keele

Wolfgang Schivelbusch, *The Railway Journey*: Leamington Spa/Hamburg/New York: Berg publishers, 1986. xvi + 203pp. Illustrations. Hardback £16.50. Paperback £6.95.

Boldly subtitled 'The Industrialization of Time and Space in the 19th Century', Wolfgang Schivelbush's *The Railway Journey* is at once a fascinating and frustrating book, containing much to tempt but rarely enough to satiate. Taken at face value, as a linked series of meditations upon the social and cultural significance of railway travel, it is certainly worth a read.

The railway system brought some of the disciplines of urban life into the countryside. Appearing 'as one great machine covering the land', it telescoped distances, brought about standardized time, turned landscape into panorama, and eventually transformed the world into 'one huge department store of countryside and cities'. Familiar stuff, perhaps, but Schivelbusch puts it over well, and often through contemporary eyes. He is at his best in exploring the curious mix of social and technological reasons why the American railroads adopted big open railway carriages, modelled on the classless steamboat saloon, while Europeans saddled themselves with isolated compartments, modelled on the stagecoach and segregated by social class.

The second half of the book takes off into the more rarefied territory of psychology as Schivelbusch first traces the origins of Freud's theory of neurotic trauma back beyond the First World War to the 1880s, when the delayed shock syndrome suffered by railway-accident victims came to be understood, and then attempts to apply Freud's theory of the 'stimulus shield' to explain how people adjusted to the anxiety and confusion sowed by dangerous technologies such as the railway. Psychological adjustment to technology, he suggests, is as important a process as urban socialization. There is also a re-examination of the thinking behind Haussman's drastic reconstruction of Paris in the 1860s, which was in part inspired by the methods of the railways with which the new boulevards connected.

Even within its own terms as a work of 'critical sociology', however, the book is open to criticism. It deals mainly with the bourgeois experience of railway travel, and long-distance railway travel at that. Schivelbusch too often resorts to the easy quote from some technology-struck continental commentator to display a point. There is little here of the world of the third-class passenger, the porter or the engineer, and nothing at all of the world of the pottering rustic branch-line with its mail bags and milk churns. The typical witness is a Parisian novelist travelling by first-class sleeper to Lyon, not a Lancashire excursionist or an Italian sleeping-car attendant.

Occasionally, Schivelbusch loses his grip on reality altogether, as when we are informed that in the department store, 'The price tag interposed itself between goods and customer as the train's speed interjected itself between traveller and landscape', or when we are asked to believe that contemporary fascination with the detail in early photographs had its roots in dissatisfaction with the elusive panorama visible through train carriage windows. But urban historians will not need reminding to take this sort of thing with a good pinch of salt. *The Railway Journey* is a diverting and stimulating read, and just the thing to keep an urban historian occupied on a railway journey – the London-York express, perhaps, if not the Bangor to Scarborough trundle.

**Robert Poole**
University of Lancaster

S. Martin Gaskell, *Model Housing. From the Great Exhibition to the Festival of Britain*. London and New York: Mansell, 1987. x + 180pp. Bibliography. £26.50.

This is an unusual, attractive and interesting book. Section I is an essay of a dozen pages dealing with the origins and concept of the model house, and Section III assesses in some thirty pages the evolution and impact of designs and proposals for model housing. The long central Section II constitutes the essential purpose of the volume: twenty separate designs, proposals or discussion documents are presented as case studies. They incorporate quotations from contemporary sources, illustrative diagrams and pictures and some further explanation and commentary by the author. The book is a sandwich, an appetizing filling between two layers of healthy wholemeal bread.

The case studies begin with the designs for the Prince Consort's model houses erected at the Great Exhibition (1851) and include model dwellings for agricultural labourers (1850), Henry Darbishire's plans for the Peabody Estates (1863), Bannister Fletcher's model houses (1871), the model bye-laws circulated by the Local Government Board (1877) and plans for Akroyden (1860s) and for Bournville as described subsequently by its architect W. A. Harvey (1906). Later we come to designs built for the Garden City Cheap Cottage Exhibition (1905), extracts from the local Government Board Manual for State-Aided Housing Schemes (1919), Kensal House (1936), pre-fabricated housing (1946) and, as a finale, the Lansbury Estate laid out in London's East End, for workers not 'yuppies', as part of the Festival of Britain (1951). While the principles of selection are not made explicit, we are offered variety. Proposals derive from the public and private sectors, include flats and houses, and are concerned with the wider environment of estate and community or just with single dwellings and their internal fitments. Dr Gaskell usually confines himself in this section to quotation, précis and exposition with minimal editorial comment. The result makes the book's central section effectively a documentary source, each example well worth careful study.

For further comment we may turn to the embracing essays which on the whole successfully thread these studies on to interpretive themes. The origins of model housing are traced back partly to utopian schemes derived from Plato via More and Bacon but more practically to medieval new towns, to sixteenth-and seventeenth-century town planning and especially to the design of eighteenth-century agricultural model villages. A concern for the proper design of house or cottage and its contribution to the larger estate, village or community continued into the mid nineteenth century when perceived urban and industrial requirements came to dominate discussions. Making the running were a handful of paternalistic industrialists, a coterie of social reformers, and anxious health experts. Belated converts belonged to the architectural profession, lowering their sights to contemplate the design of mere working-class homes. There was to be no easily found agreement between designers and sponsors as to the model to be adopted, and cottage houses were challenged by tenements or flats, aesthetic ideals could clash with practical obligations and proposals to build new towns might conflict with the claims of suburbia or the need to resettle inner city sites.

But what emerges from the debates is evidence of a broadly-based belief amongst those advocating improved housing that the raising of standards was a social and political obligation, to improve the health and economic efficiency of workers, to exercise managerial control over them, to improve their moral qualities, to defuse class tensions, to ensure social stability. Dr Gaskell stresses the didactic purpose of the model housing movement and its essentially conservative aims, 'a practical means of encouraging the dominant values of society and of extending the process of social control' (p. 16). In addition, he rightly identifies the greatest single restraint on the provision of better quality housing for the working class to be their inability in a free market society to afford the higher rents which improved, unsubsidized housing invariably required. Tenements, building on cheaper suburban land and communal lavatories were among the options devised to lower the cost of working-class housing, while leaving the wage levels of tenants unaffected, and yet still allow investors a 'decent' return on their capital. But Dr Gaskell notes the failure to square this circle. Few employers even offered improved quality housing, and those that did were sensitive to their rates of return. Building societies found themselves catering for the better-off working-class and lower-middle-class market. The scale of the garden cities and garden suburbs was too small to affect the housing of more than a minority of working-class families. What was required was the imposition of higher standards by the state, first by issuing model bye-laws from 1877, second by the publication of LGB and Ministry of Health manuals to guide local authority housebuilding, and third and most important the lowering of rents by taxpayer subsidies from 1919. State intervention, as well as the raising of popular expectations by the pioneers of model housing design, did much to improve and sustain the quality as well as quantity of housing in Britain from the late nineteenth century to the mid twentieth century. It is a conclusion readers, and government, might care to contemplate in the last decades of the twentieth century as British society again faces the obscenities of homelessness, inner city decay and relative deprivation in a wealthy society. Dr Gaskell's sandwich provides food for thought.

**Stephen Constantine**
Department of History, University of Lancaster

Kenneth T. Jackson, *Crabgrass Frontier: The Suburbanization of the United States*. Oxford: Oxford University Press, 1985. £19.50. Pbk £7.95.

When the US Census announced in 1890 that there was no longer a 'frontier' line within the United States, it inspired a young Wisconsin historian, Frederick Jackson Turner, to reflect on the significance of this frontier for American development. Almost a century later, Kenneth Jackson publishes a study of American suburbanization that evokes the Turner thesis in more than just its title.

Jackson, like Turner, sees the American experience as exceptional, and to his credit, bolsters his claim by regularly referring to the experience of other countries.

For Jackson, the characteristics of American suburbia are its low population density which he contrasts with that of Swedish suburbs; its high levels of homeownership in contrast not only to Sweden but Germany, Switzerland, France and Norway as well; its clear correlationship between high socio-economic status and suburban residence which he contrasts sharply with the experience of developing countries in Latin America and Africa and even contemporary Paris; and finally, the longer average journey-to-work of Americans, whether the journey is measured in miles or minutes.

Clearly described in his introduction, these distinctive features are ultimately explained by a classic 'push/pull' combination of forces. Massive and sustained urban population growth, which ensured that the republic was one-third urban when the frontier allegedly closed, has been one factor pushing American cities outward but the overriding sources of suburban growth have been racial and economic. Fear has pressed 'old' Americans into flight from both new immigrants and the black native-born.

As a scholar of the Klu Klux Klan, Jackson knows well the force of racist passion, yet he judges economic causes more important than racial antagonism in the process of American suburbanization. After 1870, living standards in America began an unprecedented rise which gave its vast middle-class the economic abundance to 'waste' on low-density housing on the metropolitan fringe. Moreover, abundant land meant cheap land and so, despite the passing of the frontier, the American real-estate market has never experienced the prohibitive prices familiar to Japanese home-hunters. Reinforcing the economic common sense of a suburban real-estate purchase have been government policies encouraging deconcentration, most notably the tax system which allows Americans to deduct mortgage interest and local property taxes but gives no deduction for rent. Jackson also includes such governmental policies as the 'red-lining' practices of the FHA and the ghettoization of public housing by the USHA. All these incentives have pushed Americans to the urban periphery at the same time as a widely held suburban ideal has drawn them away from the inner city.

Awarded the Bancroft and Parkman prizes on its first publication and already acknowledged as the authoritative work in its field, *Crabgrass Frontier* must surely be recommended for purchase by all urban historians, now that the paperback edition makes it affordable for undergraduates. A masterpiece of synthesized scholarship, it nonetheless possesses two faults worthy of note. The first lies in its attempt to sustain a nineteenth-century definition of suburb into the contemporary period. The relocation of places of work as well as residences since 1945 has surely produced a pattern of deconcentrated living which deserves its own title. Second, while Jackson acknowledges in his concluding remarks the inter-dependence of American suburbanization and the capitalistic system itself (p. 296), he seems oblivious to the work of David Harvey and others who see spatial relations as expressive of the fundamental capitalistic processes of capital accumulation, legitimation, and class reproduction. Unwilling to address this highly ideological debate, Jackson is ultimately ambivalent in his approach to suburbanization, deploring the injustices it leaves behind it, yet applauding the energy and the variety with which it has been pursued. Those who follow him as students of this field may wish to remedy these deficiencies. Let us hope they also match his brilliance.

**Peter Ling**
History Division, Leicester Polytechnic

Gilbert A. Stelter and Alan F. J. Artibise, *The Canadian City. Essays in Urban and Social History*. Ottawa, Canada: Carleton University Press, 1984. vi + 503pp. Plates. Figures. Tables. $14.95 Canadian.

This is a second edition of that excellent collection first published in 1977. Eight articles have been added, three and the bibliography have been dropped. The function of the bibliography is now filled by *Canada's Urban Past. A Bibliography to 1980*, edited by the same team, and the regular updates by Elizabeth Bloomfield in the October issues of *Urban History Review* (published from the Institute of Urban Studies, University of Winnipeg).

The *Canadian City* together with its companion volumes *The Usable Urban Past. Planning and Politics in the Modern Canadian City* (1979) and *Shaping the Urban Landscape. Aspects of the Canadian City Building Process* (1982) provide a very full teaching set of articles which British urban historians might rightly envy. The price at around £8 sterling for 500 pages and 20 items is one which British publishers might ponder. It makes multiple library purchase and strong purchase recommendations to students possible. These books, together with a run of the *Urban History Review*, would provide a secure Canadian component to any urban history course.

Canadian urban historians have always had a welcome and instinctive certainty as to the nature of urban history. It is 'an attempt to explain some of the basic phenomena of modern history – the growth of cities and the urbanization of society.' The self-doubt of British and even US urban historians is little to be seen, perhaps because the new school of Canadian urban historians represented in these books was part of that discovery of Canadian identity that went with the maple leaf flag, multiculturalism, *la révolution tranquille* and the liberation of Canadian history from prime ministers, governors general, staples theory and Laurentianism. Although the socio-economic geographical structure of Canadian cities has entered a post-industrial dispersing phase, social and political identities are still firmly linked to cities, towns and municipalities. Montreal, and its attendant municipalities, has so far kept the power of its regional governmental agency, CUM, firmly at bay. In Winnipeg, fragmented jurisdictions have been reorganized but as a Uni-City. There is none of the reorganization into districts and regions like those of Britain in 1974 which left urban historians puzzled as to the current location of their curiosities.

The layout of the book, with a short introduction to each section, makes this a text which could be used in any survey of eighteenth- and nineteenth-century urbanization, and which perhaps could be set off against British and other European literature. Amongst the new articles Gil Stelter gives an account of early Canadian urban development. The cities moved from being forts with markets to being markets within a nation state – the spatial configuration changing at each stage. The central square, often within a walled area, played a much greater part in Canadian urban history than in that of the 13 colonies, reflecting Canada's longer history as a state on the receiving end of the imperialist game and as an investment at the sharp end of formal and informal empires. One fascination of Canada for the urbanist is the chance to examine Europe's traditions of politics, planning and social structure working their way in empty capitalist economic space. For example, land was certainly used in latent and overt forms of social engineering. Linteau and Robert demonstrate the French-Canadian participation in the land ownership of Montreal which was a factor which drew that elite into a *cohabitation* with the mercantile anglophones. As with many of these articles the full story needs to be followed in more recent literature (see Paul Andre Linteau, *Maisonneuve, ou comment des promoteurs fabriquent une ville*, Montreal, 1981; Brian Young, *In its Corporate Capacity. The Seminary of Montreal as a Business Institution, 1816–1876*, Montreal, 1986). Toronto, with its large 'Park Lots' was the most dramatic example of attempted social engineering by land allocation. The results have been discussed by Isoble Ganton in the volume *Shaping the Urban Landscape*.The section on urban social structure has been greatly strengthened by the addition of six new articles. Some welcome old favourites remain: Katz on Hamilton and Cross on women in Montreal. These are in a sociographic tradition which despite the occasional references does not delve deeply into the forms, mechanisms and motivations of the power and class structures which shaped the distributions described. In many ways Alan Artibise's article on the prairie city, like his work on Winnipeg, provides a clearer sense of the distinctive dynamic of the Canadian class system working through the urban property developing and wholesaling elites which manipulated city government and the local tax base. Other contributors need to give more attention to the distinctive nature of Canadian urbanization, rapid in growth, distant in its sources of migration as well as that empty economic space. Sheva Medjuck, in a fascinating sociographic vignette of family and household in Moncton New Brunswick, makes an attack on Laslett (*The World We Have Lost*, London, 1965) and Anderson (*Family Structure in Nineteenth Century Lancashire*, Cambridge, 1971) without taking the opportunity to analyse how far the nature of Canadian socio-economic experience influenced the differences between Moncton and Europe. Central to this section is a new survey article by Chad Gaffield. He ends with a very North American agenda for research, demographic behaviour, transiency, occupational structure and social mobility but in the course of his survey places all the emphasis on changing urban-rural relationships, developing urban systems, urban *mentalité* and class formation. That perhaps sums up the mood of the collection - a Canadian urban history poised between a placid sociographic cum land and buildings tradition on the one hand and a more fundamental enquiry into the structures of class, power and ethnic identity on the other. In any case, this is a valuable collection which I shall continue to use for teaching.

**R. J. Morris**
Dept of Economic and Social History, Edinburgh University

## 2 INDIVIDUAL TOWNS AND REGIONS

Miri Rubin, *Charity and Community in Medieval Cambridge.* Cambridge: Cambridge University Press, 1987. xiv + 365 pp. Tables. Bibliography. £30.00.
A society reveals much about itself in its manner of identification and treatment of the poor. Where modern western society has created a new territory of poverty in the gap between welfare and self-help, in the Middle Ages the lines were differently drawn, though the contrast between sufficiency and deprivation was no less harsh. The principles invoked to justify or compensate for social inequality have also varied. But the proclamation of alleged 'Victorian values' in our own day and that of Christian sacrifice in the Middle Ages have this in common, that theory is an unreliable point of departure for any study of the living reality of need and assistance. Miri Rubin's book presents, on the one hand, an extended account of medieval theories of charity and, on the other, a description of some institutions of practical welfare which existed in and near Cambridge before the Reformation. The study demonstrates the sophistication of the former, the lack of sophistication of the latter, and the methodological difficulties of establishing the relationship between the two.

This is a courageous book, for it aims to elicit, from reticent source materials, the human motivations which lay behind the endowment of a hospital in the thirteenth century, or of an almshouse in the fifteenth. Dr Rubin inclines to a view that social changes transformed these motivations, from an earlier readiness to share resources, into a later, individualistic concern with private salvation, to which the poor (the recipients of welfare in return for intercessory prayers) were marginal adjuncts. This is a controversial and interesting suggestion; thoroughly to substantiate it would have required a more detailed analysis of the particular social context of medieval Cambridgeshire than the scope of this book has permitted. The precise geographical area under scrutiny is not defined, but in practice includes Cambridge and several other places in the region. Dr Rubin reasonably looks for distinctive 'urban' and 'rural' patterns of charitable giving, though since both Cambridge and Wisbech are equally described as 'urban', the reader is uncertain of the implications to be drawn. There exist sources, not used here, relating both to Cambridge and to such villages in the county as Bassingbourn, which might have clarified the distinctions between town and country.

But the hardest problem which the author opens to discussion is the identification of the poor themselves. Almshouses founded in late medieval Cambridge
are said to be designed in part for 'the treatment of an urban problem in a controlled
and effective manner' (p.128). But what, precisely, was this problem, and in what
sense was it new? The recurrent difficulty, faced here and elsewhere in the book, is
that medieval records tend to be more informative about the external administration of welfare institutions than about their inmates. This is underlined by Dr
Rubin when, in her account of the Cambridge hospital of St John (which occupies
one-third of the book), she tells us (p.162) that we can know nothing of those whom
the hospital assisted. In the absence of better information any conclusion must be
tentative; but one line of thought stimulated by this book might question its
argument that the earlier-founded institutions (such as St John's hospital) were
the more practically organized for the relief of hardship (p. 293 and elsewhere).
Late-fifteenth- and sixteenth-century almshouses and hostels (sometimes established by guilds, as Dr Rubin shows) were more closely controlled by their lay
creators than were the semi-monastic foundations of the twelfth and thirteenth
centuries. The later institutions, though usually small, may have represented a
deliberate, practical (if hardly adequate) response to new social problems,
particularly in towns, in a period of rapid population growth. The 50 page
bibliography reveals the author's impressively wide reading, and also the extent of
interest in this subject. Yet Dr Rubin herself would be the first to say that attitudes
to the poor, and their changes over time, remain tantalizingly difficult to study.
The findings concerning medieval Cambridgeshire presented and discussed here
will be a stimulus to future work in this fascinating area.

**Gervase Rosser**
Department of Medieval History, University of Birmingham

Tim Harris, *London Crowds in the Reign of Charles II. Politics and propaganda
from the Restoration until the Exclusion Crisis*. Cambridge: Cambridge University
Press, 1987. xv + 264 pp. Illustrated. Bibliography. Index. £27.50.

The best historical works are surely those which change a whole category of
history as well as illuminate a particular period. To this honourable company Tim
Harris's first book belongs. His decisive shift of interpretation is signalled in his
title, for by it he declares war upon the concept of 'the Crowd'. Study of crowd
behaviour is of course a well-established genre: a decade ago a friend of mine
remarked that the periodical *Past and Present* ought to be rechristened *The
Journal of Riot Studies*. But in this comfortably short volume Dr Harris provides
three large-scale corrections to the existing historiography. First, he insists that
populous communities could contain different crowds articulating different beliefs,
so that 'the fickle multitude' should be separated into distinct multitudes loyal to
conflicting ideas and active at differing times. Second, he believes that riots must
be placed in a context of 'peaceful' demonstrations, ceremonies and pamphleteering,
instead of being analysed as entities in themselves. And third, he rejects the
concept of 'popular politics', arguing that in seventeenth-century London, at least,
commoners shared political ideas with the elite, and that divisions tended to run
vertically through the community.

The dreadful paradox of academe in the 1980s is that it is at once starved and
congested, and some of these points have been prefigured by others during the last
couple of years. Robert Shoemaker has pointed out the conflicting viewpoints of
London mobs during the early eighteenth century, while Gary De Krey has
provided a picture of vertical divisions in the society of that city under the last
Stuarts. But in no sense has Dr Harris derived ideas from these colleagues, for their
work appeared even as his was in the press, and his book states these beliefs with a
clarity, and a wealth of illustration, never known before. It is an extremely easy
read, being divided into brief sections with an introduction and a summary to each
chapter, and having a logical development of themes. Dr Harris employs the trick,
shared only to the same extent by Keith Thomas, of providing a case and then

pointing out its weaknesses in order to build a stronger one. Time and again, the reviewer is preparing to note a faulty line of reasoning when the author himself tackles it and takes it into account. It is a technique which is not only charming in itself but allows Dr Harris to be remarkably gentle with predecessors, praising them while positing the 'false' picture which agrees with their teaching, and then blaming his own thought, not theirs, as he goes on to demolish it.

The overall picture of London politics provided may be summarized as follows. At the Restoration most Londoners welcomed the monarchy, but with different expectations of it. Although scarcely any of these were realized as the new regime proved both profligate and expensive, the main division lay between those who wished to tolerate religious dissent and those who did not. This rift remained throughout the reign, and represented the fundamental fault-line separating Whigs from Tories. Nevertheless, it is part of Dr Harris's subtlety of method that he recognizes shifts of opinion as well as long-term differences in it. Thus, he substantiates that amongst all classes support switched from the Whigs to the Tories between 1679 and 1683. Some niggling criticisms of detail could be made. The Excise was contracted at the Restoration, and not extended as Dr Harris believes, while hostility to the French among Londoners was powerful before the late 1660s, from which he dates its inception. But it is more interesting to consider the wider implications of his ideas. Despite his unfailing courtesy to Christopher Hill, it is clear that he has dealt another blow to those who persist in seeing the seventeenth century in terms of a class struggle. On the other hand, his work marries well with the recent heavy stress upon religious tensions in the period, whether in John Morrill's essays upon the Civil War or Jonathan Clark's portrayal of England as a 'confessional state' until 1832. To historians of the reign of Charles II he performs two principal services. One is to consider, far more deeply than before, the nature of the opposition to the Whigs in the metropolis: in fact, one could mimic J. R. Jones's seminal work and dub the second half of the book *The First Tories*. Second, by showing how much popular support Charles's government enjoyed in London throughout the last decade of the reign, it greatly increases our impression of its strength in these years. In fact, can we now describe the 'Exclusion Crisis' as any sort of crisis at all?

**Ronald Hutton**
Department of History, University of Bristol

David Garrioch, *Neighbourhood and Community in Paris, 1740–1790*. Cambridge: Cambridge University Press, 1986. xii + 278 pp. 24 illustrations. 12 tables and graphs. Bibliography. £27.50.

This is an important book, which graphically illuminates the neighbourhood life of eighteenth-century Paris, then the second largest city in Europe. Garrioch's welcome contribution takes its place alongside Daniel Roche's pioneering work, *Le Peuple de Paris* (Paris, 1981), which is currently being translated into English. The history of the French capital under the *ancien régime* has been severely hampered by the loss of municipal archives in the great conflagration of 1871. As a consequence historians have been obliged to employ considerable ingenuity in discovering alternative resources and, in this case, the author has sampled the copious dossiers of the *commissaires du Châtelet*, two or three of whom were attached to each *quartier*. The *procès-verbaux* meticulously compiled by these police officers provide a rich source, offering countless individual case-studies of the themes which Garrioch has selected for analysis, on the basis of certain neighbourhoods and particular years. His longest and most fascinating chapter is devoted to the subject of work and, like the section on recreation, it superbly delineates the ways in which different activities kept residents on the streets of their local community or, contrariwise, carried them beyond the *quartier* and across the city . His consideration of the family and still more so of religion, which receives short shrift presumably because the sources were more reticent in this respect, is less absorbing. However, Garrioch is able to demonstrate that the neighbourhoods of Paris were far from constituting the anonymous amalgams of strangers that contemporaries and historians have often made them out to be. Despite the huge impact of immigration – perhaps two-thirds of the inhabitants had originated outside Paris – the gradual withdrawal of the elites and growing cross-city traffic, local communities are clearly discernible in the shared behaviour patterns of their members. Of course changes were at work, altering as much as undermining this consensus, and the final chapter on the evolution of the Parisian neighbourhood effectively relates this particular study to developments in pre-industrial urban social organization in general. This forms a valuable conclusion to the work but it is a pity that Garrioch has chosen to avoid much reference to the French Revolution, indeed to politics as a whole. For we know a good deal about the 1790s when the *quartiers* of Paris, recast as *sections*, played a short-lived but crucial role in the history of France. Garrioch's analysis of a *quartier populaire*, the Faubourg Saint Antoine where pre-revolutionary neighbourhood solidarity remained especially strong, would certainly suggest that the communal norms elaborated under the *ancien régime* were a vital component of the *sansculotte* movement. Unfortunately the connection is not explored here, but to criticize the omission is perhaps demanding too much of a book which succeeds in throwing a great deal of light upon the hitherto neglected role of communities within the expanding towns of late-eighteenth-century Europe.

**M. Crook**
Department of History, University of Keele

R. A. Cage (ed.), *The Working Class in Glasgow 1750–1914*. Beckenham: Croom Helm, 1987. xix + 203 pp. Bibliography. £25.00.

A collection of essays, if it is to be successful as a collective project, must be one thing or the other. It should either have a theme sufficiently strong to sustain the reader's attention through both interesting and indifferent pieces or each essay must be vital enough to carry the exercise in spite of an ill-conceived organizing topic. Unfortunately very few collections are successful and they seem to rely upon one or two brilliant contributions to save them from almost total neglect. Raphael Samuel in particular specializes in the saving of such otherwise doomed volumes. The work presently under review falls some way between the criteria outlined above.

This is a collection of six essays which, according to the editor who also supplies half the contributions, serves as an intervention in the standard of living debate. Therefore, apart from having pieces on employment, poor relief, health (all by R. A. Cage) and housing (John Butt) it also includes sketches of working-class politics (I. G. C. Hutchinson) and popular culture (Elspeth King). The collection's title, however, suggests that the editor also had another aim – to produce a history of the working people of Glasgow. It is a pity that in attempting to do two things Cage failed to do either of them sufficient justice. He has as a consequence produced a schizophrenic collection – the last two essays on politics and leisure seem completely at odds with the previous four and would probably have been more at home in another volume.

Of the essays themselves Elspeth King's is the most successful. Both Cage and Butt are worthy but stick too closely to statistical evidence of which they fail to make much use: their conclusions are too guarded. It is not much of a revelation to discover that the structure of Glasgow's population underwent 'significant changes' (p. 27) nor that there was 'some improvement' (p. 51) in working-class housing during the last half of the nineteenth century. Hutchinson's contribution is similarly solid but uninspiring. Although he quite rightly plays down the independent nature of working-class politics in this period he fails to account completely for Labour's success after 1914. Is the effect of the Great War really meant to explain everything? He would have us believe that it was only the intervention of the European conflict which guaranteed the party power. It is in King's piece on popular culture that the people of Glasgow slowly emerge from beneath all the statistics, liberated from too-tightly fitting census data. She reveals a number of interesting ambiguities: some historians might feel that there was some contradiction in ILP councillors owning picture houses (p. 143). She is also able to qualify the prevalent notion that the music hall was an arena for the expression of conservative and imperialist sentiments. In some of Glasgow's theatres employers were attacked and strikers assumed the mantle of heroes (pp. 171–2).Such a collection definitely requires a conclusion to tie the pieces together. A broader perspective might have allowed the editor to escape from minutiae into meaning – as E. P. Thompson showed in *The Making of the English Working Class* (1963) the standard of living debate can be made interesting. A conclusion would also have answered one question surely fundamental to this volume: why Glasgow? Any city's history – especially that of Scotland's largest – has its own particular story to tell, but this should be related to the experience of the rest of the country and to the period as a whole. This task the editor leaves undone.

A map of the city would have been a help, as would a more complete bibliography. It is not pleasing to be so negative about any piece of work, but with a little imagination this collection could have been so much better.

**Steve Fielding**
Centre For the Study of Social History, University of Warwick

Edward Royle, *The Victorian Church in York*. [Borthwick Paper, no. 64] University of York, 1983. 49 pp. + 1 map. £1.80. Edward Royle, *Nonconformity in Nineteenth-century York*. [Borthwick Paper, no. 68] University of York, 1985. 39 pp. + 1 map. £1.80.

Edward Royle is a rare example of an historian who is able to write sympathetically and authoritatively both on Secularism and on Christianity. Admittedly, these essays on the churches and chapels of Victorian York are much less ambitious than his histories of Freethought. He has here no novel thesis to argue, and with so little space available, there can be no question of a definitive study. As a brief overview, however, they are excellent. York is interesting and unusual as a city which had *too many* Anglican churches in the mid nineteenth century. In 1841 the 22 parishes inherited from the Middle Ages contained 31,000 people. With the Anglican revival of the 1840s, an era began of cut-throat competition between clergymen with few parishioners, but each with a large church and a growing body of parochial institutions to maintain. When in the 1860s, the Minster, previously something of a scandal, began to organize special services for working men (and to attract good congregations), hard-pressed incumbents of neighbouring churches were none too pleased. Royle gives the clergy high marks for energy and dedication, but argues that their efforts were vitiated by excessive reliance on wealthy patrons and anachronistic social assumptions. This, he suggests, was a major reason for the success of the Nonconformists in recruiting shopkeepers and the better-off sections of the working-class. The most important group of Nonconformists were the Wesleyans. The common view that Methodism grew most strongly in areas where the Church of England was weak clearly does not apply to York. On the contrary, York Methodism initially benefited from the strength of evangelicalism in the city, and the support of several clergy. At least as late as 1815, the Wesleyans retained close links with the Church. Nonconformity in York was highly volatile. Disputes and schisms played a large part in the story. The fortunes of individual chapels fluctuated wildly, as did those of the numerous denominations. There is an interesting section on the relative participation of women and men in the congregations, membership, church meetings and management committees of various denominations – a subject that historians have seriously neglected. In one respect, however, the statistics of church attendance are misleading. Royle juxtaposes the results of the national religious census of 1851 with those of Rowntree's local census of 1901, without explaining that the former included children, whereas the latter was limited to adults. He thus implies that the late-Victorian decline in churchgoing was considerably more drastic than it really was.

One other small criticism: Royle eschews all comparisons between York and anywhere else, feeling, no doubt, that these would be a luxury in a brief paper. Surely this is a mistake. The successes and failures, strengths and weaknesses of Victorian Christianity in York cannot be judged by any absolute standard, but only by comparison with other places that are to some extent similar. Comparison with, for instance, other medium-sized cathedral cities, newer industrial towns in the West Riding, or surrounding villages, would help us to make better sense of York.

**Hugh McLeod**
Department of Theology, University of Birmingham

A. J. Kidd and K. W. Roberts (eds), *City, Class and Culture: Studies in cultural production and social policy in Victorian Manchester*. Manchester: Manchester University Press, 1985. Pbk £8.95.

Gary S. Messinger, *Manchester in the Victorian Age: The Half-Known City*. Manchester: Manchester University Press, 1985. Pbk £5.95.

Our understanding of Victorian cities has increased considerably since Asa Briggs's pioneering book of that title. Not only are the significant differences between them more readily acknowledged but our view of each city has also changed significantly. Nowhere is this more true than in Manchester. No longer is it viewed primarily as an overgrown cotton town distinguished by a skyline dominated by the chimneys of monster factories and a social structure simply divided into mutually antagonistic classes of industrialists and operatives. This crude classification which seemingly explained so much – Peterloo, the Anti-Corn Law League, Chartism, free trade Liberalism and so on – has been convincingly demolished through the work of such historians as Derek Fraser, John Seed and, most prominently, Vic Gatrell. One of these books both recognizes the value of this work and seeks to build on it; the other, alas, does not.

Messinger's book fails to live up to the promising description on its back cover. Admittedly there are passages which are clearly based on what was probably a fairly competent Ph.D. on imagery and perceptions of Manchester in the Victorian age, as opposed to the reality of the city itself, but even these are rather unsystematic and idiosyncratic comparisons and allusions occasionally being decidedly ill-informed; the Irish Land League, for example, was not contemporaneous with the ACLL. Neither is there much for the elusive 'general' reader keen to find out more about the city itself. The wealthy's conditions, we are informed, were 'quite pleasant', even 'especially comfortable' but the poor lived in lodging houses where 'bedding was sometimes changed so seldom that filth simply accumulated until eventually a lodger protested'. One is struck by the blandness on the one hand and the unexplained intimacy on the other. A discursion on Peterloo occupies most of a chapter entitled 'The creation of public order' but ends with a plea for someone, 'perhaps psychologists and anthropologists' to look again at the 'surviving documents'. Elsewhere Oldham is transformed into a North Lancashire weaving town. It is a strange book which sadly fulfils no obvious purpose: Manchester remains a 'half-known city'.

The volume by Kidd and Roberts has a clearer idea of its purpose and market, and its contributors display a firmer grasp of the realities of Manchester life. Focusing on the middle classes, the articles contribute to what might generally be called an exploration of the nature and inconsistencies in Manchester's Liberal tradition. Kidd's introduction provides a thoughtful resumé of recent work on the structure of Manchester society and he goes on to build on this in his specialist study of the promoters of the city's charities and the way they both complemented and undermined the administration of poor relief for the casually employed and the permanently destitute. The poor feature again in Stephen Daviss piece on the underlying motives for, and the changing tactics, of the corporation's police force, although the controlling elite's attitudes to such restrictions on individual freedom are possibly obscured by initiatives from the professional force itself. Chronicling traces of anti-semitism in some of the late-Victorian periodicals, Bill Williams detects a weakening of the tolerance which had characterized earlier business and commercial circles but he suggests that the strenuous efforts of Jewish leaders to Anglicize immigrants restored confidence and acceptance, although they sacrificed the distinctiveness of a Jewish culture in the process. It was integration on the host population's terms. Michael Rose's exposition of the 'ever widening range of cultural and intellectual interests' which an active minority supported ends Part I and provides a natural bridge to the second section which concentrates on cultural and literary output.

The difficulty of incorporating popular recreational appeal with the aesthetic and instructive environment of a museum dominates Michael Harrison's essay on T. C. Horsfall and his lifelong attempt, through his promotion of the Manchester Art Museum, to bridge the social gulf he so feared and deplored. The philistine reviewer must admit a detestation of poetry which can be traced back to his own early instructional environment, but after reading Brian Maidment's contribution he is willing to agree that it is indeed 'a complex and fascinating subject', if taken in its historical context. The constraints of genre and place which hindered bardic dialect poets, the standard bearers for a provincial culture in the battle against superior (in strength if not in quality) metropolitan culture, are clearly explained. The ultimate irony of the connection of such work with a growing conservatism runs through this and Margaret Beetham's study of popular periodicals. Provincial differences, once the source of Liberal strength, became the essence of everything that was English and traditional and therefore to be preserved for the nation. The journals themselves were little more than the medium by which a 'dominant group, metropolitan, middle class and male, attempted with varying success to shape a local culture'. The concluding essay, a selective but nevertheless absorbing study by Trefor Thomas of the changing representation of the working class in fiction, also traces what is recognizable as a national trend; a slow but perceptible shift from an emphasis on self-made men to the plight of those unable through circumstances to help themselves.

This volume, then, poses and attempts to answer important questions about the structure of the city's middle class and its liberal values, and the distinctiveness of provincial culture and its uneasy relationship with corrosive metropolitan influences. These are all potentially exciting areas of future interdisciplinary study. It is to be hoped that the staff of Manchester Polytechnic, who have contributed all bar two of these worthwhile essays, will continue to contribute as effectively in the future and that they will find a publisher with as much foresight as MUP to make such work available at the same reasonable price. Cultural production in Manchester does indeed continue to thrive.

**Michael J. Winstanley**
University of Lancaster

Fiorella Bartoccini, *Roma nell'Ottocento* (Storia di Roma, vol. xvi). Bologna: Istituto Nazionale di Studi Romani 1985. 872 pp. Bibliography. 20 tables. No price given.

Dr Bartoccini's massive study of Rome in the nineteenth century is one volume in a series which is planned to contain 31 volumes, to cover the history of the city from its beginnings, and to include two volumes on Latin literature, and five volumes on art from classical times to the twentieth century. The publishers, Cappelli, were unwise to produce so heavy a volume, of which the binding falls apart long before the book can be read. The beautiful volumes of the Einaudi *Storia d'Italia* suffer from the same fault, of which British publishers are fortunately no longer guilty. But the volume is attractively illustrated with reproductions of nineteenth-century engravings and paintings, including a wonderful Piranesi engraving, and an astonishing painting of the ghetto, by Roesler Franz. The book is dedicated to Alberto Ghisalberti, who, until his death in 1986, was a doyen of Risorgimento historians. Dr Bartoccini writes in a vivacious style, reminiscent of Ghisalberti. The subtitle of the work is 'The sunset of the "holy city". The birth of the capital', and it is inevitably divided into two parts by the acquisition of Rome by the Kingdom of Italy in 1870.

Rome is a unique city in several obvious respects, but also in one which is less obvious, and which Dr Bartoccini brings out. All other European cities which have survived from classical or medieval days have spread beyond their walls. But Rome in the second century AD had a population usually estimated at something in the region of 1,200,000. No European city was to be so large again until the nineteenth century, and Rome herself had only about 155,000 in 1840. From the decline of the empire until, and throughout, the nineteenth century Rome was too small to fill the space within the Aurelian walls. Dr Bartoccini gives interesting figures for 1841: 55.2 per cent of the area within the walls was virtually countryside. Even Trastevere, today so densely urban, was only 53.1 per cent built up. These figures are easier to believe when it is remembered that in 1987 the tourist making the statutory trip to the Catacombs of San Calisto passes through the Porta San Sebastiano and is immediately surrounded by green fields.

The book provides a very thorough study of the city from every point of view – topographical, economic, sociological, archaeological, architectural, political and historical. In the first half the Papal States as a whole are inevitably discussed, but Dr Bartoccini stresses the isolation of the holy city, an isolation both from Europe and Italy, and an isolation made more complete by the bare, uninhabited countryside, without resources, which surrounded it. It had no political life, but was still the centre of Christendom. As Gregorovius said, it was nourished, protected, punished and rewarded by the priests. Under Leo XII, in the 1820s, even the taverns were closed, and Rome became, in Massimo d'Azeglio's words, 'an establishment of spiritual exercises'.

Few cities can have experienced so sudden a change as that caused by the annexation of Rome to the Kingdom of Italy in 1870. The Italian authorities who then entered the city experienced a strange historical moment. Rome had been for them a symbol of national unity, even though she was ruled by what they saw as a foreign power – the Papacy. Suddenly she became, as Dr Bartoccini suggests, not just a symbol, but a reality, a living city with its poor, its markets, its hospitals, its streets to be lit, and its refuse to be collected. While the Italians of 1870 might seek encouragement from a past which they now possessed in material terms – in the ruins of the Colosseum and the Forum, they could also look across the river at St Peter's and the Vatican, which unlike imperial Rome, were 'intact, vital, even if the Pope was hidden behind his walls'. After 1870 Rome appeared to be a capital city as London and Paris were, but the appearance was superficial. Whereas Paris and London had developed for centuries as undisputed capitals, Italy had, so recently, contained several capitals. Inevitably becoming the capital of Italy also brought economic dislocation for the people of Rome, but Dr Bartoccini shows that the city soon entered a period of growth, so that by 1901 she had a population of 462,783, although she was still only the third of Italy's cities, after Naples and Milan.

This highly readable and detailed study will be a work of interest and value for urban historians.

**Harry Hearder**
Department of History, University College, Cardiff

Shirley Fitzgerald, *Rising Damp. Sydney 1870–1890*. Melbourne: Oxford University Press, 1987. xvi + 264 pp. 50 illustrations. 16 figures. Tables. £25.00.
The belief that the Australian colonies represented (by British standards) a working-man's paradise was widespread for nearly four decades after the gold discoveries of the mid nineteenth century, and it has been central to accounts of Australian history ever since. In particular, economic historians have emphasized the high real wages made possible by Australia's impressive rate of economic growth before the 1890s depression. However, it has not always been easy to reconcile this picture of prosperity with the growth of industrial militancy and the rise of socialism in the 1880s, before the 'long boom' broke. Shirley Fitzgerald's

book tackles this problem by subjecting the concept of 'paradise' to close scrutiny, and by contrasting the myths accepted and perpetuated by certain Australians with the harsh facts of city life. And she explains the outbreak of class conflict in 1890 by the growing perception of a wide gap between the *expectation* of 'a radical Australia which was classless and egalitarian' (p. 224) and the *reality* of 'just another capitalist society, reproducing the same antagonisms as in the Old World' (p. 229).

In concentrating on Sydney between 1870 and 1890, Dr Fitzgerald is, of course, highlighting one of the main reasons for the gap between hope and experience. Australia's prosperity was underpinned by the discovery and exploitation of the natural resources of the interior, and by its integration into the world economy as an exporter of primary products. But at the same time, Australia also contained some of the world's fastest growing cities: they absorbed capital and labour on a colossal scale, but their expansion was little regulated by either colonial governments or municipal authorities. The result – particularly marked in the case of Sydney – was the rapid reproduction in a new world of most of the urban problems of the old. Dr Fitzgerald divides her study into two sections – 'Living' and 'Working' – in order to illustrate these problems. In the first, she draws attention to the social segregation which emerged as the built-up area expanded; to the shortcomings of the urban transport system; to the lack of building regulations; and to the inadequate provision for public health. In the second, she challenges the traditional assumption that 'paradise' was characterized by a high level of opportunity for occupational mobility; scrutinizes the generally worsening conditions of work in the city; and deplores the plight of working-class women, for whom 'marriage was the primary occupation' (p. 195). Overall, while not disputing the case for 'high' real wages, her 'conclusions for the standard of living, defined as human satisfaction, [are] negative' (p. 229).

Can Fitzgerald's reinterpretation of 'paradise' be accepted in its entirety? Some readers will doubtless quarrel with her stridently feminist views on marriage – a joyless condition, apparently uninformed by lust, preference, or affection by either part, at any time. Some will criticize the characteristically Australian myopia, which not only regards as irrelevant any attempt to establish a historical yardstick of 'acceptability' in living standards which would permit comparisons between, say, London and Sydney (p. 201), but which also fails to ask whether life in Sydney might not have been 'worse' at this period than it was in Melbourne and Adelaide (or even in Goulburn and Bendigo). Others, while applauding the author's zeal to overcome the lack of detailed occupational statistics, might yet feel unconvinced by conclusions about mobility which are apparently derived from self-descriptions by a small sample who got married in two particular years. But despite these reservations, *Rising Damp* is a valuable and stimulating contribution, not just to urban history, but to a proper understanding of the overall development of Australia in the nineteenth century.

**Duncan Bythell**
Department of History, University of Durham

William H. Hubbard, *Auf dem Weg zur Grossstadt. Eine Sozialgeschichte der Stadt Graz 1850–1914*. Wien: Verlag für Geschichte und Politik, 1985. 283 pages, including 14 graphs and 33 pages of tables. Price 386 Schillings (c. £20) pbk.

In 1970 William Hubbard published an article in the *Canadian Journal of History* entitled 'Politics and society in the central European city: Graz, Austria 1861–1918'. This book is an extension of that article and rests on the same basic premise, that in its general development and growth nineteenth-century Graz was a typical central European city, far more typical than capitals such as Vienna or areas of rapid industrial expansion such as Bochum or Essen, all of which have been the subjects of earlier studies. This city was an administrative, military and university centre with a small industrial sector, its urbanization was slower than that of the more celebrated cities, but no less 'modern'.

The book is detailed, using a (dare one say?) liberal array of statistics, tables and graphs to track demographic, economic, social and political developments. Indeed, one minor criticism is that occasionally the statistical evidence is too prolific and too dense, obliging the reader to wade through columns of figures in order to discover the relevant section. A similar flaw, the overabundance of data, is also evident in parts of the text, particularly the chapter on economics, where few conclusions are drawn. However, the basic theme of the book, the transition of the city's society from one based on rank (Stände) to one based on class, remains interesting.

Hubbard begins with an intensive study of population, highlighting the large proportion of elderly residents (60 and over), whose presence won Graz its title, 'Pensionopolis'. The city was a popular retirement area for army officers and state officials and this affected both its political and cultural atmosphere and its economic structure: the other side of the coin was a low proportion of economically active residents in comparison with other Austrian cities. This may have also influenced migration. The city attracted few unskilled migrants from the immediate vicinity and more propertied people, many of whom came from German-speaking enclaves in the Austro-Hungarian Empire. 'Praktisch alle Zuwanderer waren deutscher Nationalität' (p. 25). (Practically all immigrants were of German nationality.) The political consequences of this are not lost. In the 1890s Graz became the centre of German-nationalist opposition to the Badeni Decrees, which sought to give linguistic rights to national minorities in the Habsburg Empire. Riots and demonstrations led to serious conflict with the central government which eventually suspended the city council, and this is covered in the final chapter of the book. The discussion on migration also includes a discussion of social mobility and some interesting material on the impact of residence laws.

In the section on economic development the author argues that geographical disadvantages, such as the distance from Vienna and high transport costs, hindered industrial growth. Attempts by local officials and the business community to stimulate growth were dampened by the depression of the 1870s. Although this section is as detailed as the rest of the book, it is less satisfactory, relying heavily on lengthy discussions of wage and production trends, but avoiding some interesting questions. For instance, mention is made of problems which arose from internal and external politics, but this is not elaborated. Little reference is made to the large-scale expansion of heavy industry in the 1880s and 1890s in Upper Styria, just 50 miles to the north, and the impact this had on Graz's economy.

The most interesting part of the book lies in the final sections which discuss changes in social structure and the development of class politics. At this point the statistics are complemented by a commentary on the declining political dominance of the aristocracy and haute bourgeoisie and the growing dissension within the bourgeoisie itself. The central arena for the latter was the city council. Hubbard describes the complex curia electoral system, the battle for reform in the 1870s and Graz's emergence as the 'mouthpiece of radical nationalism' and anti-clericalism in the 1890s. At this point his book provides a useful, if slighter, companion to Charles Boyer's *Political Radicalism in Late Imperial Vienna*. As he points out, German nationalism (of the Austrian variety) had been stronger in Vienna in the 1870s than in Graz. The extraordinary success of Karl Lueger's Viennese Christian social movement fused romantic Catholicism and anti-semitism into a popular petty bourgeois movement, so undermining national liberal dominance of Viennese city politics. This movement foundered in Graz, partly because of the strength of anti-clericalism in the city and partly because of the strength of nationalism. The conflict between liberal nationalists and Catholics split the petty bourgeois vote and enabled the Austrian Social Democratic Party to win its first major victory – at the Graz council elections of 1897.

In conclusion Hubbard points out that it was ironic that it was this city, the garden city and 'Pensionopolis', which provided the Social Democrats with their only effective electoral representation before 1918. But this was only one of the peculiarities of Graz. As the first section shows, it had a relatively old population, a higher proportion of civil servants, administrators and people dependent on unearned income such as rents and pensions. It also, for a short time, gave women taxpayers a vote – though only indirectly. The size and influence of the university was also unusual, as the discussion of the division between the 'educated' and 'trading' bourgeoisies illustrates. The book is a useful study of urbanization in the Habsburg Empire, but at the end, this reader was left wondering whether this really was a description of urbanization in a 'typical' central European city, as the author maintains.

**Jill Lewis**
University of Swansea

Hans Jürgen Teuteberg (ed.), *Homo Habitans*. Zur Sozialgeschichte des ländlichen und städtischen Wohnens in der Neuzeit. Studien zur Geschichte des Alltags, Bd.4. Münster: Coppenrath, 1985. 471pp.

This volume is the outcome of a conference on the social history of housing from the sixteenth to the twentieth century held in Münster in 1983. There is a long introduction by the editor, and each of its four sections is in turn preceded by a short introduction. Among the eighteen papers are several contributions by leading British housing historians, Enid Gauldie, John Burnett, Richard Rodger, Walter Minchinton, all painfully translated into German. If this review touches on their contributions only in passing it is because their work is likely to be available to readers of *UHYB* in other more accessible places.

Those who pride themselves on their command of German may wish to tackle the subtle and systematic categorization of information that should be included in an ideal history of the subject as the editor conceives it. Others will do well to turn to the introduction primarily for its useful survey of the German historiography.

The section on traditional rural housing and the impact of modern urbanization and industrialization contains a survey of housing types in Holstein (K. S. Kramer), two analyses of furniture by social grouping based on inventories, one for an area near Amsterdam around 1860 (A. J. Schuurman), the other for the Dukedom of Brunswick (R. E. Mohrmann). Similar in spirit is a study of Warsaw houses in the sixteenth and seventeenth centuries later in the volume. This section also contains Gauldie's study of the development of Invergowrie near Dundee. It would appear from the introduction to this part of the book that the study of housing types and furniture is still at the stage of the small-scale monograph.

The subject matter of the remaining three sections overlaps to such an extent that it is best to treat it as a single group of contributions ranging over such themes as the social segregation of housing (in eighteenth-century Göttingen and ninteenth-century Swiss cities), the layout of working-class housing and the relation of housing standards to family income (in mid-nineteenth-century Düsseldorf, in Copenhagen 1840–1914, in Britain, and in German cities 1900), long-term studies of the nineteenth-century housing market in Germany and in Britain, and the provision of working-class housing by cooperative building association, by employers both in Germany and in rural England, and by German municipalities prior to 1914.

The outstanding paper at the conference may well have been Richard Rodger's bold and far from uncontroversial interpretation of the crisis of British housing 1830–1920, but I shall pass over it so as to draw attention to the more important German contributions. Richard Tilly and Thomas Wellenreuther provide a highly technical study of nineteenth-century population movements and building-cycles in German cities, which analyses the operation of the market and comes to the conclusion that there was on the whole no market failure. Tilly's other contribution, his introduction to Section 3 of the book, is the only one that seizes the opportunity for comparative reflection and the identification of unresolved questions. He there contrasts his own assessment of the German housing market with the strongly pessimistic view expressed by Rodger about the british one. By highlighting the difficulty of dating improvements in housing standards as evidenced by disagreements between Rodger's paper and that by John Burnett, by contrasting Rodger's presentation of the reasons for British housing reform with the information given in subsequent papers on German employers' reasons for subsidizing housing costs, and by other probing comments, Tilly shows the potential value of conferences such as this.

Another outstanding contribution is that by Clemens Wischermann on housing standards, ideal and reality in pre-1914 Germany. This is an interim report on the analysis of an exceptionally detailed survey of housing conditions for Munich in 1904–7. It also uses a database relating to housing conditions across a range of German cities, compiled at the University of Münster. This combination of sources provides the basis for an excellent paper on the working-class family economy in relation to housing. He draws attention to the contribution that lodgers of all kinds made to the family income at the stage in the family cycle when dependent children prevented the wife from going out to work. This showed up in the overcrowding statistics, since the number of lodgers was greatest in the most overcrowded households and falls off as the number of dependent children declines.The paper contains a nice discussion of sleeping arrangements in terms of the number of occupiers per bed, the implication of these findings for children, as well as comparative information on space-utilization for cooking, living, sleeping, and so on. Wischermann's future publications should be of great interest to housing historians; even this paper is well worth the attention of anyone who can cope with the language.

Mention should also be made of Günther Schulz on the provision of housing by German employers up to 1945. He provides a systematic outline of the subject and shows yet again how important a watershed 1918 is in the history of German social policy. Complementary to Schulz's outline is Gertrud Milkereit's richly documented study of the policy of the firm of Thyssen.

Finally,Walter Steitz and Wolfgang Krabbe show how marginal municipal housing provision was in German cities before 1914. The famous initiatives in Frankfurt were as unrepresentative of German cities as those of the LCC were of British ones. The paper suggests that what positive action there was took the form of the provision of building land and loan finance more frequently than was the case in England. This is a paper whose statistics will be useful to the specialist.
**E. P. Hennock**
Department of History, University of Liverpool

## 3 METHODOLOGY AND SOURCES

John Schofield and Roger Leech (eds), *Urban Archaeology in Britain*. The Council for British Archaeology Research Report 61, 1987. x + 234 pp. 103 figures. Tables. Bibliographies. £19.50.

Psychoanalysts have identified a personality type whose characteristics consist of an obsessive compulsion 'to dwell long and unproductively upon uncompleted tasks' and whose chief pleasure consists of hoarding: the miser with his money; the collector with his stamps or book (D. Stafford-Clark, *What Freud Really Said*, 1967, p.96). To the sceptic, it often seems as if the discipline of archaeology has become fixated at this stage of development, although it must be said that much documentary history is equally representative of the type. Such sceptics will doubtless find evidence for their beliefs in *Urban Archaeology in Britain's* reminder that there are now over 70 years of unpublished excavations at Glastonbury Abbey (p. 172) and in John Schofield's plea for archaeologists to actually do something with the information they have so laboriously acquired (p. 6). Indeed, a recurring theme of the volume is the need for archaeologists to see their site excavations in some broader context: a model or problem; the town as a whole; the region served by the town. David Palliser quotes Sawyer's famous claim that archaeology can be 'an expensive way of telling us what we knew already' – although it may be equally true to say that archaeology can be an expensive way of telling us what we already knew we did not know (p. 54).

Nevertheless, this volume should convince even the hardened cynic about the value of archaeological evidence for the study of British towns in the period before 1500. Indeed, it is a powerful reminder that the discipline of urban archaeology, which we now take for granted, is largely the creation of the last 25 years. *Urban Archaeology in Britain* thus celebrates the achievements of the last three decades and examines the problems and prospects for future development.

The volume falls into three parts. Part I provides a general survey of the nature of urban deposits and issues a call for archaeologists to construct and test models of urban development rather than merely collecting more and more information.

The four chapters of Part II outline the problems facing the archaeologists of Roman, Anglo-Saxon, medieval and post-medieval towns and the evidence available to solve such problems. Part III gives more detailed study to specific forms of urban evidence: defences; castles; Roman public and domestic buildings; medieval domestic buildings, churches and religious houses; waterfront archaeology; and pottery.

Part III is, at times, rather breathless, simply because of the wealth of material which it has to cover and, occasionally, treads on some of the ground covered in Part II. The chronological chapters themselves suffer most from a lack of a common framework or problems: each contributor is free to survey his period, with its own unique problems and evidence, as he sees best. Thus David Hill devotes much attention to the 'central issue' of defining the essence of urban status while Palliser emphasizes the dangers of using archaeological evidence to solve specifically historic problems but then, very valuably, spends much time doing just that. It is not clear why Hill (or indeed Jones and Wacher) should be so concerned with defining a town (pp. 27, 47–8), an issue of semantics rather than substance (see K. Popper, *The Open Society and its Enemies*, vol. II, 1945, pp. 10,17 on the futility of the search for definitions). Finally, P. J. Davey reminds archaeologists of the need to explore the period after 1500, a need confirmed by the rest of the volume where the modern period is conspicuous by its absence: the chapters on urban defences and castles ignore the Civil War; the chapters on churches and religious houses stop at the Reformation while post-medieval waterfront archaeology is excluded since it comes within the province of 'industrial archaeology' (p. 198).

For its mass of references to archaeological work and its summaries of findings often neglected by documentary historians, *Urban Archaeology in Britain* is essential reading for all those interested in the development of British urban society. Palliser rightly castigates those historians who ignore archaeological evidence but if archaeology is truly to come of age, then archaeologists themselves must begin to intervene in historical debates and to organize their own material in terms of the paradigms and hypotheses which their evidence can deal with. But this brings us back to our starting point: the need to end all forms of antiquarianism in the study of the society of the past.

**S. H. Rigby**
Department of History, University of Manchester

James Elliot, *The City in Maps, Urban Mapping to 1900*. London: The British Library, 1987. 88pp. 13 plates. 45 figures. Bibliography. £9.95.

This attractive booklet has been published to accompany an exhibition with the same title mounted by the Map Library of the British Library for the 18 months following June 1986. This was the first exhibition of the Map Library's copious treasures to be devoted to an urban theme, which says much about the poor state of urban cartographical studies in Britain, as compared with other parts of Europe and North America.

The book follows closely the organization of the exhibition and provides illustrations of more than three-quarters of the maps on display. Since many of the maps were large, the publishers faced the inevitable problem of illustrating complete maps, and thereby losing much of the detail, or printing only parts so that details could be properly appreciated. They chose to reproduce most of the maps complete, or nearly so, many of them spread over two pages (which poses further problems for serious study). The illustrations provide a sample of the highlights of the exhibition, therefore, rather than a source for academic analysis.

Book and exhibition fall between a number of stools. There is a temporal framework, though it is a very loose one; there is a regional framework relating developments in Britain to mapping elsewhere; and there is a thematic framework, with sections on medical and warfare mapping. This does not make for a very easy progression and is symptomatic of the lack of more comprehensive investigations of urban cartography in Britain. The most successful of the sections are the first, dealing with the medieval city (though, since it includes maps published as late as 1575, the period is loosely interpreted), and the second, on the seventeenth century. The succeeding section, which deals with these two periods in Britain, also works quite well. There are, however, some notable cartographers and maps omitted, including William Hollar and the early plans of Irish towns drawn for Lord Burghley. Thereafter, the riches of the eighteenth and nineteenth centuries, and the attempt to sample not just Europe but North America and the Far East as well, overwhelmed both the writer and the exhibition and the book loses coherence. All this suggests that there is need of a much more detailed examination of the chronology and themes of urban mapping in Britain and its relationship to developments elsewhere, and need of a much more substantial book. However, this publication is sufficient to whet the appetite, to introduce to a wider public the rich fare of the Map Library, and to provide a good sample of well-produced illustrations, many of them in colour, to entice readers to further study.

**T. R. Slater**
Department of Geography, University of Birmingham

P. R. Coss (ed.), *The Early Records of Medieval Coventry* [with T. John (ed.), *The Hundred Rolls of 1280*] (Records of Social and Economic History, n.s. vol. xi). London: Oxford University Press/British Academy, 1986. xlii + 450 pp. 2 maps. 2 plates. £72.00.

This useful anthology of Coventry documents appropriately follows D. Owen's *Making of King's Lynn*, though the range of documents selected for publication is not so wide, because except for the plea rolls of the thirteenth century and T. John's edition of the Hundred Rolls for the city, the bulk of the volume is taken up with more than 800 charters and deeds of the twelfth and thirteenth centuries. The end-date of the selection, 1307, was presumably chosen for reasons of practicality and not because it has any special significance for the history of Coventry, but it would have been an advantage if this had been explained in the introduction. The deeds have been arranged mainly by street and district. This must have been a difficult decision to make, because at the end there are two groups printed under the heading of property owners, Robert de Stoke and Combe Abbey. An archival arrangement throughout, perhaps enabling the reader to appreciate the scattered properties of individuals and the rise and fall of urban estates, would have had many advantages. However, the present classification has the merit, as Dr Coss shows in the introduction, of indicating the extent to which crafts gathered in particular streets and suburbs.

Fortunately for the growing numbers of potential users who have little or no Latin, the bulk of the documents have been calendared in English and the needs of specialists have been served by quoting difficult and unusual passages in the original. The occasional editorial lapse can thus usually be corrected: for example, in 1247 the unfortunate Alice Oselot was scalded not by the unlikely 'cauldron of boiling meal', but by a vat of mash, being boiled preparatory to the brewing of ale (p. 50). The index has been prepared with care and has been provided with a wide range of subject headings. This reviewer experimented with a current research interest, 'gardens' and found, unlike in most indices, a subheading under the general category of 'land' which served his purposes very well, except that the many references to the West Orchard (*in vasto gardino*) were indexed under the street name, not as a garden. Considerations of space force modern editors to index place names under their modern form, giving the medieval variants after the modern name, which puts the editor under extra pressure to identify the name correctly. In this case the unwary should note that surnames incorporating 'Brugges' probably belong not to Flemish migrants from Bruges but to people from the less exotic Shropshire town of Bridgnorth, and the archaic name of Dry Marston, which is not identified, conceals the modern Warwickshire village of Long Marston.

Urban historians will gather much valuable information about urban growth in the thirteenth century from this volume. The names of the parties and witnesses reveal a great deal about the early town. For example, the smattering of deeds dating from the period 1200–26 produces names derived from 34 different occupations, the majority being crafts and trades. Judging from the personal names formed from place names, Coventry picked up a good number of its new citizens from surrounding smaller towns, such as Coleshill and Warwick. Trade contacts provided the basis for longer distance migration, like the smattering of Lincolnshire places such as Boston and Spalding, through which Coventry traders gained access to the coast, but also more remote places like Winchelsea which scarcely lay on any of Coventry's normal trade routes. The physical consequences of growth are of course reflected both in the many streets, lanes and suburbs, and in the size and intensity of use of the plots of land conveyed by the deeds.

Coventry's origins still remain mysterious. Dr Coss in his introduction sheds a little more light on the controversy over the two 'halves' of the town and stresses the unity of the citizens in disputes with the Priory in the late thirteenth century. It is time for Coventry's historians to turn from constitutional to topographical problems. Dr Coss points out that among the group of settlements around Coventry at least one, Bisseley, has disappeared completely because of the main centre's early growth. Can it be that Coventry's origins should be sought, like those of Norwich and Lincoln, in the coalescence of a number of small settlements? In this case the archaeologists should not necessarily expect to find the remains of the pre-Conquest town under the city centre. One cannot avoid a train of speculation from the index entry of the early forms of the suburban manor of Wyken: *Wic, Wica*, a name which has so often been found attached to an early trading settlement.

**Christopher Dyer,**
School of History, University of Birmingham

John M. Wasson (ed.), *Records of Early English Drama: Devon.* Toronto: University of Toronto Press, 1986. lxxii + 623 pp. Maps, Glossaries. Bibliography. No price given.

Audrey Douglas and Peter Greenfield (eds), *Records of Early English Drama: Cumberland, Westmorland, Gloucestershire.* Toronto: University of Toronto Press, 1986. xi + 547 pp. Maps. Glossaries. Bibliography. £60.00.

The latest two volumes in the *Records Of Early English Drama* (REED) are, superficially, the least appropriate for review in this *Yearbook*, though they are the first to be reviewed. The five earlier volumes have all focused on a single city, namely York (1979), Chester (1979), Newcastle (1981), Coventry (1982) and Norwich 1540–1642 (1984). Other town studies, including Bristol, are promised shortly, but here we have two county-based collections, one for Devon and the other bringing together two editors' work on Gloucestershire and on Cumberland and Westmoreland. But, despite the county titles, the towns of Barnstaple, Exeter, Plymouth, Gloucester, Tewkesbury, Carlisle and Kendal form the chief subjects, with some discussion of other towns such as Ashburton, Dartmouth, Totnes, and Appleby.

The primary aim of the REED project is to reprint, with total fidelity, every primary reference to dramatic activity in the English provinces before 1642. The

REED editors have wisely adopted a very broad classification of drama, which includes any civic ceremony with a pageant element, all secular music-making, entertainments such as juggling and animal-baiting and non-liturgical aspects of church festivals, such as boy-bishop ceremonies, as well as amateur and professional performances of plays,. Their earliest point of reference is determined solely by the sources, creating a marked contrast between the Devon volume, extending back into the thirteenth century and quite strong for the fourteenth and fifteenth, in Exeter and Barnstaple especially, and the north-western evidence which is overwhelmingly post-1575. Within these parameters the editors have searched and reproduced material in every kind of source, although with a strong bias, one senses, towards material in the local not the central record offices. They make considerable use of parish records, mostly churchwardens' accounts, and some use of episcopal and quarter-session records, supplemented by other court cases, diaries and contemporary printed references to drama. But the backbone of their studies are borough records, chiefly accounts and council minutes or orders. Only in Exeter do they have Hooker's invaluable descriptions of civic procedure and ceremony to add substantial flesh to the skeleton of events revealed by these laconic sources. A great deal of editorial care is therefore required to work out which entries are relevant to the REED story, and to establish from them a coherent local pattern. Each editor is expected to master the historical context of dramatic activity in the major centres covered; unlike some literary projects this is, in conception and execution, a firmly historical undertaking. The introductions attempt to set the necessary background on each town, while each document used is carefully described; indeed these volumes would prove a useful, if extravagant, starting-place for discovering the early sources available on particular towns.

Nevertheless the urban historian may look askance at these mighty red volumes, each beautifully produced, and wonder whether the effort involved in the project is best served by these publications. Extravagant is certainly the word for the volumes which can include 120 pages of translations, set separately from the original text and reiterating all the source details. The Latin and English glossaries run to about 40 pages in each volume, and include words such as ballad and battlement! The indices are excellent, and are supplemented by a section listing all the places that travelling companies visited, and giving biographical details of their patrons. The latter is frankly ridiculous, taking 70 pages in the Devon case and listing material easily available from the *Dictionary of National Biography* or else quite unnecessary. By contrast the volumes have slender editorial introductions and relatively brief endnotes, especially the Devon volume. This seems to reflect a basic misunderstanding about how the volumes can and should be used, namely the hope that scholars will be able to use these volumes, by themselves, to recreate a rounded picture of provincial drama. The chief effect of trying to digest these volumes, however, is to reinforce the sense that it is only with the guidance of someone who can place the materials in the context of urban life that they can really make sense. If one is merely going to establish the itinerary of the travelling companies, then perhaps the local setting is not very important, although even here one needs to understand why some towns were apparently more receptive than others, and why the mood changed to hostility at some point, varying in each case, between 1575 and 1625. One also needs to understand local government well enough to know whether one should expect the records to make reference to the entertaining of actors or musicians, and so what to infer from silences. If one is rightly intending to broaden the study to include locally generated drama, such as civic ceremony and music and folk activity, then the local element becomes paramount. The editors clearly agree with this but they have not, generally, had proper scope for this editorial role here. The fullest interpretation and editorial guidance is offered in the north-western section, helped perhaps by the limited time-scale, and by the ability to compare and contrast the experiences of Carlisle and Kendal. The other editors offer some useful ideas on the minor towns and parishes, but say little about the riches of Gloucester, Plymouth and above all Exeter.

These volumes will undoubtedly help those wishing to chart, at a basic level, the provision of various forms of entertainment, and the chief festivals observed in the late medieval and early-modern town. They will reinforce awareness that the Reformation did not destroy civic ceremony, showing the continued vitality of Shrove Tuesday, Mayday, perambulations and midsummer watches, and that 'puritan' hostility to drama is not easily demonstrated and did not imply opposition to civic musicians, as the Gloucester material shows. But historians seeking a deeper understanding of urban culture will either have to hope that the REED editors publish fuller studies elsewhere, or be prepared to till the ground themselves, armed with this expensive set of perfect transcriptions of some of the key material.

**Jonathan Barry**
Department of History of Archaeology, University of Exeter

David Galloway (ed.), *Records of Early English Drama: Norwich 1540–1642*. Toronto: University of Toronto Press, 1984. xciv + 501 pp. Appendices. Glossaries. Bibliography. £70.

This book forms part of a series in which the volumes for York, Chester, Coventry and Newcastle-upon-Tyne have already appeared. As was noted for the Coventry volume: 'The aim of the Records of Early English Drama is to collect written evidence of drama, minstrelsy and ceremonial activity, not to interpret it.' Professor Galloway, although not totally eschewing interpretation, has largely conformed to this stipulation. The volume under review is thus essentially a compilation of anything and everything remotely appertaining to drama and the performing arts, and to those concerned with such activities, in Norwich between 1540 and 1642.

Professor Galloway begins his volume with a general survey of Norwich history and its character, the government of the city and the Guild of St George and goes on to deal briefly with plays, players and other entertainers and with the waits of the city. This is followed by a minute survey of the documentary sources used, including the Assembly proceedings, the Chamberlains' and Clavors' accounts and the records of the Guild of St George as well as those of the Dean and Chapter. Some reference is also made to apprenticeship and freemen's lists. The sources are described in considerable detail and in a form which should be of assistance to historians concerned with areas other than drama as such. This, in turn, is supplemented by detailed appendices describing Elizabeth I's entry to the city in 1578, an extract concerning Kemp's dance from London to Norwich in February 1600, and very full information on the various patrons and travelling companies as well as a detailed listing of the Norwich waits and information gleaned from the Norwich antiquarian, Kirkpatrick, concerning the Grocers' Company. Translations of all extracts in Latin, English and Latin glossaries and a comprehensive index complete the fullest supporting information that one could reasonably wish for in such a volume.

Apart from references to the Grocers' pageant, the bulk of the documentary material concerns the city waits and the appearance on the scene of the various travelling companies supported by patrons of note, as well as those individuals described by Professor Galloway as being on the fringe and usually referred to as vagrants. By 1540 the pageants performed by the various city companies were in decline. The Grocers' play, however, was performed intermittently after this date but by the 1560s the pageant itself, described as 'a Howse of Waynscott paynted & buylded on a carte with foure whelys', was in storage. Because of rent arrears it was subsequently placed in the street and allowed to rot away, to be finally disposed of in 1570 when one Nicholas Sotherton took it away in pieces as payment for a debt of 20 shillings due to him from the corporation. If interest in the pageants declined, the travelling players continued to be welcomed if they were supported by a suitable patron. Not surprisingly, the more prestigious the patron the greater the welcome they were given. Queen Elizabeth's company performed in the city on some two dozen occasions, those of her favourite, the Earl of Leicester, on 13, and they were rivalled in the seventeenth century by the players of Anne of Denmark, Elizabeth of Bohemia and Charles I, all of whose companies performed on more than 20 occasions.

Changing attitudes, at both local and national level, however, meant that the city fathers became increasingly worried by such activities. A letter from the privy council in 1623 referred to the 'multitudes of people and familyes ... drawn away from ther buisnes and laboure' with resulting damage to the community. In such an atmosphere little tolerance could be expected for individual performers and there are frequent references to such people being whipped, or threatened with a whipping, before being sent on their way. A particularly poignant example occurred on 13 July 1606 when one John Balsomme, fiddler, was whipped and returned to King's Lynn with the usual passport, but without his son. Over a month later, on 16 August, the boy, aged six, was apprehended in Norwich and ordered to be sent back to his father. The boy *may* have been staying with relatives in the intervening period but it seems much more likely that he had been living by his wits and when caught was expected to tramp the 40 or so miles to Lynn to be reunited with his father. There was no suggestion that he was to be accompanied on the journey. Equally poignant in its own way was an episode concerning the city waits. They were sufficiently well known beyond the city's confines to be invited to join Sir Francis Drake when he set out on his Portugal voyage in 1589. Suitably kitted out the five waits undertook the journey but only two of them returned.

Limitations of space prevent any detailed discussion of other examples. Mistakes are relatively few. Thomas Bilney was burnt at Lollards' Pit in Norwich in 1531, not in London. The Ridolphi Plot was in 1571, not 1569 as is implied here. But these are minor blemishes in a volume which succeeds admirably in its chosen purpose and which will provide a valuable quarry for all historians and others interested in this particular area. The cost of the book, however, is prohibitive and at £70 a copy many libraries may think twice before purchasing a copy. Few, if any, individuals are likely to do so.

**J. F. Pound**
School of Education, University of East Anglia

Lawrence Manley (ed.), *London in the Age of Shakespeare: An Anthology*. London: Croom Helm. 372 pp. £22.50.

London has long been a source of inspiration to writers, and many publications about the early-modern capital, including the one reviewed here, have been based upon published sources. It is still tempting to rely upon such documentation, particularly since many university libraries now possess microfilms of all books printed in English between 1475 and 1700. But for some time students of metropolitan history have gone beyond published records in their researches and, as a result, have gained a greater understanding of London's striking expansion in this period. Beginning in the 1930s, F. J. Fisher, using archival sources and quantitative methods demonstrated London's growing predominance in the sixteenth- and early seventeenth-century economy. Then in the 1950s and 1960s Robert Ashton and Valerie Pearl, employing similar approaches, showed the critical role of the City in national politics under the early Stuarts. More recently, a new generation of urban historians, archaeologists and demographers has begun to explore new areas of metropolitan history. Their researches concern social structures and policies, housing, immigration, epidemics, dress and hygiene, as well as more traditional subjects such as domestic and foreign trade. Even some old chestnuts – e.g. who made up Shakespeare's audiences? – are being re-examined by historians, while those who take a new 'historical' approach to literature are finding materials in the archives that are relevant to their traditional texts.

Sadly, few of these developments are echoed in Professor Manley's anthology. Indeed, it is unclear what the book offers to those who study London history. Perhaps, as the dustjacket states, students of history and literature will find it a helpful resource, but to make any sense of the 227 snippets in this collection they will need to consult a wider literature. Admittedly, the editor's introduction creates some order out of the chaos and his prefaces to the individual chapters are relevant and well-informed. But the introduction often glosses over the rougher edges of contemporary historiography. Not all would agree, for example, that 'despite the strains of economic and social change, the life of London remained fundamentally orderly' (p. 11). Further, his figures for metropolitan population and plague deaths will require major surgery in the light of the work of Roger Finlay, Beatrice Shearer and Paul Slack. The book's chapters, despite the editor's prefaces, are a Babel of subjects and sources. Some bring together excerpts concerned with themes — e.g. 'Portrait of a city', 'The order of society', 'Coming and going', and 'London in love'. But many are just examples pulled together from a certain genre – e.g. 'From the pulpit: sermons', 'London in jest: from the jestbooks', 'Songs of the streets: broadside ballads', and 'The City in a nutshell: epigrams'.

This anthology will probably be of most interest to that elusive person, the 'general reader'. It covers a long period, from the late fifteenth to the late seventeenth century, and it includes a wide range of published materials, particularly from the poetry and popular literature of the age. These convey something of the flavour of London life, but will otherwise be of limited assistance, for the reasons set out above, to the serious student. The book's limitations are greatly exacerbated by a poor index, which includes no more than proper names.

A. L. Beier
Department of History, University of Lancaster

John Bourne (ed.), *Georgian Tiverton: The Political Memoranda of Beavis Wood 1768–98* (Devon and Cornwall Record Society, New Series, vol. 29). Torquay: Devonshire Press for the Devon and Cornwall Record Society, 1986. xvii + 180 pp. Biographical index. Index. No price given.

Beavis Wood was town clerk of Tiverton from 1765 to 1803 and the effective 'manager' of its oligarchic and increasingly lethargic corporation. He was the town's most prolific correspondent of the Ryder family, which for four generations had sat in Parliament for the borough and regarded it with a proprietorial interest. Wood's political memoranda – 84 letters reviewing political and social events in the town – provided the largely absentee Ryders with invaluable local intelligence. He was an enthusiastic and trustworthy correspondent, a shrewd political tactician and detailed observer of local affairs; indeed the ideal political middle-man.

This is not to suggest that Beavis Wood was merely a cynical political operator. Rather, in marked contrast to many around him, he was a man of firm political principles. Tory, loyalist and supporter of the Established Church, he was by nature a staunch traditionalist. He strongly disapproved of change, yet until the 1790s at least, was neither inflexible nor intolerant. As he put it in 1782, 'moderation, kindness and good humour are the best qualifications for a friend to true liberty and the British Constitution' (p. 66). Such qualities were the more necessary in a town where squabbling between the members of a faction-riven local corporation was endemic. They were also used to advantage in dealing with the town's labouring population. Wood was able to gain their trust by his active presence, by organizing charity at times of distress, and above all by his committed defence of traditional marketing regulations against engrossers and forestallers. He was, in sum, the archetypal paternalist, a man who combined humanity with an awareness that, in the small communities which comprised much of Georgian England, consent was critical to effective rule.

Stability through tradition was, however, an increasingly elusive goal. In late-eighteenth-century Tiverton, as elsewhere, the problems facing local government were beginning to mount. The 1790s were years of particular difficulty. The French Revolutionary and Napoleonic Wars decimated the Tiverton serge trade, which depended upon its markets in Germany and the Netherlands, leaving the town facing economic ruin. At the same time, local 'Jacobins' attacked the self-electing nature of the corporation and its effective control of the town's parliamentary representation. In confronting these challenges, Wood was hindered by the obstructionism, bickering and indolence of his fellow members of the town's ruling elite. His philosophy of moderation, perhaps unsurprisingly, gave way to a reactionary intolerance. When he resigned, aged 70, in 1803, the principles of unity and stability for which he had fought throughout his career already seemed outmoded. A new world was opening up which he could neither sympathize with nor understand.

The value of this collection of letters lies in its ability to encapsulate and bring to life the pressing realities of late-eighteenth-century local government and political management. Through the detail of Wood's memoranda, we see the problems which conscientious magistrates throughout England increasingly faced, and feel their frustration as they attempted to conjure unity and order out of self-interest and lethargy. Above all we can appreciate how difficult it was for local elites to respond effectively to changing circumstances. In his introduction to the volume, John Bourne provides us with a rounded account of late-eighteenth-century Tiverton, and an excellent portrait of its leading figure and his patrons, the Ryders. If the footnotes to the letters themselves are at times frustratingly brief, this is felt the more keenly because the reader is drawn so strongly by the documents into the complex world of Georgian local politics. In bringing this valuable collection to our attention the editor deserves the thanks of all students of late-eighteenth-century urban politics and society.

**Alan Booth**
Department of History, University of Nottingham

Mass-Observation, *The Pub and the People: A Worktown Study*. Intro. Godfrey Smith. Cresset Library; Century Hutchinson, 1987: First published 1943. xx + 354 pp. 9 illustrations. 15 diagrams. Bibliography. £5.95.

Originally published in 1943 without the benefit of Humphrey Spender's atmospheric photographs, the material for *The Pub and the People* was collected in a Mass-Observation survey of Bolton life between 1937 and 1939. Unfortunately, the war brought the project to an end before the survey had been completed. In his introduction to the 1943 volume, Tom Harrisson, co-founder with Charles Madge of Mass-Observation, gives as a stated aim of the book to allow 'some the the people of Britain to speak for themselves'. The collection of data about ordinary people would, Harrisson and Madge believed, provide the working classes with the information necessary to act to shape the future pattern of their own lives in a time of flux. The work is thus of particular relevance to those currently interested in 'people's history'. Today many historians espouse Harrisson's aim of allowing people to 'speak for themselves' via the media of oral history, autobiography and the community history. Indeed Raphael Samuel and History Workshop have taken over the Mass-Observation mantle to some extent with their innovative study of the 1984-5 miners' strike, *The Enemy Within*[1]. As Godfrey Smith notes in the new introduction to the book, a similar study of 1980s pub life is long overdue. To anyone contemplating the current debate with regard to the nature of memory and its use as historical source material, [2] the Mass-Observation archive also provides a unique opportunity to test the impact of time upon this most elusive, but often uncritically relied upon, faculty.

The book also demonstrates, however, that practical application of the 'speaking for themselves' technique is not without its own difficulties. Using participant observation and personal accounts from a panel of volunteers, combined with a rudimentary form of statistical analysis, the methodology adopted by Mass-Observation is perhaps the most problematic aspect of the book. In places the style is idiosyncratic, switching disconcertingly between merely recording information without comment to a semi-polemical approach more in keeping with the underlying desire to promote social consciousness. Occasional value judgements by the investigators also detract from the aim of objective and impartial observation.

More importantly for anyone considering using the book as primary source material, there is a strong underlying sense that Harrisson and his co-workers are 'exploring a lost continent'; a persistent intrusion of the contemporary intellectual and artistic climate of opinion, with its interest in the 'iconography of industrial ruin'.[3]

Nevertheless, the book has an immediate quality and is a vibrant and rich social document. The reportage style has the capacity to cross the half-century in a way that much other source material lacks. Mass-Observation is the twentieth-century historian's 'Pete Marsh'. The cultural life of Bolton's public house customers has been captured and their conversations frozen, giving the reader a sense of eavesdropping on the past. The pub, with its spittoons and sawdust floors, tubercular staff, sexual segregation, rituals of treating, Royal and Antediluvian Order of Buffaloes, bookies' runners, and racing pigeon fancy, is portrayed as being under assault not merely from its traditional rivals for the free time of Bolton's inhabitants (the churches and temperance organizations), but from the more pressing threat posed by the new leisure industries. In an interesting subtheme (again reflecting contemporary preoccupations, in this instance regarding the perceived impact of 'mass culture'[4]), Harrisson draws new battle lines. In this new configuration the collectivist, democratic and community-orientated pub (which he endows with a social conscience mediated by the pub landlord) and the similarly located Church, are allied against the individualistic, conscienceless cinemas, dance halls, football pools, radio, and 'car culture'. Regionally and socially defined activities centred on the pub, where the cost of entertainment is low and group activity high, can, Harrisson argues, be contrasted favourably with the new, national culture being promoted by heavily commercialized, profit-orientated and distant organizations like the American film industry.

Whatever the particular problems of this ambitious undertaking on the part of Harrisson and his colleagues, in the final analysis it is a tribute to their vision of the possibilities which the 'mass-observation' technique presented, that the material contained in the book and the questions which it raises are as relevant to today's society as they were fifty years ago.

## NOTES

1  R. Samuel, B. Bloomfield, G. Boanas (eds), *The Enemy Within: Pit Villages and the Miners' Strike of 1984–85* (1986).
2  See for example J. Murphy, 'The voice of memory: history, autobiography & oral memory', *Historical Studies, 22*. 87 (Oct. 1986) and J. Vansina, *Oral Tradition as History* (London and Kenya, 1985).
3  D. Mellor, 'British art in the 1930s: some economic, political & cultural structures' in F. Gloversmith (ed.) *Class, Culture and Social Change: A new View of the 1930s* (1980); 185–207, 199.
4  For a full discussion of 'mass culture' theory see S. Jones, *Workers at Play: A Social and Economic History of Leisure, 1918–1939* (1986).
**Carol L. Jones**

Gordon Cherry and Leith Penny, *Holford: A Study in Architecture, Planning and Civic Design*. London: Mansell Publishing, 1986, pp. 293. £25.00.
The great stage of post-war reconstruction in Britain seems so dated now as to be almost antediluvian. Yet gradually we are starting to see the various dramas enacted upon it more clearly and fairly. Gordon Cherry and Leith Penny's monograph on Lord Holford, once one of the most powerful and applauded stars in a now bedraggled-looking cast, marks a major step in that direction.

Holford stood foremost among the ranks of important architectural bureaucrats thrown up by reconstruction. What was his achievement? Urbane, quick, methodical, productive but elusive, he baffled his contemporaries as much as he has intrigued the authors of this book. As an architect, Holford designed nothing of distinction.

As a planner, he failed to put a personal stamp on any major executed scheme save the pre-war Team Valley Industrial Estate outside Gateshead (the first in a long succession of consultancies) and the sadly botched precincts of St Paul's Cathedral. Yet Holford did more than any other technician to lay down the lines for physical reconstruction in post-war Britain, and was for a quarter of a century venerated with a godlike awe.

The enigma resolves itself, or at any rate shifts, once Holford is accepted in his true light, as a public administrator. We expect architects (and used to expect old-style physical planners) to be in some sense creative. Administrators do not often have that chance, unless they are in the right place at the right time and concentrate their talents accordingly; which is why biographies of even the ablest administrators can make boring books. One of Holford's weaknesses, as Cherry and Penny unflinchingly show, was that he spread himself too thin to be personally creative. A list of his commitments round about 1960 borders on the ludicrous. He ran a firm of architect-planners with four or five offices in different cities, was President of the RIBA, Professor of Town Planning at University College, London, Chairman of the Historic Buildings Advisory Council, member of the Royal Fine Arts Commission, adviser to the Central Electricity Generating Board, while also being crucial to the counsels of the Royal Town Planning Institute and other bodies. Apart from the professorship none of these jobs was neglected; in many respects Holford's way (some would say genius) with committees bore fruit. We owe it to Holford, argue the authors, that the CEGB has made concerted and responsible attempts to landscape its projects over the past 30 years. But it was not Holford who landscaped the power lines and stations but 'Holford's men', the numerous friends and allies in the close-knit world of British post-war building to whom he extended indirect patronage. Here, as in many fields, it is well high impossible to say: 'This Holford did'.

Cherry and Penny squarely confront and overcome the methodological difficulties posed by his career. A mass of Holford's papers, some of them surprisingly personal, survives in the possession of his *alma mater*, the University of Liverpool. Together with the recollections of such important friends and colleagues as Gordon Stephenson and Myles Wright, these have saved the authors from being sucked in by the volume of public records which have drained all sense of purpose or direction from some other books on British post-war planning. This material prevents Holford's mature career from being conflated utterly with the history of the sundry organizations which he served. The most illuminating example is the authors' account of his role in the infant Ministry of Town and Country Planning between 1943 and 1947. This was the central episode in Holford's development, investing him with the authority which he carried in the post-war world. Cherry and Penny rightly linger over it. They do not flinch from technical detail beyond the immediate bounds of Holford's own preoccupations. As well as the expected assessment of his part in the development of planning controls, we get (for instance) a lucid exposition of the 'floor space index', that tool of urban planning which so much affected central-city development in Britain in the 1950s. But we also see Holford struggling vainly for a regional, synthetic, Geddesian concept of post-war planning, an ideal broadly disappointed in the 1947 Town and Country Planning Act. This disappointment seems to have led to his all-too-characteristic early withdrawal from the Ministry – to which many at the time, probably wrongly, attributed the failure of impetus in official planning after 1947. Altogether this chapter, precisely because it fuses the official and the personal, provides the most accessible account we yet have of central government activity in these vital years for British planning. Many will turn for guidance to these pages.

To return to Holford the man, one of the curiosities of his career is how he managed to advance so far so fast. By any standard he was singularly lucky. A bright lad but with no very distinguished school career, he drifted into architecture in his native South Africa, came over to the Liverpool School of Architecture almost by chance and at first showed scant individuality. What he could and did do was to absorb others' ideas quickly, first those of his mentor the theatrical Professor Reilly, then the socio-political approaches to architecture and planning championed by the younger generation, especially his friend Gordon Stephenson. Three years in Rome (1930–3) widened his horizons, but he was lucky to secure a lectureship on his return to Liverpool and outrageously fortunate to be chosen as Abercrombie's successor there as Professor of Civic Design in 1935. This was then one of still only a handful of full-time jobs in British planning and brought with it the certainty of private commissions. Team Valley followed immediately on, and hence Holford's wartime employment first as coordinator for a programme of building ordnance factories and hostels, then as Lord Reith's technical supremo for reconstruction. Thus was his reputation established.

It is hard after reading this biography to aver that Holford, at the critical moment in 1935, was a worthy successor to Abercrombie. He was a compromise candidate, chosen because he was not tarred with the worn-out old garden-city brush. He was a moderate modernist of the type that the Liverpool School tended ideally to produce, charming, mildly left-wing but not too much so, residually sympathetic to Beaux-Arts principles of physical layout but alive to the collaborative radicalism coming out of German architecture and planning. Holford was chosen, as so often later, because he offended nobody. That is not to say he was a cipher at this or indeed any stage in his career. Among the most interesting 'finds' of the book are the excerpts from letters Holford wrote to Stephenson from Rome in the early 1930s. They exhibit high intelligence and self-conciousness, a wide cultural range, and an awareness of the difficult choices facing contemporary architecture. Already Holford was having problems making a commitment. Despite his worldly success he never in a sense did so; that, retrospectively, is the problem of his career. He will never be a popular or heroic figure in the annals of British architecture and planning, but he will always be an important one. Cherry and Penny have given us a shrewd and just estimate of that importance. Theirs would be in all respects a model study in planning history, were it not let down by a thoroughly inadequate index.

**Andrew Saint**
University of London

# List of books reviewed

*page*

## 1 GENERAL AND THEMATIC

174 Black J. *The English Press in the Eighteenth Century* (Joyce Ellis)

175 Corbin A. *The Foul and the Fragrant. Odor and the French Social Imagination* (Bill Luckin)

171 Coss P.R. and Lloyd S.D. (eds) *Thirteenth-Century England I: Proceedings of the Newcastle Conference, 1985* (C.H. Lawrence)

177 Doughty M. *Building the Industrial City* (Nicholas J. Morgan)

172 Garden M. and Lequin Y. *Habiter la ville. XVe–XXe siècles* (Geoffrey Crossick)

181 Gaskell S.M. *Modern Housing. From the Great Exhibition to the Festival of Britain* (Stephen Constantine)

182 Jackson K.T. *Crabgrass Frontier: The Suburbanization of the United States* (Peter Ling)

178 Lees A. *Cities Perceived. Urban Society and European and American Thought 1820–1940* (Bruce Coleman)

173 Sharpe J.A. *Early Modern England: a Social History 1560–1760* (Jonathan Barry)

180 Schivelbusch W. *The Railway Journey* (Robert Poole)

183 Stelter G.A. and Artibise A.F.J. *The Canadian City* (R.J. Morris)

179 Stephens W.B. *Education, Literacy and Society 1830–1870* (David Vincent)

## 2 INDIVIDUAL TOWNS AND REGIONS

191 Bartoccini F. *Roma nell Óttocento* (Harry Hearder)

188 Cage R.A. (ed.) *The Working Class in Glasgow 1750–1914* (Steve Fielding)

192 Fitzgerald S. *Rising Damp. Sydney 1870–1890* (Duncan Bythell)

187 Garrioch D. *Neighbourhood and Community in Paris, 1740–1790* (M. Crook)

186 Harris T. *London Crowds in the Reign of Charles II* (Ronald Hutton)

193 Hubbard W.H. *Auf dem Weg zur Grossstadt. Eine Socialgeschichte der Stadt Graz 1850–1914* (Jill Lewis)

190 Kidd A.J. and Roberts K.W. (eds) *City, Class and Culture. Studies in Cultural Production and Social Policy in Victorian Manchester* (M.J. Winstanley)

190 Messinger G.S. *Manchester in the Victorian Age* (M.J. Winstanley)

189 Royle E. *Nonconformity in Nineteenth-century York* (Hugh McLeod)

189 Royle E. *The Victorian Church in York* (Hugh McLeod)

185 Rubin M. *Charity and Community in Medieval Cambridge* (Gervase Rosser)

195 Teuteberg H.J. (ed.) *Homo Habitans. Zur Sozialgeschichte des Landlichen und stadtischen Wohnens in der Neuzeit* (E.P. Hennock)

## 3 METHODOLOGY AND SOURCES

203 Bourne J. (ed.) *Georgian Tiverton: the Political Memoranda of Beavis Wood 1768–98* (Alan Booth)

205 Cherry G. and Penny L. *Holford: a Study in Architecture, Planning and Civic Design* (Andrew Saint)

198 Coss P.R. (ed.) *The Early Records of Medieval Coventry* (Christopher Dyer)

199 Douglas A. and Greenfield P. (eds) *Records of Early English Drama: Cumberland, Westmorland, Gloucestershire* (Jonathan Barry)

197 Elliot J. *The City in Maps. Urban Mapping to 1900* (T.R. Slater)
201 Galloway D. (ed.) *Records of Early English Drama: Norwich* (J.F. Pound)
202 Manley L. (ed.) *London in the Age of Shakespeare: an Anthology* (A.L. Beier)
204 Mass-Observation *The Pub and the People* (Carol L. Jones)
196 Schofield J. and Leech R. (eds) *Urban Archaeology in Britain* (S.H. Rigby)
199 Wasson J.H. (ed.) *Records of Early English Drama: Devon* (Jonathan Barry)